Gambling in Britain in the Long Eighteenth Century

English society in the eighteenth century was allegedly marked by a 'gambling mania', such was the prevalence and intensity of different forms of 'gaming'. *Gambling in Britain in the Long Eighteenth Century* subjects this notion to systematic scrutiny, exploring the growth and prevalence of different forms of gambling across Britain and throughout British society in this period, as well as attitudes towards it. Drawing on a vast range of new, empirical evidence, Bob Harris seeks to understand gambling, its growth, and significance within the context of wider trends and impulses in society. The book asks what light gambling practices and habits shed back onto society and the values, hopes, and expectations that informed the lives of those involved. This is a book, therefore, as much about the character of British society in the long eighteenth century as it is about gambling itself.

BOB HARRIS is Professor of British History at the University of Oxford, and Harry Pitt Fellow in History at Worcester College. He has written numerous books and articles on the history of Britain in the long eighteenth century, including *Politics and the Nation: Britain in the Mid Eighteenth Century* (2002) and *The Scottish People and the French Revolution* (2008). His book, *The Scottish Town in the Age of Enlightenment, c.1740–1820* (2014), co-authored with Charles McKean, won the Saltire Society's Scottish Book of the Year in 2014.

Gambling in Britain in the Long Eighteenth Century

Bob Harris
University of Oxford

Shaftesbury Road, Cambridge CB2 8EA, United Kingdom

One Liberty Plaza, 20th Floor, New York, NY 10006, USA

477 Williamstown Road, Port Melbourne, VIC 3207, Australia

314–321, 3rd Floor, Plot 3, Splendor Forum, Jasola District Centre, New Delhi – 110025, India

103 Penang Road, #05–06/07, Visioncrest Commercial, Singapore 238467

Cambridge University Press is part of Cambridge University Press & Assessment, a department of the University of Cambridge.

We share the University's mission to contribute to society through the pursuit of education, learning and research at the highest international levels of excellence.

www.cambridge.org
Information on this title: www.cambridge.org/9781009066228

DOI: 10.1017/9781009067348

First published 2022
First paperback edition 2024

A catalogue record for this publication is available from the British Library

Library of Congress Cataloging-in-Publication data
Names: Harris, Bob, 1964- author.
Title: Gambling in Britain in the long eighteenth century / Bob Harris, University of Oxford.
Description: 1 Edition. | New York, NY : Cambridge University Press, 2022. | Includes bibliographical references and index.
Identifiers: LCCN 2021029004 (print) | LCCN 2021029005 (ebook) | ISBN 9781316512449 (hardback) | ISBN 9781009066228 (paperback) | ISBN 9781009067348 (epub)
Subjects: LCSH: Gambling–Great Britain–History–18th century. | Gambling–Law and legislation–Great Britain.
Classification: LCC HV6722.G8 H37 2021 (print) | LCC HV6722.G8 (ebook) | DDC 306.4/820941–dc23
LC record available at https://lccn.loc.gov/2021029004
LC ebook record available at https://lccn.loc.gov/2021029005

ISBN 978-1-316-51244-9 Hardback
ISBN 978-1-009-06622-8 Paperback

Contents

Figures

Tables

Preface

This book has been a long time in the making. In 2005, I was privileged to be awarded a personal chair in history by the University of Dundee, and at the 'Discovery Day' lecture series held for new chairs I gave a talk titled 'A Modest Defence of Gaming', the title plundered from a rare eighteenth-century pamphlet actually defending gambling. The talk was supposed to be a taster of the sorts of theme which I then thought would inform a new research project on gambling in Britain and its first empire between c. 1660 and 1830. Very quickly thereafter, however, another research project, a major collaborative one on provincial towns in Enlightenment Scotland, took over the bulk of my attention, although I kept collecting material from various archives and keeping my eyes peeled for leads and helpful reading on gambling. Even when the project on Scottish provincial towns was completed, which was in 2014, I turned not to gambling but to writing an account of the life of the later eighteenth-century Scottish aristocratic Republican radical, Lord Daer. Once gambling did become the main preoccupation of my research, it rapidly became clear that identifying further sources was not going to be easy, and these were going to be dispersed across many, geographically disparate collections. Confronted with this challenge, and the difficulties raised by framing a convincing study of gambling, my confidence in the project, it must be said, waned at times. There is plenty of impressionistic comment, and rumour and gossip about the gambling of certain individuals and groups, but not much in the way of hard evidence. I recently heard Penelope Corfield speaking of projects for which the sources were necessarily diffuse and were perforce a long-term endeavour. This has definitely been one of those projects. Even now, I am acutely aware that more could and perhaps should be done to unearth material, or that I might well have looked in various other collections which I have ignored. Nevertheless, projects require limits, and while others might well set different ones to those which I have chosen, this endeavour has already involved a prodigious amount of archival searching. Only a portion of this effort is visible in the scholarly apparatus which accompanies the text.

The result of all this research is this book, which seeks to offer a fuller, more detailed account of gambling in Britain in the long eighteenth century than has existed hitherto, but also relate gambling, in its diverse forms, to wider impulses and patterns of change in British society in this period. Hopefully, it will offer something to people who are interested in Britain in the long eighteenth century, as well as to those with a particular interest in recreation and leisure in this period. No doubt, people will take different views about what should be in a book about gambling in this period. This one has relatively little to say, for example, about several high-profile gamblers, such as Charles James Fox or the Duchess of Devonshire. This is partly because their gambling has, to the extent it can be reconstructed in any real detail, been examined elsewhere, but also because I wanted to direct attention on to other aspects of gambling or other personalities. Nor does it say as much as it might about financial speculation and insurance, both of which had important gambling aspects to them, and attitudes towards risk in economic life more generally, which are topics which would certainly repay further investigation. To pursue all potential avenues of enquiry would, as already hinted at, be a Sisyphean task for a single historian. My choices have been, to a significant degree, led by the sources and those which I find to be most illuminating, and the desirability of drawing at least some clear boundaries around the topic. Throughout the approach is calculatedly illustrative rather than comprehensive.

For all the uncertainties which I have entertained at times about the viability of this project, I remain convinced that gambling offers a powerful lens through which to view eighteenth-century British society; it is, to paraphrase a well-known scholar, good to think with; it makes us question certain things about society in this period which have in recent years been too often taken for granted. I hope this book may motivate others to take up this challenge, and pursue it in ways different from those I have adopted.

This is not a topic which has produced a great deal of historical writing. Indeed, one might be struck by how little many historians of eighteenth-century Britain have had to say about gambling in recent years, although literary scholars have been slightly more forthcoming about representations of gambling. I should acknowledge, nevertheless, the stimulus which I have drawn from, amongst other things, the work by Thomas Kavanagh, who has written about gambling in France, and various historians of sport in this period, including David Underdown, Wray Vamplew, and Mike Huggins, as well as the authors of several very helpful unpublished doctoral theses on different aspects of sport and leisure and, in one case, the French lotteries of the eighteenth century. My substantial debts to historians, who have written about different aspects of British society in this period, will be obvious from the footnotes.

Some of the ideas and material in this book overlap, although substantially revised and refined, with earlier writings of mine published elsewhere. I thank the editors and publishers of the *English Historical Review* for permission to use material in Chapters 3 and 4, which first appeared in the journal.

As always, I owe a great deal to the staff in various private, corporate, and public archives for providing assistance. Deserving of particular mention are Pamela Hunter, the archivist of Hoare's Bank in London; Tracey Earl, who occupies a similar position at Coutts & Co.; Margherita Orlando and her team at the Bank of England Archives; Lyn Crawford and Sally Cholewa at the Royal Bank of Scotland Archives in Edinburgh; Justine Taylor, archivist at the Honourable Artillery Company; Jane Stephenson and her successor as archivist at Blair Castle, Keren Guthrie; Sir William Macpherson for his kind permission and hospitality in making accessible his archive at Newton Castle; staff at the National Records of Scotland, the National Library of Scotland, the British Library, the National Archives, the London Metropolitan Archives, and the special collections of various university libraries, notably, the universities of Edinburgh, Nottingham, and Hull; and the staff of county and local record offices in England and Scotland, too numerous to mention individually here. I record here my gratitude to Blair Castle, Perthshire, for permission to use and cite from the Atholl Papers; the owners of the Hamilton papers for permission to consult documents from their collections; the owners of the papers of the Campbell family, Marquesses of Breadalbane, for permission to consult documents from their collections. I would like to record special thanks to Ian Maun, who very kindly shared his meticulous researches on cricket in the eighteenth century, which currently run to four volumes containing a comprehensive collection of references to cricket matches found in newspapers, periodicals, and other sources. This is an invaluable resource to anyone interested in cricket and its development in eighteenth-century England. I have benefitted from suggestions about sources from, amongst others, Aaron Graham, Margot Finn, Perry Gauci, Eamonn O'Keefe, and Hazel Tubman. Jessica Davidson, my former DPhil student, very kindly undertook several research tasks for me in various archives. I am happy to record my debt to successive cohorts of students at the University of Oxford who have taken 'The London Crucible' Further Subject, several of whom have gone on to do very important research on aspects of eighteenth-century English society and culture. It has been enormously stimulating and helpful to discuss with them how we might read such sources as Boswell's 'London Journal' or *The Life and Political Opinions of the Late Sam House*. I want to record my thanks to colleagues at the University of Oxford and Worcester College for their intellectual companionship and support. I have benefitted greatly from financial support from the Lightbody Fund, and am extremely grateful to the donor who makes this available to support historical research by fellows of Worcester College. Thanks are also due to the Division of Humanities, Faculty of History, and the Provost and Fellows of Worcester College for granting me a period of extended research leave which allowed me to make substantial progress on the research underpinning this book.

Several anonymous readers have commented on earlier drafts of this book, and their criticisms and suggestions have been enormously helpful, if at times a bit daunting in respect of what might reasonably be expected of a single book. I am grateful to them; good readers are key to any halfway decent piece of scholarship. I am very grateful to Liz Friend-Smith and her team at Cambridge University Press for their support for this project and book.

This book is dedicated to two historians who have very different interests and approaches to the study of the past: Susan Whyman and Chris Whatley. Both are tenacious and brilliant researchers, and they have influenced me profoundly in how I see eighteenth-century Britain. I hope they may read this book with some perplexity perhaps, but also interest.

Abbreviations

BARS	Bedfordshire Archives and Records Service
BL	British Library
CalM	*Caledonian Mercury*
CRO	Cumbria Record Office
DA	*Daily Advertiser*
DRO	Derbyshire Record Office
ECA	Edinburgh City Archives
EdinA	*Edinburgh Advertiser*
GA	*General Advertiser*
GEP	*General Evening Post*
HJ	*Historical Journal*
HRO	Hampshire Record Office
KARC	Kent Archives and Records Centre
LA	Lincolnshire Archives
LEP	*London Evening Post*
LMA	London Metropolitan Archives
MChr	*Morning Chronicle*
NA	Nottinghamshire Archives
NLS	National Library of Scotland
NRAS	National Register of Archives of Scotland
NRO	Norfolk Record Office
NRS	National Records of Scotland
NYRO	North Yorkshire Record Office
PA	*Public Advertiser*
PKCA	Perth and Kinross Council Archives
PP	parliamentary papers
RBS	Royal Bank of Scotland
RMA	Royal Mail Archives
SCA	Sheffield City Archives
SHC	Surrey History Centre

SJChr	*St James's Chronicle*
SRO	Shropshire Record Office
TNA	The National Archives
WEP	*Whitehall Evening Post*
WSRO	Wiltshire and Swindon Record Office

Introduction

'England was gripped by gambling fever.' 'Men bet on political events, births, deaths – any future happening,' while 'Cards were the opium of the polite.' So Roy Porter informed readers of his 1982 history of eighteenth-century English society.[1] It was a common observation in accounts of this period written in the second half of the previous century, being asserted by historians as different in type as J. H. Plumb and P. G. M. Dickson.[2] Gambling cut across gender and class boundaries, and its hold on society was, Gillian Russell remarked in 1980, one of the 'enduring themes of eighteenth-century commentary'.[3] Roger Munting, in his general history of gambling in Britain and the United States, published in 1996, asserted with equal assurance, 'There is no doubt that this interest in gambling reached a peak in the eighteenth century and was one which affected all levels of society.'[4]

Insofar as general explanations were offered, two were favoured. In the first, gambling was viewed as a response to the harsh, brutal side to life in eighteenth-century England, performing an important role as a necessary, or entirely comprehensible at least, form of escapist pleasure-seeking. The second emphasized the impact of the changing moral and religious climate. According to this explanation, this was a period when restraints on pleasure were decisively loosened – wedged between what sceptical philosopher and historian David Hume was wont to

1 Roy Porter, *English Society in the Eighteenth Century* (London, 1982), p. 255.

2 J. H. Plumb, *England in the Eighteenth Century (1714–1815)* (London, 1950), p. 13; P. G. M. Dickson, *The Financial Revolution in England: A Study in the Development of Public Credit, 1688–1756* (London, 1967), p. 45.

3 Gillian Russell, '"Faro's Daughters": Female Gamesters, Politics, and the Discourse of Finance in 1790s Britain', *Eighteenth Century Studies*, 33 (2000), 481.

4 Roger Munting, *An Economic and Social History of Gambling in Britain and the USA* (Manchester, 1996), p. 115; Janet E. Mullin repeats this notion of a 'rampant gambling culture' as she puts it, in her recent book, *A Six Penny at Whist: Gaming and the English Middle Classes 1680–1830* (Woodbridge, 2015), p. 7. It also informs Mike Huggins, 'Racing Culture, Betting and Sporting Protomodernity: The 1750 Newmarket Carriage Match', *Journal of Sport History*, 42 (2015), 327–39.

describe as the 'gloomy spirit of the Puritans' of the sixteenth and seventeenth centuries, and the Evangelically inspired respectability of the Victorians. This has the advantage at least of invoking a specific historical context; after all, misery and hardship were hardly peculiar inventions of the eighteenth century. If neither explanation was sufficient, however, it was still possible to invoke the idea that an impulse to gamble derived in some way from human nature, merely awaiting opportunities to find expression. Gambling was not a new phenomenon, going back to Roman times, if not earlier; it can also be found in most societies. When the chance arose, or was provided in a variety of new ways, as in England and Britain in this period, gambling inevitably flourished.[5]

More recent historical scholarship has tended to relegate gambling to the periphery of views of British society in the long eighteenth century. A recent book on the metropolitan fashionable elite includes not a single word on the subject.[6] Studies of sport and recreation have also become less common than they were twenty years ago, which may partly explain it.[7] It may also be because, while contemporary commentary on gambling is, as Russell says, abundant and has been studied in some detail,[8] direct evidence for gambling is by its nature limited and highly selective. The silences are clamorous ones, and the question of how to interpret these is one to which we will need to turn at various points in this book.

More importantly, however, this neglect is symptomatic of major trends in the social and cultural history of the period during the last twenty years or so. To a quite striking degree these were set by Paul Langford in his now classic contribution to the New Oxford History of England series, *A Polite and Commercial People: England 1727–1787* (Oxford, 1989). The main theme around which Langford's account was organized was the growing influence of the urban middling sort. It was the achievement of this expanding, diversifying social stratum not just to create unexampled levels of economic dynamism and prosperity,

[5] See e.g. John Habakkuk, *Marriage, Debt and the Estates System: English Landownership 1650–1950* (Oxford, 1994), pp. 294–6.

[6] Hannah Greig, *The Beau Monde: Fashionable Society in Georgian London* (Oxford, 2013).

[7] Although see David Underdown, *Start of Play: Cricket and Culture in Eighteenth-Century England* (London, 2000); Mike Huggins, *Horse Racing and British Society in the Long Eighteenth Century* (Martlesham, 2018); Mike Huggins, 'Popular Culture and Sporting Life in the Rural Margins of Late Eighteenth-Century England: The World of Robert Anderson, "The Cumberland Bard"', *Eighteenth Century Studies*, 45 (2012), 189–205.

[8] Russell, 'Faro's Daughters'. See also Donna T. Andrew, *Aristocratic Vice: The Attacks on Duelling, Suicide, Adultery and Gambling in Eighteenth Century England* (New Haven, CT and London, 2013); Phyllis Deutch, 'Moral Trespass in Georgian London: Gaming, Gender, and Electoral Politics in the Age of George III', *Historical Journal*, 39 (1996), 637–56.

but to reshape society and the social order. They did so, Langford suggests, through a 'revolution by conjunction', quietly and subtly transforming cultural and social identities to reflect their priorities and preoccupations.[9] The principal vehicle for this process was 'politeness', a set of values and code of manners which served to draw together the different elements of propertied society, and in so doing enabled the middling sort to gain enhanced social recognition whilst also subordinating the aristocratic elites, or at least a significant proportion of them, to the new cultural economy. This, amongst other things, led to the rise in the later eighteenth century of an increasingly sharp critique of aristocratic mores and culture, focused on upper class adultery and gambling.[10] Where this left gambling *practices* is unclear – it coincided after all with what Langford dubbed 'the age of vanity' of the 1770s and 1780s, with its many episodes of high profile aristocratic delinquency, among which gaming featured prominently.[11] Gambling was viewed, however, as an example of the immoral behaviour of an irresponsible aristocracy or conversely a dangerous contagion among the lower orders, the two groups positioned on opposite sides of the moral and social high-plateau inhabited by an increasingly self-assured middling sort. What we are seeing here is the prefiguring of patterns and divisions which are often seen as characterizing Victorian society. Where gambling features, in short, is mainly in terms of why *opposition* to it rose to become a powerful force in later Georgian England.

To be sure, not everyone accepts Langford's portrayal of eighteenth-century English society. Notoriously, a few years prior to publication of Langford's volume, Jonathan Clark portrayed England between 1660 and 1832 as an 'ancien regime', characterized, so he said, by the hegemonic influence of monarchy, aristocracy, and the established church.[12] Others have sought to question Langford's emphasis on emulation of those above them on the social ladder as the dominant and

[9] Langford, *Polite and Commercial People*, p. 67, where the author writes, 'This was a revolution by conjunction rather than confrontation, but it was a revolution none the less, transforming the pattern of social relations, and subtly reshaping the role of that governing class which was the object of imitation.'

[10] See also, more recently, in a work which in many ways mirrors and confirms Langford's narrative, partly by emphasizing the role of the press as a vehicle of middling opinion, Andrew, *Aristocratic Vice*.

[11] Langford, *Polite and Commercial People*, pp. 582–90.

[12] J. C. D. Clark, *English Society, 1688–1832: Ideology, Social Structure and Political Practice during the Ancient Regime* (Cambridge, 1985). In the revised edition of this book, published in 2000, Clark pays greater attention to towns and politeness as forces in society, but portrays the latter, *contra* Langford, as symptomatic of the cultural hegemony of the aristocracy and court.

binding social dynamic at work within the diverse middling sort, whilst at the same time questioning the extent of the influence of polite values and ideals at this level of society. The lives of many professionals, merchants, tradesmen, and shopkeepers were rather, it is argued, focused on industry, amenity, propriety, and self-government. This, in turn, meant contriving better means to regulate uncertainty and manage risk in their lives, which also meant, crucially, regulating themselves and those over whom they were expected to exercise control – wives, children, servants, and apprentices.[13] Trade or the market on this view bred its own distinctive culture and values, with an emphasis on hard work, a rejection of 'extravagance', and strict, methodical accounting both for one's conduct and income, an outlook which was (often) compatible with and reinforced by religious belief.[14] In an economy which relied on widely extended chains of credit, such as prevailed in eighteenth-century England, an ideal of virtuous or prudential masculinity took an even tighter hold among the expanding ranks of the middling sort, while notions of female propriety, especially in respect of consumption and leisure, were constructed as complementary to this ideal.[15] As Julian Hoppit neatly put it some years ago now, 'credit went to the creditable'.[16] Gambling, as a form of idleness and exemplifying rejection of self-government and equanimity, was something to be shunned and of which sternly to disapprove.

[13] See esp. Margaret R. Hunt, *The Middling Sort: Commerce, Gender, and the Family in England, 1680–1780* (Berkeley, CA, 1996), and, more recently, in an account which both supports and qualifies Hunt's in various important ways, Karen Harvey, *The Little Republic: Masculinity & Domestic Authority in Eighteenth-Century Britain* (Oxford, 2012).

[14] See esp. Hannah Barker, 'Soul, Purse and Family: Middling and Lower Class Masculinity in Eighteenth-Century Manchester', *Social History*, 33 (2008), 12–35; Hannah Barker, 'A Grocer's Tale: Gender, Family and Class in Early Eighteenth-Century Manchester', *Gender & History*, 21 (2009), 340–57; Hannah Barker, 'A Devout and Commercial People: Religion and Trade in Manchester during the Long Eighteenth Century', in Elaine Chalus and Perry Gauci (eds.), *Revisiting the Polite and Commercial People: Essays in Georgian Politics, Society and Culture in Honour of Professor Paul Langford* (Oxford, 2019), pp. 136–52; Matthew Kadane, *The Watchful Clothier: The Life of an Eighteenth-Century Protestant Capitalist* (New Haven, CT, 2013); John Smail, 'Coming of Age in Trade: Masculinity and Commerce in Eighteenth Century England', in Margaret Jacob and Catherine Secretan (eds.), *The Self Perception of Early Modern Capitalists* (New York, 2008), pp. 236–40.

[15] This is most starkly argued in Woodruff D. Smith, *Consumption and the Making of Respectability* (New York, 2002).

[16] Julian Hoppit, 'Attitudes to Credit in Britain, 1680–1790', *Historical Journal*, 33 (1990), 319. For a recent affirmation of the new importance of 'reputation' in this period as a source of creditworthiness, see also Alexandra Shepard, *Accounting for Oneself: Worth, Status and the Social Order in Early Modern England* (Oxford, 2015), pp. 278–302.

Or, as Janet Mullin proposes in an important exception to the general neglect of gambling, card playing was taken up and simultaneously tamed by middling people, being reconstituted as a near ubiquitous activity which served to confirm and inculcate their priorities of prudence and self-control. 'The well documented restraint, moderation and discretion of the trade and professional classes', she declares, 'permeated their hours away from work and shaped their choice of leisure activities, both in deciding what games to play and where and how to play them.'[17] On this view, Langford's 'polite and commercial people' eagerly took to carding as an important element in their wider, developing culture of sociability. Typically, the games played – among which whist was preeminent – involved elements of calculation and cooperation, were for modest stakes, and were engaged in within strictly delimited time frames. Card playing was firmly embedded within a culture of gentility which emphatically lacked the individualistic performance, the hyper-competitiveness, the marathon sessions, and the heedless risk-taking which were (supposedly) the stuff of elite gambling.[18] Alongside building and perpetuating social and business networks, card playing might also serve as a training for the young in the financial, numerical skills, and accounting which enabled the middling sort to exert greater control over themselves and their fortunes.

If there was a gambling mania in eighteenth-century Britain, therefore – we will shortly return to the question of Britain – the story to which more recent historiography seems to be leading us is one of a 'mania' that was being cumulatively drained of energy, or repressed, from the final third of the eighteenth century, if not earlier, and which was, in any case, less widespread than we might once have supposed. Or, more pointedly, oppositions between those who did and did not gamble were becoming more visible, pervasive, and decisive in impact. Certain qualifications to this account would be required. The early eighteenth century was hardly lacking after all in hostility to 'immoral' activities such as gambling, as testified to by the rise of the Reformation of Manners movement in the 1690s, which battled on with its campaign to eliminate 'lewdness and bawdry' for several decades in the face of mounting opposition and

[17] Mullin, *A Six Penny at Whist*, p. 7. Mullin is fully aware that not all among the middling sort followed these protocols, that some among this group gambled in a much less prudent manner.

[18] This is not to imply that self-presentation and concern about image were not very much part of the middling world of prudent card playing, but this was about subordination to a collective identity not a highly resistant, exhibitionist individualism.

indifference, before finally fizzling out in the later 1730s.[19] It also presumes that attitudes towards gambling map fairly neatly onto social class or rank, a proposition which, while frequently repeated, is, as will be argued in subsequent chapters, highly doubtful.

I. A British 'Gambling Mania'?

A new history, therefore, of gambling in eighteenth-century Britain should begin by looking afresh at the notion of a gambling mania which has cast its long historiographical shadow. It barely needs pointing out that the term is very ill-defined. It is, nevertheless, usually used in two, closely related senses: first, to imply a deep-seated and widespread impulse to gamble; and, second, to suggest something of the distinctive character of this impulse – as being marked by a peculiar intensity. Gambling, on this account, is portrayed as being essentially irrational.

To begin with the first of these notions – the remarkable social and geographical extent of the impulse to gamble: the salient question is *not* whether this was true – plenty of evidence for this will be provided at different points in this book – but how exceptional in this was eighteenth-century Britain. Was the eighteenth-century 'gambling mania' a peculiarly British phenomenon? Or, rather English, since it needs to be stated from the outset that Scottish society in this period has never been so described, and with good reason. For, even if the dread power of the 'parish theocracy' in Scotland can easily be exaggerated, the conjoined influences of the Kirk and a Calvinist Presbyterian religion that was overtly hostile to secular pleasures were evident enough.[20] Scottish society was also significantly poorer than its neighbour to the south, while its urban and rural middling strata were smaller and collectively less influential before the early nineteenth century. Moreover, wealthy Scots disposed to gamble for large sums of money were more likely to do so in

[19] R. B. Shoemaker, 'Reforming the City: The Reformation of Manners Campaign in London, 1690–1738', in Lee Davison et al. (eds.), *Stilling the Grumbling Hive: The Response to Social and Economic Problems in England, 1689–1750* (Stroud and New York, 1992), pp. 99–120; T. C. Curtis and W. A. Speck, 'The Societies for the Reformation of Manners: A Case Study in the Theory and Practice of Moral Reform', *Literature and History*, 3 (1976), 45–64. Gaming was not a major preoccupation of the reformation of manners movement, or rather was only very intermittently so. For which, see Chapter 5, pp. 247, 252. The Reformation of Manners campaign was revived briefly in the later 1750s, before its much stronger revival in the 1780s.

[20] This is not to deny the importance of the growing spirit of accommodation with secular currents in the Kirk, which lay behind the rise of so-called Moderate ascendancy from the middle of the eighteenth century. This, however, was not based on numerical or geographical hegemony, but political control; and the Popular Party remained well entrenched and dominant in many parishes, especially in the western lowlands.

London, Bath, or another of the English resort towns. We will meet several such people in this book.

Nevertheless, Scots *in* Scotland did gamble, albeit extant evidence for this is sparse. There was plenty of gambling, of various kinds, in the taverns which huddled on and off old Edinburgh's main street, the High Street. In 1753, an Edinburgh vintner's (wine merchant's) was the site for a bet between a writer (lawyer) and a merchant for a hogshead of wine to see who could walk the fastest from the High Street to the top of Arthur's Seat.[21] At the end of the eighteenth century, the infamous William 'Deacon' Brodie and his cronies were to be found gambling in clubs which met in taverns, such as Clark's in Fleshmarket Close, one of the narrow alleys which ran off the High Street.[22] The rare glimpses afforded by the archives of gambling among the Scottish middling and lower orders suggest much more going on of this than that for which we have a record. In 1724, to cite one example, Robert Lermont and his wife were summoned before the Hawick kirk session for keeping a 'gameing house'. Lermont had previously promised to desist from allowing 'boyes and apprentices to resort to his house for gameing att ye cards'. He appeared before the session on 17 January, and was admonished for not keeping to his promise, but several days later he was back in trouble when it was reported 'that manie did still haunt' his house, for 'gameing at cards'. Eight years earlier, a meeting of the same kirk session had rebuked several people, including the innkeeper where the incident took place, an excise officer, the town's Baillie, and a merchant, for a brawl that had taken place after a raffle had been held to dispose of three-cornered hat.[23]

Politics, war and diplomacy, and various sports – golf, bowling, cock-fighting, and from the second half of the century, horse racing – furnished plentiful opportunities for members of the Scots landed and urban elites, and, indeed, those below them on the social scale, to make wagers.[24] In 1801, a rather grumpy, elderly John Ramsay of Ochtertyre described for his neighbour and regular correspondent, Elizabeth

[21] NLS, Acc 6257, memorandum of wager in pocket book of David Bruce of Kinnaird, 14 Feb. 1753.

[22] *The Trial of William Brodie Wright and Cabinet Maker in Edinburgh and George Smith Grocer There, Before the High Court of Justiciary* (Edinburgh, 1788).

[23] Scottish Borders Archives and Local History Centre, Hawick, CH2/1122/2, Hawick Old Kirk Sessions, minutes and accounts, 1711–25, 29 Jan., 12 Feb. 1716; 12, 17, 24 Jan., 2 Feb. 1724.

[24] For betting on politics, see e.g. NRS, Montrose Papers, GD220/5/454/9, Lord Justice Clerk to the Duke of Montrose, Edinburgh, 22 Jan. 1715; John Strang, *Glasgow and its* Clubs; *Or Glimpses of the Condition, Manners, Characters, & Quiddities of the City, during the Past & Present Century* (London and Glasgow, 1856), p. 465; NLS, Acc 11208, Papers of

Graham, visiting the cockpit in Edinburgh where he had been 'astonished at the mixture of peers and sharpers, lawyers and pickpockets'. For Ramsay, this offered the perfect excuse to bemoan, as he put it, the 'sad landscape of modern manners'. His particular target was the 'young men of fashion', brought up in 'unprincipled, half-educated style'. 'They are', he grizzled, 'little less frivolous and licentious than the late French noblesse – heaven grant they are not visited a similar scourge.'[25] Such words might be dismissed as no more than the conservatism of the old, sharpened in this case by the turmoil and violence unleashed by the French Revolution, but the shifts they reflected in leisure habits and manners that had occurred in recent decades were far-reaching. Ramsay's picture, shorn of the moral disapproval, might well fit a good deal of the life of the Edinburgh merchant Alexander Anderson. His later eighteenth-century world was one replete with fashionable clothes, entertainments, race meetings, golf, balls, assemblies, and card playing, at which he often seems to have lost a few pounds.[26] As we will see in later chapters, we can also find a good many Scots, including among the labouring classes, adventuring in the lottery.

However, to talk of a gambling mania in eighteenth-century Scotland would simply be bizarre. If many Scots were speculators, it was in a rather different sense; their energies went into making money or securing career advancement. These traits, long present in Scottish society, were ones which became increasingly and starkly visible in the eagerness with which Scots seized on such opportunities beyond their country's borders, which in the eighteenth century meant pre-eminently London, and even more strikingly North America, the Caribbean, and India.[27]

the Honourable Company of Edinburgh Golfers, 36–42, Bet Books, 1776–1826. In the absence of newspaper evidence, which historians of such things south of the border have mined very profitably to chart incidence of such events, the frequency of cockfighting matches north of the border is uncertain. Cockfighting came to Dunfermline in 1705, and appears to have been an annual occurrence on handsel Mondays until 1797. (Ebenezer Henderson, *The Annals of Dunfermline and Vicinity from the earlier authentic period to the present time AD 1069–1878* (Glasgow, 1879), p. 376.) Bowling greens were present in a good number of Scottish burghs. One of the best sources for this is town maps, where these exist. For horse racing, see ch. 1, pp. 49–62.

25 *Letters of John Ramsay of Ochtertyre 1799–1812*, ed. B. L. H. Horn (Edinburgh, 1966), pp. 43–5, Ramsay to Elizabeth Graham, 24 Mar. 1801. According to the Edinburgh bookseller and occasional writer, William Creech, the Edinburgh cockpit was established in 1785 (Hugo Arnot, *The History of Edinburgh, From the Earliest Accounts to the Present Time* (Edinburgh, 1788), Appendix, p. 667).

26 NLS, MS 8899, Account Book, 1771–96, of Alexander Anderson, merchant and burgess of Edinburgh.

27 The literature on the importance of empire as a means of gaining or recovering fortunes for Scots in the eighteenth century has grown hugely in recent years, and is far too large

The comparison, nevertheless, usually made in this context is not one between England and Scotland, although it must be borne in mind in what follows: rather, it is that between England and continental Europe, or more narrowly England and France. The British/English were unusual, so it is sometimes said, in their habit of betting on the outcome of political and international events and wars, while horse racing and cricket were among English exports to France in the eighteenth century.[28] Whether this contrast really holds up is extremely doubtful. High stakes gambling – 'deep play' as it was commonly known – was readily found on the European mainland. It was this reality which enabled the Venetian adventurer Casanova to gain an entrée into the world of the European aristocracy – in France, Italy, the United Provinces, Russia, Spain, and various German states. The gambling capital of eighteenth-century Europe was the watering hole of Spa in Liège in the Austrian Netherlands (present-day Belgium).[29] Britons on or contemplating a grand tour were repeatedly warned about the dangers of gaming and other entrapments.[30] Lord Lincoln, heir to the 2nd Duke of Newcastle, contrived to lose £6,000 to a Venetian sharper in Florence in 1771.[31] At the start of his grand tour forty years earlier, Edward Mellish declared to his father, Joseph Mellish of Blyth Hall, Yorkshire:

> My uncle desires … that I would make my observation of the People at Paris, & avoid all Play and Extravagance, which is very good advice. The French only regard strangers according to the money they spend and figure they make with their Equipages and provided you game and play you will be well received in the best company at Paris, where one risques [sic] losing five ten or fifteen pounds sterling in two hours time, besides at Games of Hazard [a dice game], the French of the very best Fashion make no scruple of cheating you …

A few months later, from Saumur on the Loire, Edward informed his mother, in words which need to be taken note of: 'I avoid Gaming as

to list in detail here. But see, T. M. Devine, *Scotland's Empire, 1660–1815* (London, 2003); Douglas Hamilton, 'Scotland and the Eighteenth-Century Empire', in T. M. Devine and Jenny Wormald (eds.), *The Oxford Handbook of Modern Scottish History* (Oxford, 2012), pp. 424–38. For London Scots, see Stana Nenadic (ed.), *Scots in London in the Eighteenth Century* (Lewisburg, PA, 2010).

28 C. H. Lockitt, *The Relations of French and English Society (1763–1793)* (London,1920), pp. 45–8.

29 Thomas M. Kavanagh, *Dice, Cards, Wheels: A Different History of French Culture* (Philadelphia, PA, 2005), pp. 85, 89.

30 On which, see Henry French and Mark Rothery, *Mans's Estate: Landed Gentry Mentalities, 1660–1914* (Oxford, 2012), ch. 3.

31 University of Nottingham, Manuscripts and Special Collections, Newcastle (Clumber) Collection, Ne C 3023, G. Chamberlayne, Pisa, to the Duke of Newcastle, 20 Dec. 1771; 3022, same to same, Florence, 28 Dec. 1771; 3280, Lord Lincoln, Naples, to the Duke of Newcastle, 30 Jan. 1772.

much as it is possible, which is a most pernicious entertainment, & there is no Country in the World free from *except England*' (my emphasis).[32] Writing about the later eighteenth century, Leslie Mitchell notes that a young man who refused to gamble in Paris was known as 'inutile'.[33]

The strict limits to British exceptionalism in this context are also strongly suggested by the history of official lotteries in eighteenth-century Europe. While the Dutch and English led the way from the 1690s in using such devices to raise public money, royal and public lotteries spread very widely in Europe – to Rome in 1732, Vienna in 1751, Brussels in 1760, Madrid and Berlin in 1763, and Warsaw in 1768, to name but a few places.[34] In France, prior to 1776 and the establishment of the *Loterie Royale*, lotteries were mainly charitable or religious in purpose. Either they were a response by hospitals to climbing numbers of poor resulting from the combined effects of war and subsistence crises in the late seventeenth and early eighteenth centuries, or they were devices by congregations to finance church construction projects. Sales of tickets were not confined to Paris, and all operated under the oversight of the royal administration. Several of them became permanent. By the mid eighteenth century, lotteries were being more widely used in France to finance public projects, including, from 1757, a military school which had opened in Paris six years earlier, a lottery recently described by one historian as 'by far the largest lottery Europe had ever known'.[35] These lotteries were all suppressed, however, in 1776, when the *Loterie Royale* was founded. The French state lottery was a huge bureaucratic enterprise, with a presence throughout the country. Following the example of the *Loterie de L'École Militaire*, it used the Genoese style lottery, rather than, as was the case in England and earlier French lotteries, the Venetian one. Participants bet on a series of numbers being drawn, with the maximum sequence being five. They could also bet on the exact order in which the numbers were drawn.

The French state lottery in the eighteenth century was, in short, the gambler's lottery *par excellence*. What it allowed was seven possible wagers – starting with one on any single number being drawn, then the

[32] University of Nottingham, Manuscripts and Special Collections, The Mellish Collection, Me C 24/3/18, Edward Mellish, Paris, to Joseph Mellish, 8 Nov. 1730; 24/3/10, Edward Mellish, Saumur, to Mrs Mellish, 25 Feb. 1731.

[33] Leslie Mitchell, *The Whig World 1760–1837* (London and New York, 2005), p. 17.

[34] Marie-Laure Legay, *Les Loteries Royales dans L'Europe des Lumières (1680–1815)*, (Lille, 2014).

[35] Robert Kruckeberg, 'The Royal Lottery and the Old Regime: Financial Innovation and Modern Political Culture', *French Historical Studies*, 37 (2014), 35. This paragraph draws heavily on Kruckeberg's article.

precise order in which it was drawn, then two numbers and their precise order, then on three, four, and five numbers. What is more, the sum paid out in prizes was 'of an order of magnitude greater than any previous lottery' anywhere. For five numbers, the so-called *quine*, the amount paid was a million times the player's wager. Wagers could, moreover, be for sums as low as six deniers, an option deliberately intended to encourage participation among the lower orders. The aim was to make it more attractive than any foreign lottery, and thus confer on it an effective monopoly in France. It was hugely successful, to the extent that participation may well have become an almost normal activity for Parisian workers.

Anyone still tempted to believe that gambling in England was more pervasive than on the European mainland would do well to take heed of comments made by François de la Rochefoucauld, son of the duc de Liancourt. Visiting Britain in the early 1780s, Rochefoucauld noted that 'in general' gaming in England was of a 'very modest kind'.[36] No doubt he had in mind partly the card play which, in Porter's witty phrase, had become the 'opium of the polite', and forms the focus of Mullin's study, referred to above, in which small sums were wagered by women and men of the upper and middling classes on the outcome of games such as whist or piquet. On the other hand, he also noted that every town had its 'group of men' who played for 'very high sums', as well as the existence of men whom he called 'black legs' who staked very large sums on betting on horse races. English gambling may in the end simply have become more visible than elsewhere in Europe; or rather it was *made* more visible by the existence of a uniquely free, bold, ebullient and creative print media, which encompassed multiplying newspapers, periodicals and, not least importantly, satirical cartoons, as well that great 'English' literary innovation of the period, and significant export and agent of English cultural influence, the novel.[37] Whether it was more common is altogether more questionable.

There are, therefore, good grounds for thinking that the impulse to gamble in England/Britain in this period was less distinctive than is sometimes supposed. However, as an analytical tool the notion of a gambling mania is blunt in the extreme – so blunt, in fact, as to be well-nigh useless. In the first place this is because of its evasiveness and

[36] *A Frenchman in England 1784: Being the Mélanges sur L'Angleterre of François de la Rochfoucauld*, ed. Jean Marchand (Cambridge, 1933), pp. 59–69.

[37] For the prominence of gambling as a theme in contemporary novels, and an important explanation for this, which has some similarities with views advanced in this book, see Jessica Richard, *The Romance of Gambling in the Eighteenth Century British Novel* (Basingstoke, 2011).

slipperiness with respect to the matter of chronology. As long ago as 1965 Lawrence Stone argued that high stakes gambling in the seventeenth century was a form of 'conspicuous expenditure' which was 'deeply ingrained' in what he characterized as, at its apex, 'an idle and exhibitionist society'. 'It was', Stone wrote, 'as important [for a gentleman] to know how to play cards or handle the dice as it was to be able to ride a horse or dance a galliard.'[38] Another scholar has pointed out that critiques of gambling became *more common* after 1689, in reaction to the libertinism of the Restoration.[39] Gambling among the rest of society, including the lower orders, was hardly rare before 1689, one symptom of which was the remarkable growth in the manufacture of packs of cards during the seventeenth century, reaching, as Nicholas Tosney has shown, over a million a year in the 1680s. This, rather astonishingly, equated to something like one pack per household *per annum*.[40] When and where in society the gambling mania began, whether it waxed more strongly at certain moments and within some social strata, or, indeed, when it ended may well be unanswerable questions; however, they are usually ignored by historians.

This and other limitations of the notion will become only more apparent in the course of this book as we examine different practices and cultures of gambling in Britain in the long eighteenth century. Here two very different illustrations suffice to highlight several further problems with which it is associated. The first concerns distinctions between different sorts of gambling as began to be described above by Rochefoucauld in the 1780s. The distances between them were so great that thinking about them as a single phenomenon is unhelpful, if not downright nonsensical; they meant and were motivated by very different things. For in one – the 'modest kind' – control or the setting of limits was, as Mullin has emphasized, very much the point; the purpose was recreational and social rather than primarily or significantly financial or self-consciously performative; in another – that of the 'black legs' the purpose was presumably one narrowly of financial gain, while in the final one – the high stakes play among groups primarily (but not exclusively by any means) of men – it was financial, but more especially and emphatically exhibitionist – hence the eye-bulging size of the stakes.[41]

Our second illustration moves us well away from the metropolitan and the ostensibly polite and fashionable to the Wales of small tradesmen,

[38] Lawrence Stone, *The Crisis of the Aristocracy, 1558–1641* (Oxford, 1965), pp. 571, 567.
[39] James E. Evans, '"A Scene of the Uttmost Vanity": The Spectacle of Gambling in Late Stuart Culture', *Studies in Eighteenth Century Culture*, 31 (2002), 8.
[40] Nicholas Tosney, 'The Playing Card Trade in Early Modern England', *Historical Research*, 84 (2011), 637–56.
[41] Mullin, *A Six Penny at Whist.*

innkeepers, artisans, and labourers as captured in the diary of William Thomas of Michelston-Super-Ely, Glamorgan.[42] At one level this record provides abundant support for the popularity and frequent intensity of gambling at this level of society. From the annual horse and foot races staged over three days in June on Stalling Down near Cowbridge, to frequent and frequently protracted cock matches, which could last up to three days and nights, and feats of pedestrianism, opportunities to wager money were seemingly a regular part of an annual recreational calendar and, for some, everyday life. More subtle messages are conveyed by Thomas, who regarded what he viewed mostly as the excesses of his neighbours with an oft-disapproving eye. Despite this judgemental attitude, we get from him a good sense of how gambling might function as a performance of hyper-masculinity at this level of society. On 10 October 1763, Thomas recorded the death of 'old Howel Mathew', a gardener and cousin of his mother – 'a great cock fighter and lover of all pleasure and vanity'. Several years later, it was the death by drowning of Edmondo of Port Bello, an innkeeper: 'A great cock fighter, and a reputed very unhonest, unjust sort of a man, being gone from Nothing in appearance very wealthy in a few years. Had as the report runs six or seven watches in his house.'[43] Thomas's was a world of typically rough, unruly recreations – or rather the world he observed around him was this – over which innkeepers often presided; but one also in which people sought fortunes, and appearance could readily deceive as people 'lived pompous', as he put it. In the entry in his diary for 8 July 1768, he noted:

> This night Aquila, the great innkeeper in the New Inn at Cardiff, escaped from under the Bailiffs hands by deceiving them to go to bed, and absconded. Being in the matter of 400£ debt. Debt, not 15 months since he began business, keeping such entertainment that any lord could desire. Had one bed worth 40£ and here most of the nobility resorted. He began from nothing, *wholly on credit* ...[44] (My emphasis.)

Thomas begins to tell us of a society where the gentry remained firmly at the apex, but in which in various other ways social order was in considerable flux. It was also one in which reputations were shaped by gambling in different, contradictory ways, reflecting the frequent collisions between very different values and beliefs, and different notions of masculinity, which informed behaviour. One individual was simply, but approvingly, described as a 'polite, saving man'. On 15 June 1778, it was the death of 'Old David of Cymmer', a yeoman of ninety-five, that was

[42] *The Diary of William Thomas of Michelston-Super-Ely, near St. Fagans Glamorgan, 1762–1795*, abridged and edited by R. T. W. Denning (Cardiff, 1995).

[43] *Diary of William Thomas*, ed. Denning, pp. 87, 232. [44] Ibid., pp. 206–7.

recorded, 'formerly one of the greatest gamblers about racing and cock-fighting in these parts'.[45] It was also one in which certain people actively opposed gambling and sought its suppression. It was, in short, a society that produced a multiplicity of cultures and types of speculation, but also where there was much more nuance and complexity in attitudes towards gambling *throughout society* than are commonly acknowledged by historians.

Was gambling irrational – the second element of the idea of a 'gambling mania'? This is almost too easy to rebut. Rationality depends very largely on context, and in relation to what we view it. Contemporary critics calling for its suppression, not surprisingly perhaps, condemned gambling – or 'gaming', as they more usually called it – as irrational. Their attacks, however, were highly selective, and they tended to see what they wanted to see. It was only certain types of gambling that they attacked, or, as often, the gambling of certain types of people – frequently, although not always, that of the lower orders.[46] As the modern literature on gambling acknowledges, people gamble for all sorts of reasons, many of them quite rational ones – recreation, stimulation, gain, aspiration, as well as acquisition of social status or identification with a particular group.[47] In some cases, they are staking their money on chance pure and simple, in others on judgement and skill, and sometimes on a mix of all three. There are 'problem gamblers', who are a special case; but self-mastery, the exercise of careful judgement and gambling are not intrinsically opposed.[48] If gambling were merely irrational, it is hard to see how it could be the subject for serious historical study, apart from charting its presence in different parts of society.

II. New Perspectives: Reconnecting Gambling and Its Contexts

Thomas Kavanagh has declared in a wide-ranging history of gambling in France over several centuries that 'there can be no general or universal history of gambling. The way people gamble, and what that activity says

45 Ibid., pp. 286, 365.

46 The strong class bias of criticisms of gambling in Britain in the eighteenth century but also later periods has been emphasized elsewhere. For a recent argument regarding this in relation to the lottery, see James Raven, 'Debating the lottery in Britain c.1750–1830', in Manfred Zollinger (ed.), *Random Riches: Gambling Past and Present* (Ashgate, 2015), pp. 87–104.

47 See e.g. Alistair Bruce, 'Betting Motivation and Behaviour', in Leighton Vaughan-Williams and Donald S. Siegel (eds.), *The Oxford Handbook of the Economics of Gambling* (Oxford, 2013), pp. 1–24.

48 See e.g. Ross McKibbin, 'Working-Class Gambling in Britain, 1880–1939', in Ross McKibbin, *The Ideologies of Class: Social Relations in Britain 1880–1950* (Oxford, 1991), pp. 101–38.

of them, are parts of a larger cultural whole defined by the contours and tensions of a given society at a given time'.[49] It is firmly with this notion in mind that the research underpinning this book was undertaken. The reason for exploring gambling can only be partly to identify and reconstruct gambling practices in the past; the deeper purpose is to try and show what light these shed back onto society and the values, hopes, and expectations that informed the lives of various groups within it. To put this a bit differently, gambling cannot be understood independently of the contexts and broader cultural, social, and economic currents in which it was enfolded and from which it gained its specific meanings. The remainder of this Introduction sketches a series of arguments in relation to this which are pursued in the rest of this book.

The first of these, borrowing from behavioural studies of modern gambling habits, concerns the relationships between 'chance', speculative impulses, and social fluidity, and between these and gambling.[50] Britain in this period may not be best characterized as a 'risk society'.[51] Nevertheless, it was one in which questions of fortune and chance came to preoccupy people in novel ways. Paradoxically, one reason for this was a consequence of attempts to diminish the potential impact of misfortune. As briefly alluded to above, an important development in eighteenth-century Britain was the rise and spread of new ways of attempting to minimize and manage misadventure. This was a development that was associated with, but not driven by before the later eighteenth century, new probabilistic forms of reasoning that had been generated in part by consideration of gambling problems, and which were linked in turn to the emergence of a new figure in gambling

[49] Kavanagh, *Dice, Cards, Wheels*, p. 4.

[50] Reuven Brenner with Gabrielle Brenner, *Gambling and Speculation: A Theory, A History, and a Future of Some Human Decisions* (Cambridge, 1990). The emphasis in this book is on lottery-style wagering, especially among the poor. However, one of their main arguments is that people of *all* classes who have not previously gambled will decide to do so when they are confronted by increased economic insecurity. They also emphasize that perceptions of one's wealth are relative. 'When people are outdone by their fellows, they pin their hopes on undertaking risks they shunned before. Some play games of chance and others venture into entrepreneurial or criminal acts.' Risk-taking thus increases when people perceive threats to their economic security and that others are doing better than them.

[51] 'Risk' is a very specific idea, although it is frequently conflated, in potentially confusing ways, with uncertainty. 'Risk', strictly defined, is a category of understanding based on the measurement of potential outcomes. It is, in short, a matter of *measured* uncertainties. Emily C. Nacol has recently suggested, however, that the idea of 'risk' became generally current 'through a slow transformation in the late seventeenth and early eighteenth centuries' (Emily C. Nacol, *An Age of Risk: Politics and Economy in Early Modern Britain* (Princeton and Oxford, 2016), no. 3, p. 131).

culture – the 'professional gambler'.[52] The most important means was the burgeoning practice of insurance, including fire and life insurance, as part of a much wider penumbra of schemes and organizations formed in this period to protect and provide for, amongst others, widows and children of different groups – for example, and most famously, clergymen – although in some cases they were replacing older means, such as those provided through membership of guilds and other bodies.[53] 'Despite initial hesitations', Keith Thomas asserts, 'insurance established itself during the eighteenth century as one of the most basic sources of security for the English middle classes.'[54] Yet, if a new sort of security was the promise thereby held out, it was only very partially realized.

This was true in two main ways. First, for all that this period saw unexampled economic development and growth – frequently somewhat loosely given the label 'the industrial revolution' – economic life continued to be characterized by frequent, sharp fluctuations.[55] While these might commonly derive, as had been the case previously, from the state of the harvest and the weather, the general pattern was powerfully reinforced by economic expansion and modernization, and from the mid eighteenth century the extent to which these depended on widely extended systems of circulating credit which were highly susceptible to crises of confidence.[56] When such occurred – as in 1772, when the Ayr Bank collapsed, for example, or in 1793 when Britain entered the French Revolutionary wars – bankruptcies cascaded across economy and country. Credit, made increasingly accessible by the multiplying country banks in the second half of the eighteenth century, may have helped to encourage the risk-taking on which growth and economic development more broadly depended. The boundary, however, between judicious speculation and a simple gamble was constantly shifting, and only really discernible in retrospect. The lure of great profit resulted in as many failures as successes. '[L]arge profits', declared a guide to the young

[52] One such figure was the notorious Scots financier John Law, for whom, see Antoin E. Murphy, *John Law: Economic Theorist and Policy Maker* (Oxford, 1997) and Larry Neal, *'I am Not Master of Events' The Speculations of John Law and Lord Londonderry in the Mississippi and South Sea Bubbles* (New Haven, CT and London, 2012).

[53] Geoffrey Clark, *Betting on Lives: The Culture of Life Insurance in England, 1695–1775* (Manchester, 1988).

[54] Keith Thomas, *Religion and the Decline of Magic* (London, 1971), p. 782.

[55] T. H. Ashton, *Economic Fluctuations in England, 1700–1800* (Oxford, 1959). For recent comment on the profound impact on the general population in the British metropolis of cold spells, through increases in fuel prices or fuel shortages, see William E. Cavert, *The Smoke of London: Energy and Environment in the Early Modern City* (Cambridge, 2016), pp. 103–21.

[56] Julian Hoppit, 'Financial Crises in Eighteenth-century England', *Economic History Review*, 2nd ser., 39 (1986), 39–58.

trader in 1783, 'are baits to the avaricious, who adventure on remote traffic to accumulate … a fortune soon; but, alas, it frequently turns out a mere delusion, and brings on the trader's ruin.'[57] Opting as a merchant or manufacturer to invest in fixed capital – in a factory, say, or new machinery – or new processes; experiment with new crop rotations if you were a tenant farmer; or as a tradesman or merchant purchase a wider range and quantity of goods on credit for the purposes of domestic or overseas trade or, indeed, invest in a shipping or wartime privateering venture: such decisions were always necessarily gambles of sorts – on rapidly shifting market opportunities, calculations about the likely behaviour of others, and various people's creditworthiness.[58] Meanwhile, as Tawny Paul has recently very powerfully reminded us, debt, managing debt, and freeing oneself from debt – the other side to the availability and ubiquity of credit – cast their long, dark shadows over the lives of many among especially the middling sort.[59]

The instability that counted in this context was felt first and foremost at the level of the individual and the household, and can be traced in the frequent, and to the modern eye, bewildering twists and turns in the fortunes of specific individuals across their lives, and in the repeated acts of self-reinvention in which they were compelled to engage. For some, such as John Hatfield, the latter and deception of others were much the same thing. Hatfield would eventually be charged with counterfeiting the signature of an MP in order to avoid paying the postage on letters. (Letters franked by an MP went free in the post after 1764.) The son of a clothier, Hatfield was apparently born in Derbyshire in around the later 1750s. He followed his father into the textiles trade, but his life changed, or rather he changed his life, when he married a 'Lady of Family', in other words one of established social rank. Marriage was a very significant vehicle of social mobility in this period, providing access to money and (often) social capital. At this point our hero transformed himself into a gentleman, presumably meaning very publicly adopting the trappings – the clothing, the type of accommodation and furnishings, the leisure

57 *The Management and Oeconomy of Trade or the Young Trader's Guide* (1783), p. 20, cited in Julian Hoppit, 'Attitudes to Credit in Britain, 1680–1790', *Historical Journal*, 33 (1990), 315.

58 This feature of contemporary economic activity is brought out very clearly by Priya Satia in her book, *Empire of Guns: The Violent Making of the Industrial Revolution* (Richmond, 2018), esp. ch. 2. For one contemporary's anxiety about the impact of credit on VA, commerce, and the element of gambling which it supposedly introduced, see Richard Champion, *Comparative Reflections on the Past and Present Political, Commercial and Civil State of Great Britain* (London, 1787), p. 227.

59 Tawny Paul, *The Poverty of Disaster: Debt and Insecurity in Eighteenth-Century Britain* (Cambridge, 2019).

habits – of contemporary genteel living, setting up home first in the county town of Chester and then the fast-growing port town of Liverpool. What happened next is unclear, but he appears to have spent time in gaol in Scarborough, before turning up next in Tiverton, Devon, where he married again, entering at the same time into a merchant partnership. The latter evidently failed to prosper, or perhaps was undermined by the trade depression and straitened economic conditions of the later 1790s, especially 1799–1801. Having been declared bankrupt, in 1802 the irrepressible Hatfield embarked on a summer tour to the Lakes – now very much the fashionable thing among the polite and genteel – passing himself off as Alexander Hope, MP, and marrying – very possibly bigamously – a young woman who kept an inn at Buttermere.[60] Here the trail goes cold, but several of its key ingredients are not hard to find in the lives of other people from this period. The figure of the 'social adventurer' stalked the social imaginary of the period.[61] More pertinently, for many more people moving from occupation to occupation was part of the adaptability and versatility required to survive economically in this period, that and the fact that barriers to entry in occupations were generally quite low, and professional structures still fairly embryonic.

Moreover, dependency – the condition of many – brought its own nagging insecurities. This was especially the case for single women, widows, and spinsters, who often lived on incomes derived from and invested in mortgages and bonds, and other investments, which might fail or go bad.[62] Such occurrences were the counterpoint to the more optimistic side to eighteenth-century economic life: the risks and speculations that paid off, the riches and wealth gained, and the upwards social

60 RMA, printed notice, G.P.O. 12 Nov. 1802.

61 See e.g. Donna Andrew and Randall McGowen, *The Perreaus and Mrs Rudd: Forgery and Betrayal in Eighteenth-Century London* (CA, 2001).

62 Securing a dependable income from investments, and the element of risk involved, is a topic which needs further investigation, and would shed further important light on how contemporary economic conditions shaped attitudes towards risk and chance. Before the mid nineteenth century, portfolio investment was limited to a narrow range of public stocks. The main alternatives were property and lending on mortgage and bonds. Increasingly important were annuities, which were, for example, used to fund improvement projects by local authorities, or were a form of lending, and from the end of the eighteenth century commercial tontine schemes. At the beginning of the eighteenth century, the spinster Elizabeth Freke directed her cousin, John, to purchase 100 lottery tickets in one of the classis lotteries, costing just over £3,000, including commission. She would, however, not accept his memorandums as security for this investment, choosing instead to invest around two-thirds of the sum in a mortgage and bond. *Remembrances of Elizabeth Freke, 1671–1714*, ed. Raymond A. Anselment, *Camden Fifth Ser.*, 18 (2001), pp. 276–7.

mobility. Many people in eighteenth-century British society, especially those below the level of the elites, were preoccupied by wealth – gaining it, translating it into independence, social status, and 'happiness' – a term that echoed through contemporary social commentary – but acutely conscious also of its likely transience. Against this background, speculation and insuring against an uncertain future were much closer bedfellows than in more modern times. This was partly why insurance and making wagers were very closely associated in the decades leading up to 1774 and the passage of the so-called Gambling Act (1774), which sought to establish a clear separation between them. As the leading modern historian of the early insurance industry remarks: 'Until 1774 wager policies were both commonplace and fully integrated with other lines of insurance business.'[63]

Second, while Britain in the long eighteenth century may have been a less 'catastrophic' place than in the past, as, for example, plague disappeared and famine was banished from England and from *most* of Scotland after 1700, although spikes in mortality rates did not entirely disappear, as witnessed, most notably, in 1727–1730. In the British capital infant mortality probably peaked in the mid eighteenth century, when two-thirds of children, irrespective of social background, appear to have died before their fifth birthday. Thereafter, child mortality seems to have fallen quite markedly, by around a half by 1850, while adult mortality fell less sharply, but still appreciably, by around a third.[64] While the impact of typhus in Britain generally lessened, at least before the 1830s, when it returned on a new scale to the industrial cities, along with a deadly new arrival, cholera, fatal disease remained strikingly present across this period.[65] The big killers were smallpox and tuberculosis (TB), both of them rigorously socially egalitarian in their impact. It was only the widespread adoption of vaccination which conquered smallpox in the nineteenth century; the effects of earlier inoculation were much more uneven and patchy, and in London almost certainly fairly marginal before 1800.[66] A cure for TB would have to wait a lot

[63] Clark, *Betting on Lives*, p. 44.

[64] P. E. Razzell and Christine Spence, 'The History of Infant, Child and Adult Mortality in London, 1550–1850', *London Journal*, 32 (2007), 271–92.

[65] For a recent work which emphasizes the pervasive nature of 'contagion anxieties' in eighteenth century London and England, see Kevin Siena, *Rotten Bodies: Class & Contagion in Eighteenth Century Britain* (New Haven, CT and London, 2019).

[66] R. J. Davenport, Jeremy Boulton and L. D. Schwarz, 'The Decline of Adult Smallpox in Eighteenth-Century London', *Economic History Review* (2011), 1289–1314. But see also P. E. Razzell, 'The Decline of Adult Smallpox in Eighteenth-Century London – a Commentary', *Economic History Review* (2011), 1315–35; and R. J. Davenport et al.,

longer.[67] In England and Wales, the consensus is that accelerating population growth after 1750 was driven less by falling mortality – although this did contribute – than rising fertility rates, which were, in turn, partly a product of the lowering of the age of marriage of women.[68] London was almost certainly distinctive here, in that the age of marriage was already low at the beginning of our period.[69] Fears, meanwhile, of food shortages remained, and, indeed, grew significantly from the central decades of the eighteenth century, although more efficient and integrated markets, market intervention at central and local levels, and imports of grain from Ireland, the Baltic, and America meant that such episodes did not develop into full-blown mortality crises.[70] Among the majority of the population – the labouring poor – destitution and poverty could, as Jeremy Boulton writes, 'happen to almost anyone'.[71] With no or very few effective safety nets, the shadow of disaster was never far away, for much of the middling sort and the labouring classes.

Keith Thomas famously viewed the transition to a less menacing, capricious world as part of the explanation for the growing disenchantment of society, as older frameworks for explaining the vagaries of life, which invoked magical and religious beliefs, fell apart, to be replaced by a world in which it was believed that risks and uncertainty, and human misfortune, might be brought under much greater control through the application of reason and technology.[72] Other historians have talked about this period seeing the secularization of notions of 'fortune', as God receded as a director of events, to become the figure of the watchmaker, who operated through stable, secondary laws.[73] General providence, in short, replaced specific providences. Yet, even if we assumed that these shifts in attitudes occurred and spread fairly rapidly – which

'Urban Inoculation and the Decline of Smallpox Mortality in Eighteenth-Century Cities – A Reply to Razzell', *Economic History Review* (2016), 188–214.

[67] Helen Bynum, *Spitting Blood: The History of Tuberculosis* (Oxford, 2012). The inventor of the separate steam condenser, James Watt's desperate, sadly unavailing efforts to find a cure to help his daughter, Jessie, are eloquent testimony to the depth of suffering caused by TB and its impact on families. See Bob Harris, *A Tale of Three Cities: The Life and Times of Lord Daer 1763–94* (Edinburgh, 2015), pp. 205–6.

[68] E. A. Wrigley and R. S. Schofield, *The Population History of England 1541–1871: A Reconstruction* (London, 1981).

[69] Razzell and Spence, 'The History of Infant, Child and Adult Mortality in London'.

[70] The spectre of famine was not entirely banished, however, for which see R. A. E. Wells, *Wretched Faces: Famine in Wartime England, 1793–1801* (Gloucester, 1988).

[71] Jeremy Boulton, '"The Meaner Sort": Labouring People and the Poor', in Keith Wrightson (ed.), *A Social History of England 1500–1750* (Cambridge, 2017), p. 321.

[72] Thomas, *Religion and the Decline of Magic*, ch. 22 'The Decline of Magic'.

[73] Lorraine Daston, *Classical Probability in the Enlightenment* (Princeton, NJ, 1988), pp. 131–2.

Thomas, it should be noted, accepted was almost certainly not the case – the effects were rather different to how they are sometimes presented.[74] First, they served to make 'chance' visible as people began to think about their worlds differently.[75] For one saturated with providential or superstitious explanations had no real place for the idea of 'chance' – all was either the hand of God or of other hidden forces. Moreover, as material betterment held out the prospect and reality of lives of enhanced comfort, amenity, and plenitude, and the idea that mischance or misfortune could be controlled or mitigated took firmer hold, so this only served, paradoxically, to bring into sharper focus the extensive realm of chance.[76] What if life was essentially a lottery? What if clearly speculative activity were rewarded – as undoubtedly it was in the burgeoning commercial and fledgling financial markets of eighteenth-century Britain and overseas? In a world as heavily driven as that of eighteenth-century Britain by the vagaries of patronage, contemporaries seeking their fortunes could not but be acutely conscious of the fragility of present fortunes – death or removal of a patron often made the difference between success and failure, between hopes realised and hopes dashed.[77] Might not some gambling make much better sense against this background, or derive from similar impulses?[78] The deeper point here is that the growing fixation with 'improvement', with using reason to create a

[74] Thomas, *Religion and the Decline of Magic*, pp. 769, 772.

[75] The rationality of people in the eighteenth century should, it almost goes without saying, not be exaggerated, and attitudes towards 'chance' were almost certainly more contradictory than this might seem to imply. Indeed, it may be the contradictions and tensions between the ideas of 'chance' and 'luck' that partly account for the success of the lottery in Britain in the eighteenth century, for which see Chapter 4, below.

[76] Thomas talked of an inevitable rise in 'human self confidence' and 'the emergence of a new faith in the potentialities of human initiative' (Thomas, *Religion and the Decline of Magic*, pp. 778, 791–2). These broad shifts have recently been the subject of new examination in Paul Slack, *The Invention of Improvement: Information & Material Progress in Seventeenth-Century England* (Oxford, 2015).

[77] The importance of this was only too apparent in India by the 1780s, for example, where many, especially younger sons of gentry families sought their fortunes, and where competition for places and the patronage of major office holders was intense, military employment by Indian rulers could bring large rewards, and changes to domestic political conditions had a great bearing who gained influence and power. This is quite apart from the risks entailed in the various means of repatriating funds from India. For some of these realities, see NRAS 2614, Papers of the Macpherson Family of Blairgowrie, Perthshire, bundle 158, letters from James Macpherson to Allan Macpherson, 1783–91; Mitchell Library, Glasgow, TD219/10, Campbell of Succouth Papers. See also, more widely, G. S. Byrant, 'Scots in India in the Eighteenth Century', *Scottish Historical Review*, 64 (1985), 22–41.

[78] Some would argue that luck plays a much less significant role in investment, whether in business or financial products. Gamblers also, in a sense, create risk, rather than confront risk where it is inherent in the activities in which they are engaged.

more regulated, amenable environment, in no way banished anxieties about failure and misadventure. Rather, the latter was to a significant degree the dark side of the former, especially for the middling sort, which included many of the gentry. Their dreams were delicately poised between deep pessimism and surging optimism.

To be clear, a number of things are being suggested here. First, that the history of a good deal of gambling is inextricably linked to the history of 'chance' and 'fortune' and how groups and individuals viewed and sought to deal with this as a facet of their lives. The argument is not that uncertainty was in any way new as a pervasive presence in people's lives, but 'chance' was beginning to be seen in new ways and that speculative activities, including gambling, need to be seen partly against this background, and the pursuit of wealth and greater amenity, although this was far from the full story since, as we will see, much lottery adventuring was apparently predicated precisely on the misunderstanding of 'chance' and its conflation with 'luck' which might not be – so people managed to convince themselves – random at all.

Second, on a slightly different tack the lines between legitimate and unacceptable speculative activity are entirely arbitrary. One might be called 'gambling' and the other 'speculation', but that, crudely, was and is a matter of ideology and perspective.[79] This was even more true of eighteenth-century Britain. Get-rich-quick schemes proliferated in the later seventeenth and early eighteenth centuries, enticing unwary investors, while the rapid growth of the stock market from the 1690s, and the vast land speculation schemes launched in the North American colonies in the mid eighteenth century, raised difficult questions about speculative economic impulses. Contemporaries struggled to make sense of this new economic world. The national debt and public stocks which underpinned it might facilitate diversification of assets and much needed financial liquidity, but prices of stocks fluctuated sharply on news of wars and the outcomes of military engagements, or rumours about these. Exchange Alley was 'Gambling Alley'.[80] As one contemporary lamented in 1772, 'The gaming table in Change Alley has ruined more families than all the gambling Coffee-Houses in London.'[81] Recurrent debates about and attempts to legislate against stock-jobbing were testimony to the salience

[79] See relevant comment in Ann Fabian, *Card Sharps and Bucket Shops: Gambling in Nineteenth-Century America* (Ithaca, NY, 1999) and David C. Itzkowitz, 'Fair Enterprise or Extravagant Speculation: Investment, Speculation and Gambling in Victorian England', *Victorian Studies*, 35 (2002), 121–47.

[80] Samuel Gale, *An Essay on the Nature and Principles of Public Credit* (London, 1784), esp. p. 81.

[81] *MChr*, 12 June 1772. I owe this reference to Carlo Tanghetti.

of these issues, and the difficulties which trading stocks presented to legislators who sought to distinguish between legitimate trading and 'stock-jobbing or other species of gaming'.[82] Widespread forms of contemporary personal finance, purchasing and borrowing on life annuities and buying shares in commercial tontine schemes, the latter of which emerged in the later eighteenth century, might very plausibly be viewed as gambling. As the cosmopolitan radical Joel Barlow pointed out in the early 1790s: 'A tontine partakes at once of the nature of lotteries and of simple life-annuities, and involves itself in the principal vices of both. Like a lottery it is founded in the spirit of gambling.'[83] Markets in agricultural products and other goods were subject to speculative practices which some equated with gambling.[84] Some even argued that the canal mania of the later eighteenth century was a form of gambling, as subscribers bargained on large future profits from tolls.[85] Was eighteenth-century Britain a place where many people rashly speculated on 'fortune' as the best route to wealth and independence, or was it one where people increasingly sought methodically to calculate risks and pursue 'sober, regulated commerce'?[86] Both were true, of course, although the gap between them was much smaller than many contemporaries affected to believe.

Third, *pace* Langford, the pursuit of upwards social mobility, or sometimes recovery of social status, gripped the imaginations of many in

[82] See H. V. Bowen, '"The Pests of Human Society": Stockbrokers, Jobbers and Speculators in Mid-Eighteenth Century Britain', *History*, 78 (1993), 38–53; P. Kosmetatos, *The 1772–73 British Credit Crisis* (Basingstoke, 2018); Larry Neal, 'The Evolution of Self- and State Regulation of the London Stock Exchange, 1688–1878', in M. Debin and J. van Zanden (eds.), *Law and Long-Term Economic Change: A Eurasian Perspective* (Stanford, CA, 2011), pp. 300–22; For a more general discussion, see Stuart Banner, *Speculation: A History of the Fine Line between Gambling and Investing* (New York, 2017).

[83] Joel Barlow, *Advice to the Privileged Orders in the Several States of Europe* (London, 1793), p. 44. See also *The Commercial and Agricultural Magazine* (6 vols., 1799–1802), vi, 199. Tontine schemes were those in which investors shared the proceeds of the collective sum invested, according to their shares, and when an investor died their share was allocated to the remaining investors. Annuities were widely used as a form of borrowing to fund improvement schemes and so forth, and as a means of personal borrowing. For payment of an agreed sum of money, the purchaser would receive a life annuity. Those paying the annuity were in a sense taking a gamble on the duration of the life of the purchaser.

[84] See e.g. John Arbuthnot, *An Inquiry into the Connections between the Present Price of Provisions, and the Size of Farms* (London, 1773), p. 59.

[85] James Anderson, *General View of the Agriculture and Rural Economy of the County of Aberdeen, with Observations on the Means of its Improvement* (Edinburgh, 1794), p. 137. Anderson viewed this negatively, but for a positive portrayal, see John Billingsley, *General View of the Agriculture of the County of Somerset, with Observations on the Means of Improvement* (London, 1798), p. 307.

[86] The phrase 'sober, regulated commerce' comes from H. T. Colebrooke, *Remarks on the Present State of the Husbandry and Commerce of Bengal* (Calcutta, 1795), p. 287.

eighteenth-century English/British society, although, *contra* Langford, this did not necessarily entail emulation of the gentry among the middling sort. To be sure, this preoccupation waxed more strongly at certain moments than others, for example, briefly during the frenzied months of the South Sea Bubble in 1720 or in the 1760s and 1770s, when the figure of the 'nabob' pushed its way to the front of debates about social *arrivisme* and the impact of 'luxury'.[87] But the perception that the social order was being constantly reshaped was commonplace throughout. How much social mobility was there has been the subject of vigorous debate among historians, although this has focused mainly on *entry into* the landed elites.[88] Yet, even those who are sceptical of the idea that England boasted a peculiarly 'open elite' in this period acknowledge the importance of mobility downwards, and the quite remarkable turnover in smaller estates in certain parts of the country, particularly places close to London or large provincial towns and cities. What is disputed, in other words, is how many stormed the final citadel and joined those at the very apex of society. Equally importantly, the rapidly expanding urban societies of provincial Britain in the later eighteenth century often seem to have produced both quite sharply delineated social hierarchies, but also, and especially when viewed over time and more broadly, to have been highly fluid socially. Recent research in this context has tended to support some elements at least of Plumb's typically boldly drawn, disarmingly gendered, picture of these places which he penned well over half a century ago:

> The provincial towns were like London, but with less wealth and more poverty, more despair, less social order, less charity, more disease, but, like London, full of opportunity for men of tough temperament, endless vigour, and resource to acquire the modest affluence necessary to enter the demi-paradise of comfort and ease which the eighteenth century afforded for hard cash. With property came standing in society and a future for one's children, for in the early part of the century it was relatively easy to pass from one social class to another – a fact which amazed Voltaire and others.[89]

[87] See esp. Julian Hoppit, 'The Myths of the South Sea Bubble', *Transactions of the Royal Historical Society*, 12 (2002), 141–65; James Raven, *Judging New Wealth: Popular Publishing and Responses to Commerce in England 1750–1800* (Oxford, 1997).

[88] On which, see, notably, Lawrence Stone and Jeanne C. Fawtier Stone, *An Open Elite? England 1540–1880* (Oxford, 1986); John Cannon, *Aristocratic Century: The Peerage of Eighteenth Century England* (Cambridge, 1984). But see also I. R. Christie, *British 'Non-Élite' MPs 1715–1820* (Oxford, 1995); Marcus Ackroyd, Laurence Brockliss, Michael Moss, Kate Retford, and John Stevenson, *Advancing with the Army: Medicine, the Professions, and Social Mobility in the British Isles, 1790–1850* (Oxford, 2006).

[89] Plumb, *England in the Eighteenth Century*, p. 17. For more recent relevant discussion, see esp. Maxine Berg, *Luxury & Pleasure in Eighteenth-Century Britain* (Oxford, 2005); Bob Harris and Charles McKean, *The Scottish Town in the Age of the Enlightenment, 1740–1820*

What may have really mattered here, however, was not so much the actual extent of social mobility, both upwards *and* downwards, although there was much highly visible evidence of social success in the changing built environment, in the multiplying villa properties which came to encircle many a growing town, but the strength of the conviction that moving upwards was eminently possible, and the habit of thinking in these terms. To a very considerable number of people, gambling may well – like a fortunate marriage, usually viewed in monetary terms, or the opportunities for rapid wealth creation represented by overseas empire, or, indeed, other get-rich-quick schemes – have been viewed as yet one more means of gaining or recovering a substantial sum, which might be used to gain or maintain independence, or even brokered into 'making a figure' in society. Gambling in this context can be viewed as another form of speculative economic activity, as well as a form of consumption.

This may equally have been true of many among the labouring classes. Their expectations and hopes operated on a continuum with those entertained by those above them on the social scale rather than being of a completely different order. They were, however, almost certainly frustrated more frequently – increasingly so by the later eighteenth century as apprenticeship was progressively diluted, the gap between journeyman and master widened, and labour was increasingly subject to tightening control and the chilly discipline of the wage economy.[90] In closed systems, modern theorists of gambling tell us, gambling can act as a safety valve, providing the means to people to speculate on gaining the fortune who would otherwise lack these.[91] The lottery habit of domestic servants was the subject of much sniping criticism from the later eighteenth century; but this was hypocritical and at the very least a product of a lack of any real imaginative engagement with the lives of these individuals. Gambling (including the lottery) may, as its critics feared, have

(Edinburgh, 2014), esp. ch. 6. Susan Whyman's recent book on William Hutton, the Birmingham stationer, offers much food for thought on this theme, and on the limits as well as opportunities for social mobility in the rapidly growing and relatively open society of Birmingham in the later eighteenth century, from the perspective of the self-made (Susan Whyman, *The Useful Knowledge of William Hutton: Culture and Industry in Eighteenth-Century Birmingham* (Oxford, 2018).

90 Peter Linebaugh, *The London Hanged: Crime and Civil Society in the Eighteenth Century* (London, 1991); Douglas Hay and Nicholas Rogers, *Eighteenth-Century English Society: Shuttles and Swords* (Oxford, 1997); Leonard D. Schwarz, *London in the Age of Industrialisation: Entrepreneurs, Labour Force and Living Conditions 1700–1850* (Cambridge, 1992); C. A. Whatley, *Scottish Society: Beyond Jacobitism, towards Industrialisation* (Manchester, 2000).

91 Charles T. Clotfelder and Philip J. Cook, *Selling Hope: State Lotteries in America* (Cambridge, MA, 1989); Edward C. Devereux Jr., *Gambling and Social Structure* (New York, 1980).

undermined the work ethic of people. Yet, it was also a product of the socially fluid, consumer society that was greatly expanding its influence in this period, and of the resulting aspirational motivations that could also – and, if certain historians are correct, did – inspire 'industriousness'.[92]

If chance, risk, and social mobility – both the reality and the myth – offer, therefore, important lenses through which to view gambling and the large historical forces that shaped it in Britain in this period, gender furnishes us with another vital perspective. For, as other scholars have noted in various different contexts, and has been intimated above, gambling was often ineradicably linked to performance of gender identities. One historian has argued that for much of the eighteenth century, gender was notably mutable, making its performative aspects only more significant.[93] Be that as it may – it is not a view easily, if at all, susceptible to proof – for some men the association between gender and gaming was forged through a particular, externalized notion of honour, and the compulsion to enact this. The operative word, however, is *some*, not all, even within the same social rank.[94] The issue may well be why *some* elite men (and, indeed, women) saw the need to or wished to gamble in particular ways, and others did not, and why and how this changed over time. Such individuals might be seen, temporarily at least, as consciously stepping outside alternative notions of appropriate conduct, as rejecting the imperatives of duty, moderation, and self-restraint which governed

92 See esp. J. de Vries, *The Industrious Revolution: Consumer Behaviour and the Household Economy, 1650 to the Present* (Cambridge, 2008). See also D. N. McCloskey, *Bourgeois Dignity: Why Economics Can't Explain the Modern World* (Chicago, 2010); C. Muldrew, *Food, Energy and the Creation of Industriousness: Work and Material Culture in Agrarian England, 1550–1780* (Cambridge, 2011); R. C. Allen and J. L. Weisdorf, 'Was there an 'Industrious Revolution' Before the Industrial Revolution? An Empirical Exercise for England, c.1300–1830', *Economic History Review*, 64 (2011), 715–29.

93 D. Wahrman, *The Making of the Modern Self: Identity and Culture in Eighteenth Century England* (New Haven and London, 2004).

94 It has been argued influentially that notions of honour were being transformed in the eighteenth century, brought under the sway of civility and internalized. Honour became less a matter of maintaining reputation in the eyes of others through outward show and more one of conscience. For which, see esp. Robert Shoemaker, 'The Taming of the Duel: Masculinity, Honour and Ritual Violence in London, 1660–1800', *Historical Journal*, 45 (2002), 525–45; Robert Shoemaker, 'Male Honour and the Decline of Public Violence in Eighteenth-Century London', *Social History*, 26 (2001), 190–208. See also Lynn Abrams, 'The Taming of Highland Masculinity: Inter-Personal Violence and Shifting Codes of Manhood, c. 1760–1840', in Lynn Abrams and Elizabeth L. Ewen (eds.), *Nine Centuries of Man: Manhood and Masculinity in Scottish History* (Edinburgh, 2017), pp. 80–98. The notion of honour mobilized in gambling, however, stands outside of this change, further evidence that very different ideas of honour coexisted in eighteenth-century society.

much of the rest of the propertied classes.[95] Or, accepting that English and, indeed, British society sustained and nurtured multiple models of masculinity (and femininity) in this period, they might assume quite different identities in different contexts.[96] The figure of the 'polite gentleman', reconstructed mainly from prescriptive literature, which has tended to dominate discussions of masculinity in the eighteenth century, was only one of several viable normative models of manhood, and not necessarily the most powerful. Moreover, as Shepard and others have observed, normative ideas of manhood contained tensions within them.[97] Among the landed classes, at the core of their understandings of manhood was the idea of personal autonomy, tempered at the same time with a strong sense of responsibility and duty.[98] Critics viewed gaming as characterized precisely by the loss of personal autonomy, as abject surrender to the sway of destructive passions or emotions. As one judge very starkly declared from the bench at the beginning of the nineteenth century, gaming was the 'offspring and parent of the basest passions that disgraced the human mind'.[99] Yet, this was the view from the outside. One can argue that for its practitioners, it represented exactly the opposite – the ultimate expression of the autonomous self, albeit within a clear set of accepted protocols surrounding gaming which defined 'honour', the code of the 'gentleman'. The argument – beyond emphasizing the self-consciously theatrical aspects to much contemporary gambling activity – is that the picture here was a shifting, complicated one, and that the force and meaning of different values varied according to generation, family background, marital, social, and professional status, and, indeed, context or milieu. The patterns of gambling activity which

[95] This is the argument which seems to be made by Anthony Fletcher in *Gender, Sex & Subordination in England 1500–1800* (New Haven and London,1995), ch. 16. Fletcher observes (on p. 345), 'beneath this façade of sophistication ... there was a deeply selfish set of sexual mores and an unabashed male hedonism'. See also Philip Carter, *Men and the Emergence of Polite Society: Britain 1660–1800* (Harlow, 2001); Vic Gatrell, *City of Laughter: Sex and Satire in Eighteenth-Century London* (London, 2006); Keith Thomas, *In Pursuit of Civility: Manners and Civilization in Early Modern England* (New Haven and London, 2018), pp. 63–4.

[96] See esp. Helen Berry, 'Rethinking Politeness in Eighteenth-Century England: Moll King's Coffee House and the Significance of "Flash Talk"', *Transactions of the Royal Historical Society*, 11 (2001), 65–81.

[97] Alexandra Shepard, *The Meanings of Manhood in Early Modern England, 1560–1640* (Oxford, 2003); Tim Hitchcock and Michèle Cohen (eds.), *English Masculinities 1600–1800* (London, 1999); Karen Harvey, 'The History of Masculinity, c.1650–1800', *Journal of British Studies*, 44 (2005), 296–312; William Stafford, 'Gentlemanly Masculinities as Represented by the Later Georgian *Gentleman's Magazine*', *History*, 93 (2008), 47–68.

[98] French and Rothery, *Mans's Estate*, esp. introduction.

[99] *Times*, 11 Feb. 1800.

are revealed by the evidence are in various ways heavily contextual and cyclical as much as linear.

Much gambling was basically recreational, although this did not in any way preclude elements of the performance of hyper-masculinity – rather the reverse. Or, it might also at the same time be economically motivated, as in the case of pedestrianism (or foot-racing). Or it might be all of these things, and involve mobilization of other identities at the same time – for example, patriotic and geographical ones. As McKibbin argues in the case of specifically working-class gambling of a later period, on its own this is not in itself very revealing of why people chose this activity as a form of stimulation and entertainment as opposed to any other.[100] It is, as already alluded to, recreational gambling for modest stakes among the propertied classes which has recently received the most attention, and partly for this reason is given less emphasis in this book, although it is certainly not ignored.[101] More attention is given to gambling among the lower orders, among both women and men, although we are heavily reliant on the press and, to a lesser extent, the records of the courts, for our knowledge of this, and much that we might wish to know about, say, motivations and patterns of participation remains hidden from the historian's gaze. Part of the point in doing so, however, is to underline a theme that will feature throughout: the degree to which gambling and opportunities to gamble in eighteenth-century Britain were the products of a rapidly commercializing society. This allows us to link the history of gambling to larger forces shaping and reshaping eighteenth-century Britain.

III. Organization, Coverage, and Sources

Contemporaries were, unsurprisingly given what has been said above, notably inconsistent in what they labelled as 'gaming' or 'gambling', and it could mean no more than taking risks in hope of gaining some benefit or advantage.[102] This book, partly reflecting this reality, takes a broad

[100] McKibbin, 'Working-Class Gambling', 118. [101] Mullin, *A Six Penny at Whist.*

[102] In his dictionary, Samuel Johnson defined the term 'gambler' as a cant alternative to 'gamester', as a 'knave whose practice it is to invite the unwary to game and cheat them'. 'Gaming' was defined by Johnson as 'To play wantonly and extravagantly for money.' Gaming was a term thus used pejoratively, as in the main were the terms 'speculative' and 'speculation'. They implied risky pursuit of immoderate profits at the expense of others. Those who saw 'stock-jobbing' as a form of gaming or gambling might emphasize its illegality – they had in mind here trading in options prohibited (ineffectually) by Barnard's Act (1734) – but also the extent to which it was supposedly exploiting and taking advantage of the 'credulity of the public, by entering into dishonourable combinations, as the Gambler makes use of false dice,

view of what constituted gambling, although it excludes, for the most part, financial speculation. There is a history yet to be written about financial speculation and activity, which would, as already suggested, overlap with one about gambling, and plenty of hints about what this might contain can be found in this book at various points. The gambling, however, on which this book focuses is in the main related to leisure, recreation, and different forms of sociability – betting on the outcome of events or sports, wagering, and playing games and engaging in contests for stakes. The lottery is a special case, in that, especially prior to 1769 purchase of a lottery ticket was usually an investment as well as a gamble. It could also be construed as patriotic, as supporting the national interest. To this extent, the lottery had a hybrid character. Which mattered more – investment or gamble – depended to a significant degree on the terms of particular lotteries, but also the individual lottery adventurer. Nonetheless, quite apart from the intrinsic gambling element, the official lottery spawned a whole array of derivative activities that emphatically were forms of gambling. It also spawned what can legitimately be described as the first modern British gambling business. When its critics complained that the state was endorsing and encouraging gambling through staging lotteries to raise funds, they were incontrovertibly correct.[103] This was acknowledged by ministers, and their supporters, who cited fiscal utility in this context as their main defence, and also the argument that lotteries at least had the merit of turning the ubiquity of gambling to public advantage. As Porter summed it up, through the lottery 'gambling itself became nationalized'.[104]

This book takes up the story of gambling in the 1690s, when the combination of the growth of the press, following the lapsing of pre-publication censorship in 1695, and the establishment of the official lottery in the previous year, together served to make gambling among a widening cross section of society much more visible, and, therefore, susceptible to systematic scrutiny. The end point is c.1830. The opening

the Stock-jobber makes use of false intelligences'. (*The Beauties of All Magazines Selected* (3 Vols., 1762–174), ii, 4.)

103 See e.g. Thomas Howard, Earl of Effingham, *An Essay on the Nature of a Loan. Being an Introduction to the Knowledge of Public Accounts* (London, 1782), pp. 11–14. *An Enquiry into the Present Alarming State of the Nation. Shewing the Necessity of a Reform in Government, and a Speedy Resolution of Taxes; an Adequate Representation of the People; and Restoration of Triennial Parliaments* (London, 1793), pp. 27–31, esp. p. 27, where the author writes, 'Lotteries keep up a spirit of Gambling amongst every class of the people, from the Peer to the Beggar'; John Fellows, *Seasonable Words of Advice to All Such as Are Concerned in the Lottery; In Which Are Pointed Out the Evils that Have Attended on Gaming, Especially in Buying Chances, Policies, and Insuring* (London, 1780).

104 Porter, *English Society*, p. 256.

decades of the nineteenth century represented, as we will see, a distinct phase in the history of gambling, one which sheds important light backwards on to the eighteenth century, but which also underlines the relevance of several central underlying themes, notably the persistent importance of gender performance and conceptions of honour, where change was not simply linear, as too many histories of this period tend to imply. However, 1830 is not an entirely arbitrary date on which to close. From that date a new social order began to take much clearer shape under the impact of industrialization, one in which, at least in rapidly expanding industrial towns and cities, basic horizontal social divisions became ever more clearly discernible. Gambling did not disappear or obviously diminish – far from it, although it may have become somewhat less visible. Parliament abolished the lotteries in 1823 – the final one was staged in 1826 – although it did this less for moral than financial reasons, while cockfighting was made illegal in 1849. Horse racing probably continued to be considerably more widespread than at the beginning of the nineteenth century, and pedestrianism in certain parts of Britain showed every sign of flourishing.[105] There may have been decline in some areas, but growth in others; weighing them against one another would be a heroic enterprise.

Whether gambling did or did not peak in the eighteenth century is, nevertheless, only partly the point. This is, as already emphasized, a book as much about the interactions and relationships between gambling and British society in the long eighteenth century as it is one about gambling *per se*.

It is also selective in how it approaches its subject, offering a series of pictures of different facets of gambling. This is done partly because gambling is, as already implied, a diffuse subject, and reconstructing a fully comprehensive picture would in any case, given the nature of the evidence, be an impossible task. Chapters 1 and 2 provide analyses of gambling at different social levels. Chapter 1 explores gambling among mainly the elites, focusing particularly on horse racing and the various types of gambling associated with the rise of socially select gaming clubs in the capital, London. This enables us to bring within a single frame the gambling of a certain section of the elites, but also the growth in this period of professional gamblers. This chapter also examines the gambling habits and careers of certain specific individuals, notably, James Boswell, the biographer of Johnson, and William Grant of Congalton, who moved in similar circles to Boswell in the Scottish capital before

[105] Adrian Harvey, *The Beginnings of a Commercial Sporting Culture in Britain, 1793–1850* (Aldershot, 2004).

departing for the gambling clubs of London and Bath, and Lord William Murray, second son of the third Duke of Atholl. Lord William's life of gambling, which ended with his sorry death in 1796 in Newgate gaol, was one mainly conducted in London, North America, and India. Chapter 2 looks at the gambling of the lower orders and sections of the diverse middling sort, focusing particularly on the locales and characteristics of popular gambling in the British capital, and, second, the development of pedestrianism and associated gambling activities in the early nineteenth century. This begins to bring into focus several of this book's other key themes, especially the influence of commercialization as a force shaping gambling and opportunities to gamble, but also the relevance of the revival, or rather perhaps reinforcement and greater visibility, of traditional models of masculinity against the background of a quarter of century of war against Revolutionary and Napoleonic France. The militarization of British society in this period had various and profound effects on gambling and its meanings, but we can also plot several developments that continued to shape especially popular gambling long into the nineteenth century. Chapters 3 and 4 explore the lottery, especially the state and official lotteries of 1694–1826, which have left a good deal of evidence of their remarkable and growing presence in British society, together with the lottery adventuring of different groups and individuals among the population. These chapters explore, in turn, how it was that the lottery rose to such a prominent position in society, and what lay behind its magnetic appeal. The final chapter examines shifting attitudes towards gambling from the perspectives of the law and efforts by the authorities to constrain and suppress gambling. It is a story of the profound limits of the law as an influence and restraint on gambling, and one which enables us once again to see how diverse and, indeed, contradictory were contemporary attitudes towards gambling, even if for some these were straightforwardly positive or negative.

In pursuit of gambling of different kinds and its various meanings, this book draws on a wide range of sources, including newspapers, pamphlets, periodicals, account books, bank accounts, diaries and journals, letters, betting books, and legal records, amongst others. These come from public and private collections deposited in archives located across Britain. While not ignoring representations of gambling, it deliberately seeks to move, where possible, beyond these, as well as impressionistic comment and reportage, to focus on specific, well-documented cases of gambling. This is, in other words, a mainly empirical study. As in all such histories, we are necessarily dependent on the vagaries of archival survival and compilation, together with contemporary habits and practices of record-keeping and sharing of information. This inevitably means the gambling of some people is more visible to us than that of others. This is equally true of types of gambling. It is probably fair to say that committed, heavy gamblers were not disposed to divulge the details of their activities. Or, they either sought to hide their gambling or thought it not worthy of recording. Legal records are similarly capricious, both in respect of their survival and what was considered by the courts in the first place since the laws on gambling were only very sporadically employed by contemporaries, and gambling debts above a small sum not recoverable through legal action. Most gambling activity took place, in short, beyond the consideration of the law. Nevertheless, sufficient traces survive to enable general patterns and impulses to be reconstructed, even if a comprehensive picture remains elusive.

1 Gambling for High Stakes or 'Deep Play'

> If gallantry was the characteristic of Charles the Second's reign and religion of his father's, politics of Queen Anne's, and chivalry the times of yore, gaming is undoubtedly the predominant feature of the present. *Anthony Storer to Lord Carlisle*, 13 Feb. 1777[1]

The idea that 'gaming' reached unexampled heights in Britain in the 1770s and 1780s was frequently expressed. London and Bath were the primary sites for this activity; and the main protagonists were the 'fashionable classes'. Yet, if it was reports of dizzying sums casually lost and won among the fashionable, or those aspiring to such status, which preoccupied contemporaries, an equally commonly articulated concern was that through the power of emulation gaming was rapidly spreading down through society. Extravagance or dissolution might start with those at the top of the social ladder, but it would surely not cease there. Indeed, there was disturbing evidence to the contrary, as gaming clubs proliferated across the British capital.[2]

Such concerns were nothing new; they had, for example, been widely expressed in the early 1750s.[3] The view that gaming corroded the moral fibre of the nation was voiced throughout the eighteenth century, reaching another noisy crescendo in the 1790s as, under the impact of the French Revolution, concern was refocused onto the suspect morals of the upper classes, or 'aristocracy' as they began to be termed by hostile

[1] Historical Manuscripts Commission (HMC), *Fifteenth Report, Appendix, Part VI: The Manuscripts of the Earl of Carlisle, Preserved at Castle Howard* (London, 1897), p. 319.

[2] Donna T. Andrew, '"How Frail Are Lovers Vows and Dicers Oaths": Gaming, Governing and Moral Panic in Britain, 1781–1782', in David Lemmings and Claire Walker (eds.), *Moral Panics, the Media and the Law in Early Modern England* (Basingstoke, 2009), pp. 176–94; Bob Harris, 'The 1782 Gaming Bill and Lottery Regulation Acts (1782 & 1787): Gambling and the Law in Later Georgian Britain', *Parliamentary History*, 40 (2021), 462–80.

[3] Bob Harris, *Politics and the Nation: Britain in the Mid Eighteenth Century* (Oxford, 1992), pp. 295–305.

radical commentators.[4] Nor was Storer strictly correct in his characterization of change. Gaming among the elites had been very much a feature of the later Stuart era, and continued to be so during the early Hanoverian period. One might well argue, therefore, that in the end what was distinctive about gaming in the 1770s and 1780s was its unexampled visibility coupled with the strength and amount of criticism which it aroused. If Joseph Addison and Richard Steele, to name but the most influential spokespersons for such a view, had sought in the 1710s to divorce the concept of honour from activities such as gambling, their moral outlook had conquered much of society by George III's reign. That the court under George III was no longer a prime site of gaming – the annual twelfth-night custom of the monarch playing 'hazard' or cards with Groom Porter having been abolished in 1761 as part of the inauguration of a new style of patriotic kingship – rendered the high-stakes gambling of some of the elites only more starkly revealed and susceptible to disapproval.[5] What gave contemporary concerns added urgency was the unfolding drama of British failure and defeat in the War of American Independence. Britain's elites were, it appeared, revealing themselves to be unfit to lead the nation, with the result that the country's status as a great power was being placed in grave peril. It was the fate of the prominent opposition Whig, Charles James Fox, with his heavy gambling debts and utterly insouciant attitude towards their accumulation, to become a prime symbol of elite corruption, while the unsullied and relatively untried William Pitt the Younger became the figurehead from 1783 to 1784 of a widespread mood of national revival, which had a conspicuous moral as well as political dimension, insofar as these can be separated.[6]

This case is very plausible and contains several important truths. Britain's 'age of extravagance' in the 1770s and 1780s, as Paul Langford dubbed it, was at least partly the creation of its critics, empowered by an ever-expanding, evermore influential, uninhibited press and a burgeoning voyeuristic obsession among the reading public with the activities of the fashionable.[7] White's, the St James's Street

[4] Gillian Russell, '"Faro's Daughters": Female Gamesters, Politics, and the Discourse of Finance in 1790s Britain', *Eighteenth Century Studies*, 33 (2000), 481–504; Amanda Goodrich, *Debating England's Aristocracy in the 1790s: Pamphlets, Polemics and Political Ideas* (Woodbridge, 2005).

[5] *SJChr*, 8 Jan. 1775; *Belfast Newsletter*, 27 Jan. 1761.

[6] See esp. Joanna Innes, 'Politics and Morals: The Reformation of Manners in Later Eighteenth-Century England', in Eckhart Hellmuth (ed.), *The Transformation of Political Culture: England and Germany in the Late Eighteenth Century* (Oxford, 1990), pp. 57–118.

[7] Paul Langford, *Public Life and the Propertied Englishman 1689–1798* (Oxford, 1991), esp. pp. 540–58.

chocolate house which was transformed into a highly exclusive all-male club in 1736, and whose membership encompassed much of the early Hanoverian political elite – including the dukes of Newcastle and Bedford, Henry Pelham, and William Pitt the Elder – had been the scene of high-stakes gambling much earlier in the century.[8] Gambling of a similar kind had occurred elsewhere, such as, most obviously, Newmarket, Bath, and at court. Yet, while this was the subject of occasional gossipy comment in the correspondence of the elites, it attracted strictly limited coverage in the press.[9]

However, the intense concern expressed in the 1770s and 1780s was not simply the invention of anxious minds and a more sharply critical, bolder press. The 'extravagance' of some among a generation who emerged into adulthood in years when, as Leslie Mitchell puts it, 'conventional religion and morality were at a discount', was real enough.[10] London clubs such as Almack's and Brooks's, both of which were established in 1764, were sites of spectacular, intense gaming that was all too visible, bidding, as one contemporary termed it, 'defiance to all decency and police'.[11] This gaming involved women and men, although Brooks's had an exclusively male membership. Moreover, the type of gambling favoured by patrons of such places depended purely on the operations of chance.[12] Why it should have been such a prominent feature of gambling culture and fashionable recreation in this period defies easy explanation.

This chapter re-examines high-stakes gambling in Georgian Britain by, in the first place, reconstructing an overall, properly differentiated picture of elite gambling in eighteenth-century Britain. What role did gambling, of different kinds, play in the lives of people at or towards the top of society, and what sorts of pattern of change are we able to detect in this sphere? Given the patchy evidence which survives, the emerging picture will necessarily be somewhat impressionistic, although several reasonably

[8] W. B. Boulton, *The History of White's* (2 vols., London, 1892). See also Erasmus Lewis, *A Letter to the Club at White's* (1750).

[9] See e.g. BARS, Lucas (Wrest Park) Papers, L30/8/39/20, London, 5 Oct. 1732: 'Lady Jane Russell was here last night who seems to speak very feelingly of ye Duke of Bedfords losses at play. She says he lost forty thousand pounds in one night just before he went & thirty-two thousand of it was to one Fleetwood.' See also for comment on Bedford's gaming losses, *Daily Post*, 13 Feb. 1731; *Daily Courant*, 15 Feb. 1731. The press provided occasional comment on the sums won and lost on twelfth night at court. See e.g. *Weekly Journal, or British Gazetteer*, 14 Jan. 1727; *PA*, 8 Jan. 1752, 11 Jan. 1755.

[10] Leslie Mitchell, *Charles James Fox* (Oxford, 1992), p. 15.

[11] HMC, *Fifteenth Report, Appendix, Part VI*, p. 496: George Selwyn to Lord Carlisle, 11 June 1781.

[12] See further below.

clear conclusions suggest themselves. The category 'elite' is quite broadly defined for this purpose. The focus is primarily on the landed classes, ranging from county gentry at the bottom end to the 'great', the upper echelons of the titled nobility, at the apex. This is not to imply, however, that gaming for high stakes or any other amount was a monopoly of these sorts of people. Indeed, an insistent criticism of gaming was that it promoted promiscuous social mixing, that the gaming tables and cockpits of Britain were patronized by those from the very top to the very bottom of society. As Lady Boscawen snidely observed to a correspondent in December 1780, in a reference to the notorious gamester and nabob General Richard Smith, who was fabulously wealthy, although definitely not high-born:

> You woud [sic] be sorry to see our finest ladies & greatest Beauties D[uchess]'s of Rutland & Devonshire sitting at a gaming table … with one Gen[era]'l Smith sitting between Them who was a cheesemonger's son & who wins All their money & says "I have strip'd [sic] the poor women of all their Pin Money to Night."[13]

There was another version of this concern; namely, that gaming rendered the young, callow heirs to landed fortunes prey to the wiles and skulduggery of sharpers.[14] Individuals who lived wholly or partially by the proceeds of gambling probably merit separate treatment. By the early nineteenth century, such people had become a conspicuous feature of the 'Turf', the sporting set associated with horse racing, as well as betting on other sports, such as cricket.

One further preliminary note of caution should be sounded. If the social boundaries delimiting the landed elites were blurred, increasingly so in the eighteenth century, gaming among the elites was, as hinted above, part of wider cultures and habits of gambling. Any distinctiveness and exclusivity had less to do with the activity itself than the settings in which or among whom it took place. Developments such as the increasingly strong appeal to landed notability from the later seventeenth century of urban-based forms of sociability and leisure reinforced this pattern. The eighteenth-century 'man of fashion' was to a significant degree the product of quite deliberate choices, and often age; he tended typically to be a bachelor. But he was also, as importantly, socially

[13] TNA, Chatham Papers, 30/8/2, 149v–150r, Lady Boscawen to Lady Hester Pitt, Audley St., 23 Dec. 1780. For Smith, see G. J. Bryant, 'Smith, Richard (bap. 1734, d. 1803)', *Oxford Dictionary of National Biography* (2004), available online at http:ezproxyprd.bodleian.ox.ac.uk:4563/1o.1093/ref:odnb/63539.

[14] See e.g. Edwards, Frederick, *The Ill Effects of the Game of Rowlet, Otherwise Rowley-Powley* (London, 1744).

amphibious, neither solely of country nor solely of town, but of both. His social origins were also not unambiguously clear; he might equally well be a scion of a landed family or that of prospering mercantile and professional families. Take the Edinburgh merchant, Alexander Anderson, whom we met briefly in the Introduction: the son of a lawyer, James Anderson of Newbiggin in Fife, in 1772 Alexander's annual personal expenditure was of the order of £80, rising to £220 or so in the mid-1780s to around £350 in the 1790s. He was every inch the fashionable gentleman.[15] By the 1790s he had a house in Hanover Street in Edinburgh's New Town and another in St Andrews, fast becoming a genteel resort at the end of the eighteenth century.[16] He fitted himself out with 'fine shoes', 'a hat with velvet', 'lace ruffles and gloves', 'silver buckles'; he had an Italian master for two months; he took a six-week-long 'London jaunt' in the spring of 1774, visiting the British capital again two years later, when he went to the Ranelagh pleasure gardens. He was a member of several gentlemen's clubs and societies;[17] dined at Edinburgh's fashionable hotels (Dunn's and Bayle's), and had a subscription to Walker's Coffee House; attended the George Square assemblies, as well as assemblies in St Andrews; played bowls and golf; and was a visitor to race meetings held in Leith and Cupar, Fife. He played cards regularly, especially at race meetings, such as in November 1786 at the Cupar Race Meeting where he lost £5.13. An English equivalent from the same period would be the prosperous Hull underwriter Robert Carlisle Broadley, son of Hull merchant Thomas Broadley. Robert, whose personal expenditure was around £120 a year in the 1760s – who along with his group of friends who came from similar backgrounds has been described by Gordon Jackson as representing 'as formidable an array of wealth and power as ever assembled in Hull' – was a frequent gambler.[18] He was also, seemingly, fairly successful, having won, for example, just over £64 in 1770.[19] The rise of fashionable 'urban gentry', such as Anderson and Broadley, made social boundaries in Georgian Britain all the more porous. For every 'man of fashion', moreover, there was an equivalent 'woman of fashion'.

15 NLS, MS 8891, account book of Alexander Anderson, 1771–96.

16 Anderson paid subscriptions to the St Andrews ballroom (1789) and assembly (1794).

17 The accounts mention a 'catch club', St Andrews Society, 'Hum Drum Club', the Vocal Harmony Society, and the Harmonic Society. References are also made to golfing dinners and balls, and a skating dinner.

18 Gordon Jackson, *Hull in the Eighteenth Century: A Study in Economic and Social History* (London and New York, 1972), p. 265.

19 University of Hull, Brynmor Jones Library, DP/146, Journal and Personal Account Book of Robert Carlisle Broadley of Hull, 1768–1773.

1.1 Gambling amongst the Elites

Gambling of different kinds was well integrated in the lives of the eighteenth-century British elites. In the first place, this was reflected in the contents of the myriad conduct books which poured from the printing presses in the eighteenth and early nineteenth centuries. Such guides to genteel or, as it was more commonly denoted, 'polite' conduct acknowledged the prevalence of and, more often than not, the harmlessness of some gambling. This was emphatically not, however, to condone high-stakes gambling or 'deep play'. Rather the point, reiterated time and again, was to play with and in moderation. Gambling was a bad and dangerous master, just as it was a legitimate, even desirable diversion. As the author of one of these guides from the later seventeenth century declared, 'To play sometimes, to entertain company, or to divert your self, is not to be disallowed; but to do it so often as to be called a Gamester is to be avoided.'[20] The essential message here was to be repeated, in various forms, for most of the subsequent century and beyond, to women and men. The hack writer of the later eighteenth century, John Trusler, a helpfully reliable guide to conventional views, and whose publications were probably read mostly by those who aspired to gentility as opposed to those for whom it was the privilege of birth, counselled that the mark of a gentleman was 'to play … genteely'. What this meant was playing for small sums and showing 'neither excessive disappointment or eagerness'. For women, Trusler's words took on a more monitory tone, 'To play occasionally at cards, for your own amusement, or that of your company, provided you do not play deep, nor often, is harmless.' He continued, 'If gaming is a vice in men, it is much more so in women.'[21] Another guide, adapted from a French one, acknowledged that if one wanted to be 'in the world' – in other words, in society – one had to play, but it warned 'never to play deep, that neither winning nor losing may have any Effect upon you, and that you may preserve the same Harmony and evenness of Temper, which you are so remarkable for … upon all other occasions'.[22] One should play, therefore, but in such a way as was consistent with maintaining an agreeable, sociable, and

[20] *The Lady's Year's Gift: Or, Advice to a Daughter* in *The Works of George Savile, Marquis of Halifax*, ed. M. N. Brown, 3 vols. (Oxford, 1989), ii, pp. 404–5.

[21] J. Trusler, *Principles of Politeness and Knowing the World, Containing Every Instruction Necessary to Complete the Gentleman and Man of Fashion* (16th ed., London, 1800), pp. 41, 75.

[22] *The Lady's Preceptor, Or, a Letter to a Young Lady of Distinction upon Politeness Taken from the French of the Abbé D'Ancourt, and Adapted to the Religion, Customs and Manners of the English Nation* (London, 1743), p. 67.

polite disposition. This was the real subject matter of this guidance. Ultimately the only difference between the gamester and the polite gambler was 'character'. The 'gamester' in polite literature was figured as an antitype, as someone governed by the extremity of his or her passions, disfigured (quite literally) and denatured by the tempestuous, swirling energies of the gaming table. The barely suppressed anxiety, which can be read between the lines of these conduct books, was that the gamester and the polite gambler were at one and the same time opposites *and* threateningly proximate.

Tensions and attitudes apparent within this advice were felt in different ways in the lives of individuals. One such, at the beginning of our period, was the Catholic gentleman George Hilton of Beetham, Westmorland, who was to play a minor part in the Jacobite rising of 1715.[23] Hilton's principal and, it is fair to say, great weakness was drink, something which would dog him throughout his life. He once worked out that his drunken 'bootes', or 'fuddle' days, as he sometimes called them, had cost him 620 days of his life in just the eight years between 1714 and 1722, as well as nearly £50 a year.[24] Given the amount of time he spent in inns and taverns, it should perhaps come as no surprise that he was an inveterate gambler. His game of choice was backgammon, which he played at home, in the homes of his acquaintances, in a London coffee house, and in various inns; on occasion he also played card games and bowls. He may well not have recorded all his gambling, and much of it was seemingly for relatively small sums, a matter of a few shillings. Not quite all, though, as suggested by an entry in his journal for 15 July 1700:

> Memorandum for this weeks worke I'll not play at any game for 2d in hard silver this 3 months and then never to play at any game for above 2s and 6d per game whatever; never will I play at any quick game vizt hazed [i.e. hazard, a dice game] &c nor above 7 games at one sitting be my fortune what it will.[25]

Needless to say, he was incapable of keeping to such an admirable regimen. In December 1700 he was to be found in London spending the night at Aldersgate, ostensibly looking for a coach to carry him home, playing backgammon all night until 10 a.m. the next morning, on which occasion he, as he described it, 'lost well'.[26] Hilton played with pretty much anyone whom he chanced to find in his company – tradesmen,

[23] *The Rake's Diary: The Journal of George Hilton*, transcribed by Ann Hillman (Curwen Archives Texts, Berwick upon Tweed, 1994).

[24] Ibid., p. 70. Hilton marked his 'fuddle' days with the symbol of a bottle and glass in his diary.

[25] Ibid., pp. 11–2. [26] Ibid., p. 23.

craftsmen, yeomen, and tenant farmers, as well as local gentry; his world was far from being rigidly compartmentalized along social lines.

John, Lord Hervey, first Earl of Bristol, was a very different kind of person, inhabiting an entirely different social sphere. Similar kinds of tension are, nevertheless, discernable in his life in relation to gaming. If Hilton's existence was basically that of an impoverished, often feckless and disputatious, country gentleman in a comparatively poor region of England – although one which encompassed regular visits to towns, such as Kendal, and trips to London – Hervey, with his seat at Ickworth Park, Suffolk – 'Sweet Ickworth', he once called it – and a house and stables in St James's Square in the British capital, was a courtier who, together with his second wife, Elizabeth, boasted a place at the very heart of elite fashionable life in the early eighteenth century. His diaries, together with the regular letters written to him by his wife when they were apart, are only partially revealing of his and, indeed, her gambling.[27] He made various adventures in lotteries, most notably in the state lottery in 1710, when he purchased 155 tickets – 110 for himself and 45 for his wife and their children. He played cards, as did his wife with her London acquaintances.[28] Female card playing was very well entrenched in London fashionable circles by the early eighteenth century.[29] In June 1703, Hervey made a vow – 'to play no more'.[30] He gave six reasons for this, and his decision was clearly partly aimed at influencing his children in their choices. First, it was a waste of time. Second, he declared, 'no money prospers well that's gained by play'. What he meant by this we cannot say for sure, but presumably it was something along the lines that only money properly earned was likely to prove productive. This moralizing view of wealth was one with a long history and future. Third, gaming that was not fraudulent was almost inevitably going to lead to losses. Fourth, it led to moral degeneration – swearing, keeping 'loose company & conversation'. Fifth, it led to maintaining late hours, weakened the health, and rendered someone 'altogether unfit for any sort of business either publick or private'. Sixth, it left a 'man of great estate' susceptible to sharpers. And seventh, while fighting in a good cause 'should never be declined by any man' – or rather *gentle*man – gaming led to quarrelling and unnecessary personal disputes. As he

27 *The Diary of John Hervey, First Earl of Bristol, 1688–1742* (Wells, 1894).

28 See e.g. *Diary of John Hervey*, pp. 52, 127.

29 James E. Evans, '"A Sceane of Uttmost Vanity": The Spectacle of Gambling in Late Stuart Culture', *Studies in Eighteenth Century Culture*, 31 (2002), 1–20; Hon. C. C. Cowper (ed.), *Diary of Mary, Countess Cowper, Lady of the Bedchamber to the Princess of Wales, 1714–1720* (London, 1865), pp. 14–5, 22, 125, 171.

30 *Diary of John Hervey*, p. 39.

concluded, 'On commence par ester [sic] dupe – on finit par être fripon', which is, he continued, 'ye best abstract of a gamester's character' and should be sufficient to 'cure any wise or honest man of so fatal a passion.' These were points calculated to warm the hearts of critics of gaming throughout the eighteenth century.

Several facts make Hervey's vow all the more intriguing. He was certainly not thereafter beyond making a bet. In late November 1719 he made a wager with a Colonel Campbell for a hundred guineas that French Mississippi stock would not be above 100 in a year's time, which he duly won.[31] Such betting was commonplace among male members of the landed classes, as attested to by, among other things, the betting books of various clubs and associations, such as White's or the Board of the Honourable Brotherhood, the Tory members of which met at the Cocoa Tree Coffee House in London.[32] Bets of this kind were made on an extraordinary range of topics, from the political and topical – the outcome of elections, battles, and sieges – to marriage, death, or, during the 'balloonmania' of the early 1780s at Brooks's, whether the Marquess of Cholmondeley would have sex with a courtesan in a balloon suspended 100 feet above the ground.[33]

The gambling of his sons was a recurrent cause of concern to Hervey. In 1717, he paid 50 guineas to a certain individual on behalf of one son, Jack (John Hervey, from 1723 2nd Baron Hervey), extracting from the latter a promise that he would never play again at Basset 'as long as he should live'. Jack had form. In 1711 he had been ordered home from Newmarket, but appears to have ignored the instruction in order to play dice in the 'chocolate House'.[34] In 1732 he paid over £1,000 to discharge debts accumulated through gaming of another of his sons, Thomas.[35] Controlling, or seeking so to do, the gaming of sons was a major pre-occupation among landed families, testimony not only to its ubiquity but also to the extent to which counter-pressures existed on their conduct and behaviour. As Hervey counselled another of his sons, John and

[31] Ibid., p. 69.

[32] White's betting book records bets of club members from 1743 to 1878 (Boulton, *History of White's*, vol. 2). LMA, A/BLB/1 & 2, Minutes of the Board of the Honourable Brotherhood. The bets among the Brotherhood were for bottles of claret.

[33] Henry S. Eles and Earl Spencer, *Brooks's 1764–1964* (London, 1964), esp. pp. 35–47; Leslie Mitchell, *The Whig World 1760–1837* (London and New York, 2005), p. 50. The sums staked ranged from 10 guineas to 500 guineas. See also R. Fulford, *Boodle's 1762–1962: A Short History* (1962), pp. 27–8; Boulton, *History of White's*, vol. 2.

[34] *Diary of John Hervey*, pp. 66, 296–7.

[35] Ibid., p. 82. See also William R. Jones, 'Hervey, Thomas (1699–1775)', *Oxford Dictionary of National Biography* (2008), available at http://ezproxy-prd.bodleian.ox.ac.uk:2095/10.1093/ref:odnb, p. 13119.

Thomas's half-brother, Carr, on his twelfth birthday, that what he hoped for from him was that he would become 'so pious, charitable, just and usefull a member in your generation, that not only you may be ye joy and support of my age & family, but one of the shining ornaments of your country.'[36] There was a landed variant of the model of 'virtuous masculinity' which, or so it has been argued, the middling sort cleaved to with increasing conviction in this period, one that was much more than an appropriation of the middling version, and that (in various forms) became ever more influential during the eighteenth century. This emphasized duty and responsibility, alongside personal autonomy and honour.[37] This had very considerable bearing on how gaming was viewed at this level of society. Contemporaries sometimes pictured society, especially from the later Georgian period, as divided between a dissolute aristocracy or elite and a middling sort pre-occupied by the twin imperatives of propriety and moderation; it is important not to fall into the trap of thinking that this describes anything like the reality.

Even more striking in the present context was another aspect of Hervey's life: he was part of the Newmarket turf set of the later seventeenth and early eighteenth centuries. He also attended or ran horses at several Suffolk races – Swaffham, Thetford, and Ipswich – as well as at the famous Burford meeting in Oxfordshire, Nottingham, and Quainton. Racing at this level was very costly; Hervey was spending between £600 and £700 a year maintaining his horses at Newmarket.[38] He was staking very considerable sums on races, anywhere between a few hundred guineas to over a thousand guineas.[39] Hervey took particular pride in one of his horses, named Wenn, which he bred himself and which won more than twenty races for him, referring to the horse on several occasions as 'my famous horse called Wenn'.[40] During the spring meeting at Newmarket in 1698 he won over £600 on one match – it is not entirely clear whether this was involving one of his own horses, but it seems likely – also winning matches with two other horses, which he appears to have backed heavily. We know this because he described the events in detail in several letters to his wife, who took a keen interest in his racing activities; indeed, they envisaged it as a kind of joint enterprise. Hervey on occasion placed bets on races for her at Newmarket.[41] The letter he

36 Ibid., pp. 190, 202–4 See also p. 48, where on 4 June, Hervey wrote, 'Friday, my dear son Carr went to Cambridg[e]. I hope in God that he will prosper him in his studies there & make him an useful instrument of his glory in this wicked generation.'

37 On which, see esp. Henry French and Mark Rothery, *Man's Estate: Landed Gentry Mentalities, 1660–1914* (Oxford, 2012).

38 *Diary of John Hervey*, p. 123.

39 Ibid., pp. 27–9, 42, 44–5, 47, 51–2, 58.

40 Ibid., pp. 47, 51–2.

41 Ibid., pp. 253–4, 277, 282, 296–7.

wrote to his wife describing one of his victories is worth quoting at length, because it tells us much about what horse racing meant to Hervey:

> ... but honest Lubcock by ye most supernatural invincible goodness that ever was shown in any creature at last betterd Looby, tho' he run much too fast for him, & had beat him ye first 7 mile of ye 8 they run; but upon Lubcock's being whypt & spurd from shoulder to flank, he at last conquerd his adversary & won us 325 guineys; ye odd 25 was a bett ye King made with me against Lubcock, who was more pleas'd with this match than all he ever saw before. I have been ye more particular in this relation, because I am sure twill be some satisfaction to thee to know how much this victory must have pleas'd me; which indeed it did more than ever any match did before, *because it succeeded almost to a yard according to ye presumption on which I made it.*[42]

For Hervey, then, the crucial element appears to have been not really so much the bet, but what it represented, which was his judgement about the qualities of his horse relative to the one he had chosen to match it against. Racing was a form of competitive display of 'public masculinity', which took place in the full glare of the 'world's' attention. At stake was a sportsman's prowess and judgement, and the meaning of the bet needs to be viewed within this context.[43] After losing a match to the Duke of Rutland in 1712, Hervey decided to give up racing; his wife may have given up 'play' at the same time.[44] This was related to, if not driven by, the debts which their children were running up through gaming, and, for Hervey at least, the powerful appeal of activities that were more fundamental to his sense of identity – namely, custodianship of Ickworth, which included, in addition to extension of the estate, demolition of the old mansion house, and a major programme of tree planting and landscaping.

Gambling of different kinds was thus a prominent element in the lives of many of the elites at the beginning of the eighteenth century. Recreational gambling – playing cards, nine-pins, or bowls for stakes – was closely integrated in elite sociability, be this hetero- or homosocial.[45] For women, especially those who formed part of fashionable court circles, betting on card games, played with other women and men, was the most common form of gambling. As the example of Lady Hervey

[42] Ibid., pp. 137–8.

[43] The term 'public masculinity' is used by Jane Rendall, in 'The Clubs of St James's: Places of Public Patriarchy, Exclusivity, Domesticity and Secrecy', *The Journal of Architecture*, 4 (1999), 167–89.

[44] Ibid., pp. 323–24.

[45] For an example of one elite woman who played 'nine pins' for modest stakes, see LA, BNLW 4/6/18, Account Book of Eleanor, 1st Viscountess Tyrconnel, 1715–19, entries for 2 June, 27 Oct. 1716. The Duke of Argyll's country house at Petersham was equipped with both a nine-pin alley and a bowling green.

illustrates, although such women may not typically have attended the Newmarket races, they took a keen interest in the racing and placed bets, in her case through her husband. Among and between elite men, apart from racing, gambling was commonly a matter of betting on games of bowls or, in Edinburgh, golf, or on games such as backgammon, dice, billiards, or cards. Betting on these games was, it should be emphasized, typically for fairly modest sums in terms of personal expenditure. In the mid-1700s, Nicholas Carewe, later (from 1715) 1st baronet of Beddington, Surrey was gambling a few shillings at a sitting in London taverns and coffee houses, such as the Grecian and White's, or at various races and cockfights.[46] He appears to have gambled somewhat larger sums at the Newmarket races in 1706, including a little over a £1 at 'raffling'. Raffling or dice led him on occasion to gamble for slightly larger amounts. In 1707 he may have lost 17 sh. on the dice tables at Hampstead, and he certainly lost another 16 sh. raffling at Tunbridge Wells. In 1707, he seems to have lost a total of around £39 in what he termed 'play' and another £2 at cards. The dangers of betting on dice games, with their potential for quickly producing large losses, were well recognized.[47] Larger sums were regularly staked on and in side bets on cockfights, the dedicated pursuit of many among the gentry and titled nobility[48], and by some individuals on dice and cards, as well as on horse races, especially at Newmarket to where fashionable London and the court, at least the men, decamped during the reigns of William III and Queen Anne, as they had done during the reigns of Charles II and James II. There was fierce interest in fashionable court circles in sport and in major wins and losses.[49] This was an extension of habits of high stakes gaming among some of the nobility and members of the court in this

[46] BL, Add MSS 30,355, account book of Nicholas Carewe, afterwards 1st Baronet Beddington, Surrey, 1707–8. See also BL, Add MSS 74,245, account book of Robert Walpole [i.e. Sir Robert Walpole's father], 1693–8. The most he spent on cards was 2sh. 6d. at Lady Hobart's in November 1698. In 1695, he gave 'Bob', presumably his son, the future Sir Robert Walpole, 4 sh. which the latter had lost at cards. Otherwise his expenditure on gambling was limited to entering various private lotteries, which proliferated in the 1690s. And WSRO, Marquis of Ailesbury Papers, 1300/894, 'earl of Ailesburys Account, 1689–92'.

[47] See e.g. the bond of obligation which Sir John Sherard gave to Sir John Brownlow in 1687, which obliged Sherard to pay Brownlow £1,000 were he to pay at hazard for money or goods. LA, Brownlow Papers, BNLW 4/11/2, Bond of Oligation, 4 July 1687.

[48] We lack modern studies of cockfighting in this period, although see Iris Middleton, 'Cock Fighting in Yorkshire in the Early Eighteenth Century', *Northern History*, 40 (2003), 129–41; R. F. King, 'Aspects of Sociability in the North East of England 1600–1750', unpublished Ph.D. thesis, University of Durham (2001), pp. 164–78.

[49] See e.g. *Hervey Diary*, pp. 125–6, Lady Hervey to John, Lord Hervey, 5 Apr. 1698, where Lady Hervey writes, 'We are all day a fancying what you are doing in every minute. The town is empty. It affords no news; nor no body talks of any thing but Newmarket.'

period. Yet, as the case of Hervey illustrates, even within such circles attitudes towards gaming could be more ambivalent, even contradictory, than is sometimes supposed by historians.

The relationship between the elites and gambling, if anything, only deepened during the eighteenth century. One important contributory factor, in addition to the continuing development of the London 'season' after 1689, was the remarkable growth of spas and resorts, including from the final quarter of the century seaside resorts such as Scarborough or Brighton. Bath, however, was by some distance the most influential, in terms both of the numbers, type and range of people who visited it, and the power of its example. The relationship between spas and gaming had long been a close one. As a modern historian of English spas has noted, it had been apparent as early as the late sixteenth century, and as the record of Carewe's gambling testifies, places such as Tunbridge Wells and Hampstead were sites of dicing and raffling in the 1700s.[50] It continued to be a prominent feature of such places. John Macky, the Scottish spy and travel writer, made much of this at the beginning of the 1720s, as well as the sometimes quite fine variations in the character of these places, reflecting in part who typically frequented them, and, more pertinently for present purposes, who gambled there.[51] Lady Jane Coke, writing from Tunbridge Wells in 1750 to her regular correspondent, Mrs Eyre of Derby, tartly observed: 'There was a good deal of company, and some beauties, but by all I heard the men's attachment was to the gaming tables.'[52]

Much (probably most) of the gambling which occurred at Bath and other spas – those 'theatres of fashion' as one contemporary writer dubbed them – took the form of playing card games for low stakes; it reflected how far, as Janet Mullin has recently emphasized, cards became the preoccupation of the 'polite' across the British Isles in the eighteenth century.[53] The conservative moralist, James Fordyce, grumpily moaned in 1775 that card playing had 'now become so strangely predominant, as to take the lead of everything else in almost every company of every rank'.[54] In 1766 John Penrose, a retired clergyman from Cornwall,

[50] Phyllis Hembry, *The English Spa, 1560–1815: A Social History* (London, 1990), pp. 3, 22.

[51] John Macky, *A Journey through England. In Familiar Letters. From a Gentleman Here to his Friend Abroad*, 2 vols. (2nd ed., London, 1732), i, pp. 94–6 [Tunbridge Wells], 110–11 [Epsom]; ii, 4–5 [Belsize].

[52] *Letters from Lady Jane Coke to her Friend Mrs Eyre at Derby 1747–1758*, ed. with notes by Mrs Ambrose Rathorne (London, 1899), p. 54: Mrs Jane Coke to Mrs Eyre, 21 Aug. 1750.

[53] Janet E. Mullin, *A Six Penny at Whist: Gaming and the English Middle Classes 1680–1830* (Woodbridge, 2015).

[54] J. Fordyce, *Sermons to Young Women*, 2 vols. (London, 1775), i, p. 198.

described a scene that was endlessly replayed, with the odd variation, in Bath: 'Our visit to the Leighs [Mrs and Miss] was not protracted to any considerable length: for one Mr Hutchinson, Capt. of an India-man, and his Lady, drank Tea with us, and immediately after, sat down to Quadrille.' When the Leighs left Bath, making a present to the Penroses of the 'remains' of their household, these comprised 'a little salt, a little vinegar, 2 large Pieces of candle, half a lemon, some ink, and' – naturally – 'a Pack of cards'.[55] To not play cards was to place oneself decidedly on the margins of polite company. The assembly rooms, which sprang up in towns across Georgian Britain, frequently featured card rooms; while card assemblies joined dancing assemblies as key ingredients of polite leisure.[56] As Fordyce sourly pointed out, carding had taken over domestic as well as public leisure; more and more homes, from those of the landed elites to the prospering middling sort, featured card tables.[57] One young lady, who disliked playing cards in 'A mix'd Company' – by which, she meant with those whom she was not intimately acquainted – and was evidently frequently a loser financially thereby, gently complained from Nottingham in 1780 that 'so general' were card parties 'that the lady's [sic] cannot spend Afternoon Agreeably without them'.[58] While it was, to be sure, not only women who played cards in 'company' in the eighteenth century – both men and women played in homosocial and heterosocial gatherings and parties – there was many a polite woman of the period who was devoted to 'carding', although the frequently disparaging comments about this preoccupation overlook the relative independence and equality with men which this activity afforded women.

55 *Letters from Bath 1766–1767 by the Rev. John Penrose. With an Introduction and Notes by Brigitte Mitchell & Hubert Penrose* (Sutton, 1983), pp. 37–8, 71.

56 Mark Girouard, *The English Town: A History of Urban Life* (New Haven and London, 1992); Bob Harris and C. A. McKean, *The Scottish Town in the Age of the Enlightenment 1740–1820* (Edinburgh, 2014), pp. 397–9.

57 Fordyce, *Sermons*, i, 198. Glamis Castle, Strathmore Papers, 185/5, inventory of the furniture & household goods, plate & China at Gibside, 29 Oct. 1761, which shows six card tables in the house, one made of walnut in the 'Foreparlour'; a mahogany one in the 'Back Parlour'; another walnut one in the 'Prayer room'; a mahogany one and a Mississippi table in the servants' hall; one in the steward's room; and one in the 'The Bath West Room'. TNA, Chancery Masters Exhibits, C104/146, Catalogue of Sale of Contents of Sir George Colebrooke's house in Arlington Street, Christie and Ansells, 1778, which indicates that he had a mahogany hazard table in 'The Cove Room next the Park'; a pair of mahogany card tables in each of the 'Lesser Library', the 'Stucco Parlour', and the 'India Paper Drawing Room', as well as another such table in 'The Ball Room'.

58 NA, DDFJ/11/1/5, fos. 3–6, Ann Warde to John Hewett, Nottingham, 9 Jan. 1780. See also fos. 99–100, same to same, 28 Jan. 1781, where Ann noted that, while there were no concerts or plays, 'card routs there are in abundance'.

However, this was never the full story of the gambling at spas and resorts. In the first place, such places attracted gamblers of a different ilk. As John Macky reported, they were typically sites of what George Hilton, who we met earlier, called 'quick games', in other words games of chance which were principally designed to promote betting.[59] In the 1770s a certain Thomas Kent was lured by Sir Alexander Leith into playing hazard, a dicing game, at Brighton, the sums involved amounting to over £10,000. This may have been a sharper's trick, for Kent was later enticed into a further dicing game in London, where he lost another £500.[60] Towards the end of the eighteenth century one writer remarked that, apart from the environs of St James's in London, there was 'no part of the world … where gaming is carried on so high a pitch as at Bath'. This they attributed to the presence of 'swarms' of sharpers or 'blacklegs', such as appear to have deceived Thomas Kent. These individuals were, they lamented 'suffered to patrole our streets, arm in arm, with the flower of our nobility, whom they pillage at their leisure, under the assumed and specious mask of gentlemen'.[61]

Deep play at Bath, and certain other resorts, was commonly associated with people from the very highest social echelons. This was especially true among women. As early as 1709, Margaret Cave observed in relation to Bath:

> This town is full of company & highly entertain[e]d with singing & musick by the famous Nicolino & Valentino, besides Plays, baths, puppet shews, <…?> Dancing & some gameing, *but I don't see much of that high, among the Ladys being but few of Quallity at this place now.*[62] (My emphasis.)

Sixty years or so later, and for a further thirty years, the spinster Grace Trevor provided regular reports on goings on at Bath to her friend, the Countess of Chatham, widow of William Pitt the Elder. Trevor was part of a circle of older women, most of them single (widows and spinsters), that engaged in 'low play', which meant tables of cribbage on most evenings. The contrast, explicitly drawn by Trevor, was with the 'Ton', a term which, as Hannah Greig has emphasized, was primarily culturally rather than socially defined, which only makes identifying who it actually encompassed all the more trickier.[63] One regular Bath resident who

[59] It was Richard 'Beau' Nash who, as Master of Ceremonies, introduced 'E.O.' tables to Bath and Tunbridge Wells. Nash appears to have prevented private individuals keeping gaming tables in Bath during his reign as master of ceremonies there. *PA*, 23 Feb. 1768.

[60] NLS, 'A Narrative, Thomas Kent', 13 Apr. 1783.

[61] *A Tour Through England and Wales in* 1791, extracted in the *Edinburgh Magazine*, XVIII (1793), pp. 125–6.

[62] BL, Verney Papers, 636/54, Margaret Cave to [Sir Thomas Cave?], Bath, 3 Feb. 1709.

[63] H. Greig, *The Beau Monde: Fashionable Society in Georgian London* (Oxford, 2013).

might have qualified was Henrietta Pelham-Holles, the Duchess of Newcastle, wife and then (from 1768) widow of Thomas Pelham-Holles, 1st duke of Newcastle. In the year beginning 1 May 1760, she won just over £84 playing brag, and lost just over £192. The equivalent figures for commerce were £88 and £71; quadrille £7 and £16; tredille £78 and £64; and whist £9 and £34.[64] The sums for the following year were of a similar order, and while she appears to have reduced the sums she gambled in later years, when she was widowed, she was still winning and losing up to £16 at a sitting. This was playing quite deep, although not on the leviathan scale of the exclusive male gaming clubs or female devotees of the faro tables in the 1780s and 1790s.[65] It was also well within her means.

Opportunities, therefore, to gamble for many male and female members of the elites, especially those who were part of metropolitan fashionable society, increased from the end of the seventeenth century. Indeed, the change for women may well have been more marked than for men, since the latter, as in the cases discussed above, long had inns, taverns, and from the later seventeenth century, coffee houses in which to game, as well as, when younger, university and the inns of temple. Whether the development of polite society offered new freedoms to women, or rather how much it did so, is debated among historians.[66] One can certainly argue that it constrained them more powerfully than men. For all that there are examples of especially young men, such as Dudley Ryder, the future attorney general, or Ralph William Grey from the north east of England, for whom the challenge of fashioning a polite self was a source of acute anxiety, behaving 'impolitely' did not threaten their social status, as it did, unerringly, for women.[67] Recall here the monitory counsel to women relating to gaming, although this was also

[64] BL, Add MSS 33,628, private accompts of the duchess of Newcastle, 1757–1776.

[65] Lady Spencer's advice to her daughter, Georgina, Duchess of Devonshire, in 1775, was to 'Play at whist, commerce, backgammon, trictrac, or chess, but never at quinze, lou, brag, faro, hazard or any games of chance.' Quoted in Phyllis Diane Deutsch, 'Fortune and Chance: Aristocratic Gaming and English Society 1760–1837', unpublished Ph.D. thesis, New York University (1991), p. 65.

[66] See, *inter alia*, Amanda Vickery, *The Gentleman's Daughter: Women's Lives in Georgian England (New Haven and London, 1998)*; Joyce Ellis, '"On the Town"; Women in Augustan England', *History Today*, 45 (1995), 20–7; H. Barker and E. Chalus, *Women's History: Britain 1700–1850: An Introduction* (London, 2005); Rosalind Carr, *Gender and Enlightenment Culture in Eighteenth Century Scotland* (Edinburgh, 2014). For marked scepticism about the extent of change for women, and an emphasis on basic continuities, see King, 'Aspects of Sociability in the North East of England'.

[67] *The Diary of Dudley Ryder, 1715–1716*, ed. W. Matthews (1939). Grey's almost painful uncertainties about how to fashion a polite identity are exhaustively recorded in his memorandum books (Northumberland Record Office, 753, box 1, G, memorandum books of Ralph William Grey, 1731–50).

related to the flagrant sexual double standard which prevailed in the eighteenth century. On the other hand, it is hard to dispute the proposition that polite leisure culture furnished women with new opportunities to socialize, both in public venues and homes, with what appears often to have been a striking degree of independence. For many women, across Britain, 'carding' became something of an obsession, while some women among the 'quality' and metropolitan fashionable elite, who usually had access to their own money, whether through annuities and other sums settled on them, or annual sums provided by their husbands, played for considerable stakes, usually in one another's houses and at fashionable resorts such as Bath.[68]

New opportunities to gamble in the eighteenth century were not restricted to card playing, dice, or other games of chance. Later chapters explore the growth and appeal of lotteries, especially the official and public lotteries. What they show is how far adventures in the lotteries became a regular activity, or even habit, among a large cross section of female and male members of the landed classes, especially those with good links to the British capital, which was an expanding number in this period.[69] As striking, however, was the growth of horse racing, the subject to which we now turn.

1.2 Horse Racing and Gambling

Several decades ago in his seminal study of provincial English urban renewal in the century after 1660 Peter Borsay emphasized the very marked expansion of horse racing in the half-century or so leading up to 1740.[70] Borsay may actually have underestimated this because of an overemphasis on town, as opposed to rural, races, and reliance on data derived from the *Racing Calendar*, which from 1727 provided an annual listing of race meetings. Not all of the race meetings which sprang up in the early decades of the eighteenth century were, to be sure, well attended; nor did they always attract more than a handful of entrants;

[68] Almack's was relatively unusual among the exclusive clubs in that it admitted women to its premises. One other factor which contributed to gaming among elite women was ready access to credit. Georgina, Duchess of Devonshire, for example, depended heavily on borrowing from Coutts Bank to meet her gambling debts. For which, see Deutsch, 'Fortune and Chance', pp. 80–5.

[69] Susan Whyman has emphasized how John Verney and the Verney women participated keenly in lotteries in the 1690s, including attending the draws (S. E. Whyman, *Sociability and Power in Late Stuart England: The Cultural Worlds of the Verneys 1660–1720* (Oxford, 1999), pp. 76–7).

[70] P. Borsay, *The English Urban Renaissance* (Oxford, 1989), pp. 184, 355–67.

most only lasted for a single day or possibly two.[71] An exhaustive unpublished study has indicated that race meetings in Northumberland and County Durham in the decades before 1740 were at least double the number of what is revealed by the *Racing Calendar*.[72] Whether the pattern is similar elsewhere is unknown, although it is highly unlikely that expansion was uniform across the country.[73] Because of the nature of the sources – we are heavily dependent on the existence and survival in this context of provincial newspapers – tracing in comprehensive detail the chronological and geographical expansion of racing is impossible. The rate of growth appears to have quickened markedly in the 1730s, leading the early historian of York, Francis Drake, to declare in 1736 that it was 'surprising to think to what a height this spirit of horse racing is now arrived in this kingdom, when there is scarce a village so mean that has not a bit of place raised once a year for this purpose'.[74] Yorkshire was a racing county, so Drake's comments may be exaggerated, and certainly cannot simply be assumed to apply to other places. Nevertheless, and further testifying to the strength of the forces for growth at work, larger race meetings extended the number of days over which they were held, also increasing the number of prizes and races. In 1716 in the Northumbrian market town of Morpeth there were two days of racing; just over two decades later this number had risen to five.[75]

As early as 1737, the nation's legislators were evidently sufficiently concerned about the expansion of racing, and consequent encouragement of 'idleness' among the wider population, for the press to report that they were considering a bill to suppress all races other than royal plates.[76] Three years later an act was passed to restrict racing, by placing a minimum limit on prize money for any race of £50, a measure which was renewed and made permanent in 1745.[77] This led to a period of rationalization and retrenchment during the central decades of the eighteenth century. Although limited work has been done on this, the effects

[71] See various letters in the Verney papers in the British Library referring to problems attracting participants at various race meetings in the 1710s. BL, Verney Papers, 636/56, Margaret to Sir Thomas Cave, 19 Sept. 1716 [referring to Lutterworth]; Lord Fermanagh to Ralph Verney, 7 Oct. 1716 [referring to Aylesbury]; 636/54, Sir Thomas Cave to ?, 14 Sept. 1712 ['indifferent sport at Quainton']; Mary Lovett to ?, 27 Oct. 1713 [Stamford].

[72] King, 'Aspects of Sociability', p. 131.

[73] The popularity of racing varied quite markedly across the country, with Yorkshire and the north east being two areas where it was unusually prominent.

[74] F. Drake, *Eboracum: Or, the History and Antiquities of the City of York* (York, 1736), p. 241.

[75] King, 'Aspects of Sociability', p. 138.

[76] *Old Whig*, 20 Oct. 1737.

[77] 13 Geo. II, c. 19; 18 Geo. II, c. 34.

of the legislation appear to have been broadly those hoped for by its architects, in that most of the more popular, often rural, meetings disappeared after 1740.[78] By 1779, many English market or county towns (e.g. Lewes, Worcester, Salisbury, Grantham, Ludlow, Lincoln, and Hereford) and a smaller number of fast expanding ports and manufacturing towns (Liverpool, Hull, Sheffield, Manchester) were hosting annual three-day race meetings, while a handful of towns (such as Canterbury and Morpeth (four days) or Newcastle, Carlisle, and Durham (five days) held longer ones.[79] York was holding a six-day meeting by the same date, while Newmarket staged six race meetings during the year, representing a total of thirty-nine days of racing. Strong growth resumed in the final decades of the eighteenth century, in a second wave of major expansion which continued into the 1830s; there followed another period of consolidation in the mid-nineteenth century.[80] As in the earlier expansionary phase, this new one involved the emergence of additional sites of racing, the establishment of new and longer race meetings at established courses, but also the development of a more clearly defined calendar of big races, with the foundation of the St Ledger (1776), the Oaks, and the Derby (both in 1779), and the 1,000 guineas and 2,000 guineas at Newmarket. As Adrian Harvey has shown, there was a near doubling of stake money between 1793–1804 and 1805–1815 as financial investment in racing significantly increased at the beginning of the nineteenth century.[81]

The fortunes of horse racing north of the border followed a markedly different trajectory. In stark contrast to England, the picture before c.1760 was one of stagnation – even perhaps decline between the 1740s and 1760s. The sources for this are very patchy and sparse, and the pattern is at best dimly discernible; we know that racing was held in several places – Stirling in 1734, Dundee, Peebles, and Cupar in 1735, Perth in 1740 – only because of stray references in gentry

[78] Using data from the *Racing Calendar*, Borsay estimated a reduction in the number of race meetings by two-thirds between 1739 and 1749 (Borsay, *English Urban Renaissance*, pp. 184–5). Rebecca King estimates an even starker decline in the north east of England, of 82 per cent (King, 'Aspects of Sociability', p. 181).

[79] James Weatherby, *Racing Calendar: Containing an Account of the Plates, Matches, and Sweepstakes, Run for in Great Britain and Ireland, in the Year 1779* (London, 1779).

[80] Adrian Harvey, *The Beginnings of a Commercial Sporting Culture in Britain 1793–1850* (Aldershot, 2004); Wray Vamplew, *The Turf: A Social and Economic History of Horse Racing* (London, 1976), ch. 1; Mike Huggins, *Flat Racing and British Society 1790–1914: A Social and Economic History* (London, 2000).

[81] Harvey, *Beginnings of a Commercial Sporting Culture*, p. 23. Even by 1823, nevertheless, eighty-seven out of ninety-five race courses were holding only one race meeting a year.

correspondence or accounts.[82] Nevertheless, such evidence as exists points uniformly to a similar conclusion. Perth, for example, appears to have held no races between 1740 and 1761, while there were no races on Leith Sands between 1741 and 1748.[83] Races may have continued in the early eighteenth century in the Borders, but these probably attracted only local interest, and had a decidedly popular character, being linked to the annual ritual of the riding of the marches.[84] The final third of the eighteenth century saw the establishment or revival of racing in several Scottish towns, although the overriding impression is that race meetings flourished for relatively short periods and sustained success proved elusive. Racing, for example, revived in Montrose at the end of the eighteenth century, but in 1803 only four horses were entered to contest three races. There followed a hiatus until 1821; a gold cup race was held there in 1822, but racing then ceased four years later.[85] The main historian of Scottish racing suggests that already by the 1780s patronage of Leith races by the Scottish gentry and nobility was on the wane.[86] Elsewhere, the viability and success of racing was heavily dependent on the support of the Royal Caledonian Hunt, established in 1777, which, while it gave this in early years solely to Kelso, from 1787 shared its patronage between Dumfries, Stirling, Hamilton, Ayr, Edinburgh, Perth, and the aforementioned Borders town.[87] The result was that there were some years when these towns offered no races, or racing was very poorly supported.[88] Other probable reasons for the underlying weakness of Scottish racing was that there were relatively few Scottish 'turfites', while leading Scottish owners of race horses tended to focus their efforts on the more prestigious meetings south of the border. It also almost certainly reflected differences in the structure of landed society north and south of

[82] NRS, GD 112/21/77, personal account books kept by John, Lord Glenorchy, later 3rd Earl of Breadalbane, entry for 6 Mar. 1740, 'To a subscription of last year for Perth Races – 5-5-0.' It is not entirely clear whether this was a subscription for 1739 or 1740. NRAS 2177, Hamilton Papers, Bundle 2808, letter to the Duke of Hamilton, Hamilton, 18 Apr. 1735, refers to 'Cowpar [i.e. Coupar] races'; same to same, 4 Mar. 1735, which refers to 'two plates' at Dundee in April, and to plates at Milnefield and Peebles.

[83] J. Fairfax-Blakeborough, *Northern Turf History, Vol. IV, History of Horse Racing in Scotland* (Whitby, 1973), p. 41.

[84] Harris and McKean, *The Scottish Town*, pp. 366, 374; NRAS 2177, Hamilton Papers, Bundle 2808, letter to the Duke of Hamilton, 6 June 1735, which describes the plate races at Peebles.

[85] Fairfax-Blakeborough, *Northern Turf History, Vol. IV*, p. 280.

[86] Ibid., p. 45.

[87] Ibid., pp. 116–9

[88] Racing at Hamilton, for example, seems to have lapsed after 1811, the last visit there of the RCH. See NRAS 2177, Hamilton Papers, Bundle 765, memorial of the provost, magistrates, and town council of Hamilton, 5 Nov. 1838, calling on the Duke of Hamilton to use his 'powerful influence' with the Royal Caledonian Hunt to restore racing to the town. There was no racing at Kelso in 1794 and 1795.

the border, with the pyramid of landed wealth in Scotland being considerably more steeply sided.[89]

However, in the present context, the causes of these patterns are not our primary concern. What does matter is their importance for habits and practices of gambling among the elites.

Racing's appeal was always social as well, or as much, as sporting. As has long been recognized, the main race meetings in England and Wales were important moments of elite sociability, taking their place in the annual recreational calendar of the landed classes.[90] Along with the racing, such events typically offered assemblies and concerts in the mornings and evenings. In 1716 Mary Lovett remarked that the 'company and Diversion' at that year's Lutterworth races had been 'both very small'. The key indicator was the number of coaches which had been present, no more than twenty. Nevertheless, as she went on: '... the Lady's picked up Beaus enough for A Country Dance ... Balls at Mrs Cole's House ... we were all very merry and easey and the Company that did not care for Dancing played at Cards ...'[91] In Newcastle, during race week in the 1730s and 1740s the composer Charles Avison organized a series of morning concerts, which were typically attended by women while the men were engaged in or in attendance at cockfighting matches. Cockfighting normally took place in the mornings before the racing in the afternoon.[92] The importance of 'Company' to the success of a race meeting was widely acknowledged; 'there is nothing', one contemporary wrote in the mid-eighteenth century, 'will make the Swaffham races florish [sic] so much as making 'em Commodious for the Fair Sex'.[93] The provincial theatre manager of the later eighteenth century, Tate Wilkinson, noted in his memoirs that the salaries of his theatre company

[89] One index of the general weakness of participation in racing north of the border is the relatively low number of Scottish subscribers to Weatherby's *Racing Calendar* – just twelve in 1779.

[90] Of 225 race meetings identified at York and Hambleton between 1700 and 1739, all but five were connected to assize dates, when the country gentry would be in York. Iris Middleton and Wray Vamplew, 'Horse Racing and the Yorkshire Leisure Calendar in the Early Eighteenth Century', *Northern History*, 49 (2003), 62. See also Angela Dain, 'Assemblies and Politeness 1660–1840', unpublished Ph.D. thesis, University of East Anglia (2000), esp. pp. 41–3.

[91] BL, Verney Papers, 636/56, Mary Lovett to [?], 29 Sept. 1716. See also LA, Mass 13, correspondence of Mrs Carte, 13/21, letter begun 4 June and ended 7 June: 'Shilton race was yesterday, & I was there, indeed but for ye name of one I might see as much company at Bosworth Church almost every Sundy [sic], there was only Lady Dixies coach ours & one Mr Trotmans from Nun Eaton S.r <Wolton?> & his daughters but not his Lady...'

[92] King, 'Aspects of Sociability', p. 156.

[93] NRO, copy of a letter from A. Wodehouse, Kimberly, 13 July 1755.

were doubled during race weeks, such were demands on them for performances.[94] Major race meetings were viewed as significant gatherings of the landed elites, and judged for their success by most contemporaries by the range and number of the 'quality' present.[95]

Eighteenth-century horse racing had a dual character, in that its growth and attraction were driven, on the one hand, by powerful commercial forces and entrepreneurial energies – in the form of innkeepers, ambitious civic elites seeking to bring people and money to their towns – and, on the other, a marked impulse to exclusivity. This tension was common to much elite leisure activity in the eighteenth century, but it was starkly apparent in the case of racing, and continued to be a major, even intensifying, strand in its development in the subsequent century when the Jockey Club, always a very exclusive body, sought to impose greater control over and standardization of racing, including eliminating irregularities and flagrantly underhand practices.[96] While the popularity of racing among a wide cross section of society is amply attested, and some race meetings in the second half of the eighteenth century, for example, those at Cowbridge, Glamorgan, had an emphatically popular character, at the larger, more important meetings – such as at Newmarket, York, Epsom, and Doncaster – strategies were carefully employed to promote and enforce social separation.[97] This was typically done through the device of subscription, which conferred access to the growing number of purpose-built stands or the famous meeting rooms at Newmarket.[98] Access to such spaces was an obvious mark of social status. One Hull gentleman recorded his purchase of a ticket for the Beverley race stand in 1771 in his journal 'that I may not have to look

[94] Tate Wilkinson, *The Wandering Patentee, or, The History of Yorkshire Theatres, from 1770 to the Present Time* (York, 1795), p. 271.

[95] See e.g. Edinburgh Central Library, Y DA 1861.789, Journal of Andrew Armstrong, 1789–93, fos. 27, 51, 125–7, 285, 366.

[96] Vamplew, *The Turf*, ch. 6; Huggins, *Flat Racing*, ch. 7. For lists of Jockey Club membership from 1828 and 1829, see CRO, Lonsdale (Lowther) Papers, D/Lons/L9/2/31.

[97] For the Cowbridge races, see *The Diary of William Thomas of Michaelston-Super-Ely, Near St Fagans, Glamorgan 1762–1795*, abridged and edited by R. T. W. Denning (Cardiff, 1995), pp. 146, 163, 183, 230. Thomas regularly moaned about the 'noise and riots' which accompanied the racing on Stalling Down outside Corbridge, where there were horse and foot races, as well as cockfighting.

[98] When the New Rooms at Newmarket were built in 1771, the subscription was 10 guineas for noblemen and 5 guineas for commoners plus a further 5 guineas every October in advance of the October meeting. See CRO, Carlisle, D/Lons/L9/2/31, list of members of the New Rooms, 1829. The Bibury Club meeting at Burford in June was confined to club members.

back at the original Purchase in case I shd lose it'.[99] Landed patronage of county race meetings was crucial to their success. As Borsay has noted, surviving lists of subscribers for the Warwick races show that around 30 per cent had the title of knight or above, while around 15 per cent were from the titled nobility.[100] Subscribers to the York and Lincoln races display a similar pattern.[101] In Scotland, as alluded to above, the importance of landed patronage of racing in the later eighteenth century would be hard to overstate. The original membership of the Royal Caledonian Hunt, the body whose support was crucial to the eighteenth-century revival of Scottish racing, comprised just twelve individuals, only two of whom were commoners: John Nesbit and John Rutherford. The others were the Dukes of Hamilton, Buccleuch, Roxburgh, and Gordon, the Earls of Eglinton, Haddington, and Glencairn, and Sir Thomas Wallace, Sir William Don, and Sir William Cunnyngham. Membership of the Royal Caledonian Hunt was fixed at forty-five, being extended somewhat in later years, but the firmly landed character of the body was very much retained. The Perth Hunt, which supported annual Perth race meetings from 1784, comprised local landed notables led by regional magnate, the Duke of Atholl.[102] The revival of racing in later eighteenth-century Scotland was, from one perspective, a symptom of the renewed cohesion and confidence of the Scottish landed classes following the turmoil and instability of the first half of the century.

Entering horses in races in this period was by no means the preserve of the landed elites. Much depended in this context on the prestige of the meeting; and plenty of meetings of the later eighteenth and early nineteenth centuries continued, as earlier in the century, to hold races aimed

[99] University of Hull, Brynmor Jones Library, DP/146, journal and personal account book of Robert Carlisle Broadley of Hull, entry for 21–26 May 1771.

[100] Borsay, *English Urban Renaissance*, pp. 189–90.

[101] LA, Monson Papers, 10/9/6, an account of the receipts and payments on the money collected for the Ladies Plate at Lincoln, 1733; W. Pick, *An Authentic Historical Racing Calendar of all the Plates, Sweepstakes, Matches, &c, Run at York, From the First Commencement of Races There in the Year 1709, to the Year 1785 Inclusive* (York, 1785), gives lists of subscribers to the York assemblies during York race meetings between 1752 and 1777, pp. 53–4, 56–7, 59–60, 62–3, 66–7, 69–70, 72–3, 76, 79–80, 85–6, 90–1, 94–5, 98–9, 102–4, 108–9, 112–4, 117–8, 123–5, 129–30, 134–5, 141–2, 146–8, 152–3, 157–8, 162–3.

[102] Fairfax-Blakeborough, *Northern Turf History, Vol. IV*, pp. 167, 172. See also NLS, MS 8251, Andrew Stuart to [?], n.d. but prob. 1801, where the author reported that he has been attending the Hamilton races 'which was a very good one – the company more select than numerous'. After dining at the ordinary – presumably in the Hamilton Arms – the ladies had retired to Hamilton House, while the men 'amused' themselves with tea, coffee, and cards; there was a ball in the evening.

at lesser gentry and tenant farmers usually riding their own horses.[103] However, cost restricted competition for the most valuable prizes at fashionable meetings to the seriously wealthy. We have already seen that John, Lord Hervey, 1st Earl of Bristol in the early eighteenth century was spending up to £1,000 a year simply on maintaining his race horses. Reconstructing the costs of racing at different points in the eighteenth century is impossible because the records are usually incomplete, and clearly it depended on the scale of the involvement. At one end of the spectrum were the racing interests of a 2nd Earl of Rockingham or Duke of Hamilton, while at the other were those of country gentleman such as John Swinburne from the north east, who had a handful of race horses in the 1730s and 1740s, but who still was expending considerable sums in stud fees, payments to saddlers and smiths, drugs for his horses, and employing a jockey.[104] One scholar has recently estimated that Lord Harley spent between £3,600 and £4,000 in a somewhat half-hearted attempt to resuscitate the famous Welbeck stud between 1717 and 1725, while a newspaper declared, in what was probably a gross exaggeration, that the Prince of Wales had been spending £30,000 a year on his stud towards the end of the eighteenth century.[105] Lord Archibald Hamilton's racing accounts for 1790–1791 and 1802–1803 show expenditure,

[103] In the first half of the eighteenth century, races were on occasion reserved for people of the middling sort. At Durham, for example, in 1732, there was a prize of £8 open to anyone who was 'deemed a Trading man', while at the Newcastle races in 1734 there was a prize for horses belonging to freeman of the town. King, 'Aspects of Sociability', pp. 152–3. In 1712, Margaret Cave reported to her husband from the Lutterworth races that a 'handsome cup' raced for on Wednesday had been won by 'an honest innkeeper at Northampton' (BL, Verney Papers, 636/54, Margaret Cave to Thomas Cave, 1 Sept. 1712). For the later period, see James Weatherby, *Racing Calendar* (1823), for various races for non-thoroughbred horses which were the property of farmers. These were typically linked to hunts. The Tradesmen's Plate at Swansea was for non-thoroughbred horses, the property of gentlemen residing in the south west from 30 Dec. 1822. In the 1800s, races were held for members of yeomanry cavalry companies. For example, at the Wrexham races in 1806, Sir Watkin Williams Wynne donated a £50 prize for a race of horses who were the property of non-commissioned officers and privates of the North Wales Yeomanry Cavalry (*Literary and Fashionable Magazine* (1806), 'Sporting Varieties', 60). Races for ponies and galloways were held in Hampshire in the later eighteenth century (*The Salisbury and Winchester Journal*, 20 May 1799).

[104] Northumberland Record Office, Swinburne (Capheaton) MSS, ZSW 454, Sir John Swinburne, account and diary from 11 June 1730 to [?]Nov. 1744.

[105] Peter Edwards, 'The decline of an aristocratic stud: The study of Edward Lord Harley, 2nd Earl of Oxford and Mortimer, at Welbeck (Nottinghamshire), 1717–29', *Economic History Review*, 69 (2016), 870–92; *Diary, or Woodfall's Register*, 15 Mar. 1792. In 1785, one contemporary bemoaned, in relation to the spring meeting at Newmarket: '...the Prince has been here fetlock deep in the Turf – how much the Nation must pay for this, the Carlton house business & his other follies'. (*The Diary of Sylas Neville 1767–1788*, ed. Basil Cozens-Hardy (London, New York and Toronto, 1950), p. 325.)

respectively, of £1,324.13.1 and £1,414.9.3. These included sums for sweepstakes.[106] Set on the other side were sums realized through sales of horses and winnings, which in some years could be considerable.[107] Hamilton was a very successful owner of racehorses, winning the St Ledger on no less than seven occasions. Whether he spent more than he won on racing was evidently of no concern to him, as he wrote from the continent in September 1792:

> … I rec'd yours with ye list of York. I have only to say that whoever plays must expect rubs. It gives me more concern when I think that those who might have been a little particular to my stable may have lost their money than any thing else (for as for me) I don't mind it in ye least; …[108]

Lord Kinnaird spent £428.12.11 on stud fees in 1808, and paid nearly £80 to the jockey William Clift for his services between April and November 1810.[109]

The costs referred to above are those only for maintaining a stud of racehorses, and employing jockeys and so forth, not for entering them in matches, or, indeed, betting. Matches between racing notability could involve huge sums. When Sir Lawrence Dundas's filly, for example, beat the Duke of Buccleuch's at Leith in 1772, the sum at stake was 1,000 guineas.[110] Dundas, the 'nabob of the north', whose vast wealth derived from military contracting, had been systematically brokering this wealth into property and the search for social status since at least the end of the Seven Years' War.[111] When attending the April 1773 meeting at Newmarket he carried with him bank notes, bank bills, and gold to the

106 NRAS, Hamilton Papers, Bundle 4032, racing accounts, 1 Nov. 1790–1 Nov. 1791, 1 Nov. 1802–1 Nov. 1803.The major expense was stud fees at Breckengill, Yorkshire.

107 In 1793–4, Lord Archibald Hamilton raced horses at Doncaster, York, Durham, Leith, Newcastle, West Chester, Reeth, Boroughbridge, Manchester, and Penrith. His colt, Phlegan, won at Reeth, West Chester, Manchester, York, Boroughbridge, and Penrith. In all his winnings in this year came to £911.5.0, which represented a gain on the year of £123.10.7 (Bundle 3520, racing account, 1 Nov. 1793–1 Nov. 1794). In 1798–9, his expenditure was £1,151.5.0, but sums realized through winnings and the sale of three horses came to £932.10.10 (Bundle 3521, racing account, 1 Nov. 1798–1 Nov. 1799). See, however, Lord William Lowther's sensible comments in the entry in his diary for 21 Jan. 1813: 'After breakfast drew a detailed account of the outgoing expenses necessary for the establishment of a stud of Race Horses. The outgoings I am confident exceed the usual calculations. He is very lucky & fortunate who is not a loser' (CRO, Carlisle, D/Lons/L2/13, diary of William, Lord Lowther, 1813).

108 NRAS 2177, Bundle 3527, Lord Archibald Hamilton to [?], 20 Sept. 1792.

109 PKCA, Kinnaird Papers, MS 100, bundle 1064, account with Richard Prince, 1808; payments to William Clift, 1810.

110 Fairfax-Blakeborough, *Northern Turf History, Vol. IV*, p. 41.

111 Helen Clifford, 'Accommodating the East: Sir Lawrence Dundas as Northern Nabob? The Dundas Property Empire and Nabob Taste', accessed online, 24 Aug. 2020 at http://blogs.ucl.ac.uk/dist/1/files/2013/02/Aske-Hall-final-pdf-19.08.14.pdf.

sum of £2,000. He won £560, including two forfeits, lost £150, and paid a forfeit of £105.[112] At the first meeting at Newmarket in 1780, his losses and expenses on stakes amounted to £1,005, while his winnings may have come to £1,380.[113] In 1810, Lord Kinnaird at the 2nd October meeting at Newmarket paid out £1,240 for stakes for four horses, a forfeit, and £500 to the Duke of Grafton, which may have been for a bet.[114]

Amounts placed on matches varied widely. There were those for whom the main point was the breeding, training, and racing. One such was the Suffolk MP Sir Charles Bunbury, a steward of the Jockey Club for over half a century until his death in 1820, and owner of the winner of the Derby on three occasions. Of Bunbury, it was recalled, his 'nearly invariable rule was, safe play and moderate gains'; he was best known for pioneering a new, kinder form of training of horses.[115] Yet, there were others for whom the competitive gambling was more clearly a major part of the attraction. From 1772 until 1792, together with Thomas Foley, Charles James Fox maintained a stud at Newmarket. In 1774, one his horses, Pyrrhus, was matched against a horse of Lord Grosvenor's for 2,000 guineas. It was later reported that Pyrrhus won in stakes and matches a total of 10,400 guineas, and received 1,625 guineas in forfeits.[116] In the early nineteenth century one commentator suggested that during Fox's time at Newmarket the sums laid for stakes and matches, and for side bets, were consistently larger than in other periods.[117] There is no way of adjudicating on this definitively, although it was reported that Fox spent £16,000 on betting at Newmarket in 1772, while Mrs Delaney reported that Foley had lost £50,000 at Newmarket in the following year.[118] In 1771, the Duke of Richmond, who had been staying

112 NYRO, ZNK X, 1/14/25.

113 NYRO, ZNK X, 1/14/37, memorandum, Newmarket, Apr. 1780.

114 PKCA, MS 100, Bundle 1064, account of Lord Kinnaird with James Weatherby, first and second October meetings, 1810.

115 *Monthly Magazine* (1821), 432–6, 'Memoirs of Sir Charles Bunbury'. Another who took an almost obsessive interest in such matters was the 5th Duke of Hamilton. When he was in London a regular refrain in his letters back to Hamilton was a request for information about the condition of his horses. E.g. NRAS 2177, Bundle 2867, the Duke of Hamilton to Inglis, 25 Apr. 1735, where Hamilton writes, 'Let me hear how all the Horses are by the first post and whats a doing at Hamilton.' Hamilton expected to be kept closely informed about all his sporting concerns – fox hounds, hawks, as well as horses – and the key decisions about their maintenance and where, for example, his horses should run were very much his.

116 *The Literary and Fashionable Magazine* (1806), 60–1.

117 Ibid., 61.

118 Cited in John Brooke, 'Foley, Thomas (1742–93), in *The History of Parliament: The House of Commons 1754–1790*, eds. L. Namier and J. Brooke (London, 1964) (www .history of parliamentonline.org/volume/1754-1790/member/foley-thomas-1742-93).

at Rockingham's house at Newmarket, declared to his host: 'As to the gambling & match making it is very entertaining to observe, but as prudent not to be concern'd in it.'[119] Matches for very large sums had, nevertheless, long been a feature of racing at Newmarket, and this continued to be the case in later decades.[120]

About other types of betting associated with racing, including the side bets, it is even more difficult to establish secure facts. Because gambling debts were matters of honour, and, from 1711, not recoverable at law when they were over £10, they rarely surface in the archives. The only appeal in the case of racing before 1846 was to the Jockey Club, but its officials, meaning usually its president, adjudicated only on the circumstances of a bet or the conditions under which it should stand.[121]

Anecdotal evidence, including reports in the press, indicates that betting at races, certainly by the later eighteenth century, was very widespread, and frequently heavy. The diarist Sylas Neville described the scene at Newmarket on a visit there during the October meeting in 1771:

> It is a strange collection of Lords, Lacqueys, Jockeys & Blacklegs, where all are on a level. It is curious to hear them make their bets at the Betting or Distance Post. One calls out 'I'll lay £150 to £100.' If any one take the bet, which any one may do, each makes a memorandum in his pocket book & they settle when the race is over. It is a sad thing to see these noble jockeys throwing away their hundreds & thousands with as much indifference as if they were so may shillings. They are fascinated by a strong infatuation & many of these men are our Governors. God deliver me from such Governors![122]

119 SCA, Wentworth-Woodhouse MSS, 1411, Duke of Richmond to Lord Rockingham, 2 Nov. 1771.

120 See e.g. the race between Sir Harry Vane Tempest's 'Hambletonian' and Mr Cookson's 'Diamond' at the spring meeting at Newmarket in 1799. This match was for 3,000 guineas and the owners also placed a further side bet of 800 guineas. *Times*, 27 Mar. 1799. On 24 May 1799, the *Times* reported: 'The Rage for RACING, which has been on the decline for many years, is now reviving. The famous match between *Hambletonian* and *Diamond* has contributed to render Newmarket once more the grand mart for fashionable gambling.' In 1767, Rockingham's matches at Newmarket drew sharp criticism from one disappointed, anonymous correspondent, and calls for him to live up to the character supposedly expected of someone who might again occupy high office and who had what was described as 'known dislike to vice'. SCA, Wentworth-Woodhouse MSS, 795, anon. to Rockingham, May 1767.

121 NYRO, Zetland Papers, ZNK X, 1/2/251, letter from Lawrence Dundas to Lord Eglinton, 25 Mar. 1777: 'I understand you have been enquiring people's opinions regarding the bet you think depends betwixt you and me upon the sweepstaker at Kelso. I entreat you there may not be any sort of difference upon that matter, as I think there is no bet, yet I think perhaps there is the only way determining the matter is to stat the cases to the stewards of the Jockey Club who you know are like the Marshals of France of that sort…'

122 *Diary of Sylas Neville*, p. 131.

In 1803 the leading Jamaican planter, John Tharp, lamented the added expense which his son incurred through living close to Newmarket, which, he claimed, involved him in 'promiscuously' mixing with 'such people who only come down to gamble & make a gay appearance'.[123] Symptomatic of the quantity of betting was the regular reporting in the press by this period of odds on races, including on occasion by the 1790s those given by Tattersalls Betting Room in London. Many bets were, as Neville observed, agreed between the individuals involved, and this may well have been common practice among gentlemen. Robert Carlisle Broadley, who regularly attended the Beverley races in the 1760s, records several bets with individuals on races in his journals.[124] Mike Huggins suggests that at the beginning of the nineteenth century, and probably for considerably longer, heavy betting was dominated by the upper ranks, although self-styled fashionable 'sportsmen' were increasingly visible in this realm. He notes that the introduction of races such as the St Ledger and Derby, where horses were entered as yearlings, enabled larger fields of competitors and ante-post betting, which could begin many months before the race, and which introduced a new level of sophistication to betting on races.[125] And, while large bets were mostly the monopoly of the upper ranks, jockeys and stable lads can be found betting from the late eighteenth century.[126] Hamilton's accounts include a record of what his stable boys won and lost on various sweepstakes in 1789.[127] Other race-goers can be found making bets in booths or betting rooms at courses. At the Durham races in 1735, a John Wall claimed to have made a bet of just two shillings with a Richard Wilson.[128]

Race meetings were closely associated with various other forms of gambling. This was to be the source of much criticism of racing by the 1840s, but it was hardly new. Recall here Jack Hervey defying his parents to stay in Newmarket in 1711, and playing dice in the chocolate house there. Fox and his gambling cronies, including the Prince of Wales,

123 Cambridgeshire Record Office, Shire Hall, Cambridge, Tharp Papers, R/55/7/21, John Tharp to?, Good Hope, 24 Jan. 1803.

124 University of Hull, Brynmor Jones Library, DP/146, entries for 14 Jan. 1771, 12 Aug. 1773.

125 Huggins, *Flat Racing*, pp. 54–60.

126 Ibid., p. 95. Evidence on the scale of side bets made by the upper ranks is patchy. The second marquis of Rockingham quite commonly staked £10.10 on the outcome of races in the 1750s. In June 1754, he lost 'by betts' at Stamford races £7.7 while in April 1753 he lost £52.10 betting on a match involving one of his horses, 'Sophy'. SCA, Wentworth-Woodhouse MSS, WWM/A/995, cash book of the second marquis of Rockingham, 1751–54.

127 NRAS 2177, Hamilton Papers, Bundle 3856, racing account, 1789.

128 King, 'Aspects of Sociability', pp. 138–9.

reportedly played cards for high stakes during Newmarket meetings.[129] 'E.O.' tables were frequently set up at race meetings. In 1796, the *Times* reported that E.O. tables were being licensed at Ascot for 12 guineas a table, while the so-called Gold Table was rentable for 40 guineas. The money thereby gained by the race promoters helped to defray the cost of the plates for the races, and thereby enabled five days of racing.[130] Periodic attempts were made to prevent such occurrences, such as in the early 1750s, but these had at best a short-term impact.[131]

This might be because, as one historian of sport in the later Georgian period has written, the 'English were obsessed with gambling'.[132] But it was also symptomatic of how far the organization and staging of horse racing was driven by commercial imperatives, as well as the demands and activities of the 'betters', as one commentator called them in the early nineteenth century. The French traveller, François de la Rochefoucauld, towards the end of the eighteenth century called these people the 'blacklegs'.[133] They were essentially professional gamblers, and their growing influence at major race meetings was one factor which began to change the character of racing and gambling more widely in the later eighteenth century. How far and how rapidly such a shift in racing culture, and its reputation occurred is hard to say given current knowledge.[134] The existence of people who lived partly or wholly by gambling had long been acknowledged, particularly in metropolitan society; these were the sharpers who haunted the gambling dens of the capital, but also spas and resorts, and who presented a menacing threat to the gullible young landed gentleman tempted to engage in gambling. The existence of 'Newmarket conjurers' was acknowledged well before the end of the eighteenth century.[135] Yet, the transformation was symptomatic of broader, deeper-lying changes in the cultural economy of gambling in the later Georgian period. Another sign of

129 *Edinburgh Magazine*, 18 (1793), 434–5. 130 *Times*, 11 June 1796.

131 King, 'Aspects of Sociability', p. 159, quoting a report from the *Newcastle Journal*, 4 Sept. 1750 that organizers of the Stockton races had banned 'any Gaming Table, or unlawful Games, in the Street or Market Place' during the races. The *Times* reported on 2 Aug. 1802 that the recent act prohibiting 'Little Goes', a form of private lottery, had put an end to raffling at Brighton races and that no E.O. tables were to be seen on the course.

132 Harvey, *Beginnings of a Commercial Sporting Culture*, p. 152.

133 *A Frenchman in England 1784, Being the Mélanges sur L'Angleterre of François de la Rochefoucauld*, ed. Jean Marchand (Cambridge, 1933), pp. 59–69. The term was coming into general use, for which, see *Times*, 11 June 1796, which reported that 'The betting room [at Ascot] was full; and exhibited a sad mixture of gentlemen and blacklegs.'

134 Huggins describes their activities in the nineteenth century, basing his comments partly on the records of those of John Gully between the 1820s and 1840s (Huggins, *Flat Racing*, pp. 58, 78).

135 WSRO, Marquis of Ailesbury Papers, 1300/1786, Lord Castlehaven to Lord Bruce, Grovely, 17 Jan. 1765.

this was the rise of the 'sportsman', or 'Man of the Turf', as more sharply defined figures who were increasingly viewed with marked ambivalence, if not overt disapproval by contemporaries. His urban, metropolitan counterpart was the 'Dandy'.[136] Such men can be seen as fashioning reactionary forms of public masculinity, which often consciously flouted strengthening notions of respectability, a development which needs to be viewed in terms of the political reaction associated with the impact of the French Revolution, the effects of participation in the French Revolutionary and Napoleonic Wars, and a contemporaneous reconfiguration of parts of fashionable metropolitan society.[137] Earlier wars had seen tendencies towards the militarization of civilian life, through the embodiment (from 1757) of the militia, and a marked taste among the elites – rural and urban – for military uniforms and military reviews and parades.[138] Yet, while there was much continuity in the 1790s and 1800s in this context with these earlier periods, there were also significant changes and greater diversity in terms of the responses it evoked. The effects of all this were to reveal only more sharply, and re-emphasize, tensions that had, as we have seen, long been present among the elites in respect of attitudes towards and habits of gaming and gambling. But what was also different by this period was how far commercial forces, and growing power of publicity, were reshaping gambling; and what this placed under pressure was its (always relative) exclusivity as well as its meanings. We will explore this further in the conclusion to this book. Suffice it to say here, while 'deep play' and gambling was still engaged in by members of the titled nobility and landed elites, its connotations were shifting, and its associations with the 'quality' were becoming ever more ambiguous. Another of the effects of war and political reaction was to re-emphasize the responsibilities of landownership, a development which, as Peter Mandler has shown, in conjunction with a changing religious mood, re-energized and redirected the sense of public duty among a generation of aristocratic Whig politicians who were to come into office in the 1830s and 1840s.[139]

1.3 'Deep Play' in the Later Eighteenth Century: Gambling Scotsmen

We can now return to the 1770s and 1780s, and the 'deep play' of the fashionable which so antagonized its highly vocal critics. Viewed against

136 Christopher Breward, 'Masculine Pleasures: Metropolitan Identities and Commercial Sites of Dandyism, 1790–1840', *London Journal*, 28 (2003), 60–72.

137 For the latter, see Rendall, 'Clubs of St James's'.

138 M. McCormack, *Embodying the Militia in Georgian England* (Oxford, 2015).

139 Peter Mandler, *Aristocratic Government in the Age of Reform* (Oxford, 1990).

the eighteenth century as a whole it begins to look much less exceptional. The structures of experience and opportunity, the habits and dispositions, which led to high-stakes gambling were very well established in society by this date. Nevertheless, the contexts were changing in various ways, which in turn altered fashionable gaming in certain respects, together with its meanings, as well as how it was viewed. These changes were quite subtle and protracted, but cumulatively their impact was considerable. We can begin to trace some of them in the related, and in certain aspects overlapping, cases of two gambling Scotsmen: the biographer of Johnson, James Boswell; and William Grant of Congalton.

Boswell, son of an Ayrshire laird and lawyer, was one who repeatedly struggled against the 'rage of gaming', a compulsion he seems to have developed in the many taverns nestling off the High Street of the Scottish capital in the later 1750s. At one point, probably at the end of the 1750s or beginning of the subsequent decade, he made a promise not to play at all for three years, and later undertook not to play for above 3 guineas at any one sitting.[140] When he came to London in the early 1760s he scrupulously avoided playing cards, even though it led to his being on the margins of fashionable social gatherings, including 'routs' held at the duchess of Northumberland's town house.[141] For Boswell, who craved social recognition, this was an act of strenuous self-denial. Back in Scotland a few years later, he relapsed, and played again at games of chance; 'the fever', he wrote to his close friend William Johnston Temple, 'still lurked in his veins'. Having lost around 14 guineas, he resolved never again to play games of chance, and only to play whist in company for 'a trifle'.[142] But Boswell was ever making such promises to himself or, indeed, about not drinking heavily; the lure of the cards and being 'rakish' was simply too great, as was the simple fact that it was almost impossible to avoid play within the circles in which he moved in the Scottish capital, where, if anything, polite manners were even more precariously superimposed on a society in which older conventions of easy, often indecorous familiarity were more strongly embedded than in the British capital, and the consequent contradictions in male conduct on occasion more startlingly juxtaposed. It is hard to believe that the 'vulgarity' of a Lord Braxfield would have been acceptable or, indeed, conceivable in London.[143]

140 *Letters of James Boswell: 29 July 1758–29 Nov. 1777*, ed. C. B. Tinker, 2 vols (Oxford, 1924), pp. 161–5: James Boswell to William Johnston Temple, 24 Aug. 1768.

141 *Boswell's London Journal 1762–1763*, ed. Frederick A. Pottle (New Haven and London 1950), pp. 126–7.

142 *Letters of James Boswell*, ed. Tinker, pp. 161–5.

143 *Boswell's Edinburgh Journals 1767–1786*, ed. Hugh M. Milne (Edinburgh, 2003), pp. 124, 193, 245, 277, 287–8, 305–6, 387, 403; Bob Harris, *A Tale of Two Cities: The Life and Times of Lord Daer, 1763–1794* (Edinburgh, 2015), pp. 50–1.

Grant learnt to play in many of the same Edinburgh taverns and locales as those frequented by Boswell.[144] Grant's main partner in gambling was Gilbert Innes of Stow. They were part of a tight-knit group of young men, mostly from upwardly mobile, prosperous families who achieved considerable social status in eighteenth-century Edinburgh. Among their number was George Webster, one of the three sons of the Edinburgh clergyman, Dr Alexander Webster, a man who, despite being a leading figure in the Evangelical popular party in the Church of Scotland, was himself no stranger to Edinburgh's boozy conviviality, hence his nickname, recalled by the moderate clergyman and recorder of enlightenment Edinburgh Alexander Carlyle, of 'Magnum Bonum'.[145] George was a frequent companion of Boswell's, on one occasion joining him, Alexander Kincaid, the printer and son of a future Lord Provost of the city, the advocate Andrew Balfour, and one 'young Hay', a surgeon, at Wares' tavern off the north side of the High Street for an all-night session of whist, where, as Boswell describes, 'the rage of play so heated me that I abandoned myself to it'. At one point during the night, Boswell had lost about £6, but his eventual losses came out at a little under half that sum.[146] Webster's two older brothers pursued military careers; George was a cloth merchant. Gilbert Innes of Stow, whose father, George, had risen to the post of cashier of the Royal Bank and who purchased the Stow estate in Peebleshire, followed his father as a banker, becoming in later life Deputy Lieutenant of Edinburgh, and a leading figure in Edinburgh society, patron of the arts and culture, and charitable donor. In 1781, he was (naturally enough) one of the managers of the scheme for building new assembly rooms in the Scottish capital, which eventually, after several false turns, led to the construction of the magnificent George Street assembly rooms in the New Town.[147] In the early 1770s, Gilbert and William were making bets and playing at billiards and hazard for sums of money ranging between a few shillings and several pounds. On 9 November 1773, for example, the former noted that Grant owed him £18 from games of billiards. Just a few days later, the sum had climbed to

144 Innes of Stow refers to the following places where he played games for money: Walker's Tavern; Fortune's Tavern; Francis Ware's Tavern (formerly Macduffie's); Munro's Tavern; the Princes Street Coffee House; Ewen's; Balfour's; Moncrieff's club; the skating club at Duddingston.

145 Others referred to by Innes of Stow include: Munro Ross; Capt George Munro; Sir James Baird; George Dempster; William Brodie; Doctor Nairn; Sir John Lauder; Alexander Gordon; Sir James Murray; Andrew Erskine; Charles Kerr; William Fullarton; Sir John Whiteford; Capt. Wallace.

146 *Boswell's Edinburgh Journals*, ed. Milne, p. 203.

147 NRS, GD113/4/156, item 263, minute of the meeting of subscribers to the scheme for erecting new assembly rooms, 14 Mar. 1781.

nearly £50. They were playing for 20 guineas a match at this point. Innes of Stow was also losing up to around £20 a night at hazard. On 13 June in the following year it was double this sum at one sitting in Fortune's Tavern. They were betting on horse races, purchasing lottery tickets, and passing bonds between them to pay off gambling debts.[148] In 1776 Dr Alexander Webster wrote to George Innes to complain of the distress to which the 'pernicious vice of gambling' had reduced his son, George; for Webster senior it was Gilbert and William Grant who were to blame by accepting a bond from his son for a gambling debt supposedly at a fraction of its real value.[149] The Rev Dr Webster had threatened his son with pursuing a legal action before the Court of Session, if he did not recover this bond, where he and all his 'Game companions' would be called on oath to testify about the circumstances surrounding the exchange of this bond and their other 'Game transactions'. This action threatened to expose 'to infamy', as George Webster wrote, the gaming activities of him and his friends, more than hinting at the stern disapproval among many for such activities within what remained in many ways a conservative culture in the Scottish capital, albeit one that would liberalize markedly in the 1780s.[150] In the same year, 1776, Gilbert was keeping a faro bank, although not at his home.[151]

A few years later William had moved to London, where, as he wrote to Gilbert, life was a 'constant round of Dissipation'. This involved, in addition to gambling, womanizing – another shared compulsion of the two men – as well as attending masquerades.[152] Grant complained that his capital was 'much too small to play with Advantage' – a measure of the much higher stakes which prevailed in gaming circles in the British

[148] NRS, GD113/5/419/2/1, account book kept by Gilbert Innes, 1773–6.

[149] Webster appears to have lost between £250 and £260 to Innes of Stow within a matter of a single month. He then lost a further 50 guineas to him. NRS, GD113/5/365B/14, State of Facts, relating to Mr Webster's process against Mr Innes, 13 Dec. 1776.

[150] For a characterization of Edinburgh society in the 1780s, see Harris, *A Tale of Three Cities*, esp. pp. 48–9.

[151] NRS, GD113/5/419/2/1, entry 7 Feb. 1776, which reads: 'Lost at Corris at keeping a Pharaon Bank 7-10-0'.

[152] NRS, GD113/4/156, correspondence between William Grant and Gilbert Innes of Stow, item 18: William Grant to Gilbert Innes of Stow, 15 Mar. 1780. Like Boswell, Grant unsurprisingly quickly contracted venereal disease (for which, see ibid., item 75, Grant to Innes of Stow, 21 Apr. 1780 & item 92, same to same, 19 May 1780). Innes of Stow appears to have engaged in casual sex on an almost heroic scale, fathering numerous illegitimate children. Katie Barclay describes him as 'an inveterate gambler and philanderer', and has identified from his correspondence thirty-two women who became his mistresses. He maintained at least twenty-five illegitimate children and when he died sixty-seven children made a claim on his estate. Katie Barclay, 'Illicit Intimacies: The Imagined 'Homes' of Gilbert Innes of Stow and his Mistresses (1751–1832)', *Gender & History* 27 (2015), 576–90.

capital – and consequently he was contemplating moving on to Bath to try his luck there. Grant's trip to Bath gained him 33 guineas, although he had lost a further 15 trying his luck playing with a noted gambler – a 'Mons[ieu]r Phillips'.[153] Back in London, he began playing at Almack's, where he boasted he had 1,000 guineas in hard cash, in addition to 20 guineas in his pocket. But, he noted, 'the play unavowedly runs so deep that it would require 3 times the sum to give', what he described as 'the Requisite stability'.[154] He was spending substantial sums to maintain a place in this sort of society on the 'pendicles of dress and Trumpery' with the hope of making gains which would clear his debts and make his fortune.[155] He lost £350 at 'The Spring Garden Club', one of several gambling clubs to which he was admitted.[156] The impression conveyed in his letters is that he had entered a tight-knit gambling fraternity – 'The Almack Gentry' – who were playing deep and with fierce, almost professional intensity.[157] By December 1781, he was losing more often than not. On 24 December of that year, he informed Gilbert that he had lost ten stakes last night, which amounted to 500 guineas. On 22 January 1782, he observed that he was 'down above £600' since the last letter, although his fortunes appear to have improved somewhat in the subsequent few months.[158]

Gamesters were rarely, if ever, self-reflective people. As a result, historians' interpretations of their motivations tend to be highly speculative and often based on somewhat strained psychological readings of their personalities.[159] Why one person was enticed by gaming and another

[153] NRS, GD113/4/156, item 50: William Grant to Gilbert Innes of Stow, 3 Apr. 1780.

[154] NRS, GD113/4/156, item 238, William Grant to Gilbert Innes of Stow, n.d....

[155] NRS, GD113/4/156, item 238.

[156] NRS, GD113/4/156, item 243, Grant to Innes of Stow, 3 Mar. 1781; item 246, same to same, 8 Mar. 1781, which mentions his being admitted 'into another club' where he had won £100.

[157] Leslie Mitchell emphasizes how gambling in the St James's clubs of this era was a 'serious business', with gambling parties lasting through the night, and longer on occasion, and with participants sporting special clothes. Leslie Mitchell, *Whig World*, p. 49.

[158] NRS, GD113/4/156, item 365, Grant to Innes of Stow, 24 Dec. 1781; item 367, same to same, 22 Jan. 1782. On 26 Jan. 1782 he wrote: 'I dare say as Total Eclipse will be exhibited, and The Flocks shall have the Mountains before I shall have it in my power to make one at Tommy Purves's.' GD113/4/156, item 365. Tommy Purves's was Thomas Purves's tavern in Edinburgh.

[159] Lorraine Daston, for example, writes, 'It is tempting to speculate on how upper-class gambling may have provided a forum for aristocratic values no longer given military scope: display, courage conceived as a deliberate courting of large risks, a rigid and often ruinous code of honor' (Lorraine Daston, *Classical Probability in the Enlightenment* (Princeton, NJ, 1988), no. 178, p. 160). This is nonsensical given the continuing military role of the upper ranks in this period, and, as we will see later, one could

not, or one person capable of restraint in this context and another not, is usually impossible to say at this distance. Gaming certainly offered a world in which one could express and exhibit one's sense of an autonomous self, hence perhaps its potential appeal to young men of rank. At the same time, it was increasingly a coterie culture, defined by its exclusivity, fierce commitment to play, and, at the highest levels, notoriety. Grant possessed great belief in his own skills and method as a gambler, which, as modern studies of gambling have shown, is (unsurprisingly) a common feature of the psychology of gambling. But he was also pursuing wealth commensurate with his already high social ambitions, on which immersion in London's fashionable circles was now acting to amplify.[160] He and his acquaintances, many of who were friends from his Edinburgh days, delighted in preparing themselves from the King's birthday ball at St James's, an annual display of fashionable London decked out in its finery.[161] He was consciously flirting with the prospect of celebrity. 'I am', he declared to Gilbert, 'at present engag'd in a great Undertaking which in two or three months will make me the Subject of almost Every Conversation'. On another occasion, he boasted of his presence at a masquerade: 'I was amazingly bright you'l find my bon mot in *all the prints*.'[162] (My emphasis.) To make a mark in this world was to find oneself the subject of gossip in newspapers which by the later eighteenth century reported with avidity the goings-on of the fashionable metropolitan elites, even as, in some cases, editors such as Henry Dudley Bate sought to use the threat of publicity and press scandal as an additional source of income through blackmail.[163] Grant sought wealth quickly; as well as gaming, he was looking to speculate in government stocks, such as navy bills and consols. What Grant wanted above all was to make a figure in 'society', an ambition which almost certainly propelled the gambling of several notorious gamesters in this period, such as the nabob General Smith, whereas for others, such as Fox and his cronies, it was their almost complete indifference to their wider reputation, their sense of

argue that the relationship was often the other way – that it was the culture of honour nurtured in the military that fuelled gambling.

160 He was also paying off debts to his various gambling cronies.

161 By early 1782 he was lodging in Craven St, together with the Laird of Grant and Caleb Whitefoord.

162 NRS, GD113/4/156, item 42, Grant to Innes of Stow, 13 Apr. 1780.

163 The place of 'scandal' in selling newspapers from the 1760s onwards has been noted by historians, but never investigated systematically, although see Donna Andrew, 'The Press and Public Apologies in Eighteenth-Century London', in Norma Landau (ed.), *Law, Crime and English Society, 1660–1830* (Cambridge, 2002), pp. 208–29. Some individuals fought back, prosecuting newspapers for private libel. Unlike cases of seditious libel in the press, these cases have yet to attract close scrutiny.

separation, if not immunity, from the public's gaze, which was striking.[164] Reputation among their tight-knit circle of friends was an altogether different thing.

Grant was an outsider in the British metropolis, although so were many. The circles in which he moved were, if not identical to, then overlapping with those frequented by Fox and his gambling friends. The shape and conditions of their world can, as several historians have noted, be partly understood in terms of shifts in modes of sociability and associational behaviour within elite metropolitan society in the decades after 1760. If the mid-eighteenth century is associated, rightly or not, with the rise of public sites of leisure, notably the pleasure gardens of Vauxhall and Ranelagh, the later eighteenth century saw a renewed emphasis on exclusivity among the fashionable classes. One symptom of this was the ways in which their London town houses were turned into sites of exclusive entertainments, 'routs', and notable hostesses, such as the Duchess of Cumberland or the Duchess of Gordon, gained new social prominence as leaders of fashion[165]; another was the proliferation of exclusive clubs and associations. One of these, which has so far received little notice, was 'The Lady's Club', founded in 1770, and which was associated with opposition Whig aristocratic circles.[166] Others, which by contrast have attracted very considerable attention, were the gentlemen's clubs, Boodles and Brooks's, which operated a system of blackballing. Such a system, to be fair, had been operated at White's from the 1730s, and the tendency to exclusivity was nothing new at this level of society, as Hannah Greig has shown.[167] Nevertheless, and somewhat paradoxically given their pronounced exclusivity, these venues became associated with,

[164] For relevant comment on the latter, see Mitchell, *Whig World*, p. 54. See also the comments by John Crawfurd on the suicide of John Damer in 1776, son of the 1st Lord Milton, and his 'indifference to public opinion', which, as Crawfurd wrote, 'some find commendable'. Damer, who had debts in excess of £40,000, and who was not prepared to curb his expenditure, shot himself at a notorious brothel in Covent Garden, but not before being seen in the morning walking, riding, and laughing in a glover's shop in Berkeley Square, buying a pair of pistols in Bond Street, and then entertaining two girls at the brothel until 2 a.m., to the accompaniment of a child fiddler. BARS, L30/14/86/4, John Crawfurd to Thomas Robinson, 2nd Baron Grantham, 21 Aug. 1776.

[165] Attempts at exclusivity might fail, as occurred in the case of the Pantheon in Oxford Street which opened in 1772 as a new venue for fashionable assemblies. Initially the idea had been to limit admission to only peeresses or those they recommended, but this evidently was the cause of resentment among those whom one contemporary called 'the Nabobbesses in the Parish of Marylebone who having ample Fortunes chuse to rival the Nobility'. Consequently, 'all subscribers of Fortune' were admitted. Blair Castle, Atholl Papers, Box 54 (3), George Steuart to the Duke of Atholl, 14 Jan. 1772.

[166] TNA, C104/146, Cullen v Queensberry, Minutes, Accounts and Vouchers of the Lady's Club, afterwards Arlington House Club, 1770–5.

[167] Greig, *The Beau Monde*.

and developed alongside, a culture of brazen exhibitionism. This deliberately eschewed the sobriety and ostentatious domesticity cultivated by George III and Queen Charlotte, instead parading its delight in its own extravagance and excess and pursuit of hedonistic pleasure. In the early nineteenth century, it would reach its apogee in the coterie led by the Prince of Wales, whose Brighton pavilion was an appropriate symbol of its ostentatious visibility but also privacy. It was the scale and imagination on which pleasure was sought that was a good deal of the point, and how it was often staged in view of the public, but separate from it. Playing deep was at one level a further dimension to this culture, one which fully embraced women as well as men. While women were not admitted to the homo-social world of Brooks's, they hosted 'faro' tables or games of hazard in their homes, until, that is, Lord Chief Justice Kenyon temporarily decreed otherwise in the 1790s.[168]

Frustratingly, the full meanings of the 'deep play' of this period can only be inferred from the contexts in which they were enfolded, and also the types of gambling which were favoured by Fox and others, including Grant. Evidence for the size of the sums typically being staked in gaming sessions is usually based on report and rumour, which is why the testimony provided by Grant is so valuable. William Douglas, Earl of March and from 1778 4th Duke of Queensberry, who evidently made gaming his main occupation, thought nothing of losing a thousand pounds at a session, although he was a very wealthy man, indeed.[169] In 1774–1775, Fox's gambling losses were reported to be £140,000.[170] Grant, recall, was on occasion betting with stakes of 50 guineas, but also noted that to bet with safety at Almack's required sums in excess of 3,000 guineas. In 1776 Lord Carlisle lost £10,000 in one evening of gaming.[171]

The essential point to grasp about the favoured games of the 'gamesters' was that they were vehicles for betting quickly, hence the gains and losses of dizzying sums. As Thomas Robinson, 2nd Baron Grantham observed to his brother Frederick in 1779: 'I should think the rapidity of Macau [a card game which, like faro, depended heavily on chance] would make it very fashionable in England, where people are in such a hurry to be ruined.'[172] If many among the propertied classes in this period were plagued by the shadow of indebtedness, the management of debts, and potential bankruptcy, the appeal of such games was

[168] Russell, 'Faro's Daughters'.
[169] Henry Blyth, *Old Q: The Rake of Piccadilly* (London, 1967), p. 54.
[170] Mitchell, *Whig World*, p. 250.
[171] J. H. Jesse, *George Selwyn and his Contemporaries*, 4 vols. (London, 1882), iii, pp. 136–7.
[172] BARS, L30/15/54/193, Thomas Robinson, 2nd Baron Grantham, Madrid, to Frederick Robinson, 11 Apr. 1779.

demonstration that the code of manners and values which obtained among elite gamblers was of altogether different order. This was no English 'agrarian bourgeoisie', in Edward Thompson's formulation, but a culture which eschewed the moderation, self-regulation and watchfulness of the creditworthy.[173] What it was not, however, and this is equally important, was coterminous with anything like the whole of the landed elites of later eighteenth-century Britain; rather it was a very specific fragment. Whereas to frequent Brooks's in the later 1770s and 1780s was to stand, as one contemporary neatly put it, at 'the precipice of perdition', White's, increasingly the resort of the country gentlemen in London, by the same period seems, by way of contrast, to have seen only moderate gambling.[174] The original rules of Boodle's, which in its infancy was known as 'The Virtue Club', drawn up in 1762–1764, included one (the 17th) which carefully restricted the scale of betting on card games, chess, and cribbage, and side bets on the outcome of such games.[175]

1.4 Lord William Murray: The Feckless Younger Son

In the final section of this chapter, we turn to a cautionary tale of a gambler whose story is further revealing of the status and position of gambling among the landed elites at the end of the eighteenth century. Our subject is a junior member of one of eighteenth-century Scotland's

[173] E. P. Thompson, 'Patricians and Plebs', in E. P. Thompson (ed.), *Customs in Common* (London, 1991), esp. p. 84.

[174] HMC, *Fifteenth Report, Appendix, Part VI*, p. 463, George Selwyn to Lord Carlisle, 24 Feb. 1781, p. 471, same to same, 12 Mar. 1781. Almack's, founded in 1764, was also a site of high stakes gambling, although when Brooks's was established in 1778, it became the main site of such activity. For descriptions of the high stakes gaming at Almack's in the early 1770s, see BARS, L30/14/86/1, J. Crawfurd to Thomas Robinson, 29 Nov. 1771; L30/14/86/2, same to same, 25 Feb. 1772; L30/14/188/4, Lord Carlisle to Grantham, 15 Jan. 1772; L30/14/350/1a, George Selwyn to Thomas Robinson, 7 Feb. 1772. See Vickery's comments: 'While some aristocrats may have conformed to the melodramatic stereotype, recent scholarship tends to stress the canny commercialism and social restraint of noble landowners. But in any case, the vast majority of untitled landed gentlemen were far from fast, loose, and raffish' (Vickery, *Gentleman's Daughter*, p. 395). In his *English Society 1688–1832: Ideology, Social Structure, and Political Practice during the Ancien Regime* (Cambridge, 1985), pp. 107–8, Jonathan Clark presented gaming and gaming clubs as key aspects of an aristocratic ethos, also suggesting that it was adherence to the special code of behaviour in these clubs which helped to underpin aristocratic hegemony in this period. What this ignores is precisely that it was only a subsection of the aristocracy, and a relatively small one, which indulged in such conduct, that the exclusivity of the gaming clubs was relative, and that they attracted much adverse comment.

[175] Fulford, *Boodle's*, pp. 24–5.

leading magnate families, Lord William Murray, second son of the 3rd Duke of Atholl.

It begins with a tragic death – that of the 3rd Duke, who was killed in a drowning accident in the silvery waters of the River Tay in 1774. During his time as head of the family, the 3rd Duke had spent quite heavily, especially on buildings. The latter included a new London town house in Grosvenor Place, the costs of which had far exceeded initial estimates, the refurbishment of Blair Castle – the ancestral dwelling – and the family's summer residence at Dunkeld. He had also spent significant sums on the acquisition of land adjoining the main estate.[176] Under his successor, Lord William's older brother, a programme of 'prudent Oeconomy' was put in place in the months and years following his father's death, a programme which would have significant repercussions for Lord William.[177] Still minors, he and his seven siblings went with their mother, the dowager duchess, to live at Highfield near Liverpool. The education and future of Lord William was a source of considerable tension between the dowager duchess and her eldest son. One issue was an application for a commission in a highland regiment in the British Army, despite Lord William being seriously underage, an application which was facilitated by his great uncle, Lord John Murray, the commanding officer of the 42nd Foot regiment, the Black Watch. The dowager duchess later protested that she had been opposed to this.[178] The second was his education. His mother was adamant that he should not go to one of the major public schools in England, but be educated by

[176] See esp. Blair Castle, Atholl Papers, Box 54 (3), 212, George Steuart to the Duke of Atholl, 22 Sept. 1772, where he notes that the estimate for the house in 1768 was £4500, and as of May 1771 costs had been between £7,500 and £8,000. Steuart declared that he had done his best to lay out the Duke's money to advantage 'without losing sight of the character your Grace supports'. See also Box 54 (4), 234, same to same, 8 Dec. 1773, where Steuart reports the final cost of the house as £10,376.

[177] This can be followed in various letters in the Atholl Papers – e.g. Box 54 (5), 244, John Mackenzie of Delvine to the Duke of Atholl, 6 Dec. 1774; 246, same to same, 15 Dec. 1774; and Box 65 (1), esp. 6, which gives a statement of the new Duke's income; and 20, John Mackenzie of Delvine to the Duke of Atholl, 31 Jan. 1775, which listed various burdens on the estate. See also Box 65 (1) 134, Col James Murray to the Duke of Atholl, 21 Aug. 1775, where Murray notes that his nephew is the poorest Duke in Britain as far as income is concerned, and recommended that he live on £2,000 *per annum* rather than £3,000. The Atholl estates in Scotland were producing a rental income of around £6,000 in 1774.

[178] Atholl Papers, Box 61 (1), 112, Col James Murray to the Duke of Atholl, 4 July 1775, giving the dowager duchess's approval for Lord William being appointed an additional lieutenant in his great uncle's, Lord John Murray's Royal Highland Regiment, but since he was only thirteen he would not be able to join for another four years until his education was completed. In the event Lord John procured for him an ensigncy in an additional company to remain at home because of his age. See also 65 (2), 9, dowager duchess to the Duke of Atholl, 12 Jan. 1776.

a private tutor at home. In this, her views were strongly coloured by the death of one of her sons, Lord James Murray, in April 1770 from an illness contracted whilst at Eton. However, she also took a very dim view of public schools, both in terms of the quality of learning they provided and their (supposed) corruption of their charges.[179]As far as she was concerned all they really taught was how to game and drink, with the result that when the young men came of age this simply led to 'many unhappy marriages and ruind Estates'.[180] Lord William was restive under his mother's watchful eye. She had told him about the military commission, but only because she had hoped that it would act as a 'spur' to him. Disputes about his education continued, and at one point it was, apparently, the subject of threatened legal action.[181] The duke wished him to be sent to an academy in London, but this brought further protests from his mother: '... you'll not meet with any boy younger than fifteen at the Academy, ask yourself', she demanded, 'is it proper for a boy of William's spirit to be put to an Academy so near London so young without one creature to look after him.' Of Lord William and his younger brother, George, she declared: 'I shall never leave either of them (especially William) to the temptations of that sink of Polution [sic] (i.e. London) without my own Eye near him.'[182] It was this message she repeated again and again in several highly emotional letters.[183] The dilemma at their heart was one that landed families experienced generation after generation – namely, how best to equip their children, especially the sons, for initiation into society and much desired and necessary independence, but at the same time guide them away from temptations to undue extravagance and bad habits, of which fashionable London presented one, which inevitably would be placed in their path. One of many sharp ironies of Lord William's story is that Colonel James Murray,

[179] Atholl Papers, Box 65 (1), 102, Lady Charlotte Murray, Highfield, to the Duke of Atholl, 21 June 1775; 172, same to same, 20 Oct. 1775. Both the future Duke and Lord James Murray, who died, were educated at Eton. See also Box 54 (1), 201, Duke of Atholl to John Norbury, Eton, 7 Oct. 1770, which reported that the death of Lord James had upset the duchess so much that his younger sons, George and William, were to be sent to 'more private schools or academies' when in England or be taught at home or nearby in Scotland. The future Duke, the 4th Duke, also did not return to Eton (228, Norbury to the Duke of Atholl, 2 Dec. 1770).

[180] Atholl Papers, Box 65 (1), 172, dowager duchess to the Duke of Atholl, Highfield, 20 Oct. 1775.

[181] Atholl Papers, Box 65 (2), 9, dowager duchess to the Duke of Atholl, 12 Jan. 1776; 16, same to same, 24 Jan. 1776.

[182] Atholl Papers, Box 65 (2), 9, dowager duchess to the Duke of Atholl, 12 January 1776; 16, same to same, 24 Jan. 1776.

[183] Atholl Papers, 65 (2), dowager duchess to the Duke of Atholl, 29 Jan. 1776, 37, same to same, 7 Mar. 1776.

his uncle, who would enjoin him to show restraint and desist from gaming, had himself been temporarily lured into gambling as a young man at the same stage of life as Lord William.[184]

Exactly what happened next is slightly unclear, although the dowager duchess moved to London, as did William. By late 1776 the latter was evidently already behaving in a way which was the cause of serious disapproval;[185] by at least April of the following year he was agitating to be allowed to join his regiment, the Royal Highlanders (also known as the 42nd Foot), in North America, which he was allowed to do.[186] This turned out to be the first of several disastrous decisions; for it was through 'the dissipated turn of the Army' encamped in New York that Lord William was lured into heavy betting.[187] The dissipation of Howe's army in New York was notorious. As the author of a letter describing New York under British occupation, reprinted in the *London Evening Post* in 1777, expostulated:

> Never were such scenes of dissipation and luxury at any place or period, as here prevailed through all ranks, both civil and military, at New York, &c since the last campaign – gambling, wenching, and intoxication have rode triumphant – subalterns have been stript of their fortunes at play, while immense sums have been made by certain persons of higher rank, licensed sharpers, and rapacious commissaries, &c.[188]

New York was the start of Lord William's particular road to perdition. The regiment returned home in late 1778, and while Lord William had been making regular apologies to his uncle for his behaviour, his gambling debts were mounting.[189] To pay these he had been drawing bills on his mother, which were by September 1778 arriving at her doorstep every week for between £50 and £100 without 'any line of explanation or apology'. The dowager duchess had been borrowing from Drummond's Bank to pay these.[190] His mother and older brother, the duke, were wringing their hands about what to do confronted with these circumstances. The former did want him at her home (now at

[184] Atholl Papers, Box 49 (8), 161, Lieut Col James Murray, London, to the 3rd Duke of Atholl, 30 Nov. 1769; Jac C II (4), 73, Lady George Murray to John Murray of Strowan, 21 Sept. 1760.

[185] Atholl Papers, 65 (2), 79, Duke of Atholl to Col James Murray, 3 Nov. 1776.

[186] Atholl Papers, 65 (3), 8, Capt George Murray to the Duke of Atholl, 9 Feb. 1777; 10, Duke of Atholl to Col James Murray, need date; 17, Lady Charlotte Murray to the Duke of Atholl, 7 May 1777.

[187] Atholl Papers, 65 (4), 35, James Murray to Sir Eyre Coote, n.d., but 1782.

[188] *LEP*, 6 Sept. 1777.

[189] Atholl Papers, 65 (3), 44, Lord William Murray to Col James Murray, 2 Jan. 1778.

[190] Atholl Papers, 65 (3), 59, Lady Charlotte Murray to Capt George Murray, 17 Sept. 1778.

Westcombe) because of his probable bad influence on his siblings, while the duke counselled against allowing him to spend time in London. Consequently, he was sent to Dunkeld, where efforts were to be made to reform his conduct before he rejoined his regiment.[191] These had little effect, however. By March 1779, when the time had come for this to happen, as the duke explained to his uncle, Colonel James Murray, he was 'afraid' that Lord William was showing 'little sign of reformation' and could not be trusted. As the duke lamented, he would 'rather have charge of a parcel of wild beasts!'[192]

Rifts emerged between family members about who was to blame for Lord William's fecklessness. So serious had these become that Colonel James Murray was barred from the dowager duchess's house. Behind their differences were divergent views about the education and upbringing of the children. Colonel James Murray's charge was that she was bringing them up 'in idleness and ignorance', and that she was 'squandering their patrimony' through poor financial control.[193] Reading between the lines, the dowager duchess was both too controlling *and* too indulgent a parent. Contemporaries quite frequently saw flaws in upbringing and education as a major cause of an individual's excessive gambling; and some historians have followed this line of explanation.[194]

Colonel James Murray played the crucial role in the next stage of the story. He sought to arrange in 1781 an exchange between Lord William and a captain in the East India Company army. This was envisaged as a new start for Lord William, and his uncle wrote letters of introduction to important figures in the military in India for his nephew.[195] He also wrote a moving letter imploring his nephew to grab the chance that was being presented to him for a change to his conduct. His main appeal was,

[191] Atholl Papers, 65 (3), 69, Duke of Atholl to Col James Murray, 1 Dec. 1778.

[192] Atholl Papers, 65 (3), 74, Duke of Atholl to Col James Murray, 31 Mar. 1779.

[193] Atholl Papers, 65 (4), 11, Col James Murray to Lady Charlotte Murray, 19 Dec. 1780.

[194] See e.g. Nicola Phillips, *The Profligate Son: Or, a True Story of Family Conflict, Fashionable Vice and Financial Ruin in Regency England* (Oxford, 2013).

[195] Atholl Papers, 65 (4), 15, Lord William Murray to Col James Murray, 2 June 1781; 38, Col James Murray to the Duke of Atholl, 9 May 1782; 40, Col James Murray to Lord William Murray, 17 May 1782. Col Murray wrote letters of introduction for his nephew to Major General Stewart and Sir Eyre Coote. For a later, strikingly similar case involving John Lauder, son of Sir Thomas Lauder, see NRAS 771, Papers of the Macpherson-Grant Family, Bundle 141. John's reckless gambling was as an officer in the Portuguese Army, and his father used his contacts to arrange a cadetship for him in India. As he wrote to his friend, John Macpherson Grant of Ballindoch on 7 Feb. 1835: 'Your account of John is melancholy – He seems resolved to throw away cast and to cease to be a gentleman – my last hope is that the prospect which now opens to him of being allowed a fresh trial, in a new scene, and with the power of forming new acquaintances – and throwing off bad habits may yet prove an inducement to him to return to the ways of wisdom and virtue.'

significantly, to his nephew's sense of personal honour, but also the honour of his family: 'I conjure you to respect your honour, the Honor of your Family, and the peace and happiness of your most indulgent parent [i.e. his mother] … Consider it by a long continuation of uniform good and honourable Actions without admitting a suspicion of or doing a mean thing that a good Name is obtaind – And that one slip instantly destroys what requird many years to raise …'[196] If such was the plan, it did not work. Once in India, Lord William argued with his commander, seemingly about a lack of promotion. He was placed under arrest in December 1783 having challenged his commander to a duel. He had eventually apologized, but on being released quit his position.[197] More alarmingly, despite these events having been hushed up, and his resuming a military role, in October 1784 he fought a duel with a fellow soldier, a Captain Waugh, which led directly to the latter's death a few days later. What emerges from a letter penned by Lord William describing the lead-up to this incident is how its origins came from a seemingly highly developed capacity to become embroiled in personal disputes, which, in turn, derived from an equally strongly developed sense of honour and the imperative of being seen to defend this as a gentleman. Notions of honour were keenly cultivated within military circles, and duelling among military men was as a result far from uncommon.[198] Lord William seems to have reeled from challenge to challenge with fellow officers. Waugh, who had allegedly been to the fore in insulting Lord William, despite being supported within the regiment by him for his own promotion, in his view had not behaved like a gentleman. For this reason, when he met him for the duel, despite winning the coin toss to see who should fire first, he told Waugh to do this. Waugh duly did so, but his shot only grazed Lord William's hair. His shot in reply proved altogether less innocuous in its effects. Lord William returned to Britain in disgrace three years later, facing the threat of legal action from the dead man's father, and entangled in more debt.[199] How much of the latter was due to gambling

196 Atholl Papers, 65 (4), 40, Col James Murray to Lord William Murray, 17 May 1782. Bills amounting to over £1,411 were outstanding for gaming losses by Lord William at this point.

197 Atholl Papers, 65 (5), 23, Col Charles Cathcart to Major General James Murray, 30 July 1784.

198 There is very little published work on this, despite the recent interest in notions of masculinity in eighteenth-century Britain. However, see N. A. M. Rodger, 'Honour and Duty at Sea', *Historical Research*, 75 (2002), 425–47. I am also very grateful to my student Eamonn O'Keeffe for allowing me to read his 'Officers Behaving Badly: Honour, Duelling and Courts Martial in the Napoleonic British Army', unpublished M.Phil. dissertation, University of Cambridge (2018).

199 Atholl Papers, 65 (5), 14, Duke of Atholl to Major General James Murray, 21 Apr. 1784; 15, same to same, 25 Apr. 1784; 17, same to same, 20 May 1784; 113, George Farquhar to the Duke of Atholl, 3 Aug. 1786; 165, Duke of Atholl to Major

is unclear, but gambling among officers in the Indian Army – as, indeed, it was in the British Army and militia regiments – appears to have been commonplace, a product presumably of a homosocial culture and periods spent in relative isolation in one another's company.[200]

The final chapters in Lord William's sorry story need not detain us long. Suffice it to say that he married in 1789 the granddaughter of Sir James Hodges, town clerk and deputy chamberlain of the City of London, Mary Anne Hodges. Her father, also called James Hodges, had served in the East India Company in the Madras Civil Service. Lord William may have hoped this fortunate union would enable him to extricate himself from his continuing financial straits. If so, he was to be disappointed, as he reminded his brother at the end of 1791: 'As you well know – the Fortune I rec.d with Lady W.m was very small & perfectly inadequate to support the line of life *we ought to appear in*' (my emphasis).[201] By early 1791 his creditors were pursuing him through the courts, and by at least May 1792 he was detained as a debtor in the King's Bench prison.[202] There he appears to have been notable for two things: ostentatious displays of political loyalism, including chairing a

General James Murray, 20 Dec. 1786; 65 (6), 46, Lord William Murray to the Duke of Atholl, 22 Oct. 1787; 47, Lord William Murray to Mr George Steuart, 23 Oct. 1787; 53, Duke of Atholl to Major General James Murray. It appears that the opinion of Thomas Erskine was sought in relation to whether Lord William could or would be tried, presumably for murder.

200 For comment on the prevalence of gaming among civilians and military men in India, see Devon Heritage Centre, Z6/227, Robert Palk, Patna, to Robert Palk, 16 Jan. 1774; Z6/335, same to same, Fort St George, Madras, 15 Oct. 1779. For comment on gambling within regiments of the British Army, see F. P. Hett (ed.), *The Memoirs of Susan Sibbald* (1926), p. 290; BL, RP 8211, transcript of 'The Peninsular Memoirs of Lieutenant George James Sullivan', p. 3. I am very grateful to Eamonn O'Keeffe for the last two references.

201 Atholl Papers, 65 (9), 102, Lord William Murray to the Duke of Atholl, 24 Dec. 1791. In this same letter, Lord William noted that Hodges had provided £2,400, but was determined not to assist him any further than this. Lord William asked his creditors if they would grant him release from confinement for a year in view of a promise by Hodges to pay half of any sum recovered from the East India Company. They agreed if Hodges would grant a bond for half the sum recovered. See 65 (9), 96, James Hodges to the Duke of Atholl, 7 Dec. 1791; 65 (10), 4, same to same, 9 Jan. 1792; 65 (10), 6, Duke of Atholl to James Hodges, 11 Feb. 1792. Hodges's attempts to recover money were unsuccessful, however, and agreement with the creditors broke down. Lord William was a prisoner in the King's Bench by 21 April 1792 (*Gazetteer, or New Daily Advertiser*, 1 May 1792). See also Box 59(1), 337, Lord William Murray, State Side, Newgate, to the Duke of Atholl, 14 Oct. 1794, which refers to death of his father-in-law, and although all of estate had been left to his widow, Lord William still hoped a later will would be found favouring his wife and her family.

202 Atholl Papers, 65 (6), 49, Lord William Murray to the Duke of Atholl, 21 Feb. 1791. His debts may have amounted to between £13,478 and £16,169, exclusive of what he owned his mother (Box 65 (10), 5, sketch of Lord William's affairs, 1792. See also 65 (10), 6, 'L.d W.ms Debts', which state these as being £13,234.

loyalist meeting in December 1792, and, perhaps paradoxically given the former, an abortive escape plan in the summer of 1793.[203] In December 1796 he died in Newgate gaol, where he had been sent in October 1793, of what was described as an 'inflammation of the stomach'.[204] The Atholl papers in Blair Castle contain no notice or discussion of Lord William's death, bar the briefest of references in a letter written by the Duke of Atholl's man of business, George Farquhar. This alluded in passing to the unfortunate circumstance of several Edinburgh newspapers referring to his place of death, and noting that efforts would need to be made to ensure that some money be kept from the creditors to support his widow and children.[205] The near complete veil drawn over these events conveys its own very powerful message.

1.5 Conclusion

The tale of Lord William Murray highlights several important things about gaming among the elites in eighteenth-century Britain. Gaming – and other forms of profligacy – represented an obvious temptation to young men and (although in different ways perhaps and to a somewhat lesser extent) women from elite families. These temptations grew after 1689, as many of the landed elite came to stay for a good proportion of the year in the capital, as did the related hazards posed by the committed gamblers of London's exclusive clubs or the sharpers and 'blacklegs' into whose company at the race course, the spas and resorts – most obviously, Bath, but also Tunbridge Wells, or, by the early nineteenth century, Brighton – and in the capital's taverns gambling might easily draw inexperienced, overeager young gentleman with financial resources and a keenness to exhibit their independent standing in the world. The temptations and dangers were almost certainly strongly reinforced by how young these individuals could be when they were pushed out into 'the world'. Lord William was not yet sixteen when he went to America, while one of his nephews joined the navy at twelve. Tutors at school – public and private – were expected to shape and regulate the conduct of their landed charges, but their influence was not always very great. There is a close parallel here with circumstances on the grand tour, which commonly formed a key part of the education of the male elites, with tutors

203 *Diary, or Woodfall's Register*, 12 Feb. 1793; *PA*, 21 Feb. 1793; *World*, 9 Oct. 1793; TNA, HO42/26/26 & 27.

204 *Telegraph*, 31 Dec. 1796, report of Lord William's death on 30 Dec.

205 Atholl Papers, Box 59 (4), 7, George Farquhar, Edinburgh, to the Duke of Atholl, 10 Jan. 1797.

struggling to keep control of wilful charges impatient of restrictions, and often becoming all the more conscious of their elevated social rank.[206]

Nevertheless, gambling at this social level was, as at other levels, always about choices – in respect of when to gamble, how, and with whom – as well as cultural horizons and expectations, and, indeed, the sorts of social, professional, and, indeed, in the 1770s and 1780s, political networks in which a person was enmeshed. Some among the landed elites were unable to resist the allure of the gaming table, or, indeed, evidently very consciously chose to succumb. For gaming for high stakes especially could offer a rarely encountered intensity of experience, arena of competition and rivalry, but also opportunity for 'making a figure' in fashionable society. As in the case of William Grant, gaming was a means as well as an end. The highly theatrical, carefully scripted elements of certain forms of exclusive gaming in this period served to facilitate this. This was a world of highly self-conscious performance and self-fashioning, which traded on illusion at many different levels, although the ability to sustain participation in this world was anything but equally shared; it required access to very large amounts of ready income and credit. For the fashionable female denizens or visitors to London's or Bath's fashionable gatherings, gambling may have offered something similar, but it also allowed them the opportunity to display, in a very public fashion, qualities – self-mastery, competitiveness, the open flirtation with risk – typically denied to them in other spheres.

Yet, for all that *some* members of the elites played deeply and without apparent regard for the financial consequences, others (almost certainly the large majority) did not; or, like Lord Hervey and his wife, found good reasons to extricate themselves from the world of elite gaming. Probably fairly typical of the country gentry was someone like Sir John Bridger, a leading figure among the Sussex gentry in the later Georgian era, who

[206] See on this theme the letters written by Josiah Walker to the Duke of Atholl from Eton referring to the Duke's eldest son, and those by Capt Arbuthnot who accompanied the young man on his subsequent grand tour, both sets in the Atholl Papers, Box 59. The letters make very clear the recurrent dilemmas about guiding their charge into his responsibilities and into society. For example Box 59 (1), 225, 15 June 1794, where Walker recommended a trip to a watering place, a fleet, or military camp rather than his charge returning home for the holidays because he would be treated with 'undue flattery' by the servants and gamekeepers. Or Box 59 (2), 179, where Capt Arbuthnot outlined plans for their tour on the continent, stating that the aim will be to produce 'habits of regularity, study, and exercise'; and 235, 29 Sept. 1795, which reported their arrival at Neuchatel where there would be fewer opportunities for dissipation and vice and a better chance of learning French. In the event, the tour was curtailed because of the persistent reserve and supposed indolence of his charge. He was, in part as an antidote to this, entered into the army. Tragically this merely led to illness and mental breakdown.

was spending very modest sums on gaming in the early 1800s.[207] Edward Morant, a Jamaican planter, who sought very purposefully to integrate himself within the Hampshire gentry and capital's political elite, gambled in London clubs and the homes of notables such as the Duke of Bolton; but his losses – which ranged from around £200 to around £550 during the height of his gambling in the first half of the 1770s – were never more than a quarter of the balances in his account with his bankers.[208] In the early nineteenth century the 3rd Earl Spencer was gambling between a few pounds and around £20 – on, amongst other things, games of billiards, casino (a card game), and cribbage.[209]

The notion, meanwhile, that honour was a key ingredient of an aristocratic code of manners in eighteenth-century Europe is oft repeated, and is undeniably true in a fairly obvious sense.[210] It is equally true that the world of gaming was governed by the rule of honour. Thus, recourse to law in pursuit of debts or the course of disputes arising from gambling was intensely frowned upon within gambling circles, while seeking interest on debts accrued through gambling was deliberately eschewed. To do so was to violate the 'gentlemanly' code of values which governed this world. Nevertheless, notions of honour, even within aristocratic families, were no more uniform than within other social strata. As we saw in the case of Lord William Murray, individual honour and family honour could easily come into conflict. Honour was always linked, moreover, to notions of duty, and the latter also varied, depending on, amongst other things, age, position within the family, background, or religious conviction. What honour meant and how it was enacted also depended significantly on milieu. The appeal of different kinds of gambling, especially gambling for high stakes, was no more uniform, in short, among the landed elites than, as we will see in later chapters, among other social groups.

207 East Sussex Record Office, Brighton, The Shiffner Archives, SHR/1372–1385, General and Personal Cash Accounts of Sir John Bridger, 1751–1811. In 1805, for example, Bridger spent £3.9sh on gaming out of total expenditure of c. £1,570.

208 Emma Page, 'Place and Power: The Landed Gentry of the West Solent Region in the Eighteenth Century', unpublished D.Phil. thesis, University of Oxford (2016), esp. pp. 225–55. I am very grateful to Emma Page for allowing me to consult her data on Morant's income, bank balances, and gambling losses.

209 BL, Althorp Papers, Add MS 76596, account book, marked 'Play and Bets', 1811–14. One exception was on 30 Mar. 1812 when he won £241.10.0. Between 22 June and 1 Dec. 1811, he won on twenty-four occasions, with his largest gain being £6.6.0 and his biggest loss, among nineteen losses, was £21.0.0. His predecessor, the 2nd Earl, spent £413.8sh on gambling losses at Brooks's between December 1782 and June 1783, but this was less than 10 per cent of his total expenditure during that period. Add MS 76154, Account Books of the 2nd Earl Spencer, 9 Dec. 1782–17 July 1783.

210 Jonathan Dewald, *The European Nobility 1400–1800* (Cambridge, 1996).

2 In Search of Popular Gambling

Other chapters in this book explore various features of gambling by those mainly in the top third of society. But what about the majority of the population? In outline at least, the picture is reasonably clear. Common before 1700, as shown by, amongst other things, periodic bouts of concern on the part of authorities across Britain about gaming in taverns,[1] gambling among the lower orders appears to have grown significantly during the long eighteenth century. The expansion of the press following the lapse of pre-publication censorship in 1695, it is true, served to make it much more visible. To this extent, the impression of vigorous growth may be something of an illusion. Equally, we need to define clearly what we mean by growth in this context. It could mean expansion either in terms of the proportion of people who gambled, or the amount and intensity of gambling among the lower orders, irrespective of whether this involved a larger percentage of this very disparate group. Given the rapid growth in population from the mid eighteenth century, combined with accelerating urbanization (measured both by the proportion of people residing in towns and qualitative changes to the urban environment and urban living), it is likely that it was of both kinds. The authorities and Parliament in the long eighteenth century periodically sought to suppress and constrain the 'idleness' of the lower orders, which included gambling. The forces driving their growth might be temporarily contained, but, ultimately, they would have been irrepressible even had the will or, indeed, capacity consistently been present to prevent this. Yet, as the final chapter shows, this emphatically was not the case.

2.1 Cricket and Betting

An important cause of increased gambling among the many was the rise of organized sports, most obviously horse racing – 'the ruin of many persons of all Ranks', as one newspaper claimed – but also cricket and, to

[1] See esp. Nicholas Tosney, 'Gaming in England, c.1540–1760', unpublished Ph.D. thesis, University of York (2008).

a lesser extent, boxing or pugilism.[2] Beyond this was the deepening and widening commercialization of leisure with which the development of these sports was associated.[3] Boxing will be discussed briefly later. The proliferation of horse race meetings in England in the 1720s and 1730s was, as we saw in the previous chapter, striking. The new meetings often depended on the patronage and opportunism of the diversifying, expanding, and increasingly prosperous urban middling ranks. Quite commonly timed to coincide with fairs and popular holidays, and often having an overtly popular aspect, such as the staging of smock races for women, many of them drew large numbers of the lower orders as spectators.[4] While a majority of them seem to have been driven out of existence by hostile legislation passed in 1740, renewed in 1745, race meetings of the later Georgian era, when racing entered a second major phase of growth in this period, continued to attract socially very diverse crowds. As Mike Huggins notes in relation to Cumberland in the early nineteenth century: 'Local people were prepared to travel to the annual races at nearby towns ... Such annual racing events were looked forward to and, like fairs, offered times off when factory workers or farm labourers could claim a holiday.'[5] The Monifieth races in the same period, held annually in July/August and, less regularly, in the autumn on Budden Sands on the Angus coast of north-east Scotland, were the occasion of an exodus of people from all classes from the linen-manufacturing town of Dundee, as they walked, rode, were driven, and sailed the few miles up the coast to attend the event.[6] The cross-class appeal of horse racing significantly predates the mid to later nineteenth century, when it attracts most notice from historians. The opportunity to bet on the races was a major part of this appeal, although the betting habits and practices of members of the lower orders in this context have left scant evidence.[7]

Betting on cricket has left slightly more traces. From its origins as a largely disorganized, popular rural activity in the previous century, and in

[2] *SJChr*, 2 May 1767.

[3] For a good summary, see Dennis Brailsford, *British Sport: A Social History* (rev. ed., Cambridge, 1997); Richard Holt, *Sport and the British* (Oxford, 1989).

[4] See Iris Middleton, 'The Developing Pattern of Horse Racing in Yorkshire 1700–1749: An Analysis of the People and the Places', unpublished Ph.D. thesis, De Montfort University (2000), ch. 3 'The Yorkshire Horse-Racing Calendar'.

[5] Mike Huggins, 'Popular Culture and Sporting Life in the Rural Margins of Late Eighteenth-Century England: The World of Robert Anderson, "The Cumberland Bard"', *Eighteenth-Century Studies*, 45 (2012), 196–7; Mike Huggins, *Horse Racing and British Society in the Long Eighteenth Century* (Martlesham, 2018).

[6] *Dundee, Perth and Cupar Advertiser*, 17 July 1807; 17 Aug. 1810; 16 Aug. 1811. The races seem to have included on occasion foot races for men and women (*Dundee, Perth and Cupar Advertiser*, 13 June 1806).

[7] See ch. 1, pp. 59–60.

a pattern broadly similar to horse racing, cricket was transformed from the 1720s or thereabouts into a national sport with modern characteristics – namely, a set of laws and a governing body, albeit the degree of central control was strictly limited before the formation of the Marylebone Cricket Club in 1787.[8] Cricket retained a distinct geography, its heartlands comprising the southeast English counties of Sussex, Surrey, Kent, and Hampshire, although by the end of the century it was beginning to be played more regularly in the north.[9] As David Underdown has shown in his beautifully described partial lament for the super-cession of a cricketing culture rooted in village life, and the particular rhythms and patterns of labouring life in these communities, there grew up in competition with it from the 1720s and 1730s a new form of cricket shaped by the magnetic force of London, but also dependent on gentry patronage and select individuals from among the social and fashionable elites.[10] Many of these new-style cricketing contests were essentially opportunities for wagers, such as those between teams put together by Frederick, Prince of Wales, and the Earl of Middlesex in July 1735; the Duke of Bedford and the Earl of Halifax in 1741; or the duke of Cumberland and Sir John Elvill a decade later.[11] Cumberland, with his pronounced sporting interests, evidently found such contests irresistible, as hinted at in a letter sent by Robert Ord to the Earl of Carlisle in August 1751:

> You will see in the papers that Lord Sandwich has won his match at cricket against the Duke [of Cumberland], but what I think the best part of the story is not told here. The Duke, to procure good players on his side, ordered twenty-two who were reckoned the best players in the country to be brought before him to choose eleven out of them. They played accordingly, and he chose eleven.

[8] See Timothy J. McCann's summary of its condition at the end of the eighteenth century in Timothy J. McCann (ed.), *Sussex Cricket in the Eighteenth Century*, Sussex Record Society, 88 (Lewes, 2004), p. lxxvi: '… underarm bowling apart, the game at the end of the eighteenth century was recognizably a modern one. Cricket was widespread; it was played to a developed set of rules; score-cards were sold on the grounds; it was widely reported in the newspapers; and the first historians and statisticians were beginning to emerge'.

[9] John Bale, 'Cricket in Pre-Victorian England and Wales', *Area*, 13 (1981), 119–22.

[10] David Underdown, *Start of Play: Cricket and Culture in Eighteenth-Century England* (London, 2000).

[11] *GEP*, 8 July 1735; *Daily Journal*, 15, 30 July 1735; *LEP*, 18 Aug. 1741; *Newcastle Journal*, 10 Aug. 1751; *GA*, 15 Aug. 1751. I am extremely grateful to Ian Maun for very generously sharing his meticulous research on eighteenth-century cricket with me, which now comprises four volumes containing comprehensive listings of matches across the period.

The story did not end there. Those not selected decided to challenge the 'elect' to play for a crown a head. In the resulting game, all too predictably, they vanquished the chosen eleven 'all to nothing'.[12]

If certain members of the elites – including from the royal family, the English titled nobility, and the southern English gentry[13] – were important patrons of the game, behind cricket's growth was also, first, the deeply ingrained habit manifest among men of diverse social origins of engaging in and watching sporting contests for financial stakes.[14] In the case of cricket, as with various other sports, this might happily be rationalized in terms of promoting 'robust and manly exercises', of helping to deter those not born to menial labour – in other words, the propertied – from the seductions of 'idleness and effeminacy', on and about which many a writer lingered and lamented during the central decades of the eighteenth century.[15] Cricket would, it seemed, redeem British hyper-masculinity in a period when it was feared to be in full retreat under the impact of the relentless spread of 'polite' values and manners. As one newspaper correspondent declared in 1751:

> It cannot but give Pleasure to the Publick to find such manly Exercises as Cricket and Rowing so much in Fashion; which besides their healthful Influences are entirely opposite to those affeminate [sic] Diversions to sink your Youth in Idleness and Luxury, and, by debauching their Morals, disqualify them from acting a manly Part, in the great Theatre of Life.[16]

The identities of those who played cricket, beyond, that is, members of the fashionable elites, and those who attended the major public schools

[12] Robert Ord, Chief Baron of the Exchequer in Scotland, to the 4th Earl of Carlisle, quoted in G. Brodribb, *The English Game. A Cricket Anthology* (London, 1948), p. 28.

[13] Jack Fuller, proposing an annual cricket plate for the county, once described cricket as a 'Diversion more calculated to the Genius, and more agreeable to Sussex men than a Horse race…' (McCann (ed.), *Sussex Cricket*, p. 36: Jack Fuller to Charles Lennox, 2nd Duke of Richmond, 18 Aug. 1746). The popularity of cricket matches in Sussex among the gentry and freeholders of the county was such that they were on occasion drawn into electioneering contests, much as in the case of race meetings in other counties, for example, Yorkshire or Staffordshire.

[14] Another very important facet of this was the contemporary enthusiasm for cockfighting, which was widespread across Britain, at least into the 1820s. While many breeders and owners of birds were from the gentry classes, spectators were drawn from all classes of society, and one of its main attractions was that it provided a vehicle for gambling. For which, see Iris Middleton, 'Cockfighting in Yorkshire during the Early Eighteenth Century', *Northern History*, 11 (2003), 129–46; George Jobey, 'Cockfighting in Northumberland and Durham during the Eighteenth and Nineteeth Centuries', *Archaelogia Aeliana*, 20 (1992), 1–25; J. H. Porter, 'Cockfighting in the Eighteenth and Nineteenth Centuries: from Popularity to Suppression', *Transactions of the Devonshire Association for the Advancement of Science, Literature and Art*, 118 (1986), 63–71.

[15] See Eliza Haywood, *The Female Spectator*, Vol. I (London, 1755), p. 124.

[16] *London Morning Penny Post*, 17 July 1751.

and the universities of Oxford and Cambridge, are somewhat obscure. Some of the most adept cricketers were drawn from the rural labouring and farming classes, while the most commonly used contemporary social designation of players was that of 'gentleman', by at least the middle of the eighteenth century an unhelpfully baggily capacious category. The famous Hambledon Club, membership of which mainly comprised members of the gentry, was established by 1750 – although the members typically did not play, but rather paid others to do so – while cricket clubs first began to emerge in London twenty-five years or so earlier.[17] As Underdown observes, 'cricket was obviously flourishing in the London area by the middle of the eighteenth century'.[18] Formed from across the metropolis – east, west, south, and north, as well as from the City of London – and throughout its environs, the proliferation of such teams provided ample opportunities for young men drawn from all points on the social spectrum to play the game. Matches were played between, amongst others, teams made up of watermen, brewery workers from Southwark, butchers, poulterers, and gardeners.[19] In 1777, a Hackney hairdresser appeared before the Bow Street magistrates' office, accused of stealing from the master of a footman, with whom he was frequently in company, including playing cricket with him.[20] Rotherhithe in the east of London saw a flurry of cricketing contests in January 1776 staged on the ice, and played on skates.[21] Impromptu games were frequently played by metropolitan youth, as one letter writer tetchily complained to the press in 1775:

> Sir, Tower Hill would be an agreeable Resort for the Gentry in the Environs of that Part, provided it was made safe for Ladies to walk, without the Risque of their Legs being broke; but in the present Case, with a Dissolute idle Set of Fellows, it is only a Harbour for Gaming and other Vices; among which is the Play of Cricket; in itself it is a noble Exercise, but on this Hill is an Asylum for all kinds of idle Apprentices and Gentlemens servants.[22]

Several deaths of passing spectators by blows from cricket balls were reported, further testimony to the ubiquity as well as hazards posed by cricket-playing in and around London, among them a cabinet maker from Shoe Lane, struck down by a ball in Hoxton in 1771, and an eminent tailor from Fetter Lane felled a year earlier in similar fashion

[17] Peter Clark, *British Clubs and Societies 1580–1800: The Origins of an Associational World* (Oxford, 2000), p. 81.

[18] Underdown, *Start of Play*, p. 95.

[19] *DA*, 24 Mar. 1744; *DA*, 29 May, 15 Aug. 1754; *LEP*, 14 Sept. 1766, 15 Aug. 1772.

[20] *Middlesex Chronicle*, 31 July 1777.

[21] *Middlesex Chronicle*, 26 Jan. 1776; *LEP*, 25 Jan. 1776.

[22] *PA*, 26 July 1775.

on Richmond Green. Serious injuries caused by blows from cricket balls, such as loss of an eye, were also the subject of frequent press comment.[23] Matches between women, from the elites and well below this on the social scale, were staged, although women's cricket remained very much an occasional affair.[24]

Second, promoting cricket's rise were rising commercial agencies and forces. Behind the staging of many a cricketing contest can be discerned the hand of a commercially astute tavern- or innkeeper. Typically, they would advertise the staging of a contest, the stakes to be played for, and provision of food and drink. They might also offer prizes for games.[25] Or, more simply they were beneficiaries of the unusual amount of custom generated by such events. Notable commercial sponsors of cricket in the British capital in the mid eighteenth century included Robert Bartholomew of the White Conduit Tavern; Francis Ludgate of the Rising Sun and Sportsman, located nearby to Marylebone Church, and pre-eminently, George Smith of the Pied Horse, of whom more below, a man whom Underdown describes as the 'indispensable middleman' of London cricket in those years.[26] This was an aspect of a common business strategy on the part of victuallers and publicans across Britain of vigorously patronizing sports and other 'diversions'.[27] In 1759 the 'Red Lyon' inn at Stoke, near Guildford was advertised for sale, together with the lease on seven acres of adjoining land which had been used for playing cricket for the last thirteen years.[28] Three years earlier, magistrates with responsibility for licensing alehouses were reminded that cricket matches, along with cockfights, horse races, and bull and

[23] *Middlesex Journal*, 9 Aug. 1770; *GEP*, 11 June 1771; *LDA*, 10 May 1753; *British Spy, or New Universal London Weekly Journal*, 5 June 1756; *WEP*, 28 Apr. 1761; *LEP*, 31 May 1765; 28 May 1766; *WEP*, 24 July 1766.

[24] As early as 1747, two teams of women from Sussex villages played a match at the Artillery Ground (*DA*, 4, 7, 9, 10, 15 July 1747), probably sponsored by the Duchess of Richmond, while on 23 Aug. 1756 the *Sussex Weekly Advertiser* reported: 'On Friday, the 6th of this Instant was play'd a Match at cricket on Long Dow, by the most famous women of the kingdom, Sarah Chase, of the Parish of Boxgrove, and Mary Coots of the town of Chichester, for five Guineas on each side ….' In 1777, the Countess of Derby created a stir by leading a group of elite women in a game at the Oaks race meeting, an example apparently copied by eleven old maids of respectively Hanstead and Harlow in Essex. (*MP*, 26 June 1777; *MChr*, 29 Sept. 1777.) Several elite women also on occasion sponsored cricket matches. See also McCann (ed.), *Sussex Cricket*, pp. lxxiv–lxxvi.

[25] See McCann (ed.), *Sussex Cricket*, pp. lxvii–viii.

[26] Underdown, *Start of Play*, p. 93.

[27] Clark, *British Clubs and Societies*, p. 164.

[28] *London Gazette*, 7 Aug. 1759. In 1768 Robert Rutty, of the Coffee-House, Stoke Newington, advised customers of his relocation to new premises, which had 'a large field for cricket and trap-ball, besides a private ground for Dutch pins' (*GA*, 2 July 1768).

bear baitings were illegal.[29] A good number of the period's leading cricketers became or were publicans, such as Richard Nyren of the Hambledon Club.

In the central decades of the eighteenth century a high proportion of the most widely publicized, high profile cricketing contests were played on the Artillery Ground of the Honourable Artillery Company, located off Chiswell Street in Finsbury Fields in the heart of the City of London. The key figure in this context was George Smith, referred to above. Smith leased the ground and the Pied Horse tavern from the company before he left for Marlborough in 1752, where he successfully kept another inn until his death in 1761.[30] For several decades, under the direction of Smith and his successors, the Artillery Ground became the scene of matches between carefully selected teams, often picked or sponsored by elite figures, where the aim was to produce evenly matched contests conducive to spectacle and betting.[31] It was through their appearances at the Artillery Ground that rural cricketers from teams such as that from the Sussex village of Slindon in 1742, who were matched twice against a team representing London, were pulled into the orbit of metropolitan sport, which thrived on publicity, somewhat bogus competition for the title of the best team or cricketer in England, and a fledgling form of celebrity.[32] Such men might temporarily attain the exalted status of 'Heroes of the Artillery Ground'.[33] In 1745, a London lawyer declared of the first of two 'great Matches of cricket' between teams representing Kent and 'All England' of that summer, the first staged at Bromley Common, Kent, and the second at the Artillery Ground:

> The conversation of the town turns entirely upon the great match of cricket between Kent and All England, to plaid on Bromley Common next Fryday … The Prince of Wales & all the nobility in the Town will be present … I am in hopes of entertaining the club with particulars of the game, as it will certainly produce another poem, because I know a gentleman who is in fact ordered to attend on purpose.[34]

29 *The Universal Visiter* [sic], *and Monthly Memorialist. For May 1756.* […] Number V (1756), p. 418.

30 *DA*, 22 Feb. 1752; *Salisbury Journal*, 17 Aug. 1752; *WEP*, 2 July 1761.

31 See e.g. the three cricket matches staged between teams from Surrey and Sussex in 1745, where the expenses were shared between the Duke of Richmond, Lord John Sackville, Mr Taaf, the Duchess of Richmond, and Lord Berkeley. McCann (ed.), *Sussex Cricket*, pp. 34–5. Sackville wrote to the Duke of Richmond on 14 Sept. 1745: 'I wish you had let Ridgway play instead of your stopper behind it might have turned the match in our favour.' (Ibid.)

32 *DA*, 30 Aug, 1, 4, 6, 7, 8, 9, 10, 11 Sept. 1742.

33 The phrase comes from the *SJChr*, 9 June 1761.

34 Richard Saville (ed.), *The Letters of John Collier of Hastings 1731–1746*, Sussex Record Society, 96 (Lewes, 2016), p. 306: James Collier, Fig Tree Court, to John Collier, 9 July 1745.

Never mind that the country was engaged in what had become a global war, the War of the Austrian Succession, and would shortly turn into one for survival of the Hanoverian and Protestant regime in Britain as Bonnie Prince Charlie landed off the Hebridean island of Eriskay in July 1745 to launch the last of the major Jacobite risings of the eighteenth century; the attention of Londoners was instead focused on cricket. During matches the pitch at the Artillery Ground was roped off and spectators ordered not to encroach thereon. The reason for this was to ensure a fair, unrigged contest, and to prevent potential disputes about the result.[35]

That the crowds attending at the Artillery Fields, and, indeed, other cricket matches typically included large numbers of the lower orders is abundantly clear. In 1772 Kent farmers complained about the staging by Sir Horace Mann, nephew of the famous diplomat and friend of Sir Horace Walpole, of a cricket match on his Bishopsbourne estate, which led to their losing 3,000 labourers for several days during the harvest.[36] With respect to the Artillery Fields, attendance of a large, socially diverse audience was despite Smith charging spectators 2d for the privilege, and on occasion 6d, although hiking up the price of admission on occasion led to trouble from angry prospective attendees.[37] Access to the ground was through the yard of the Pied Horse, and efforts were repeatedly made to prevent people climbing onto the walls surrounding the ground.[38] In 1751, one writer complained sourly that the manner of conducting contests on the Artillery Ground was 'highly detrimental of the common people, by inticing them to spend the whole afternoon in idleness'.[39] One match, staged in 1772, the year before the H.A.C. Court of Assistants first sought to prohibit such contests on its ground, was reported to have

[35] See e.g. *LEP*, 12, 31 July 1740. On some occasions, Smith formed a ring of benches around the ground. Stewards armed with whips policed the ground. In 1757, the HAC Court of Assistants received a complaint that 'Horse & Foot Races were frequent in the Artillery Ground to the great Detriment of the Gates & other Buildings by Persons climbing over the same', leading the court subsequently to ban the keeper of the ground from allowing the staging of such events (Archives of the Honourable Artillery Company, Court Minutes, 4 Oct., 10 Oct. 1757). Whether this was effective is unclear, for the *London Evening Post* of 24 Aug. 1765 reported that some of the 'principal magistrates' of the city were considering taking action to end any more gambling on the Artillery Ground and the attendant 'tumultous and riotous assemblies'. This may, however, refer to cricket matches, which were first prohibited, unsuccessfully, by the Court of Assistants in 1773. They were eventually ended in 1780 following action by the City of London magistrates.

[36] *GEP*, 22 Aug. 1772.

[37] See *LEP*, 22, 29 Aug. 1747. On occasion tickets were evidently issued to those who left before the end of a match to enable readmission (see e.g. *DA*, 31 May 1744).

[38] See n. 24, above. See also *LEP*, 27 July 1750;

[39] *Observations on Mr Fielding's Enquiry into the Late Increase of Robbers &c* (1751), p. 36.

attracted as many as 20,000 spectators.[40] Such figures were more than likely exaggerated. Crowds of several thousands would seem, nevertheless, to have been fairly commonplace.[41] And, while much of the betting on the contests was for quite large stakes by members of the elites – or the 'idle' as one periodical denominated them in the 1750s, those who frequented the capital's pleasure gardens, gaming tables, brothels, and coffee houses – it was far from confined to them.[42] Bets were made between individuals or with professional bookmakers, who were an increasingly pervasive (and corrupting) presence at the major London cricket matches by the end of the eighteenth century.[43] In August 1765, the press reported on a match played at the Artillery Ground between teams representing Surrey and Dartford for a stake of a 100 guineas a side. According to the press, nearly 12,000 spectators were present. When the match was abandoned before being completed, the result was violence: 'The Mob (many of whom had laid large Betts) imagining foul Play, began to be outrageous, several of whom were dangerously wounded and bruised.' The press also reported on a young butcher who, entrusted with about 40 pounds by his mistress to buy cattle in Smithfield-market, instead went to the Artillery Ground, where he gambled away the whole sum on the cricket.[44]

The figures cited in the newspapers for side betting were necessarily based on rumour and hearsay. Moreover, what direct evidence we possess of betting on cricket by those from well outside the elite relates to contests between local or village teams, not to the types of high-profile match staged at the Artillery Ground. The Nottinghamshire stocking

[40] *GEP*, 2 June 1772. [41] See McCann (ed.), *Sussex Cricket*, p. lxv.

[42] *The World for the Year One Thousand Seven Hundred and Fifty-Four* (1755), p. 379. The size of the stakes played for in the 'great matches' sponsored by members of the elites is somewhat unclear, and the figures commonly cited in the press may not reflect the money which actually changed hands on such occasions. For some cautionary comment on this, see John Goulstone, *Hambledon: The Men and Myths* (Cambridge, 2001), pp. 109–15. I am grateful to Ian Maun for this reference.

[43] Underdown, *Start of Play*, pp. 163–5. Bets were made on the outcome of matches, but also key features of the contests, such as who would make the most runs and so forth. In 1742, for example, when the Sussex village team of Slindon played a select eleven from London at the Artillery Fields, many bet that one of the Slindon players would score forty 'notches', although on this occasion they lost. (*LEP*, 4 Sept. 1742.) The odds were 20 to 1 on Slindon winning the match because they had won all but one of their recent matches. In the event, the village team lost two games against the Londoners. Whether matches were corrupted by betting fixes before the early nineteenth century is unclear, although the press quite frequently would report in the final third of the eighteenth century on the 'knowing ones' being surprised by an unexpected result. The 'knowing ones' here presumably referred to those who followed closely the form of teams and individuals.

[44] *SJChr*, 22 Aug. 1765.

weaver Joseph Woolley, for example, recorded his attendance at and betting on the outcome of matches of the former kind in the 1810s.[45] So too, half a century earlier, did the Sussex shopkeeper Thomas Turner, who also on occasion played in games himself.[46] In the case of both men, the bets they placed were of the order of a few pence or at most a shilling. Yet, in addition to the impressionistic evidence cited above, there is copious testimony to betting among the lower orders on sporting contests and challenges of all sorts in eighteenth-century London, some of which will be rehearsed below. It is inconceivable that they were not taking the opportunities to bet on the outcome of the myriad cricketing contests which were staged in and around the capital from the 1730s and 1740s onwards.[47]

2.2 Perspectives and Agenda

The story of gambling among the wider population in this period is thus partly one about the impact of Britain's giant metropolis, its interactions with and shaping of patterns of leisure, not just among the elites, but throughout much of society, the continued vitality of local traditions and sporting cultures, and the shifting meanings of place and community as society was transformed by commercial and economic change. Where London led other towns and cities and strongly urbanizing regions tended to follow, but also increasingly generated their own distinctive patterns of change. As a result of this, and the early nineteenth century social crisis unfolding in southern and eastern agricultural counties – the result of relentless population growth, an overstocked labour market also caused by changing labour hiring practices, and the loss of by-employments for women and children – the regional geography of popular sporting and gambling culture shifted markedly away from the south and south east, towards the rapidly industrializing and urbanizing regions of the midlands and north west of England, South Wales, and west-central Scotland. If the world of popular gambling can only be documented in considerable depth from the mid nineteenth century, the continuities with earlier decades were, nevertheless, quite marked. They tend, moreover, to be underplayed by historians, probably because

45 NA, DD/311/4, photocopy of diary of Joseph Woolley of Clifton, 1813, entry for 9 Dec.; DD/311/6, ibid., 1815, entries for 4, 5, 6, 7 Oct.

46 *The Diary of Thomas Turner 1754–1765*, ed. David Vaisey (Oxford, 1985), pp. 46, 63, 102, 158, 322.

47 Other common metropolitan venues of cricket matches included Blackheath, Lambs Conduit Fields, Marylebone Fields, Kennington Common, Putney Common, Richmond Green, Tothill Fields, and St George's Fields.

they subvert a common periodization used to discuss the development of leisure and sport, with the early nineteenth century being depicted as a hiatus between two fundamentally different worlds, those of early modern and modern Britain.[48]

Tracing the basic contours of this world of expanding opportunities for gambling among the majority of people is fairly straightforward. Yet, much of the detail remains only very partially revealed. This is the case in respect of patterns of difference along axes of place, time, and, indeed, social groups. What sorts of gambling prevailed at different social levels, and what role it played in the lives of most people, resist easy answers. The impression of ubiquity conveyed in much of the press and contemporary print is not inconsistent, for example, with it being a regular, intense preoccupation of a minority, albeit a growing one among the lower orders; or, indeed, that many, such as Thomas Turner, referred to above, generally chose for various reasons to resist its lure, or, indeed, completely eschewed it. For Turner, the descriptor 'gamester' was one that carried clear negative connotations.[49] Equally, the contexts – social and cultural – in which this activity were enfolded, and which conferred on it much of its meanings, are somewhat occluded. What is fairly apparent is that gambling at this level of society was mainly (although by no means exclusively) engaged in by men, and linked very closely to the worlds of the tavern and various forms of male self-fashioning. If anything, this relationship deepened and took on additional layers of significance from the later eighteenth century, under the impact of the French Revolutionary and Napoleonic Wars and the development of the new industrializing society of the early nineteenth century. It was, however, already an essential feature. In this, as in other aspects, much of an older world of popular recreation and gambling became subsumed within a newer one.

Rather than furnishing a comprehensive picture of popular gambling between c.1700 and c.1830, the rest of this chapter explores its nature and development through two, separate lenses. First, we examine more closely popular gambling habits and practices in London in the long eighteenth century. This is partly because the sources, while still fragmentary and frequently opaque, are relatively abundant, but also because of the precocity of the British capital's commercialization. Leisure and culture in eighteenth-century London were as various historians have emphasized, unusually heavily shaped by commercial forces and agents.

[48] See the reflections on this in Emma Griffin, 'Popular Culture in Industrializing England', *Historical Journal*, 45 (2002), 609–35.

[49] *Diary of Thomas Turner*, ed. Vaisey, p. 208, where Turner asked, 'What can betray greater stupidity in mankind than to game for such large sums?'

London was, partly for this reason, a crucible of cultural innovation.[50] The theme of commercialization will be picked up again in the second section, which focuses on pedestrianism or foot racing. Studies of this phenomenon mostly focus on the central decades of the nineteenth century, although foot races were common long before then.[51] Bringing the development and nature of foot racing into clearer view provides us with an opportunity to explore how habits of gambling among the lower orders developed in the early nineteenth century and how this interacted with and was informed by a widening and deepening *British* national culture, alongside resurgent or rather reimagined subnational cultures and identities.

2.3 Popular Gambling in the British Metropolis

To map popular gambling habits in the eighteenth-century British metropolis is, from a certain perspective, to go in pursuit of a chimera. The distinctions between the gambling of people of different social rank were blurred, something which is emphasized at other points in this book. For its critics not the least perturbing aspect of gambling was that it often brought high and low together in promiscuous propinquity. Sharpers passed themselves off, with seemingly considerable success, as 'gentlemen', while much gaming might be thought of as occupying a liminal social space in which a highly performative form of gentility was an integral part of the experience, the point being that it was a sphere in which imposters and those who aspired to social success gained ready access. Young heirs and youthful men of rank were especially vulnerable to the sharpers and adventurers who infested the taverns of Westminster and other parts of the city, luring them into games of cards or dice in which they would be relieved of large sums.[52] This was evidently sufficiently common to be an important factor behind the passage of the

50 See esp. Peter Borsay, 'London 1660–1800: A distinctive culture?', in Peter Clark and Raymond Gillespie (eds.), *Two Capitals: London and Dublin 1500–1840* (Oxford and London, 2001), pp. 167–84.

51 See *inter alia,* Peter Swain, 'Pedestrianism, the Public House and Gambling in Nineteenth Century South-east Lancashire', *Sport in History*, 32 (2012), 383–404; Peter Radford, *The Celebrated Captain Barclay: Sport, Money and Fame in Regency Britain* (London, 2001).

52 For two such cases, one from towards the beginning of our period and the other from the end, see TNA, C6/372/12 and *Leeds Mercury*, 9 Oct. 1807. The former concerned a Gibbon Bagnall of the Inner Temple, a 21 year-old with expectations of an inheritance who had in 1709 been drawn into gaming and lost some hundreds of pounds, in payment for which he had given several notes. The latter included a report of a young gentleman from Lancashire who had recently come into what was described as 'a splendid fortune', and who had lost £6,000 in a game of cards with a 'black leg' in St James's Street.

Gaming Act of 1710, the most significant piece of anti-gaming legislation passed during the eighteenth century.[53] Betting on all sorts of things was commonplace, and involved London's shopkeepers, tradesmen, and artisans, as well as those well above them on the social ladder.[54] 'Policy gambling' – the taking out of insurance policies on the outcome of events, an activity which first attracted hostile notice in the 1690s – was, as one contemporary pointed out, the city's equivalent to the betting practices of the West End elites.[55] Rich, middling, and poor alike played the lottery.

All of which said, while there were no hard and fast boundaries, there was a loose division between popular and elite gambling, the former defined by its inclusivity, the latter its obverse. Beyond this, we can begin to discern a culture of 'inferior gamblers', one closely linked to criminality and often located in various open spaces (fields and parks), which, in its persistent, highly visible presence, defied the regulatory gaze and ambitions of moral reformers and magisterial authority. Beyond that was a world of more organized gambling which was part of a much broader process of the commercialization of popular leisure and recreation in this period. These disparate realities were perceived by those in authority as a threat to the cohesion of society, as both an expression and source of 'idleness', which in turn was believed to lead inexorably to a life of crime. Part of the difficulty in reconstructing their roles and significance in society is that we usually see them through hostile eyes.

Moreover, the distinction between 'inferior gambling' and commercial gambling at certain points begins to collapse. This is because the motivations of those who, for example, pushed wheelbarrows of oranges for which people were enticed to play with dice or ran gambling games of different kinds from barrows and booths at London's legal (Bartholomew and Southwark fairs) and illegal fairs (Tottenham Court Fair, Hampstead Fair, Welsh Fair, Mile End and Bow fairs, May Fair) were economic.[56] These were people who lived by gambling, and by luring

[53] See ch. 5, pp. 225–8.

[54] See further below. For city ward and dining clubs which engaged in betting on national affairs and city matters, see LMA, MS 2841, vol. 1, minutes of a Candlewick ward club from 1739; MS 3406, minutes of City of London dining club; MS 544, vol. 2, minutes of the Centenary Club.

[55] *MChr*, 5 Dec. 1777; City of London Sessions, Sessions Papers, presentment of Grand Jury, 16 Jan. 1693, *London Lives, 1690–1800*, LMSLPS15004000 (www.londonlives.org, version 1.1., 17 June 2012). The latter refers to four offices located near to the Royal Exchange.

[56] An order of court made against common players of interludes and keepers of gaming houses and gaming tables at Tottenham Court fair in 1724 referred to 'keepers of gaming houses, gaming booths, gaming tables, cups and balls, or any other unlawful games'

others to spend money on play. The sharpers and cheats who infested the streets, fields, and taverns of the capital, and who relied on the gullibility of the many visitors and newcomers to the capital, and the young and inexperienced, were part of the economy of make-shifts which, as Tim Hitchcock has shown, enveloped many of the poor in the eighteenth-century capital.[57] Survival in this context relied on adaptability, mobility, and relative invisibility. Such individuals almost certainly overlapped with the groups of gamblers who were commonly to be found frequenting various spots in the capital – St James's Park, Moorfields, Tower Hill, Stepney Fields, or St George's Fields south of the river, to name but a few – which formed parts of a distinctive topography of license and unrule.[58] Subsisting on the proceeds of gambling and often, it seems, theft, they stood well outside of the roles prescribed for them by the elites or those, such as Wesley and the Methodists, who desired and sought moral revival. These were people such as Richard Haddock who kept a Bagnio (i.e. bath house) in Holborn in the 1720s, but who had begun life as a shoe black earning money on the parade in St James's Park, graduating from that to becoming an 'attender on ye gaming tables … and so to street robbery'.[59] How many of them there were is impossible to say, but they were an unsettling, persistent, and very visible presence, provoking one contemporary in 1751 to describe them as a 'Race of Vermin' who were 'equally daring and dangerous'.[60]

They were also part of a rapidly developing, and increasingly well populated metropolitan recreational landscape, the scope of which historians have only begun to reconstruct. This is partly because in recent years their attention has been focused elsewhere, on the worlds of the so-called polite and the elites. The rapidly expanding realm of popular entertainment and recreation in London was, nevertheless, one that its

(LMA, Middlesex Sessions, Orders of Court, MJ/O/C/002, Jan. 1721–Jan. 1725, fos. 119–119d, Aug. 1724).

57 Tim Hitchcock, *Down and Out in Eighteenth Century London* (Hambledon and London, 2004).

58 In the 1760s and 1770s, there were persistent complaints about and apparently fruitless efforts to eliminate such people and activities from St James's Park. See *inter alia*, *Gazetteer*, 7 Jan. 1767; 29 May 1770; *PA*, 6 Jan. 1768; 11 Aug. 1769; 16 Feb. 1776; *GEP*, 16 Feb. 1773; *Westminster Journal*, 10 Aug. 1771. The role of Moorfields as a site for such things was (unsurprisingly) a major theme in John Wesley's promotion of a revived Reformation of Manners of Society in the later 1750s and early 1760s (John Wesley, *A Sermon Preached Before the Society for Reformation of Manners on Sunday, January 30, 1763. At the Chappel on West Street, Seven Dials* (London, 1763), esp. p. 6).

59 TNA, State Papers Domestic, SP36/18/23, E. Hughes to the Duke of Newcastle, 11 Mar. 1729.

60 *GA*, 25 July 1751.

critics were denouncing with increasing vehemence from the later 1730s onwards, reaching a series of clamorous crescendos in the mid-1740s and early 1750s.[61] One factor driving its growth were the relatively high real wages earned by the capital's numerous and very diverse artisan class, many of whom worked in skilled trades. Against a background of falling food prices, real wages in the capital continued to rise until the mid eighteenth century, after which they began to fall quite sharply until the 1790s, before rising again in the early nineteenth century, although it may well have been only in the 1840s that they exceeded their previous high point of a century earlier.[62] This was the general background against which Parliament passed new laws between the late 1730s and 1750s, including anti-gambling acts, aimed at restraining the expansion of popular leisure, if not driving it into reverse.[63] One symptom of change was the proliferation in the central decades of the eighteenth century of pleasure and tea gardens across the capital. At one end of the spectrum – the decidedly fashionable end – were Vauxhall Gardens (reopened by Jonathan Tyers in 1732), Ranelagh (opened to instant acclaim in 1742), but also, slightly less notorious, Marylebone Gardens (reinvented by Daniel Gough in the later 1730s) and (more briefly) Cuper's Gardens in Lambeth (which flourished for a decade or so from 1738 before finally closing in 1760). While the first two particularly have attracted considerable commentary in recent years, much less has been written about places such as Bagnigge Wells in Lambeth, after c.1760 the favoured resort of city merchants and their families, or the large number of more evanescent establishments, the typical clientele of which comprised apprentices, journeymen, as well as tradesmen and shopkeepers and their wives and families.[64] One cluster of the latter type of establishment was to be found in Clerkenwell to the north of the city.[65] These were typically

[61] Nicholas Rogers, *Mayhem: Post-war Crime and Violence in Britain 1748–1753* (New Haven and London, 2012); Bob Harris, *Politics and the Nation: Britain in the Mid Eighteenth Century* (Oxford, 2002), pp. 282–95.

[62] L. D. Schwarz, 'The Standard of Living in the Long Run: London, 1700–1860', *Economic History Review*, 38 (1985), 24–41, esp. 25.

[63] See ch. 5, pp. 228–9, 232–3.

[64] Jonathan Colin (ed.), *The Pleasure Garden: From Vauxhall to Coney Island* (Philadelphia, PA, 2012); P. J. Corfield, *Vauxhall: Sex and Entertainment, London's Pioneering Urban Pleasure Garden* (2nd ed., 2012); Hannah Greig, '"All Together and All Distinct": Public Sociability and Social Exclusivity in London's Pleasure Gardens, ca. 1740–1830', *Journal of British Studies*, 51 (2012), 50–75; Alan Borg and David Coke, *Vauxhall Gardens: A History* (New Haven and London, 2011); T. J. Edelstein, *Vauxhall Gardens* (New Haven, 1983).

[65] Warwick W. Wroth, *The London Pleasure Gardens of the 18th Century* (London, 1896), pp. 34–42, 148; Harris, *Politics and the Nation*, p. 287.

far from respectable, although what this meant, as in the case of their more famous counterparts as John Brewer shrewdly notes, was very much in the eye of the beholder.[66] They were frequented in the evenings or, more regularly, on Sundays, increasingly *the day* of recreation in the capital at this level of society.[67] Mulberry Gardens, Clerkenwell, made its appeal in 1745 to the 'honest sons of trade and industry after the fatigues of a well spent day'.[68] Another of these places, this one located south of the Thames, was described by Sylas Neville in an entry in his diary for 12 January 1783:

> With R. [to] a very large bread & butter manufactory in St George's Fields. Here we found a very large collection of idle dissipated young men, most of them clerks in the public offices or in the Commerce, drinking tea wine &c with their Dixies, for few modest women go but now & then for curiosity to see the rooms & gardens which are pleasant, & then in company of their husbands or relations.[69]

How many were associated with gambling, in addition to the more frequent sexual commerce, is hard to say; it is significant in this context, however, that sites such as Marylebone Gardens had been closely linked to gambling before their mid-century makeovers. In the early eighteenth century, the spas at Belsize and Hampstead were notorious gamblers' haunts.[70] In addition to cricket matches, the lessee of White Conduit House in Islington, Robert Bartholomew, mentioned earlier, promoted horse races on White Conduit Fields in the 1740s, which drew large crowds of 'labouring and working people' and encouraged much betting, and which drew the attention of the metropolitan authorities as being in contravention of the recent legislation aimed at eliminating such

[66] John Brewer, '"The Most Polite Age and the Most Vicious": Attitudes towards Culture as a Commodity 1660–1800', in Ann Bermingham and John Brewer (eds.), *The Consumption of Culture 1600–1800: Image, Object, Text* (London and New York, 1995), pp. 341–61.

[67] See e.g. LMA, Middlesex Justices, Sessions Papers, MJ/SP/1787/05/006 & 008 A/B, representation of the Grand Jury, 24 May 1787, which talked about the Lord's Day as the key occasion or source of 'growing vices' in reference to gambling in taverns and in public gardens which had, it was stated, 'opened all around the metropolis', with 'invitations on walls of every public street'. The same document also emphasized the spirit of dissipation which prevailed in 'Fields and Public Gardens, Tea Houses and Taverns to an incredible number'. A letter published in *Lloyds Evening Post*, 10 June 1763 complained about the streets 'being full on Sundays of gambling boys'.

[68] Wroth, *London Pleasure Gardens*, p. 42.

[69] *The Diary of Sylas Neville 1767–1788*, ed. Basil Cozens-Hardy (London, New York and Toronto, 1950), p. 300.

[70] LMA, Middlesex Sessions, Orders of Court, MJ/O/C/002, Jan. 1721–Jan. 1725, fos. 21–22, May 1722.

events.[71] White Conduit House began life as a tavern; the tea room was a later addition.[72]

2.4 Taverns, Coffee Houses, and Gaming Houses

In respect of furnishing venues for popular gambling, taverns and inns, coffee houses, and gaming houses can all be seen in a basically similar light. The gap between them in this context was often a very narrow one, insofar as it was pursuit of profit or, indeed, simple survival, which furnished the main motivation behind provision of such facilities and opportunities. Tavern keepers had little or no choice in this respect, as even their fiercest contemporary critics were forced to acknowledge.[73] In what was a saturated market, with taverns competing intensely for customers, not to do so was to imperil their survival. This was despite the fact that patronizing and encouraging gambling on their premises was illegal, and made tavern keepers vulnerable to prosecution, or loss of their ale licence, although only if someone chose to inform on them, which was a fairly rare event; gambling flourished in eighteenth-century London despite the intermittent hostility of the authorities, but also because it was supported by local communities, or a large cross section thereof. Many taverns (probably a majority of them) had skittle grounds or rooms, ninepin alleys, billiard tables, shuffle-boards, backgammon boards, or cards. More striking still is their provision of other gaming equipment, such as 'E.O.' tables or that required to play 'hazard', which comprised a table and set of dice. This feature of the metropolitan recreational economy became especially visible in the 1770s and 1780s, which begins to explain why contemporaries in those years became so concerned about the emulative effects of elite gaming. In 1782, to take two examples, an information was presented against one Savile Robinson, described as being 'late' of the Parish of Marylebone – a very rapidly growing, increasingly densely populated part of London in the later eighteenth century – for keeping a common gaming house, which included an 'E.O.' table, while in the spring Middlesex quarter sessions

[71] LMA, Middlesex Sessions, Orders of Court, MJ/O/C/005, May 1743–Feb. 1753, fo. 113d. Another place in London where races were held in the same period was Tothill Fields. The *General Evening Post* reported on 5 Sept. 1747 that a pony was to run eighty times around 'the Race' [presumably meaning race course] in Tothill Fields in 12 hours for a wager of 100 guineas.

[72] Wroth, *London Pleasure Gardens*, p. 131.

[73] See *inter alia* LMA, Middlesex Justices, Sessions Papers, MJ/SP/1787/05/110B, officers and inhabitants of Mile End, 12 July 1787; Sir John Fielding, *Extracts From Such of the Penal Laws. As Particularly Relate to the Peace and Good Order of this Metropolis* (London, 1768), p. 414.

of that year the magistrates considered the case of William Weston, a victualler from St Catherine's precinct, who had been permitting people to play 'E.O.' on his premises.[74] In the previous year, Martha Swan, the wife of a labouring man, who signed her testimony with a cross, informed on one William Smith of the Marquis of Granby's Head in Lambeth Marsh. What had prompted this action was that her husband had lost £1.15s at the 'E.O.' table which Smith kept in his tavern. She also complained of Smith's hosting frequent cockfights and 'playing of skittles'.[75]

Coffee houses, which proliferated in London from the later seventeenth century, have by contrast been depicted by several historians as constituting a very different kind of space to taverns. For these historians, such places were pre-eminently sites of open conversation, social sobriety, and even a form of democratic enlightenment.[76] This may well be a historiographical mirage. There was no single, essential coffee house experience, but instead much diversity in terms of both their typical clientele and character. This is quite apparent from, amongst other things, descriptions of them given in the early eighteenth century diary of the future Lord Chief Justice, Dudley Ryder, or the fictional characterization of their different clientele by the hack writer, Ned Ward, whose *London Spy*, published in parts in 1709, was an eighteenth-century Grub Street hit and provided an influential template for writing on London society throughout much of the rest of the eighteenth century.[77] Given their rapid growth – one historian suggests that a reasonable estimate of their number in the capital by the early eighteenth century would be between 400 and 500[78] – the diversity should perhaps be unsurprising. As early as 1693, Ellis's Coffee house in the Old Jewry in the city was presented to city magistrates along with several taverns as places where the 'lewd and dissolute' would congregate.[79] Nor is it at all remarkable

[74] LMA, MJ/SR/3146, Middlesex Justices, Sessions Roll, Apr. 1782, 8 Apr. 1782, jurors' presentment against Savile Robinson, 17 Mar. 1782; Middlesex Justices, Sessions Papers, MJ/SP/1782/04/001, 9 Apr. 1782.

[75] SHC, QS 2/6/mic/1781/52, information of Martha Swan, sworn 21 Aug. 1781.

[76] Brian Cowan, *The Social Life of Coffee: The Emergence of the British Coffeehouse* (London and New York, 2005); Markman Ellis, *The Coffee-House: A Cultural History* (London, 2004).

[77] *The Diary of Dudley Ryder, 1715–16*, ed. William Matthews (London, 1939); Edward Ward, *The London Spy* (London, 1698).

[78] Michael Harris, 'London Newspapers', in M. F. Suarez, and Michael L. Turner (eds.), *The Cambridge History of the Book in Britain, Vol. V 1695–1830*, (Cambridge, 2010), p. 414.

[79] City of London Session, Sessions Papers, presentment of Grand Jury, 16 Jan. 1693, *London Lives, 1690–1800*, LMSLPS150040003 (www.LondonLives.org, version 1.1., 17 June 2012).

that some of them became sites of gambling, although it may well be that it was mainly the elites (broadly defined) who were likely to frequent them for this purpose, as opposed to the 'journeymen and labourers' whose tavern gambling was a source of periodically acute concern to the authorities and their employers.[80] 'Policy gambling', referred to above, was firmly located in the coffee houses to be found in and around Exchange Alley at the very heart of the city.[81]

Details regarding the numbers, location, and nature of the third of our trio of institutions – gaming houses – are altogether more fragmentary. Attention to date has understandably been quite heavily focused on the small number of highly visible, socially exclusive subscription gaming houses – White's in the early Hanoverian period, Almack's and Brooks's in the later eighteenth century, and Crockford's in the Regency era.[82] Gaming houses of a rather different kind clustered in and around Covent Garden, a locale of joyous, uninhibited unrespectability richly described recently by Vic Gatrell.[83] One account in the early 1720s indicated that the number of these was at least thirty, while another put the figure at twenty-two.[84] Contemporary nomenclature was (and is) very slippery, indicative of the variety of different kinds of establishment encompassed by the term 'gaming house'. At one end of the spectrum was the lowly night cellar, almost certainly no more than dingy room under a house, such as that run by one Richard Sharples in the Haymarket in the early 1720s, where common gamblers might congregate;[85] towards the other end were premises set up specifically for gaming; while in between were, as we have already seen, tavern keepers who equipped their premises with 'E.O.' tables and other gambling equipment. Some of the most elaborate enterprises typically employed a range of people in various distinct roles,

80 See e.g. BL, Add MS 30,335, account book of Nicholas Carewe, afterwards 1st Baronet of Beddington, Surrey, 1705–1708. This records frequent payments for gaming, often in London or Cambridge and Newmarket, but also Hampstead and Tunbridge Wells. The London coffee houses in which Carewe gamed were Grecian's, the Bedford Coffee House, and White's Chocolate House.

81 See also, for relevant comment, *MChr*, 5 Dec. 1777.

82 See ch. 1, pp. 66, 68–70, for these elite gambling clubs.

83 Vic Gatrell, *The First Bohemians: Life and Art in London's Golden Age* (London, 2013). LMA, Westminster Sessions, Orders of Court, WJ/O/C/001, April 1720–April 1728, fos. 4–4d (5 Oct. 1720), refers to an instruction from the Lord Justices about the nuisance of gaming houses which spoke of their being 'more common public gaming houses in the parish of St Paul Covent Garden, than in any other part of this city and liberty'.

84 *An Account of the Endeavours That have been used to Suppress Gaming Houses, and the Discouragements that have been met with in a Letter to a Noble Lord* (London, 1722), p. 6; *LJ*, 13 Jan. 1722.

85 LMA, Middlesex Sessions, Session of the Peace and Oyer and Terminer Book, MJ/SB/B/079, Jan.–Dec. 1722, fo. 52, June 1722.

and were in their layout very carefully designed to facilitate ready escape in the event of a raid by the authorities.[86] From references in the press to gaming houses, as well as legal records, we can glean that they were to be found across much of the capital, although they were especially common in Covent Garden and nearby streets, and, increasingly from the later eighteenth century, St James's Street.[87] In the mid eighteenth century, the so-called Golden Gaming Table was kept on a boat (a lighter) on the Thames.[88]

If the actual number and full range of locations of gaming houses in the capital necessarily remain elusive, the identities of their patrons are similarly so. The latter appear to have been typically drawn from a cross section of the male population below the level of the fashionable elites. Women frequented them on occasion, and their relative absence from the sources may be less indicative of their actual non-participation than habits of reporting and prosecutorial decisions. In 1723 Barbara Bulmer was prosecuted for 'frequenting a common gaming house', although we know nothing about her apart from her name.[89] In 1754, a group of 'young Lads *and Girls*' were taken up for gambling in a public house near Leicester Fields.[90] There were female gaming-house keepers, such as Martha Barrow who maintained such an establishment in St James's Street, Covent Garden in the early 1720s.[91] Nevertheless, it was predominantly men who found their way to the gaming houses. One writer of the mid eighteenth century described gaming houses as the 'public rendezvous of gentlemen, tradesmen, servants of all degrees, journeymen taylors, barbers, butchers, bullies, highwaymen, common sharpers,

86 *An Account of the Endeavours*, esp. pp. 36–7; LMA, Middlesex Justices, Session of the Peace and Oyer and Terminer Book, MJ/SB/077, Jan.–Dec. 1720, Oct. 1720; Westminster Sessions, Orders of Court, WJ/O/C/001, fos. 107-9; *LJ*, 13 Jan. 1722. See also ch. 5, pp. 240–1.

87 See esp. TNA, Treasury Solicitor's Papers, TS11/931/3301, Rex v. Thomas Moore, keeper of gaming house and gaming room at 6 Oxenden St, Leicester Fields, 1799, which talked of five gaming houses in Oxenden St, two or three in Panton St, and 'many others in Lisle St, Orange St, Covent Garden etc.'. Other places where E.O. tables are known to have been located in the later eighteenth century include Carlisle House in Soho Square, formerly the site of Mrs Cornelys concerts and entertainments, and still in the early 1780s offering concerts and masquerades, as well as a weekly debating society; Pall Mall; Oxford Street; Cheapside; and Long Lane.

88 *GA*, 22 May 1751.

89 LMA, Middlesex Justices, Session of the Peace and Oyer and Terminer Book MJ/SB/B/080, Jan.–Dec. 1723, 9 Oct. 1723.

90 *WEP*, 20 June 1754.

91 LMA, Middlesex Justices, Session of the Peace and Oyer and Terminer Book MJ/SB/B/080, Jan.–Dec. 1723, 9 Oct. 1723.

common pickpockets [and] whores'.[92] When thirty-six people were taken in 1751 at a gaming house, located behind the Hoop Tavern on the Strand, they comprised 'Oxford scholars, Templers, merchants, officers, jews, lifeguard men, tradesmen, common gentlemen, footmen, chairmen, and others of the lowest rank'.[93] In the early 1720s, gaming houses in Covent Garden where hazard and faro were being played, were said to be frequented by 'sons, apprentices, servants of several merchants, lawyers, [and] tradesmen'.[94] In late 1796 constables netted in one raid on a gaming house in Leicester Fields:

> a notorious Highwayman – some Gentlemen of Character – two merchants – a Bankers clerk – an attorney – a hairdresser – several valets – a Capt of Dragoons, & a Black musician in the same Regiment – an Ambassador's secretary – some apprentices – a shoemaker – a Breeches maker – and two emigrant priests.[95]

The priests – exiles from revolutionary France – were apparently only there for the fire and free food customarily provided in such establishments.

'Templars' (i.e. denizens of the Inns of Temple) had a reputation for gambling, as part of a bachelor lifestyle assumed by young men seeking to establish themselves in a legal career. Similarly, there was considerable gambling, as we saw in the previous chapter, in the military. This may have been partly a consequence of hyper-masculine values associated with military service, which included a very strong emphasis on defending personal as well as collective honour. Relevant in this context is the fact that frequently younger sons of landed families sought their fortunes in the armed services, a path which, frankly, constituted a veritable lottery in respect of its outcome, a lottery with death in wartime but also patronage and opportunity. Such people could face a difficult transition into adulthood, acculturated to a fashionable lifestyle, but lacking the income to sustain this.[96] Half-pay officers were often portrayed in this period as social adventurers, frequenting resorts and pleasure gardens, in the hope of ensnaring a wealthy heiress. This stereotype may have been overdrawn, but the strength of the appeal of gambling to such men is very plausible, as is the notion that another factor that drew

92 Charles Jones, *Some Methods Proposed Towards Putting a Stop to the Flagrant Crimes of Murder, Robbery, and Perjury; and for the more effectually preventing the pernicious consequences of Gaming among the Lower Class of People* (London, 1752), p. 20.

93 *WEP*, 1 Nov. 1751.

94 *An Account of the Endeavours*, p. 6. See also *Covent Garden Journal*, 26 June 1752, which reported that the Westminster magistrate, Saunders Welsh, had raided a gaming house in Holborn, where he took up thirty 'idle persons, apprentices, journeymen, gentlemen's servants'.

95 TNA, Treasury Solicitor's Papers, TS11/931/3301.

96 See ch. 1, esp. pp. 77–8.

them, and others, to gaming was a preoccupation with cutting a fashionable figure. Many people in eighteenth-century London, particularly young men well below the level of the elites, including the serried ranks of apprentices, came under the spell of this impulsion.[97] Not all of them of course became gamblers. Some did, however, and in sufficient numbers further to diffuse the gambling habit in metropolitan society. When nine 'notorious sharpers' were seized by magistrates in the Haymarket in 1756, it is surely significant that most of them were decked out in expensive, showy clothes and swords which they had hired. They included a fiddler, who had been formerly a tapster (i.e. publican), 'dressed in rich silver tissue'; a 'broken publican'; a sausage merchant resplendent in 'brown and silver'; and a journeyman founder kitted out 'in blue and silver'.[98]

The stipendiary magistrate, Patrick Colquhoun, suggested in the early nineteenth century that there were fifteen 'superior class' gaming houses in the British capital, and fifteen 'inferior class'.[99] With his Scottish mercantile and Enlightenment background – he hailed from Glasgow – Colquhoun possessed a strong belief in the power of numbers, but his practice in this regard was heroically creative at best, and the figures look suspiciously uniform.[100] He must have known that in this context he was on even more slippery ground than was usually the case. He also

97 For the view that 'youth' were especially vulnerable to the lure of the gaming houses, see *A Charge Delivered to the Grand Jury, at the Sessions of the City and Liberties of Westminster, 16 Oct. 1754. By Thomas Lediard Esq* (London, 1754), pp. 25–6. The life of highwayman, James Maclaine, executed in 1750, was seen as exemplary of that of the 'gentleman fortune hunter'; for which, see *inter alia A Letter to the Honourable House of Commons in Relation to the Present Situation of Affairs* (London, 1750), p. 7; James Caulfield, *Portraits, Memoirs, and Characters of Remarkable Persons, From the Revolution of 1688 to the End of the Reign of George II, 4 vols* (London, 1820), iv, 87–97. Much can be learnt of the pressures on fashion on the young in London in the early eighteenth century from the diary of Dudley Ryder (*Diary of Dudley Ryder, 1715–16*, ed. Matthews). One clear distinction that Ryder drew was between an authentic form of gentility or politeness and a simple preoccupation with appearance and the figure one cut in society. Both impulses were evidently strongly present in society. That Ryder was from a religiously dissenting background only makes the evidence furnished by his diary all the more significant in the present context.

98 *Gazetteer and London Daily Advertiser*, 7 Apr. 1756.

99 Patrick Colquhoun, *A Treatise on the Police of the Metropolis* (7th ed., London, 1806), p. 143. He also estimated that, in addition to these thirty gaming houses, there were seven subscription gaming houses, and six ladies gaming houses. The political economist, J. R. McCulloch, later disparagingly referred to Colquhoun as 'this intrepid calculator'. Cited in Joanna Innes, 'Power and Happiness: empirical social enquiry in Britain, from 'political arithmetic' to 'moral statistics', in Joanna Innes, *Inferior Politics: Social Problems and Social Policies in Eighteenth-Century Britain* (Oxford, 2009), no. 209, p. 164.

100 On Colquhoun, see Ruth Paley, 'Colquhoun, Patrick (1745–1820)', *ODNB* (Oxford, 2008) [accessed online 30 August 2019 at https://ezproxy-prd.bodleian.ox.ac.uk: 4563/ 10.1093/re.odnb/5992].

intimated that their growth, or more accurately perhaps enhanced visibility, reflected the strength of the commercial interests which lay behind them. This financial resilience helped to frustrate efforts by the authorities to close them down. Thomas Miller, sentenced to imprisonment for twelve months and fined £500 in 1797 for keeping a gaming house just off Leicester Square apparently boasted that if he were to be fined £500 he would merely take the sum from his 'coffers and not miss it'.[101] Some of these enterprises may have been more purely opportunistic. In the early 1780s, when Dr James Graham's Temple of Pleasure in Pall Mall began to decline in popularity, Graham either turned over his lease or became himself involved in running the premises as a gaming house with several partners.[102] The seemingly rapid proliferation of gaming houses in the 1770s and early 1780s would appear to indicate that a good number of them were fly-by-night operations, although they were strikingly brazen in their publicity, handing out advertising cards openly on the streets.[103]

2.5 Illegal Lottery Insurance

Colquhoun linked what he described as 'partnership concerns', a development which he dated to the 1770s and the rise of 'E.O.' as the gambling game of choice, to another highly visible aspect of metropolitan gambling culture in the later eighteenth century – illegal lottery insurance.[104] The nature of this is discussed in greater detail in a later chapter, and need not be rehearsed here in any depth. Three main points are, nevertheless, worth making in the present context.

First, the 'lottery insurance' referred to was a form of betting, pure and simple; it was a wager on outcomes of the official lottery draw. Such bets were facilitated by the lengthy duration of the lottery draw before 1803, which could be anywhere between thirty-five and around forty days. Premiums rose as the draw proceeded and the odds on a ticket being drawn a blank or prize on a specific day narrowed.[105]

Second, the practice flourished because of the strength and extent of demand, which was manifest across London and its immediate environs

[101] TNA, HO 47/22/30, The Memorial and Petition of John Shepherd of Hye St, Bloomsbury, gentleman.

[102] *London Packet*, 2 Aug. 1782.

[103] *MChr*, 26 Mar. 1782. The British Museum has a substantial collection of these cards, for which see British Museum, Prints and Drawings, D. 3.261-336, seventy-six E.O. cards with decorated borders. Similar criticisms about the brazen openness of gaming houses in their activities were made in the 1790s, for which, see e.g. *MP*, 11 Jan. 1792.

[104] Colquhoun, *Treatise*, p. 143.

[105] See ch. 3, pp. 166–7.

and throughout metropolitan society.[106] Inevitably, it was the hold which it exerted over the labouring classes and the poor, particularly women, which most struck contemporary commentators, anxious about its supposedly destructive effects on families and the consequent additional burdens placed on mechanisms of poor relief.[107] The lowest premiums appear to have been 6d to win half a guinea, but even if this could not be afforded other options existed (most obviously collective purchase) which involved expending even smaller sums. James Bligh, who was a police officer in Queen Square, Westminster, which he described as a 'poor part of town', spoke at the beginning of the early nineteenth century of 'various methods of insuring in which very small sums, even the half pence in their pockets are risked in this line of gambling', while a silk manufacturer from Spitalfields – another area of the capital marked by increasing poverty, under- and unemployment, as the London silk industry declined from the second half of the eighteenth century, and as average real wages in the capital stagnated or fell – referred to women clubbing together, each paying a penny, to raise a shilling to insure a number for a day.[108]

We can only guess at the scale on which illegal lottery insurance businesses operated. Contemporary estimates put the number of illegal insurance offices (see Figure 2.1) at any one time in the capital in the later eighteenth century at between 400 and 700.[109] Yet, if anything, this seriously understates their ubiquity because of how the insurers operated, especially from the end of the eighteenth century. Many of them employed agents. These were the morocco men and women, so-called because of the small red, leather-bound books which they carried in order to record the premiums paid by clients. Such agents typically appear to have operated from their homes or in taverns and shops across the capital. When in 1791 Elizabeth Simms asked Henry Oldfield to 'insure' the number 543 for a guinea should it be drawn a blank or prize

[106] PP, 1808 (323), Reports from the Committee on the Laws Relating to Lotteries, Appendix (A), examination of Paul Groves, p. 28, where he testified that those making lottery insurances were 'very various at times; sometimes very decent people, and sometimes all orders'.

[107] See *inter alia*, *Seasonable Words of Advice to All Such as are Concerned In the Lottery* (1780); *A letter From the Grave, Communicated in a Vision By Mr Holman's Late Servant: Addressed to Servants of All Denominations* (London, 1792); *WEP*, 10 Jan. 1782; *PA*, 15 Jan. 1782; *Morning Herald*, 30 July 1782; *MChr*, 11 Jan. 1773, 21 Nov., 14 Dec. 1774, 9 Jan. 1782; *LEP*, 19 Jan. 1773.

[108] PP, 1808 (323), Reports from the Committee on the Laws Relating to Lotteries, Appendix (A), examination of James Bligh, p. 42; examination of William Hale, p. 58.

[109] See ch. 3, no. 97, p. 150.

Figure 2.1 Print of a lottery insurance office, 1790. Lottery insurance offices were present throughout the British capital by the later eighteenth century, while lottery insurance was widely believed to be particularly appealing and destructive to the labouring classes, here emphasized by the representatives of these classes – e.g. the tailor in the foreground, the butcher towards the back – depicted in ragged clothes, and captive to the delusive hopes and despair which were viewed as inextricably part of the experience of the lottery and, indeed, gaming in general. © Trustees of the British Museum.

on a stated day, Oldfield was sitting at a table in a house in Sandfield Lane in the parish of St John Hackney.[110] Two years later, Hannah David met William Bowden, a brazier by trade, in Hoxton town and went with him to the Queen's Head alehouse where she insured a number in the English lottery to be drawn a blank or prize on the 23rd day of the draw.[111] In the previous year it was claimed that 'almost all the

110 LMA, Middlesex Sessions, Sessions Papers, MJ/SP/1791/04/015, examination of Elizabeth Simms, 7 Mar. 1791.

111 LMA, Middlesex Sessions, Sessions Papers, MJ/SP/1793/04/141, examination of Hannah David, 7 Mar. 1793.

Public Houses in the City and Liberty of Westminster and County of Middlesex of every description' permitted illegal lottery insurance agents to operate on their premises, including frequently allowing them to hire rooms for this purpose.[112] Morocco men also seem to have conducted a good deal of business in shops commonly patronized by the lower orders, such as green grocers and chandlers.[113]

Third, related to this, illegal lottery insurance was a highly commercialized, tightly organized operation. In some, perhaps many, cases agents were acting for legal lottery businesses, which needed the additional revenue from this kind of insurance to make them profitable.[114] The famous lottery contractor, Thomas Bish, admitted on one occasion to trading in this way.[115] As with gaming houses, the layout of and access to illegal lottery offices were carefully designed to facilitate evasion of the unwanted attentions of agents of the law.[116] Agents who were imprisoned for being 'lottery vagrants' were, it was reported, provided with a regular financial allowance whilst under lock and key. Witnesses were regularly bribed to undermine prosecutions, and hostile legal actions launched against constables who executed warrants to search premises believed to be illegal lottery insurance offices.[117] Colquhoun hints that there was considerable coordination between the operators of illegal insurance, insofar as smaller-scale operations would sell on their premiums to larger businesses. He suggested in one place that profit margins may have been as high as between 15% and 25%, and in another a whopping 33½%, which helps to explain the enormous scale on which it operated, but also its resilience.[118] The fact that much illegal lottery insurance was clearly fraudulent – in that its operators had no intention of paying winners – and that this did not undermine its credibility speaks

112 LMA, MJ/O/C/012, Middlesex Sessions, Orders of Court, 28 Oct. 1789–5 Dec. 1795, Oct. 1792.

113 PP, 1808 (323), Reports from the Committee on the Laws Relating to Lotteries, Appendix (A), examination of Theophilus Bellis, attorney and assistant to a police magistrate, p. 26; examination of Robert Baker, police magistrate, Hatton Garden, p. 53, referring to two cases of illegal insurance, one a 'woman of respectable appearance' in a greengrocer's shop in Bloomsbury and another a waiter in an alehouse in Tottenham Court Road.

114 PP, 1808 (323), Reports from the Committee on the Laws Relating to Lotteries, Appendix (A), examination of Thomas Bish, p. 18; examination of Theophilus Bellis, p. 26; examination of Edward Shewell, p. 65. After 1803, it was also only the licensed lottery offices which could officially gain access to the numerical books in which the results of the draw were recorded, which was crucial to the illegal insurance business.

115 PP, 1808 (323), Reports from the Committee on the Laws Relating to Lotteries, Appendix (A), examination of Thomas Bish, p. 17.

116 See ch. 5, p. 240.

117 For which, see further ch. 5, pp. 246–7, 251.

118 Colquhoun, *Treatise*, p. 142, 159; PP, 1808 (323), Reports from the Committee on the Laws Relating to Lotteries, Appendix (A), examination of Patrick Colquhoun, p. 36.

volumes about the eagerness of many for opportunities to gamble in this way. Colquhoun also suggests that it was the operators of illegal insurance who were behind the 'Little Goes', small-scale private lotteries which proliferated from the end of the eighteenth century, and which were organized when the Irish and English lottery draws were not taking place.[119] These were designed, Colquhoun claims, to lure people into betting on the official draws by familiarizing them with this type of betting. There is no way to corroborate whether this was true, although it seems very plausible because their operators were selling insurances in exactly the same way as the illegal lottery offices – in other words, people were simply betting on the outcome of a draw of numbers.[120] Moreover, as illegal lottery insurance diminished, owing mainly to a reduction in the duration of lottery draws after 1803, so Little Goes became much more common, further hinting at the closeness of their relationship.[121]

2.6 Metropolitan Popular Gambling: Roles and Meanings

If gambling was common throughout metropolitan society, among women and men, can we say more about the specific roles which it played? Some people were, inevitably, lured into deep or persistent gambling well beyond what their incomes could readily bear. One newspaper reported in early April 1776 that a tradesman had in one night lost 200 guineas at a noted gaming house near St James's Market.[122] Witnesses before the 1808 Commons committee on the laws relating to

[119] Colquhoun, *Treatise*, p. 152.

[120] See e.g. LMA, Middlesex Justices, Sessions Papers, MJ/SP/1795/10/032, examination of Ann Jones of No. 6, Willow Walk in the Parish of St Leonard Shoreditch, 16 Sept. 1795. Jones was informing on a private lottery held in Goswell Street in Clerkenwell run by a certain O'Connor, a black man. Jones insured two numbers on consecutive evenings to be drawn blanks or prizes, paying on the first evening 2s to receive a guinea if one of their numbers was drawn, and 13d on the second evening to receive half a guinea in the same event. On the second evening, 100 numbers of had been drawn in the presence of around 20 people, and no prizes and no insured numbers had been drawn. See also LMA, MJ/SP/1795/10/038 I, examination of James Pegler, bookseller of Chatham Gardens and Anne Clark, 28 Sept. 1795; MJ/SP/1795/09/039 ii, Examination of Robert Banks of Phenix [sic] Street in the Parish of Christ Church, victualler & Mary Peters, widow, 24 Aug. 1795. Pegler and Clark had met one Thomas Bunhill in Islington, and paid 2s11d for insuring a number in a private lottery to gain 5 guineas if the said number was drawn on 8 August.

[121] Who actually lay behind the staging of these private lotteries is unclear, and the suspicion must be that those operating them were acting as agents for other interests. Colquhoun told a parliamentary committee in 1808 that 'principals themselves' were in the 'background'. PP, 1808 (323), Reports from the Committee on the Laws Relating to Lotteries, Appendix (A), examination of Patrick Colquhoun, p. 36; ibid., examination of Richard Baker, p. 54.

[122] *MChr*, 3 Apr. 1776.

lotteries narrated various tales of tradespeople, servants, and people from the lower orders driven to penury through contracting a rage for lottery insurance.[123] Contemporaries worried about particular groups among the population who were considered especially vulnerable to profligate gambling, notably the young in the middle and higher ranks. Those with access to their employers' money might be tempted to steal in order to gamble, such as the three clerks to city merchants who were dismissed for this reason in January 1778.[124] Domestic servants, especially those who worked for the fashionable classes, were believed to be unusually prone to illegal lottery insurance, incapable of resisting the delusory appeal of easy wealth, together with the independence, comfort, and luxury which this would bring.[125]

If illegal lottery insurance was normally viewed by magistrates, police officers, and social commentators as a pernicious, destructive snare for women and the labouring poor, there was, it bears reiterating, no single popular gambling culture in London. Rather, there existed multiple cultures and practices, which overlapped at different points, but were, nevertheless, quite different in basic character. While we can talk about the rise and growing influence of professional and semi-professional if not outright criminal gamblers seeking to gull the incautious and naïve, much gambling remained basically recreational, as it had been before c.1700, involving the playing of games – backgammon, bowls, and so forth – involving stakes of a halfpenny or penny a game, or some other similarly modest sum. This was in some ways the equivalent to the card playing for small stakes which consumed much of the leisure time of a very wide cross section of the propertied classes in the eighteenth century. There was more overlap in leisure activities between these different sections of society than the 'polite' usually wished to believe, albeit the upper ranks and middling sort were more likely to indulge this pleasure in one another's homes, and in both hetero- and homosocial gatherings.[126] Critics of popular leisure, such as Henry Fielding in the mid eighteenth century, tended to view the recreational practices of the lower orders through a very distorted lens, one informed by their often gloomy fears about social order and crime. There was a very obvious class bias here, insofar as views of gambling could be starkly bifurcated: upper class gambling might be reprehensible, but was not immediately threatening to

[123] See e.g. PP, 1808 (323), Reports from the Committee on the Laws Relating to Lotteries, Appendix (A), examination of the Rev William Gurney, rector of St Clement Danes and minister to the Free Chapel, West St, St Giles, p. 57.

[124] *GEP*, 8 Jan. 1778. [125] See ch. 3, pp. 170–1.

[126] See Janet E. Mullin, *A Sixpence at Whist: Gaming and the English Middle Classes, 1680–1830* (Woodbridge, 2015).

society; idleness among the poor, by contrast, threatened social order and prosperity. Equally striking about such commentary is how it served to occlude the habits and activities of many among the middling ranks and skilled labouring classes, eliding them with the poor or the 'mob'.

Betting, however, was an integral element of a competitive recreational culture which embraced much of particularly the capital's male population from across the social spectrum. This might just be compatible in some cases with the polite values about which historians have written extensively.[127] Yet any congruence was at best deeply uneasy, and in reality the relationship was fraught with tensions, as indicated by the fact that there was little agreement on whether cricket, for example, was a harmless 'rustick' diversion, a training for manhood, or, by contrast, symptomatic of the viciousness and corruption of contemporary society.[128] More often than not this competitive culture derived from and was a prominent facet of very firmly entrenched and pervasive currents within metropolitan leisure and recreation which were anything but polite, being characterized rather by delight in spectacle and novelty, and commonly involving violence and brutality towards other human beings or animals.[129] Such entertainments might be promoted on a thoroughly commercial basis, as in the well-publicized boxing contests put on in the mid eighteenth century by Jack Broughton at his Tottenham Court Road Booth under the patronage of the Duke of Cumberland, or cockfights and animal baiting which were sponsored by tavern keepers or, in the former case, staged in dedicated cockpits,

[127] The recent literature on this topic is too vast to list anyway comprehensively here; but see, *inter alia*, Paul Langford, *A Polite and Commercial People: England 1727–1789* (Oxford, 1989); Paul Langford, 'The Uses of Eighteenth Century Politeness', *Transactions of the Royal Historical Society*, 6th ser., 12 (2002), 311–31; Lawrence E. Klein, 'The Polite Town: the Shifting Possibilities of Urbaness, 1660–1715', in Tim Hitchcock and Heather Shore (eds.), *The Streets of London: From the Great Fire to the Great Stink* (London, 2003), pp. 27–39, 217–9; Lawrence E. Klein, 'Politeness and the Interpretation of the British Eighteenth Century', *Historical Journal*, 45 (2002), 889–98.

[128] *The World*, 14 Mar. 1754; *Gentle Reflections on the Short but Serious Reasons for a National Militia* (London, 1757), p. 9; William Buchan, *Domestic Medicine: Or A Treatise on the Prevention and Cure of Diseases by Regimen and Simple Medicines* (London, 1769), p. 105; *LChr*, 31 Dec. 1774; *London Magazine* (1775), p. 272; [Rev. J. Trusler] *Principles of Politeness and of Knowing the World. By the Late Lord Chesterfield Methodised and Digested* (London, 1775), p. 71; *LEP*, 10 Sept. 1778.

[129] When James Boswell visited the Royal Cockpit in 1762, he was shocked by the reaction of the audience to the suffering of the birds. *Boswell's London Journal 1762–1763*, ed. Frederick A. Pottle (London and New Haven, 1950), p. 87: 'I looked around to see if the spectators pitied them when mangled and torn in a most cruel manner, but I could not observe the smallest relenting sign in any countenance.' For a fascinating commentary on the persistence and depth of this impulse, see Simon Dickie, *Cruelty & Laughter: Forgotten Comic Literature and the Unsentimental Eighteenth Century* (Chicago, 2011).

such as the Royal Cockpit in St James's Park. As Underdown has noted, it could draw in people of quite high social rank, as evident in the rowing matches staged on the Thames from the mid eighteenth century, which involved young men from the elites rowing alongside professional watermen, or, indeed, many of the cricketing contests with which this chapter began.[130] A good deal of this activity, however, was spontaneous and small scale, and could involve, for example, crowds gathering around street fights and betting on the outcome. The Frenchman and visitor to London, P. J. Grosley, noted how such fights were often conducted according to an informal set of rules and sense of fair play, something closely related to the betting to which they could give rise, mirroring the drive to rule-making in those organized sports – horse racing, cricket, and boxing – patronized by the elites.[131] Challenges and contests of bewildering variety frequently emerged from a tavern-based male sociability or perhaps the distinctive occupational cultures which were such a marked feature of contemporary London. Many of these featured in brief reports in the newspapers, which is how we know about them; and while such reports were often unspecific about the identities of those involved, cumulatively they convey a strong impression of just how widely and regularly they occurred.

Some of these contests were, to be sure, between people of quite high social rank. In 1769, for example, a Barnet ostler wrote to the newspapers complaining about the derogation from the proper character of a gentleman of a young man who had, for large bets, ridden two miles across Barnet Common at a gallop, standing upright in his stirrups.[132] Such challenges might involve substantial financial stakes, or derive from the habit of betting recorded in the betting books of elite clubs of the period. Yet, equally apparent, as already stated, is that versions of this practice pervaded a much wider cross section of society. Thus, to take several examples at random: in 1788 a blacksmith wagered 20 guineas on running backwards for 1 mile in 6 minutes, which he followed by undertaking to walk a mile blindfolded in 15 minutes for a similar sum; a brickmaker moulded 1,004 bricks in a hour; a man jumped off Blackfriars Bridge; a hairdresser walked to York for 100 guineas, quickly

[130] Underdown, *Start of Play*, p. 82.

[131] P. J. Grosley, *A Tour to London: or, New Observations on England, and its Inhabitants* (2 vols., London, 1772), I, pp. 62–5. For details of circumstances surrounding the death of a Richard Aris following a fight in the Bell tavern which led to several challenges to fight in the street with betting on the outcome, see Westminster Archives, Coroner's Inquests, 1760–1771, Richard Aris, St Margaret's Parish, 9 Dec. 1766.

[132] *Gazetteer and New Daily Advertiser*, 1 Sept. 1769.

followed by a tailor who undertook to walk there and back from Bedford Row; while three years earlier, the press reported several eating contests, including one involving a cabby who choked to death.[133]

Just how enmeshed this type of betting was in the lives and culture of London's lower orders is suggested by a curious episode related in a contemporary memoir of the life of Sam House, Westminster tavern keeper and noted plebeian politician of the 1760s–1780s.[134] House, as John Brewer noted some years ago, became a very visible embodiment of plebeian political culture in London (see Figure 2.2), a culture deeply rooted in the taverns and clubs of tradesmen and artisans that flourished in London and Westminster during the Wilkite years and the subsequent rise of Charles James Fox as Westminster MP and 'man of the people'.[135] House's *Life* is not a simple record of his activities and personality; it is as much a statement of the values and ideology which informed and gave substance to a robust libertarian politics of political independence in Westminster in this period. In his steadfast adherence to his principles, depth of belief in liberty, benevolence and generosity, disregard for conventional behaviour, and even singular dress, the Sam House figured in this text was an encapsulation of a particular political identity. For our purposes, however, this almost certainly makes more illuminating and culturally significant the reported incident with which he launched a bid for metropolitan celebrity.

This incident involved an entirely naked Sam jumping off the new Westminster Bridge for a bet. It was illustrative of House's masculine bravado – the text made much of the literal exposure of his manhood, he was also apparently unable to swim – his unconcern for a certain model of propriety, and his exhibitionism, which was often unconscious but, in this instance, entirely calculated.[136] No doubt, some of what was related can be taken with a pinch of salt, in that it was clearly a deliberately exaggerated retelling of the event. Yet, this in itself tells us much about such incidents, the celebrity that they could engender, and the very public nature of this kind of behaviour. In some ways, moreover, it was merely an extension of the self-fashioning that surrounded much popular gambling engaged in by men of the lower orders. Such posturing and activity were a choice – you could obviously opt to eschew gambling, and

[133] *Times*, 8 Jan, 21 July, 24 Sept., 22 Nov. 1785; 30 May, 15, 22 July, 16 Aug., 8 Sept. 1788.

[134] *The Life and Political Opinions of the Late Sam House: Interspersed with Curious Anecdotes and Amorous Intrigues of this Singular and Distinguished Character* (London, 1785).

[135] John Brewer, 'Theatre and Counter Theatre in Georgian Politics: The Mock Elections at Garrat', *Radical History Review*, 22 (1980), 7–40.

[136] *Life and Political Opinions*, pp. 9–11.

Figure 2.2 Print by Thomas Rowlandson depicting the Westminster tavern keeper, plebeian politician, and supporter of Charles James Fox, Sam House, published in 1780. One of House's early exploits was to offer a public challenge to jump off the new Westminster Bridge. A culture of challenges was pervasive in metropolitan society in the eighteenth century, most of which were linked very closely to betting. © Trustees of the British Museum.

quite a few (even many perhaps) did – but it was, nevertheless, very much part of the world of artisans, tradesmen, and labourers in this period, and reflected a sense of selfhood constructed around sharply gendered ideas of independence. There were other conceptions of independence at this level of society, which emphasized self-improvement, the exercise of reason, sobriety, and respectability, which could be either religious or secular in origin, and which would become more influential from the end of the eighteenth century, in the following decades working to reshape and fracture in new ways the culture of the working classes of the nineteenth century. Yet, House's version, with its valorization of physical and sexual vitality, its embrace of a bibulous, unconstrained conviviality was almost certainly more common for most of this period. The widespread and ready tolerance of brutal sports, raucous recreation, and sexual license were other sides to this same culture. Nor were such things limited to the lower orders; rather men of higher social ranks frequently exhibited similar habits and behaviours, albeit on a more selective, conditional basis. As Gatrell has recently emphasized, although with reference mainly to the social elites, it was politeness that can seem somewhat precariously superimposed on top of an older set of unrespectable values, what Boswell once called those of the 'true-born old Englishman'.[137] What may also be true is that it was among the mercantile middling ranks that there was strongest resistance to its appeal, with members of this social stratum more likely to assume a form of social identity in adulthood constructed around notions of propriety or moderation, personal virtue, and trustworthiness.[138]

London saw, then, considerable continuity with earlier periods in the types of gambling that it nurtured and sustained during the long eighteenth century. Increasingly overlaid, however, on top of these were new opportunities and milieu in which to gamble, especially where sports and betting cultures intersected, but also in the form of the lottery and its various derivatives, and something which we might fairly describe as a commercial gambling industry, focused on gaming houses, Tattersalls, lottery insurance offices, and, indeed, city insurance offices. It was in London that 'professional gamblers' were most visible, from the common sharpers who infested the capital's taverns, streets, and open spaces, to the 'blacklegs' and 'gamesters' who were to be found in the gaming houses or Tattersalls, and who plied their trade in close

[137] Vic Gatrell, *City of Laughter: Sex and Satire in Eighteenth Century London* (London, 2006), esp. pp. 15–19; *Boswell's London Journal*, ed. Pottle, p. 86.

[138] See esp. Margaret R. Hunt, *The Middling Sort: Commerce, Gender, and the Family in England, 1680–1780* (Berkeley, CA, 1996).

proximity to that part of the fashionable world which sought competition, pleasure, absorption in sport and betting, a loose grouping increasingly by the early nineteenth century that was developing, or having conferred on it, a distinctive cultural identity and label – 'The Fancy'.

2.7 Beyond London

Given its dominant position in the urban hierarchy – one which was only slowly, cumulatively eroded in the decades following c.1760 – and the density of connections between the British capital and the rest of Britain, where London led other places tended to follow or exhibit similar tendencies, albeit these usually remain less visible to the historian. In Edinburgh, coffee houses and taverns furnished customers with billiard tables from the early eighteenth century, and were, it seems, common sites of gaming.[139] In 1759, Edinburgh's magistrates conducted an enquiry into the numbers of billiard tables in the city, uncovering ten within the city proper, and three in what were strictly suburbs, but still formed part of the main footprint of the Scottish capital – for example, Canongate. Convinced that 'almost the whole of these tables are frequented by Students, apprentice boyes and persones of the lowest class of Mankind', it was recommended not only that the city council suppress these sorts of tables, but that magistrates be given the authority to license tables, but only where these were patronized by 'persones of Rank & fashion'.[140] We saw in the previous chapter that it was in several of the Scottish capital's taverns off the High Street that James Boswell and his comrades gambled on this and other games. Cockpits joined bowling greens in many places, while taverns throughout Britain had long been sites of gambling of various kinds, as court records amply attest, and continued to be so. Bristol, for example, England's second city at the turn of the eighteenth century, saw an upsurge of magisterial and public concern about tavern gambling in the later seventeenth century linked to the emergent reformation of manners movement. In January 1684, one presentment complained:

That the number of ale houses & tipling houses licensed & allowed throughout the whole city is now very excessive & exorbitant & much greater than formerly;

[139] In 1704, the Edinburgh magistrates issued an order against playing at cards and dice in the city's coffee houses and taverns. (NRS, GD50/198, 12 Apr. 1704, Act against Playing at Cards and Dice, etc. in Edinburgh coiffee-houses, taverns, etc.).

[140] ECA, McLeod Collection, D, 118, item 238, report of magistrates and convenor about billiard tables, 21 Feb. 1759. See also D, 114, item 19, act of council against billiard tables, 21 Feb. 1759. This appears to have led to action being taken against four individuals for keeping billiard tables.

> By which means & by unlawfull games set up & kept by many of them who keep such houses, some of the youth are greatly debauched & others are in great danger of debauchery, diverse Artific[e]rs and labouring men misspend [sic] to much of their time & money in drinking, tipling & gaming there …

It was also claimed that inns for respectable travellers had fallen thereby into decay and the city's poor 'exceedingly increased'.[141] Six years later, the keeper of the city's bowling green was presented for hosting there a billiard table, which drew 'servants & others' to play at the expense of their masters.[142] Forty years or so later, the inventory drawn up at the death of a shipmaster and former bailie of Dundee included various pieces of gaming equipment from a coffee house, including a billiard table, chess and dame boards, with counters, and four pairs of what were listed as 'ballyalmond tables'.[143] In the early nineteenth century, a Dundee spirit dealer advertised for sale an 'excellent Billiard-table, with a wainscot top; also, a quantity of Ques and Maces'. 'The table', the same advertisement declared, 'had been long in use, and found to give general satisfaction'.[144]

Sharpers from London toured provincial race meetings and fairs in pursuit of new victims. In 1757, Sir John Fielding cooperated with Guildford magistrates, including sending two of the Bow Street runners to the Surrey town, to suppress an 'E.O.' table which had been set up by several people from London in the Red Lion tavern there during the local races.[145] A newspaper reported from Ludlow in 1778 that the 'celebrated Lord Jones', who was 'well known at Bow Street', had been apprehended at the Ludlow fair for keeping an 'E.O.' table there. The local magistrates fined Jones 40 sh., broke up his gaming table, and turned him over to a recruiting serjeant in the army, but Jones had given him the slip. The magistrates had broken up more 'E.O.' tables, reflecting, the report said, 'their determination … to root out all species of gambling whatever, as most of the games played are introduced by town sharpers, who plunder the poor, and by thieves who rob country farmers of their pocket books, and defraud them of their goods and cattle'.[146] Like horse race meetings,

141 Bristol Record Office, JQS/C/1, Presentments 1676–1700, fo. 112, and passim. Ten years later (in 1694), a similar presentment called for constables to search in their respective wards for tavern keepers who had skittle alleys, billiard tables, or any other unlawful games on their premises and to prosecute offenders with the proper force of the law because 'many poor women & their families want at home what their husbands & fathers dayly spend on such unlawful exercises'.

142 Op. cit., April 1689.

143 NRS, Commissary Court Papers, St Andrews Commissary Court, Register of Testaments, CC3/3/110, 289–93, testament of Patrick Scot, 1737.

144 *Dundee, Perth and Cupar Advertiser*, 16 Aug. 1816.

145 *London Chronicle*, June 1757.

146 *GEP*, 13 Oct. 1778.

the association between fairs – which continued to be key fixtures in local and regional recreational calendars throughout this period, and for a wide cross section of society – and gambling of various kinds – from games such as 'E.O.', dice games, to wheels of fortune and so on – was a very strong one.[147]

Meanwhile, a striking and rarely emphasized feature of the second wave of the development of boxing as an organized, commercial sport between c.1780 and c.1820 is that while many of the most notable contests were held at a location in London, or at Newmarket, where London's fashionable elite descended for the major race meetings of the year, a good number were staged in other places across Britain. What may partly explain this is the search for places where jurisdictions were disputed, which might help promoters of these contests avoid magisterial and legal efforts to prevent them. That or these sites were linked to aristocratic patrons of boxing or regular resorts of the sporting set, such as the Doncaster race course, for example.[148] But it was also a measure of the growing vibrancy and commercialization of a provincial sporting culture, as well as provincial interest in such contests, an interest which a dynamic, rapidly expanding national and provincial press served to sustain and deepen.[149] Celebrated boxers, such as Daniel Mendoza in 1790 and 1791, toured Britain, staging demonstrations and boxing lessons, following the extensive touring circuits undertaken by growing numbers of performers of various kinds, exhibitions, and scientific lecturers. This was part of a wider process of cultural blending and convergence, one in which province and metropole were, increasingly, equally

147 See e.g. notice in *London Chronicle*, 17 Nov. 1759 concerning army deserter, Richard Wingate, from Chestone, Wilts, who was said to gain his subsistence by 'Gambling and Slight of Hand, and frequents all the fairs round this part of England'. See also *GEP*, 12 Nov. 1751, for report of commitment of a man and his two sons-in-law to the Surrey bridewell. They claimed to be dealers in hardware and chapmen from Bristol, who traded at local fairs. However, a search of their belongings revealed, among other things, a wallet containing a large quantity of false dice, tetotums, painting cloths with representations on them of guineas and other figures. The court took them to be disorderly gamblers and vagrants, and they were committed to hard labour. For a recent examination of the fortunes and wider cultural significance of provincial fairs in eighteenth-century England, see Jessica Davidson, 'The Social and Cultural History of the Provincial Fair in England, 1750–1850', unpublished D.Phil. thesis, University of Oxford (2019).

148 Dennis Brailsford, *Bareknuckles: A Social History of Prizefighting* (Cambridge, 1988); John Ford, *Prizefighting: The Age of Regency Boximania* (Devon, 1971).

149 The role of the press in promoting and encouraging interest in sport in the early nineteenth century is emphasized by Adrian Harvey, *The Beginnings of a Commercial Sporting Culture in Britain, 1793–1850* (Aldershot, 2004). Harvey talks of a transformation in press coverage of sport from 1792.

active.[150] It is a pattern which becomes even more sharply discernable in the case of the rise of another sporting activity from the later eighteenth century, one extremely closely related to boxing – namely, pedestrianism or in other words foot racing. It is to certain aspects of this, and the betting cultures associated with it, that we turn in the final section of this chapter.

2.8 Pedestrianism and Cultures of Betting in the Later Georgian Period

In so far as pedestrianism has attracted attention from historians, which is, in any case, much less than boxing, it is (as already noted) in respect mainly of its popularity in the nineteenth century, especially in northern manufacturing towns and cities and their environs by the 1830s. Pedestrianism, on this view, provides a bridge between the world of eighteenth- and early-nineteenth century sports and the rise of professional football and the sporting world of the later nineteenth century. Also noted has been the emergence at the turn of the nineteenth century of national foot racing celebrities, alongside boxers such as Mendoza, among whom Captain Barclay of Aberdeen stands out.[151] What historians have not to date attempted is to plot a trajectory from Barclay's world to that of the 1830s and onwards.

Before attempting, however, to do this, we need to acknowledge a very basic, but nevertheless important, fact: while walking may have taken on new cultural visibility and freight in Britain at the turn of the nineteenth century – as signified by pedestrian travel guides, peripatetic poetry, and journals of walking tours – feats of pedestrianism (of different kinds) were common long before then and across much of Britain. The diarist Samuel Pepys attests to the widespread popularity of foot racing in the London of the 1660s.[152] In 1759, when the Rev George Woodward was returning to his parish of East Hendred, Berkshire, in a coach crossing Hounslow Heath, he and his fellow travellers espied 'a gentlemen in a white flannel waistcoat, walking very fast'. It turned out that Lord

[150] See Peter Radford, 'Lifting the Spirits of the Nation: British Boxers and the Emergence of the National Sporting Hero at the time of the Napoleonic Wars', *Identities: Global Studies in Culture and Power*, 12 (2005), 249–70; Karen Downing, 'Boxing, Manners, and Masculinity in Eighteenth Century England', *Men and Masculinities*, 12 (2010), 328–52; John Whale, 'Daniel Mendoza's Contests of Identity: Masculinity, Ethnicity and Nation in Georgian Prize-Fighting', *Romanticism*, 14 *(2008)*, 259–71.

[151] See n. 51.

[152] Earl R. Anderson, 'Footnotes More Pedestrian than Sublime: A Historical Background for the Foot-Races in Evelina and Humphry Clinker', *Eighteenth-Century Studies*, 14 (1980), 62.

Carnarvon had made a wager with this individual that he could not walk to Reading in less than 16 hours.[153] From his residence at New Inn in London in the early 1760s, Foster Powell, a native of Yorkshire, launched a career of walking feats which lasted several decades, and which featured four timed walks to York and back. In 1792, Powell walked from Shoreditch Church to York Minister in 5 days, 15 hours, and 15 minutes, which beat his previous best, set in 1773, of 5 days and 18 hours. While these expeditions were associated with gambling, and attracted much public attention, Powell died in relative poverty in 1793.[154] Joseph Strutt, who penned the first major history of English sports, declared in 1801:

In the present day foot-races are not much encouraged by persons of fortune, and seldom happen *but for the purpose of betting*, and the racers are generally paid for their performance. In many instances the distance does not exceed one hundred yards. At fairs, wakes, and upon many other occasions where many people are assembled together, this species of amusement is sometimes promoted, but most frequently the contest is confined to the younger part of the concourse.[155] (My emphasis.)

Strutt's words are ambiguous, and he may have been unduly focused on the famous contests and exploits. But as he acknowledged, races for betting purposes continued to flourish. In 1789, for example, for what was described as a 'considerable wager' the servant of an Edinburgh butcher walked 9 miles on the Queensferry Road in less than an hour and a half.[156] The diffusion of ownership of portable watches, which reached well down and across society, must have helped to facilitate the judging of these and other types of challenge against the clock, while new turnpike roads, with much better surfaces in some cases than earlier roads, made pedestrian challenges easier to stage and, indeed, spectate on.[157]

People in the eighteenth century and earlier walked, in short, far more and far further than is commonly acknowledged, for reasons of

[153] *A Parson in the Vale of White Horse: George Woodwards's Letters from East Hendred, 1753–1761*, ed. Donald Gibson (Sutton, 1983), pp. 120–1.

[154] Philip Carter, 'Powell, Foster (bap. 1734, d. 1793)', *Oxford Dictionary of National Biography*, accessed online 1 Apr. 2020 [https://ezproxy-prd.bodleian.ox.ac.uk: 2095/10.1093/ref:odnb/22645]. Powell also for a few years staged exhibitions of pedestrianism in France and Switzerland.

[155] Strutt, *The Sports and Pastimes of the People of England (1801)*, ed. J. Charles Cox (London, 1898), p. 143, cited in Anderson, 'Footraces', 63.

[156] Edinburgh Central Library, Y DA 1861.789, journal of Andrew Armstrong, 1789–93, fo. 51, entry for 19 May 1789.

[157] For watch ownership, see John Styles, *The Dress of the People: Everyday Fashion in Eighteenth-Century England* (New Haven and London, 2007), pp. 97–107.

occupation, recreation (including betting) or, indeed, their mental well-being. As a young man Samuel Johnson famously walked from Lichfield to Birmingham and back in an effort to conquer his periodic bouts of oppressive melancholy.[158] Few, however, can have matched the heroic peregrinations of John 'Walking' Stewart, who criss-crossed continental Europe on foot. In the service of the East India Company, he traversed India before taking a route around the Persian Gulf into Africa, reaching Southern Ethiopia before stepping onto and into unmapped Central Africa. In later years, he walked across the United States and Canada. Stewart's religion and politics were highly unorthodox; but the association between walking and radicalism was one which would recur down through the decades to present day.[159]

Historians of walking have barely begun to acknowledge its importance well before the end of the eighteenth century, including for the labouring classes; and the continuities in this context between the eighteenth and nineteenth centuries are strong ones. This might in the case of Londoners entail strolling out into the environs of the capital on a Sunday, but walking expeditions could involve considerably longer distances and greater time spent travelling. Dumfries merchant, William Grierson, and his close circle of male friends were regular walkers in the 1790s.[160] The Dundee radical of the 1790s, the weaver George Mealmaker was a figure in perpetual motion, but he was no more than was typical of men of his ilk.[161] This was one of the reasons that radical politics spread so readily in this era between towns and industrial villages in manufacturing regions, and could continue to exist (however debilitated by repression) beyond the fearful scrutiny of the authorities. Already by the 1810s the question of access, of provision of footpaths and public walks, was rearing its head, an issue which would become increasingly contentious by the central decades of the nineteenth century, as industrial towns and cities expanded their footprints and became ever more densely populated, and common land disappeared or was divided and rented out by town councils in pursuit of additional revenue. As one contemporary declared: 'Footpaths are chiefly used for the

[158] *Boswell: The Applause of the Jury 1782–1785*, eds. Irma S. Lustig and Frederick A. Pottle (New Haven and London, 1982), p. 100.

[159] Barry Symonds, 'Stewart, John (*called* Walking Stewart) (1747–1822)', *Oxford Dictionary of National Biography*, accessed online, 1 May 2020 [https://exproxy-prd.bodleian.ox.ac.uk: 2095/10.1093/ref:odnb/26494]. For the association between radicalism and walking, see Rebecca Solnit, *Wunderlust: A History of Walking* (2001).

[160] *An Apostle of Burns: the Diaries of William Grierson*, ed. J. Davies (Edinburgh, 1981).

[161] Bob Harris, *The Scottish People and the French Revolution* (London, 2008), p. 92.

young; who, after the toils of the day, speed to the suburbs, to breathe the fresh air of the country.'[162]

At one level pedestrianism proper was simply the product of the conjunction of just how common walking was as a form of recreation and activity and a culture of competitive betting and challenges which, as we saw earlier, flourished among men of very different social rank. This might mean no more than a group of friends or acquaintances sitting in a tavern and fixing on a particular feat, created partly in order to bet on, including races of different and often idiosyncratic sorts; or it might be a contest perhaps sponsored by an innkeeper. Joseph Woolley, a Nottinghamshire stocking weaver, describes something which may have combined both elements in his diary for 1804:

> Some time in February Thomas Cuttler ran a race a hundred yards for a leg of mutton at Nottingham wich he won and he ran forty yards with Cheetham for one shilling which he won they had the leg of mutton at mr <danns?> in narow march and they joined it to another Leg that was won by another person and had a super I was invited to it but did not Go John barker and Thomas Shallam did and a very Good Company there was at super and they spent the night quite to their satisfaction and our towns people staid all night.

A few years previously, another local man, William Barker, had lost a race for £1.2.0 and another one for 2sh. 6d.[163] Intriguingly, the winner of one of these races, a John Brooks, may well have been the same John Brooks, a shoemaker, who some weeks later put up a pair of shoes 'to shoot for', indicative of the intensely competitive culture which these men inhabited, which could as easily lead to fighting as to sporting challenges of this kind.[164] Increasingly by the late eighteenth century, however, pedestrianism involved self-styled 'professional sportsmen', such as Powell or, even more prominently, Barclay engaging in walking contests, usually under the patronage of members of the elites. In this pedestrianism has much in common with boxing. This was equally true in respect of how it was packaged, represented, and consumed, as an exhibition of patriotic manliness in an era of protracted war, one that both consciously looked backward to the ancient world's valorization of athletic masculinity, to traditional rough sports from which it claimed inheritance, but also forwards in the employment of scientific training

[162] *Dundee, Perth and Cupar Advertiser*, 1 May 1818.

[163] NA, DD 311/3, Joseph Woolley, Book of Memorandums for the Year 1804, fo. 93 (photocopy).

[164] NA, DD 311/1, Joseph Woolley, Book of Memorandums for the Year 1801, entry for 17 Feb. (photocopy). On the same occasion, in the evening two of the contenders for the shoes had a fight – it is not clear whether this was spontaneous – and one of these also wrestled with another man for a shillings worth of ale.

regimes (correct diet, the use of purgatives, sweating, and so forth). It offered reassurance of masculine virility at a moment when an unexampled proportion of the male population was mobilized in a variety of military forces, and when Britain faced invasion threats, and British and European liberty were gravely imperiled by Napoleonic tyranny. While Barclay did run in speed races, his speciality was endurance feats; they were evidence of his heroic stamina, or 'bottom' as contemporaries usually called it. Barclay was a lieutenant in the 22nd Foot Regiment, and a good number of his and other walking contests were against fellow military men.[165] With an estate in North East Scotland, Barclay was very much a *British* national hero. His feats were celebrated throughout the length and breadth of Britain, an embodiment of a conservative form of patriotism, which, in its sharply gendered emphases, and explicit invocation of manly independence, shared much in common with reformist and radical versions of patriotism by the early nineteenth century, as represented by, respectively, the Westminster MP and radical figurehead Sir Francis Burdett and in the writings of the radical journalist William Cobbett.[166]

If historians have in recent years been alert to the national significance and meanings of sport in this period, viewing it in the context of a process of nation-building in a period of acute international and domestic threat and tension, less often noticed have been how far the success of a figure such as Barclay or, indeed, successful celebrity boxers depended on flourishing local, amateur cultures of sport, ones which were encouraged and sustained by entrepreneurially minded tavern keepers. The importance of this is hinted at by references in press reports to the crowds of 'amateurs' who flocked to witness notable walking contests. The press was, it is true, crucial to the fabrication of a new kind of celebrity sports culture in this period, and men such as Barclay were acutely aware of the utility of publicity. Success was far from guaranteed, however, by the availability of the press. Rather, it was the way in which the races drew on and exploited an interest and excitement about such contests that were already deeply entrenched among the artisan and labouring classes, as well as sections of the propertied classes. The elite sportsman had many a counterpart in local town and village life, the type of individual who revelled in pitting their wits and belief in their own capacity and

165 Radford, *Celebrated Captain Barclay.*

166 See relevant comment in Ruti Ungar, 'The Construction of the Body Politic and the Politics of the Body: Boxing as Battle Ground for Conservatives and Radicals in Late Georgian England', *Sport in History*, 31 (2012), 363–80; Peter Spence, *The Birth of Romantic Radicalism: War, Popular Politics and English Radical Reformism, 1800–1815* (Aldershot, 1996).

judgement against their peers. This might involve involvement in foot racing, but it might also mean simply being willing to bet on the outcome of races both before and during them. The contests which gained national notoriety were to a large extent made possible because of the opportunity they offered notable elite sportsmen, such as Robert Fletcher of Ballinshoe in Angus, also a prominent member of the turf set, and professional gamblers to bet vertiginously vast sums of money. It is impossible to say with any certainty how widely or how far they attracted betting from people lower down the social scale, but the degree of interest they created among many below the level of the elites, including the labouring classes, is abundantly apparent, and the link between these, as well as the myriad other much less heralded contests and betting was extremely close.[167]

Second, behind national celebrities such as Barclay were an unknown number of local and regional sporting 'celebrities'. Barclay was unusual in that he was a member of the Aberdeenshire gentry, from a family with strong roots in north eastern Scottish landed society. Yet even in his case, much was made of his local roots and his family background.[168] Abraham Wood, against whom Barclay raced in 1809 in a famous endurance contest, was a Lancashire weaver, who began racing for small sums in his local region. It was these local sporting cultures, in which tavern keepers were important agents, which usually produced the national sporting celebrities. National cultures are in a sense always parasitic on local and regional cultures; one is impossible without the other. But there was more to it than this. For this was a period in which the local and regional gained new visibility and cultural significance precisely because of, first, the rise of British national culture and the impact of much greater national cultural integration; second, the fact that the idea of the British nation had become a much more intrusive force in society, owing to the impact of the French Revolutionary and Napoleonic wars and the defensive mobilization called forth by these conflicts; and third, the ways in which the forces of conservative reaction in this period, together with the strengthening sense that this was a moment of profound economic and social change, caused people to rethink their relationship to the past and in the process reinvent and rediscover popular culture. Several historians have in recent years emphasized the

167 As indicated, among other things, by the regular citing of odds on their outcome in press reports. See e.g. *Hampshire Telegraph*, 11 Aug. 1806; *MChr*, 13 Oct. 1807; *Morning Post*, 14 Oct. 1807.

168 *Aberdeen Journal*, 19 July 1809; *Leeds Mercury*, 17 Oct. 1807.

importance of regional constructions of Britishness.[169] However, local and regional identities were also projected nationally in new ways, and the development of pedestrianism reflected very closely these twin developments. It was not a case of a modern, national commercial culture meeting and interacting with a communal local one; both were modern and commercial in nature, as indicated by the continuing development of foot racing in many northern and several Welsh industrial towns. It also shows how gambling and betting among the lower orders continued to flourish in the early nineteenth century, this despite sharpened disapproval and the outright hostility of the growing ranks of religious evangelicals and an increasingly self-aware middle class for whom gambling and raucous, bibulous, and disorderly recreations among the lower orders were ideally to be suppressed in pursuit of respectability, virtue, and industry, and, not least, renewed social order.

2.9 Conclusion

As a form of discretionary expenditure, it is tempting to suppose that trends in the amount of gambling among the majority of the population broadly followed living standards – that is, higher real wages and thus disposable incomes meant more money, and potentially time – given especially that workers in many sectors of the economy were increasingly in the later part of our period paid by piece rates – to devote to gambling, whether this be merely recreational or something other. Even if this were very broadly the case – and there are plenty of serious qualifications which would need to be made to this proposition, such as the importance of cultural and religious factors in shaping leisure preferences – the myriad variations in economic fortunes according to occupation, age, household composition, and region mean that attempting to say on this basis whether gambling among the majority became more or less common in aggregate at different moments is futile. Moreover, any rises in living standards which did occur from the later eighteenth century may well have come at the cost of working for longer hours and more intensely, and because of increased contributions from children but also, and to a lesser extent, women to household wage economies.[170] People,

[169] See esp. Katrina Navickas, 'Lancashire Britishness: Patriotism in Manchester during the Napoleonic Wars', *Manchester Region History Review*, 23 (2012), 33–48; Oskar Cox Jensen, *Napoleon and British Song 1797–1822* (Basingstoke, 2015).

[170] Jane Humphries, 'Household Economy', in R. Floud and P. Johnson (eds.), *The Cambridge Economic History of Modern Britain, Vol. 1: Industrialisation, 1700–1860* (Cambridge, 2004), pp. 238–67.

moreover, do not tend to order their priorities according to the neat models of economic theory. The complaints of married women, which occasionally surface in contemporary court records, about the destructive gambling of their husbands in taverns are eloquent testimony to the competing and contested priorities which lay behind household economies in the eighteenth century, just as today. Nor were the women of the Spitalfields clubbing together to bet on a number coming up a prize or blank in the lottery draw on a specific day behaving strictly rationally in economic terms, although they may well have been in their own eyes. The evidence is impressionistic at best, but also treacherous in respect of guessing at overall trends. This is not least because set against general trends in living standards among the labouring classes, were rapid population growth from the mid eighteenth century, and the significant expansion of the share of national income accounted for by the diversifying middling ranks, especially if we include the rising class of tenant farmers in this category.[171] A good proportion of the gambling which was reflected in the press may have been as much among the middling sort as the labouring classes.

Nevertheless, as we have seen the opportunity for many people to gamble grew significantly in the long eighteenth century. This was especially true in and around London. Within and close to London, but also well beyond it, sports – both formal and organized, informal and spontaneous – with which betting was often closely associated, created the means particularly (but not exclusively) for younger, usually single men within their local communities to acquire and maintain status, and for a small number a rather broader regional and on occasion national notoriety. Betting was part of a deeply rooted culture of male competition at this level of society. Certain aspects of it, notably cockfighting, may have come under increasing criticism and challenge by the end of our period, from below as well as above. Yet, the countervailing forces were almost certainly usually equal to this. Tavern keepers were key agents within this context, as were patrons of such activities from among the elites, as testified to by the rise of pedestrianism as a highly visible popular sport and the continued strong growth in the later Georgian period of horse racing which only flattened off in the 1830s.

Finally, the very notion of popular gambling may be something of a misnomer, if by this we mean anything more strictly defined than the

[171] See Robert C. Allen, 'Class Structure and Inequality during the Industrial Revolution: Lessons from England's Social Tables, 1688–1867', *Economic History Review*, 72 (2019), 88–125, esp. 107.

gambling of some (or, indeed, many) among the majority of the population. This is partly because Methodists, for example, Evangelical Presbyterians north of the border, or artisans increasingly heavily committed to the goals of self- and collective improvement chose not to gamble, while others may have gambled, but to notably different extents and in different ways. For all the habitual gamblers – the self-styled heroes of the tavern – others may have been much more occasional in their betting, staking small sums on fairly occasional games of cards or cricket. There was, as repeatedly emphasized above, no single, uniform culture of gambling at this social level. But it is also because much gambling involved people of quite different social rank and background participating in a common activity. We should not exaggerate the extent to which this occurred, or misconstrue the nature of the social mixing it produced. It did not have to involve submerging social differences; rather it could serve to make them only more sharply visible, as, for example, at the cockpit or, indeed, at the race course or, indeed, the Artillery Ground. Equally, there was a big difference between someone relatively wealthy wagering a fairly significant sum on lottery insurance and a poor person a few pennies. The habits of gambling might also be common to various social groups – such as betting on challenges of different kinds or playing at games such as cards, billiards, or bowls – but what mattered socially speaking was with whom you played or betted. Yet, the realities could be altogether more fluid and ambiguous. In the capital's taverns or gaming clubs, for example, significant social differences were fairly often bridged or even subsumed through a shared preoccupation with playing for money, by observance of the conventions which surrounded gaming, all the more powerful for being informal, and by the highly theatrical version of male self-fashioning with which the culture of the gaming house or gaming more generally was often associated. From this perspective, the gaming house was the locus of an alternative society, one characterized by bravado and ostentation, and the flagrant rejection of the codes of moderation, self-restraint, and strict self-accounting which pervaded many areas of eighteenth-century society and which informed prevalent conceptions of patriarchy. This might be seen as politeness's underbelly, although politeness and its obverse existed in much closer proximity than those who dwell on prescriptive writings to reconstruct its history sometimes suppose. Harder to say is on whom and how many people the gaming house exerted its spell. It may well have been disproportionately young men, often in dependent positions in different ways, such as clerks; or those whose fortunes were particularly precarious, such as tradesmen and shopkeepers; or those, such as half-pay officers, seeking to broker their ambiguous status in society – as fashionable gentlemen – into more substantial gains. What we can say is that gaming house patrons, even if they only constituted a small (but still significant) minority of the population, represented a broad cross section of society, from servants and artisans to tradesmen and shopkeepers, to those who chose to style themselves as genteel. To this extent, as its critics repeatedly insisted, gaming could act in a variety of ways to dissolve established social hierarchies and identities.

3 The Rise of the Lottery

A growing number of European states, as well as European overseas colonies, established state and public lotteries in the eighteenth century. While they had been held in Italy, the Low Countries, France, England, and Southern Germany in the fifteenth and sixteenth centuries, England was in the vanguard of this new wave, closely followed by the United Provinces (today's the Netherlands), France – although a regular royal lottery was not established there until 1776 – and a lengthy list of other states, big and small.[1] The authorities in Jamaica and Barbados ran lotteries from the 1760s and 1770s.[2] In Madras the English East India Company staged them from the early 1780s, while they were common throughout the eighteenth century in the British North American colonies and early American Republic.[3]

Behind the revival of lotteries were a combination of war, surging demands of public finance, and an upsurge of financial experimentation and entrepreneurial energy witnessed in Britain and Holland in the 1690s, an era dubbed by the journalist and prolific writer Daniel Defoe in 1697 'The Projecting Age'.[4] In the predatory world of eighteenth-

1 Evelyn Welch, 'Lotteries in Early Modern Italy', *Past and Present*, 199 (2008), 71–111; Bernard Bruno (ed.), *Lotteries in Europe: Five Centuries of History* (Brussels, 1994); Marie-Laure Legay, *Les Loteries Royales Dans L'Europe des Lumiè*res (1680–1815) (Lille, 2014); Mathijs Hoekstra, 'Necessity is the Mother of Invention: The Lottery Loans of Holland during the War of the Spanish Succession', unpublished MA thesis, University of Utrecht (2010); Manfred Zollinger, 'Entrepreneurs of Chance. The Spreading of *lotto* in 18th Century Europe' (www.helsinki.fi/iehc2006/papers1/Zollinger.pdf). Anne L. Murphy, *The Origins of English Financial Markets: Investment and Speculation before the South Sea Bubble* (Cambridge, 2009).

2 The first lottery in Jamaica was authorized in 1761, with further ones following in 1772/1773, 1779, 1787, and 1788. I owe this information to a communication from Dr Aaron Graham.

3 Henry Davison Love, *Vestiges of Old Madras: Traced from the East India Company's Records Preserved at Fort St George and the India Office, and From Other Sources*, 4 vols. (London, 1913), iii, p. 222, 365–7, 445, 498, 512, 516, 521, 539; Neal E. Millikan, *Lotteries in Colonial America* (New York and Abingdon, 2011).

4 Quoted in Jonathan Sheehan and Dror Wahrman, *Invisible Hands: Self-Organization and the Eighteenth Century* (Chicago, 2015), p. 53.

century international power politics, with leading and lesser states and rulers pursuing, at different times, expansionist ambitions, securing the 'sinews of war' – of which money was the key – was ultimately what brought victory or (what was often the same thing) staved off defeat. The Glorious Revolution of 1688–1689, by which the new Protestant joint monarchy of William III and Mary acceded to the thrones of England, Scotland, and Ireland, dramatically transformed English foreign policy. Under its new ruler – William exercised sole executive power – Britain joined the fight to defeat Louis XIV's hegemonic European ambitions, setting itself on a course which in the next twenty years would turn it into one of Europe's major powers. Faced with the challenge after 1689 of financing massive expansions in the army and navy, and aiding the military efforts of continental allies, ministries in London desperately sought new means of raising funds and supporting short- and longer-term borrowing. In retrospect, this process can seem relatively smooth, with the founding of the Bank of England (in 1694) and the creation of a permanent national debt laying impressive foundations for the extension of British overseas power. The genesis, however, of this new financial world was anything but unperturbed, being characterized instead by repeated experiments, several major failures, and recurrent crisis.[5] When, therefore, the financial projector, Master of the Mint, and Groom Porter, Thomas Neale ran a very successful private cash lottery in 1693, having him hold a similar one on the behalf of the state in the following year was an option which the hard-pressed English treasury could ill afford to pass up.[6]

The first English state lottery was, therefore, as with so much eighteenth-century fiscal policy, opportunistic and experimental. Three years later, the treasury staged a second official lottery, this time far less successfully. Indeed, the Malt Lottery of 1697 has recently been described as 'one of the largest failures – if not the largest – in financial history'.[7] The consequences, however, for the future of the lottery in Britain proved to be relatively minor. In the following year, under the leadership and inspiration of supporters of the Reformation of Manners

[5] On this, see the recent discussion in A. L. Murphy, 'Demanding "Credible Commitment": Public Reactions to the Failures of the Early Financial Revolution', *Economic History Review*, 66 (2013), 178–97.

[6] Anne L. Murphy, *The Origins of English Financial Markets: Investment and Speculation before the South Sea Bubble* (Cambridge, 2009), p. 50; P. G. M. Dickson, *The Financial Revolution in England: A Study in the Development of Public Credit, 1688–1756* (London, 1967), p. 45 also emphasizes in this context the 'keen public interest in lotteries' evident between August 1693 and the following spring.

[7] Georges Gallais-Hamonno and Christian Rietsch, 'Learning by Doing: The Failure of the 1697 Malt Lottery Loan', *Financial History Review*, 20 (2013), 267.

movement, parliament passed an Act banning all public and private lotteries.[8] The moral health of the nation, it seemed, now mattered more than exploiting a relatively easy means of raising money, although legislators' willingness to impose this prohibition may well also have been influenced by the miserable fate of the second lottery. Equally significantly, the Nine Years' War had ended in 1697. In 1702 Britain entered a major new European and global conflict, the War of the Spanish Succession. When financial conditions tightened sharply in 1710, particularly in respect of short-term borrowing, and with the war bogged down in military stalemate and peace negotiations held in the United Provinces in 1709 having broken down, the then Whig ministry urgently needed new ways of securing funds. The Lord Treasurer, Lord Godolphin, revived the state lottery in 1710 as part of a bold package of measures aimed at promoting long-term lending.[9]

This time the lottery would endure. Robert Harley, who succeeded Godolphin as Lord Treasurer in that same year (1710), when a new Tory ministry assumed power, continued the policy of relying heavily on lotteries for wartime finance. Between 1711 and 1714 lottery loans assumed for the first and last time the exclusive burden of inducing lending from a cautious public.[10] Thereafter, while they carried less of this burden, and were, increasingly, mainly used as inducements to support other loan issues, especially during the Seven Years' War (1756–1763) and the War of American Independence (1775–1783), lotteries became regular features of British public finance until parliament decreed their abolition in 1823. Between 1694 and 1826, the year of the last one (before they were again revived in 1994 by John Major's

[8] For this and an earlier, 1693 unsuccessful attempt, as well as other early legislation relating to the lotteries, see Lee K. Davison, 'Public Policy in an Age of Economic Expansion: The Search for Commercial Accountability in England 1690–1750', unpublished Ph.D. thesis, University of Harvard (1990), ch. 1.

[9] Dickson, *Financial Revolution*, p. 62, See also BL, Landsdowne Papers, Add MS 829, fos. 123–34, report to the Queen on the financial situation by the Commissioners of the Treasury, 31 Aug. 1710. The individual behind the lottery proposal was probably the Scots financier, William Paterson, for which, see BL, Add MS 70155, fo. 23, William Paterson, memorial on lotterys, n.d., but prob. 1710.

[10] Key figures behind Harley's lottery policy, which was determined partly by the political imperative of relying less heavily on the Whig-dominated Bank of England and East India Company, were John Blount, secretary to the Sword Blade Bank, and director of the other significant financial initiative under Harley, the South Sea Company, established in 1711, and Edward Harley. The latter later claimed principal responsibility for authorship of the second lottery of 1711, the first of two classis lotteries, the second being held in 1712. David Hayton, 'Harley, Edward (1664–1735), of Eywood, Herefs.', in David Hayton and Eveline Cruickshanks (eds.), *History of Parliament: The House of Commons 1690–1715*, (Cambridge, 2000) (www.historyofparliamentonline.org/volume/1690-1715/member/Harley-Edward-1664-1735).

Conservative government), 170 English/British state lotteries were staged, normally before 1802 on an annual basis.[11] Parliament also from time to time permitted lotteries for public purposes, including five, for example, from 1737 to fund construction of Westminster Bridge.[12] From 1802, there were at least three state lotteries a year, and in the 1810s their frequency increased still further, although this is somewhat deceptive.[13] When the Irish lottery was abolished in 1801, as a consequence of the British-Irish Union, the number of tickets per lottery increased, and profits were shared with the Irish Exchequer. Between 1781 and 1796 there had been one Irish state lottery held each year, and two between 1797 and 1801.[14] The total number of tickets was limited annually from 1802, and these were divided between the lotteries in any given year.

The case for state lotteries in Britain was, thus, pragmatic; supporters urged their efficiency and economy as revenue-raising devices.[15] They also argued that their abolition would do nothing to lessen gambling. 'Such is the general spirit for gambling', as one writer breezily put it, 'that all the wisdom of government cannot put a stop to it; and therefore it may be applied to good purpose, and be made advantageous to the state.'[16] Doing away with the lottery would also damage the national interest because funds which might have bolstered British power would merely move into foreign lotteries.[17] It was a very plausible argument given the interest shown at different points in Britain in, for example, Dutch and Irish lotteries, the quantities of British lottery tickets sold to colonials, the Irish, and foreigners, and the international nature of contemporary capital markets.[18] While they attracted considerable criticism on moral

[11] R. D. Richards, 'The Lottery in the History of English Government Finance', *Economic History*, 3 (1933–7), 57.

[12] Details of these and of all state lotteries can be found in C. L. Ewen, *Lotteries and Sweepstakes: An Historical, Legal and Ethical Survey of their Introduction, Suppression and Re-establishment in the British Isles* (London, 1932).

[13] There were four in 1811; six in 1812; five in 1813; seven in 1814; six in both 1815 and 1816; five in 1817; and three in 1818.

[14] Rowena Dudley, *The Irish Lottery 1780–1801* (Dublin, 2005).

[15] One of the most vehement defenders of lotteries as an efficient, relatively painless, and innocuous means of raising money was Sir John Sinclair, *The History of the Public Revenue of the British Empire* (2nd ed., London, 1789), pp. 217–8.

[16] *An Address to the Sovereign, on the Ministers' Conduct in Rejecting the Petition of the Lieutenant of the Royal Navy* (London, 1788), p. 77. The author of this pamphlet proposed a naval lottery every six years.

[17] See e.g. *Considerations on Lotteries, and Proposals for their Better Regulation* (London, 1786), pp. 9–10; R. Jackson, *A Guide to Adventurers in the Lottery, or Plan of the Amicable Society of Lottery Adventurers* (n.d., but prob. 1785), pp. 4–5.

[18] For contemporary comment on Dutch demand for the 1710 lottery, see *British Apollo*, 25–7 Jan. 1710. For Irish purchase of British lottery tickets, see Dudley, *Irish Lottery*, pp. 50–6. For demand in the North American colonies, see Millikan, *Lotteries in Colonial*

grounds throughout the eighteenth century and again, in sharper form, after the end of the Napoleonic Wars, their fiscal utility ensured their continuation until by 1823 declining profitability, as much as any strengthening of the moral case against them, led to their abolition.[19]

The rest of this chapter examines the nature and scope of the lottery marketplace as it developed in Britain between the 1690s and 1820s. There is a deeper story to uncover, about how to account for the popularity and pervasiveness of lottery adventuring among Britons in this period. Before we get there, however, we need to know who adventured in the lottery, how regularly, and on what sorts of scale. This, in turn, requires us to reconstruct *how* they did so.

3.1 Creating the Lottery Marketplace

The success of the official lottery in the long eighteenth century depended in the first place on the rapid development of a (reasonably) transparent, open, and accessible market for lottery tickets, first in London and then across much of the rest of Britain. This, in turn, derived from the actions and practices of intermediaries acting as market makers and agents for the purchase and distribution of tickets. To a greater degree than elsewhere in Europe – with the possible exception of the United Provinces – official lotteries in Britain in this period relied on private enterprise for their organization and operation. At one level, this reflects key features of the eighteenth-century British state, with many of its activities being contracted out to private interests and groups.[20] However, it was also symptomatic of distinctive features of British society.

America, p. 34. It was claimed in 1769 that the Americans were boycotting British lottery tickets as part of their campaign against the Townshend duties, but that previously they had accounted for 'at least an eighth part of the lottery' (*The Cambridge Magazine* (1769), p. 479). See also more generally Larry Neal, *The Rise of Financial Capitalism: International Capital Markets in the Age of Reason* (Cambridge, 1990).

19 James Raven, 'The Abolition of the English State Lotteries', *Historical Journal*, 34 (1991), 371–89. Britain was at war in the eighteenth century for more years than any other major European power. I owe this point to Professor Hamish Scott.

20 The literature on the character of the eighteenth-century English/British state(s) is extensive, but see John Brewer, *The Sinews of Power: War, Money and the English State* (London, 1989) and, for a recent series of essays which engage directly with Brewer's seminal arguments, and open up a series of new four-nations perspectives on the character and identity of the state in the British Isles, Aaron Graham and Patrick Walsh (eds.), *The British Fiscal-Military States 1660–c1783* (Basingstoke, 2016). See also the recent relevant comments in Julian Hoppit, 'Sir Joseph Banks' Provincial Turn', *Historical Journal*, 61 (2018), 403–29.

Comparing England, France, and Germany since 1750, Jerrold Seigel has written recently of the 'precocious modernity' of eighteenth-century English society.[21] As an idea this seems overdrawn – insofar as it downplays the enduring influence of religion and social rank, the deep-rootedness of older mentalities, as well as the unevenness of change; it begs the question too of whether Scotland and Wales can be included in this framework, or, indeed, whether we should be talking here about a uniform England.[22] Whatever the notion's limitations, however, it offers a good starting point for thinking about the wider conditions which helped to shape the character and, indeed, success of the British lottery.

In describing English society in such terms, what Seigel has in mind is, first, the exceptional degree of national integration that existed in the commercial, economic, cultural, and political spheres. Second, equally unusual, he argues, was the proportion of the population who participated in the market, and, as importantly, the degree to which this influenced prevalent attitudes towards wealth creation and consumption. What stands out is the early acceptance of the legitimacy of these activities viewed both as goals and processes. As Seigel declares: 'it is clear that the thickening web of distant relations within which production and exchange were carried on, and the expanding horizons this brought, were drawing people to question the subordination of economic behaviour to ends rooted outside it, and to offer new principles derived from the operation of market networks themselves.'[23] Crucial to these developments were the presence and impact of the relentlessly expanding English, later (from 1 May 1707) British capital. Already by 1700 London boasted a population of over half a million – comprising 11 per cent of the national population – and, owing to its size (absolutely and relative to other urban settlements across the British Isles), its myriad connections to places beyond it, and the ways in which it was a terrain of connection between groups and places, exerted a type and degree of influence over the rest of society unlike any other European capital city. Less tangibly, but no less importantly, London offered unparalleled possibilities for personal reinvention, the chance to fashion oneself anew,

21 Jerrold Seigel, *Modernity and Bourgeois Life: Society, Politics, and Culture in England, France, and Germany since 1750* (Cambridge, 2012), p. 46.

22 Seigel, however, also emphasizes the 'paradoxes' of nineteenth-century British society as 'at once the most bourgeois and the least' (ibid., p. 42), a characterization of English society articulated very powerfully for a previous generation by E. P. Thompson. See esp. Thompson, 'The Peculiarities of the English', *Socialist Register* (1965), 311–62.

23 Seigel, *Modernity and Bourgeois Life*, p. 49. Paul Slack's *The Invention of Improvement: Information and Material Progress in Seventeenth-Century England* (Oxford, 2015) supports this idea but also qualifies it in important ways.

and to secure a fortune, even if the reality could be starkly different – namely, a precarious existence in a liminal social space demarcated, at one extreme, by penury and, at the other, a precarious sufficiency. Many took the high road to London in search of a livelihood, others to 'make a figure' – or, indeed, both – with the result that the capital presented an arena of unbridled social competition. As we will see below and in the subsequent chapter, tracing the diffusion of the lottery habit is, in part, to chart the extensive and close influence of the British capital on the lottery and lottery adventuring.

However, we are also peering into a world in which, as Susan Whyman has recently described it, more and more social transactions took place between people who were physically apart, where the tyranny of distance was shrunk, if not entirely defeated, by the written and printed word.[24] With growing frequency and in increasing volumes, letters, newspapers, and much other printed material were carried out from London along multiplying postal routes, while much flowed in the reverse direction. One quick measure of the expansion of the postal network in this period is the growth in the overall number of post towns. In 1741, for Britain as a whole this figure stood at 340; by 1801 it had climbed to 508. In 1770 there were 115 Scottish post towns; 20 years later there were 164. More and more places across Britain were coming to be served by six-day posts from London from the second half of the eighteenth century, while the introduction of mail coaches on an increasing number of routes from 1784 significantly reduced journey times.[25] The growth in use of postal services was striking, especially from the final decades of the eighteenth century. Between 1780 and 1800, net revenue from postage of letters in Scotland grew by just over 300 per cent.[26] In the first three months of 1823, nearly 2.4 million newspapers and only slightly fewer letters were sent out from London through the post office.[27] Lottery businesses

[24] Susan E. Whyman, 'Paper Visits: The Post-Restoration Letter as Seen through the Verney Family Archive', in Rebecca Earle (ed.), *Letters and Letter Writers 1600–1945* (Aldershot, 1999), pp. 15–36.

[25] There is no modern study of the development of postal services in this period and their broader cultural and social impact. But see K. L. Ellis, *The Post Office in the Eighteenth Century: A Study in Administrative History* (London, 1958) and Brian Austen, 'British Mail Coach Services 1784–1850', unpublished Ph.D. thesis, University of London (1979).

[26] RMA, Post 9/168, net produce of postage of letters in Scotland. In the year 5 Apr. 1780–1, this figure was £29,431.5.4; in the equivalent period 1799–1800 it stood at £92,871.6.10.

[27] RMA, Post 30/4766, an account of the number of letters and newspapers sent from London in three months, 1823.

became, as we will see further below, major users of increasingly efficient, frequent, and expanding postal services.[28]

However, fully to comprehend the lottery market and how it developed we need to take a step backwards; we need to begin at the moment of a lottery's creation. Before 1785, when lottery contractors took over the process, albeit subject to official oversight, the treasury decided on the terms of any state lottery – the number of tickets, the distribution and amount of the prizes, and so forth. As with taxes, the treasury or whoever was then first Lord of the Treasury and Chancellor of the Exchequer was typically bombarded with proposals for new lotteries from financial projectors and self-styled fiscal experts, all of them promising ever-greater returns.[29] Along with other revenue-raising measures, once settled upon by the treasury the lottery would be proposed to the Commons Committee of Ways and Means as part of the normal budgetary process. The resulting piece of legislation described the terms and conditions on which the particular lottery would proceed.

Once this legislation had passed into law, the next stage was that the terms of the lottery were published, usually initially in the official newspaper, the *London Gazette*.[30] The enabling Act specified the date on which the draw was to begin and the identity of the commissioners appointed to oversee it and ensure that it was properly and impartially run.[31] For most of the eighteenth century, before being switched first in 1802 to the Scots Corporation and then (more permanently from 1803) Coopers' Hall in Basinghall Street, the draw was held in the Guildhall at the heart of the City of London. There it quickly became part of the rich panoply of spectacle and collective drama presented by the British capital, drawing audiences during 'lottery-time' (as the period of the draw became known) from across society – from, at one end, fashionable,

[28] An undated memorandum from the early nineteenth century, which sought to establish the profit generated by the lottery over a period of five years, estimated the annual postal revenue accruing from distribution in England of 496,003 shares 'besides whole tickets' – which would appear to mean both shares and wholes – at £131,000. TNA, IR55/10, anonymous memorandum, n.d.

[29] These can be found littering the papers of successive ministers responsible for financial matters. Proposals for lotteries of various kinds were commonly published in print, and on occasion sent direct to parliament.

[30] *The London Gazette* was from inception distributed through the post office and by postmasters. Austen, 'British Mail Coaches', p. 19.

[31] The position of Commissioner of the Lottery fell under the patronage of ministers. There were forty-two of these, before Spencer Perceval as part of an economizing drive reduced their number in 1816 to twenty-eight.

elite women to, at other, artisans and domestic servants.[32] Seats in the Guildhall's galleries, which accommodated around 500 people, were sold, while the lower part of the hall was, as one newspaper described it in 1791, in plainly disapproving and no doubt somewhat distorted terms, 'crowded with poor wretches who had pawned half their clothes, and left their families starving, in expectation of miracles being wrought to relieve them from poverty, and indulge them in idleness'.[33]

For almost all of the lotteries held between 1710 and 1784, the Bank of England acted as the receiver for monies paid for the initial subscription for tickets. In this way, as in several others, the rise of the lottery was bound up with the wider changes usually referred to by the term the 'financial revolution' and the associated rapid development from the later seventeenth century of the secondary market for government debt and company stocks. Starting in 1711 a system of lists of subscribers to the lotteries operated.[34] The advantage of this was that it ensured that the initial subscription would always be filled. From 1711, payment for tickets subscribed for was also in four instalments; early payment earned rebates, essentially discounts. Part-paid tickets – as with 'scrip' in the case of other government issues – could be sold before further payments became due, normally at a premium.[35]

How comprehensively the system of subscribers' lists operated, or the degree to which the process became closed like the one that operated in most years in respect of normal public loans, is unclear. Complaints were heard as early as 1711 that only 'insiders' were able successfully to subscribe for tickets in the first of the lotteries of that year, although these no doubt reflected the very high demand for tickets and the disappointment of the unsuccessful.[36] Immediately following the initial subscription, which took just a few hours to fill, Robert Walpole, the future prime minister, phlegmatically declared to his older brother, Horatio, that it was 'certain that ye greatest part of this subscription

[32] For a contemporary account of the lottery draw, see, NRAS 2614, Newton Castle, Blairgowrie, Macpherson of Clunie Papers, Bundle 295, Harriet Macpherson to William, her brother, London, 11 Apr. 1802.

[33] *EdinA*, 15 Feb. 1791.

[34] Edward Harley organized one of these, for which see BL, Add MS 70155, fo. 43, letter to Harley about tickets not 'taken up' on his 'list', Sept. 1712 & Harley's response, 17 Sept. 1712. Another was organized by John Campbell, the Scots goldsmith banker (NRS, GD124/15/1028/2, Alex Raitt, Whitehall, to the Duke of Montrose, 15 Mar. 1711).

[35] Dickson, *Financial Revolution*, p. 77.

[36] Historical Manuscripts Commission, *Fourteenth Report, Appendix, Part IV, The Manuscripts of Lord Kenyon* (London, 1894), p. 446, Sir Roger Bradshaigh to George Kenyon, 24 Mar. 1711.

was made by stock-jobbers in order to sell again being not oblig'd to pay in above one fourth, that I am confident these Ticketts before they come to be drawn will be sold with an advantage to ye buyers'.[37] A record of first payments in the 1713 lottery reveals that a large number of bankers and dealers made substantial initial subscriptions – among them such notable figures among the capital's early eighteenth-century plutocratic financial elite as Edward Gibbon, Moses Hart, Matthew Wymondesold, Thomas Martin, John Marke, and Nathaniel Newman.[38] These and other similar individuals invested heavily in the lotteries of 1710–1714, especially those in 1711–1712, on behalf of themselves, as well as others.[39] Several decades later, in the 1740s, the leading Jewish financier Samson Gideon used his considerable financial muscle to support several lottery issues, and he dealt heavily in lottery tickets, although the full extent and nature of his activity in this context is hidden from view.[40] Lucy Sutherland, who became very familiar with this murky world through her meticulous researches on finance and politics, suggests that, following an intervention by Gideon in 1744 which involved purchasing on the market a number of lottery tickets which formed part of the public loan of that year, in order to hold up their price, it became 'customary' for the ministry to make arrangements for purchase of tickets by private bankers.[41] Stray requests for tickets in subscriptions from the 1740s and 1750s would seem to bear out this supposition.[42]

[37] NRO, Norwich, Townshend Papers, BL/T/3/1/21, Robert to Horatio Walpole, 16 Mar. 1711. It was, in fact, oversubscribed, owing to poor management by the Bank of England, with the result that, not only were there many disappointed prospective investors, those who were successful received less than (4/5ths) their original allocation.

[38] LMA, Col/CHD/LA/02/219, monies paid in upon the civil list lottery ano. 1713 being the first payment.

[39] See ch. 4, below, pp. 184–5.

[40] Lucy Sutherland, 'Samson Gideon: Eighteenth Century Jewish Financier', in *Politics and Finance in the Eighteenth Century: Lucy Sutherland*, ed. Aubrey Newman (London, 1984), p. 392. For hostile comment on the role of 'Jew stockbrokers' in raising ticket prices in 1743, see the *CalM*, 4 Apr. 1743. This report claimed that 'one of the richest Jews' was 'in so high Esteem at Court' that he had received 40,000 tickets at par. This was almost certainly a reference to Gideon, and suggests that he was active in this sphere on a very large scale at least a year earlier than Sutherland suggests.

[41] *Politics and Finance*, ed. Newman, no. 2, p. 392.

[42] University of Nottingham, Manuscripts and Special Collections, Newcastle (Clumber) Papers, Ne C 921, Earl of Hardwicke to Henry Pelham, 24 Feb. 1751; Ne C 922, same to same, 5 Mar. 1751; Ne C 507, Luke Robinson to Henry Pelham, 14 Feb. 1750; Ne C 508, Sir Dudley Ryder to John West, 20 Feb. 1750. The list system seems to have continued to operate in the 1720s and 1730s. In 1731, for example, the writer John Gay informed Jonathan Swift, then in Dublin, that he intended to buy tickets in that year's lottery at the market price rather than exploiting 'Court favours', which presumably meant foregoing the chance thereby to be included in the initial subscription

Closed subscriptions could arouse intense suspicion since people strongly suspected, perfectly reasonably, that the market for lottery tickets was susceptible to manipulation by those whom the dissenting minister and financial expert, and confidant of the Earl of Shelburne, Richard Price later disparagingly dubbed the 'moneyd harpies'.[43] A particularly blatant case, investigated by the House of Commons, was the lottery in 1753 staged to fund the purchase of the Hans Sloane collection and creation of the British Museum. The resulting Commons committee report revealed that Gideon had subscribed for 6,000 tickets, which he had very rapidly sold through a variety of brokers having paid on them only the first of the four payments.[44] Ministers were routinely accused of using lottery subscriptions to reward friends and allies, while allegations were also made throughout the eighteenth century that stock-jobbers engaged in various stratagems aimed at manipulating demand in order to inflate ticket prices.[45] The recurrence of such accusations reflected the existence (and importance) of a substantial secondary market in lottery tickets.[46]

Several points, however, need to be made about these practices and market, which begin to put them in a somewhat different light. Ministers allowed them because they were crucial to ensuring the profitability of the lottery. They also recognized that keeping up the prices of lottery tickets was helpful to the general state of public credit. As the author of an anonymous memorandum put it in 1711, public credit was a 'chain' – a fall in price of one element might well detonate a chain reaction of declining prices among the others.[47] Ministers avoided regulation of the secondary market, until, that is, Pitt the Younger changed the system under which the lotteries were organized in 1784 to one in which lottery

(C. F. Burgess (ed.), *The Letters of John Gay* (Oxford, 1966), pp. 103–5; John Gay to Jonathan Swift, 31 Mar. 1731).

43 D. O. Thomas and W. Bernard Peace (eds.), *The Correspondence of Richard Price: March 1778–February 1786*, 2 vols. (Durham, N. C. and Cardiff, 1983–94), ii, p. 178–9: Richard Price to the 2nd Earl of Shelburne, 18 Apr. 1783.

44 House of Commons Sessional Papers, vol. 19, Report from the Committee Appointed to Examine the Book, Containing an Account of the Contributors to the Lottery, 1753, And the Proceedings of the House Thereupon, 14 Mar. 1754.

45 See e.g. *Salisbury and Winchester Journal*, 15 July 1751; *MP*, 11 Jan. 1792; SJChr, 10 Jan. 1775. See also BL, Add MS 59309, fo. 10, Thomas Smith to Lord Henry Petty, 28 July 1806.

46 In the early nineteenth century, there was even a market in anticipated 'produces', which was the difference between the contract price of tickets and the gain or loss of contractors relative to this. Needless to say, this encouraged attempts to manipulate prices. TNA, T64/324, T. Wood, 'On Produces of Lotteries', n.d. but 1800s.

47 BL, Add MS 70155, f. 24, anonymous memorial on the lottery, n.d., but 1711.

contractors made bids to the treasury for the operation of the lottery.[48] Before then brokers and dealers subscribed for large quantities of tickets, with the express purpose of selling these before the draw, profiting thereby from any rise in their price. For those who understood how this market operated opportunities existed to make a substantial profit quickly. That trading of options on purchase and sale of tickets appears to have developed almost immediately underlines just how rapid was the development of this sector of eighteenth-century financial markets.[49]

Some examples reveal on what kinds of scale speculative trading of this kind occurred – 'gaming with the public' was how the Tory writer and churchman, Jonathan Swift, once described it.[50] In 1711 James Brydges, later Duke of Chandos, invested as much as £13,000 in the classis lottery, in a series of schemes which involved several other big dealers and speculators – namely, Sir Theodore Janssen, Matthew Decker, and John Blount. Another of his partners was the then Chancellor of the Exchequer, Robert Benson, who agreed to meet half the liabilities until the ticket price reached a certain level, at which point presumably he wished to sell. In July 1711 Benson wrote to Brydges agreeing with him that the opportune moment to sell was just before the start of the draw, and that he thought the best way to do this was to accept the market

[48] This did not eliminate this market, although it must have had some effect on how it operated. The treasury received one proposal from an experienced lottery office keeper, probably in the early nineteenth century, which would have destroyed it at a stroke, but it was not acted upon. What the author of the proposal suggested was essentially reducing and fixing the prices of tickets, which would then be sold on the account of the government, who, importantly, 'were not speculators in the wheel'. TNA, IR55/19, H. E. Swift, 'A Proposal For a New Mode of Disposing of a State Lottery by a Contract of Agency', n.d..

[49] For evidence of this, see Larry Neal, *"I Am Not Master of Events": The Speculations of John Law and Lord Londonderry in the Mississippi and South Sea Bubbles* (New York and London, 2012), pp. 63–7. See also BL. Add MS 70155, f. 48, [?] to [?], 9 Dec. 1713, which reports: 'And I am well [aware?] the writer of this letter has given out money to have the refusal of Tickets at 11.10 pticket before the drawing begins w.[hi]ch will be (if they arrive at that price) 15 per Cent advance [i.e. on the initial price]'. In 1714, Lord Londonderry was buying and selling 'chances' – in other words, options on ticket purchases – for which, see TNA, C108/416/14, accounts of Thomas Pitt, Jr, Lord Londonderry with George Craddock, 1714–16, Mr Sheppards acc.t ab.t Lottery ticketts &c -, 12 Feb. 1714. This includes brokerage payments for 463 chances sold, and a payment for 'daily searching 600 chances'. The chances were sold for various prices, cumulatively realizing the sum of £1,680.14.6. Londonderry also bought 'ye chance' of 600 tickets in two tranches, for which he paid £1,700 (Account current with George Craddock, 1714).

[50] *The Correspondence of Alexander Pope, 1729–1735*, ed. George Sherburn, 5 vols. (Oxford, 1956), iii, p. 285–7: Jonathan Swift to John Gay, 15 May 1732.

price.[51] Participating in the initial subscription, or purchasing early, with the intention to sell as prices rose was commonplace among stockjobbers and dealers, or those, such as Brydges, who were well versed in the arcane mysteries of Exchange Alley. Yet, it extended much more widely. In 1743, to give just two examples, two clients of Drummond's Bank in London separately engaged in transactions of this kind. One was the recently ennobled Earl of Bath, whose peerage had been the reward for the part he had played in the narrow (and for most people bitterly disillusioning) political deal that followed the fall of Sir Robert Walpole in February of the previous year. Bath made the first payment on 900 lottery tickets and £11,250 of annuity stock, costing him, respectively, £2,250 and £2,812.10. Around a month later, towards the beginning of May 1743, he sold 100 of the tickets, making a premium of £1.10 sh. on each ticket, and the annuity stock at £2,882.16.3, both on which, as just referred to, just a single payment (25 per cent of their full cost) had been made. He made the second and third payments on the remaining 800 tickets, before in September selling three tranches of 100 tickets with the three payments made on them. On these, he was making a return of around 14 per cent. To put this a bit differently, including the first 100 tickets sold, he made well over £400 in five months (roughly the equivalent of £47,300 in 2017). Having made the fourth payment on his remaining 500, he sold all but six tickets before the draw. On each ticket, he was making, less brokerage, between £1.5 sh. and £1.7 sh. per ticket. William Blair's investment was much simpler. He paid all four instalments on sixty-five tickets, selling forty-five of these before the draw, gaining him a return of rather more than 10 per cent.[52] In the 1760s, to give one further example, the upwardly mobile King's Lynn Attorney and land agent, Philip Case, several times mayor of the Norfolk port town, engaged in similar speculations involving a few hundred tickets at a time.[53]

[51] Huntington Library, Stowe Papers, ST57, vol. v, 119, Brydges to Robert Benson, 7 July 1711; ST58, vol. viii, 255, Benson to Brydges, July 1711. I owe these references to Dr Aaron Graham.

[52] RBS Archives, DR/427/23, Drummond's Bank Customer Account Ledger, 1743–4, fos. 330, 362. In 1768 and 1769, the partners of Child's Bank were engaging in similar sorts of transaction on lottery tickets. In 1769, for example, they made three payments on 1,000 tickets, and full payment on 300. Six hundred tickets were sold before the final payment became due, and the other 300 before the draw. They appear to have made a fairly modest return of £50 on these dealings. (RBS Archives, CH/203/2/1, Profit and Loss Ledger of Child & Co., 1769.

[53] NRO, Bradfer-Lawrence Collection, BL/CS6/7/15, Account Current of Philip Case with Everard Browne & Co., 1767–9.)

Such trading was a fairly safe bet because ticket prices normally rose appreciably between the initial subscription and the start of the draw.[54] Accordingly returns were, as we have already seen, high – of the order of between 10 and 15 per cent.[55] Not that it was failsafe, however, as Gilbert Innes of Stow, since 1787 deputy governor of the Royal Bank of Scotland, and his close friend, the committed gamester William Grant of Congalton, discovered in 1793. They bought well over a hundred tickets at an early stage for that year's lottery in clear anticipation of a rising market. Their problem was that the market turned out, against their expectations, to be a stagnant one – almost certainly because of the sharp, and very widespread credit squeeze that accompanied British entry into the war against revolutionary France in February 1793. Hopes of turning a quick and ready profit consequently transmuted into a desperate effort to minimize losses. On 23 February, Grant reported: 'I am at this moment sitting in judgement over the unfortunate Adventure with our friends Carteret & Callender & the Broker – We have 37 Tickets drawn which estimating the £20 prizes at £20 produce only £2,000 & cost about £600.' The dilemma was whether to sell or, as Grant put it, to 'stand the Wheel' – in other words, rely on the luck of the draw. But if they chose the latter, and a further big prize was drawn, the market would further deflate and prices tumble. Three days later Grant was still deliberating about whether to sell 100 tickets. We do not know exactly what then happened, although on 1 March he was reporting another bad day for the adventurers – three of their tickets drawn but all blanks, and the market remaining 'very dull'. Grant's hope now was that no large prize would be drawn during the rest of that day, and that the next day the market would pick up, thereby enabling him to dispose of the remaining tickets at a reasonable price.[56] What this example neatly discloses is the extent to which lottery tickets continued to be traded during the draw, and how ticket prices fluctuated sharply according to when the main capital prizes were drawn. As more and more tickets were drawn, and if the large capital prizes remained undrawn, prices of

[54] A memorial from c. 1787 noted that between 1751 and 1768, tickets had tended to double in price between their first issue and beginning of the draw. (TNA, T1/652/68–75, memorial on lotteries, n.d., but prob. 1787.) The period between the initial subscription and the start of the draw was normally around six months.

[55] Christophe Chamley emphasizes the huge profits made by bankers on trading of 'scrip' in the case of new loan issues in Christophe Chamley, 'Interest Reductions in the Politico-Financial Nexus of Eighteenth-Century England', *The Journal of Economic History*, 71 (2011), 569. Returns on consols ranged between 3.8 and 5.9%, while other loans might return between 3 and 5%.

[56] NRS, Innes of Stow Papers, GD113/4/160/20, 42, 63, 67, 68, 71.

undrawn tickets surged upwards.[57] The fact that before 1793 the draw could last up to forty-two days was what created this vertiginous prospect.

A flourishing secondary market in lottery tickets helped, therefore, to secure the profitability of the lotteries, and furnished the chance for a widening range of people – especially dealers and brokers, and those close to the corridors of power – to turn a quick profit. But how did most people buy lottery tickets, especially if they lived in places far removed from London?

3.2 Purchasing a Lottery Ticket

An important means was by visiting the capital, creating opportunities to buy tickets in person and for family members and acquaintances. People of gentry and middling status came to London in their droves. Between around 1747 and 1753 George Warrender of Bruntsfield, near Edinburgh, bought tickets through his brother, Hugh, rector of the parish of Aston in Yorkshire, who was a frequent visitor to London. On other occasions, he applied to Andrew Millar, the Scottish-born London bookseller, to buy them.[58] It was on a business trip to the capital in 1775 that a Dublin ironmonger purchased a lottery ticket.[59] Probably more common was employing the services of people, such as the bookseller-publisher Millar, who were London residents or sojourners (i.e. people who spent part of the year in London). This may have been especially true for people such as merchants or the gentry, who often had close personal and business links with denizens of the capital. In 1766 the great Glasgow tobacco merchant, William Cunninghame, bought three tickets using the services of Robert & Robert Bogle and Scott, Scots merchants in London. Colonial, Irish, Dutch, German, and other

[57] In some years, ticket prices seem to have risen at points to as much as more than twice their face value. See NRS, GD124/16/129/3, William Flint, St James, to John Jamieson, Alloa, 7 Dec. 1780, where Flint reported that he had bought a second ticket in the state lottery for £19.10s without seeking Jamieson's permission 'because if I had waited for your answer, which could not be sooner than ten days, and by that time tickets might be selling at betwixt Thirty and Forty pounds, if the £20,000 prize remained in the wheel till this time'.

[58] NRS, GD214/639/10, 12, 16, 17, 18, letters from Hugh Warrender, London and Aston, to George Warrender, 1747–53. Millar acted in a similar capacity for others, for which, see Adam Budd (ed.), *Circulating Enlightenment: The Career and Correspondence of Andrew Millar 1725–68* (Oxford, 2020), p. 297.

[59] TNA, IR55/1, bonds and affidavits relating to lost prize-winning lottery tickets, 1717–87.

foreign merchants used similar means, underlining the transnational nature of the lottery market.[60]

Family and personal connections were exploited to the same end. Jane Bonnell was a widow who came to live in London from Ireland in 1705, a few years after the death of her husband. Through her two sisters she retained very close links with influential figures in Irish Protestant society, including the family of the influential Speaker of the Irish House of Commons, William Connolly. Bonnell acted as an informal point of contact for acquaintances in Ireland wishing to buy lottery tickets, most of whom, like her, were widows or spinsters.[61] Humphrey Prideaux, the dean of Norwich, appealed to the goodwill of his cousin, the MP and merchant Humphrey Morice, to secure twenty tickets in the 1719 lottery, on the seemingly mistaken idea that MPs had privileged access to tickets:

> There being I hear a state lottery on ye Anvill I beg ye favour of you to buy 20 Ticket for me thus far I am willing to try my fortune pray this trouble from you because I am told Parliament men have ye pre-emption & I know none in yr House on whom I can more presume for the favour than yourself.[62]

In the 1730s and 1740s, Kent gentleman Sir Edward Filmer bought tickets through his brother Beavisham, a lawyer at the Inns of Court. Sir Edward wrote regularly to his sibling about lottery purchases, the optimum moment to purchase tickets, the state of the draw, the fate of his tickets, and so on.[63] Later in the century, Thomas Robinson, the 2nd Baron Grantham, when ambassador in Madrid, and his brother, Frederick, usually also resident there, employed Nathan Draper, the surveyor general of the post office in London, to buy lottery tickets for themselves, the embassy chaplain, and various other members of their family, including their sister, Anne, who remained at her marital home in Saltram, Devon.[64] Given that London depended heavily on immigrants for the continued growth of its population – already in the 1670s and 1680s it was attracting incomers at the rate of 8,000–9,000 a year – its importance as a site of trade and the professions, and of recreation and

60 Ibid., See also S. D. Smith and T. R. Wheely, '"Requisites of a Considerable Trade"': The Letters of Robert Plumsted, Atlantic Merchant, 1752–58', *English Historical Review*, 124 (2009), 545–70.

61 Anne Laurence, 'Women investors, 'that nasty south sea affair' and the rage to speculate in early eighteenth-century England', *Accounting, Business & Financial History*, 16 (2006), 252.

62 Bank of England Archives, 16A2/2/20(2), H. Prideaux to Humphry Morice Esq., Norwich, 29 Dec. 1718.

63 KARC, Maidstone, U120/C25/3, 3, 6, 8, 10-1, 19, letters from Bevisham Filmer to Sir Edward Filmer (3rd Bart.), 1733–4; U120/C26/37, 40, 43–8, same to same, 1736–7.

64 BARS, Wrest Park (Lucas) Manuscripts, L30/14/109/39, 66, 71, 79, 176, 187, 197, 203, 209, 212, which cover the purchase of lottery tickets between 1774 and 1784.

residence (both temporary and permanent) for many of the landed classes, what was significant in this context were the sheer multiplicity and density of personal and family connections to the British capital.

During the early Hanoverian period, moreover – and probably in other periods – individuals purchased tickets or arranged their purchase for quite large groups of acquaintances. One such was Walpole's House of Commons fixer, Thomas Winnington, MP for Droitwich and then Worcester, who finally gained his desired post in the treasury in 1736. In the 1730s and 1740s Winnington regularly instructed the purchase of tickets for several individuals, also buying substantial numbers on his own account, which he then distributed among his contacts.[65] Such arrangements emphasize how important kinship and other kinds of network – including, for example, military connections – were to spreading the lottery habit.[66]

Private banks, meanwhile, such as Drummond's mentioned above, represented another important means of purchasing tickets. Their clientele was predominantly an elite one – landowners, office holders, and professionals (clergymen, physicians, lawyers), and also a good number of widows and spinsters usually from similar backgrounds. These groups were, as we will see in the next chapter, well represented among the ranks of the lottery adventurers, although this may also be a bit deceptive, in that it is they who have left the greater part of records of this activity. Buying lottery tickets was part of the wider array of services that banks typically offered, including purchase and disposal of stocks, providing loans on security of stock or plate, and so on.[67] Working from his

[65] Hoare's Bank, HB/8/T/11, 1712–31, 1733/4–55, letters from Winnington and others to partners of the bank. For example, in 1737, Winnington made the first payment on 190 tickets, and the final one on 140; in 1738 he made the first payment on 100 and second on 90, and among those to whom he sold tickets were Lord Oxford and William Bromley; in 1740 he made payments on 100 tickets; in 1743 the first payment on 500 and all 4 payments on 430; while in 1744 he made payments on 400 tickets. He was acting in a similar capacity earlier, in 1731, although he may not have been buying tickets on other peoples' behalf. (HB, Ledger N/448; O/52, 321; Q/6, 411; R/277, 359.) One person who bought tickets from Winnington in 1740 and 1741 was Henrietta Cavendish Holles, Countess of Oxford (NA, DD/P/6/7/2/2, account book of the Rt. Hon. Henrietta Cavendish Holles, Countess of Oxford, 1739–55, entries for 17 May 1740 & 2 July 1741).

[66] Other individuals who, during the same period, acted in this capacity using the services of Hoare's Bank included Thomas Saunderson, MP for Lincolnshire, and the Duke of Newcastle's man of business, Peter Forbes.

[67] Peter Temin and Hans-Joachim Voth, 'Hoare's Bank in the Eighteenth Century', in Joel Mokyr and Laura Cruz (eds.), *The Birth of Modern Europe, 1400–1800: Essays in Honour of Jan De Vries* (Leiden, 2010), pp. 81–108; D. M. Joslin, 'London Private Bankers 1720–95', *Economic History Review*, 7 (1954–5), 167–86; Iain S. Black, 'Private Banking in London's West End, 1750–1830', *London Journal*, 28 (2003), 29–59.

Table 3.1. *Lottery tickets bought through Hoare's Bank, 1711–1755*

Lottery	No. of tickets	No. of individuals for whom tickets were purchased
1711 £10 lottery	2,302	113
1712 £10 lottery	2,272	119
1714	684	39
1723	789	68
1724	2,582	108
1726	1,836	102
1731	396	99
Charitable Corporation, 1733	1,293	104
Bridge Lottery, 1737	911*	82
1755	527	49

*There were several lists pertaining to this lottery, and the figures are not entirely consistent.
Sources: Hoare's Bank, HB/1/6, Ledger for Plate, 1697–c.1730; HB/5/H/1–2, Money Lent Ledgers, 1710–c.1725; HB/8/G/10, accounts regarding the Bridge lotteries, 1737–9; HB/8/G11, record of payments to the bank to complete the remaining sums due upon receipts for tickets in the lottery, 1755

premises at the sign of the Golden Unicorn in Pall Mall, goldsmith banker, John Ewer, was decidedly discouraging when people wrote to him asking if he would buy tickets for them in the early 1730s, although it is clear that, despite his own stated 'indifference' towards lottery adventures, he did so for a fair few individuals, including the Duchess of Hamilton.[68] In the case of the partners of Hoare's Bank on Fleet Street, whose high church and Tory views were shared by many (although by no means all) of their clientele, we can put some numbers on the scale on which they purchased tickets for them. For seven lotteries staged between 1723 and 1737, two of which were not state lotteries, and for which consolidated records of their activity survive, the bank's partners bought tickets for 347 clients (see Table 3.1 above).[69] Other banks – Drummond's and Coutts, for example – regularly purchased tickets for customers, although on what sort of scale is less clear. Goldsmith banker, John Campbell, forerunner of Coutts, was heavily involved in purchasing tickets for his clients in the Queen Anne lotteries, in one communication noting that he had been unable to send an account of a recent transaction

[68] Westminster City Archives, Acc. 762, letter book of John Ewer, banker, 1731–3. I am grateful to Perry Gauci for drawing this source to my attention.

[69] For a fuller discussion of the evidence, see Bob Harris, 'Lottery Adventuring in Britain, c.1710–1760', *English Historical Review*, 133 (2018), 284–322.

Table 3.2. *Drummond's Bank, lottery dealings, 1724–1760*

Year	Tickets bought	Tickets sold before the draw	No. of clients to whom tickets were sold
1724	630		60
1731	300 (first payment)		c.20
1736 Bridge lottery	866		c.39
1737 Bridge lottery	1,176 (first payment); 931(second payment)	200	49
1743	111	34	17
1745	100 (three payments only)	100 (on which three payments made)	?
1755	1,763 (first payment); 250 (final payment)	219; received cash for first payment on 105	74
1757	790		53
1758	165	160	?
1759	250	250	?
1760	500	450	?

Sources: RBS Archives, Drummond's Bank, Customer Account Ledgers

to a client in March 1711 because '[w]ee have been so busy about this lottery'.[70] In the initial subscription for the first lottery of 1711, Campbell paid into the Bank of England, for himself and his 'friends' [i.e. clients] £10,600.[71] During 1711–1712, he acted on lottery business for at least thirty-one individuals, ten of whom were peers.[72] In the case of Drummond's Bank (see Table 3.2 above), the degree of involvement varied quite significantly from lottery to lottery, although, as with other banks, some clients were fairly regular users of this service. Sometimes difficult to tell is how far banks were purchasing on their own account or for clients; in most cases it appears to have been in both capacities. Banks also bought blanks (tickets which had failed to win a prize in the draw)

70 Coutts & Co. Archives, Letter Book 6, 13 Jan. 1710–14 Oct. 1714, fo. 26v., John Campbell to Alexander Campbell, 10 Mar. 1711.

71 Coutts & Co. Archives, Letter Book 6, 13 Jan. 1710–14 Oct. 1714, fo. 27v., John Campbell to John Campbell, 15 Mar. 1711.

72 Data extracted from Coutts & Co. Archives, Letter Book 6. Later letter books indicate that clients bought lottery tickets through the bank throughout the eighteenth century. Coutts does not, however, appear to have kept consolidated lottery accounts, and the account books of individual clients are not readily accessible to historians. I am grateful to Tracey Earl, archivist at Coutts Bank, for information and assistance on this question.

and prizes from their clients. For example, in 1721, the perpetually slippery Simon Fraser, Lord Lovat used Drummond's Bank to buy two lottery tickets for £22.2 sh. on 30 June, later (in early September) selling the two resulting blanks for £15.3 sh., paying a commission on this latter transaction of a shilling. In 1743, the 2nd Duke of Atholl remitted to the same bank the difference between the price of six tickets that had been bought for his eldest son, Lord George Murray, who, ironically perhaps in the present context, would in 1745–1746 be military commander of the Jacobite forces that sought to uproot the Hanoverian regime, and six blanks that had been sold through the bank.[73] Had Lord George won a capital prize in the lottery perhaps he might have steered well clear of Bonnie Prince Charlie's highly risky political adventure.

Not only were London banks active in this capacity. By the mid eighteenth century the Edinburgh-based Bank of Scotland was buying tickets for several clients, including several members of the Ayrshire gentry.[74] Less certain is whether its rival, the Royal Bank of Scotland, established in 1727, was doing likewise, although in the later 1750s and early 1760s its accountant James Ewart was dealing in tickets, shares of tickets, and 'chances'.[75] In 1763 Ewart seems to have been running a scheme selling tickets in that year's state lottery, as well as two Irish charitable lotteries.[76] In 1764 he was dismissed from the bank, having fallen into debt and been imprisoned in the tolbooth under the instructions of one of his creditors. How or whether, indeed, his downfall related at all to his lottery dealings is, sadly, unclear.[77]

Banks continued to deal in lottery tickets in the later eighteenth century, buying and selling tickets for clients, although on an ever-diminishing scale in the case of the latter. This included the proliferating

[73] RBS Archives, DR/427/2, Drummond's Bank, Customer Account Ledger, 1722–3; DR/427/23, Drummond's Bank, Customer Account Ledger, 1743–4, fo. 27.

[74] NRS, GD113/3/487, papers of George Innes, 2nd cashier of the Bank of Scotland.

[75] *CalM*, 4 Aug. 1759; 6 Aug. 1760. John Campbell, the cashier of the bank, bought and sold lottery tickets for James Campbell of St Germains in 1744, although this may have been a joint enterprise between them. RBS Archives, RB/1480/11/8, Account of James Campbell of St Germains with John Campbell for the purchase of lottery tickets, 12 May 1744. I have as yet failed to locate other details relating to lottery ticket purchases in the records of the bank, although Lord Deskford had an agent pay cash to the Royal Bank in 1757 'obliging them to deliver 20 lottery tickets' (NRS, GD248/697/5, account of James, Lord Deskford with Mr James Philp, advocate, entry for 23 Mar. 1757), which may indicate that Ewart was acting on more than simply his own initiative.

[76] NRS, RH15/66/7, accounts and business letters addressed to James Ewart, 1762–4; Court of Session Productions, CS96/3307, James Ewart, Royal Bank, Edinburgh, lottery ticket note book, 1763.

[77] RBS Archives, RB/1480/23/1, draft letter from John Campbell to John Campbell of Achalader, 20 July 1764.

country or provincial banks.[78] In the 1790s, the Edinburgh banker and owner of the *Caledonian Mercury* newspaper, Robert Allan, bought tickets for Lieutenant Colonel Murdoch Maclaine of Lochbuie on the Isle of Mull and his son.[79] The main reason why banks became less important in this context was the growing importance of lottery offices; and it is to these that we now turn.

3.3 Lottery Offices

When lottery offices first emerged as leading players in, and creators of, the lottery marketplace is impossible to say definitively. Impressionistic evidence – derived mainly from newspaper advertisements and personal account books – points pretty strongly to the central decades of the eighteenth century as being the crucial period. Currently rather little is known about these concerns, the identity of the individuals behind them, levels of their capitalization, and scales on which they operated.[80] By the late eighteenth century the picture they present is of a core of well-established concerns, some of which had been in existence since the 1740s or 1750s, around which swarmed a larger number of much more marginal, short-lived operations, fighting for survival in a crowded, fiercely competitive market, and frequently operating on the margins of legality.[81]

Most lottery office keepers appear to have been stockbrokers for whom sales of lottery tickets and lottery-related products became the main components of their business. Charles Corbett and his son, also called

[78] For one example, the Manchester bank, Heywood Brothers, see RBS Archives, HB/36/1, Heywood Brothers Customer Account Ledger, 1791–4, f. 433, 'Lottery Tickets, 1791–2'. This appears to show the partners of the bank purchasing 1,800 tickets for £3,859.2.7 and selling them for £5,165.5.7.

[79] NRS, Maclaine of Lochbuie Papers, GD174/419/71, Robert Allan, Edinburgh, to Murdoch Maclaine of Lochbuy, 17 July 1795; 78, account current of Lt. Col. Murdoch Maclaine with Robert Allan & Co, 1795.

[80] The accounts of one lottery business, White, Benge & Co. of 16 Lombard Street can be found in the archives of the Honourable Artillery Company, HAC/As/G1/1, HAC Lottery Accounts 1775–1777. They dealt in tickets and shares, bought and sold prizes, as well as insuring against drawing a blank. The accounts are not readily comprehensible, since expenses and income are not clearly distinguished, nor are the nature of payments usually specified. Nevertheless, what is evident is the need for access to considerable capital – they, for example, bought 367 tickets in November 1776 at a cost of nearly £4,500 – together with the importance of insurance as an aspect of lottery businesses.

[81] See further below.

Charles, were more unusual in that they were booksellers. Corbett junior would be ruined in 1771 by the mis-sale of a lottery ticket.[82]

The rise of lottery offices was, from one perspective, another symptom of the maturation and specialization of eighteenth-century financial markets first charted systematically by Peter Dickson.[83] An early entrant about whom we know more than most was goldsmith banker Matthew West. His activities also begin to show just how important such people were from an early stage in driving an expansion in sales of lottery tickets. West may have begun his lottery business in 1710; but he was certainly active in 1711, offering a scheme to the public whereby individuals could purchase shares in that year's ten-pound lottery. Following the draw, the tickets would be sold, prizes and blanks alike, and the proceeds divided up between the participants in proportion to the size of their investment. West's was one of at least two such schemes which operated in that year, both of which were organized and promoted by groups of goldsmith bankers.[84] West ran similar schemes in later years, also by the early 1720s dealing in tickets in various Dutch lotteries. By at least 1731 he was advertising his services in the Edinburgh press.[85] Potential customers in Edinburgh or elsewhere could communicate their demands to West by letter. They could also, for a fee (6d), register their tickets, which meant that they would be notified expeditiously of their fate by post.

By the mid eighteenth century people were commonly distributing their lottery purchases between different lottery offices, presumably convinced (or hopeful) that this might increase their chances of scooping one of the capital prizes.[86] Lottery offices did business in person, by proxy, or

[82] James Raven, *The Business of Books: Booksellers and the English Book Trade 1450–1850* (New Haven and London, 2007), p. 240.

[83] Dickson, *Financial Revolution.*

[84] *News Supplement*, 9 Mar. 1711; *Daily Courant*, 20 July 1711; *Post Boy*, 7 Apr. 1711; *British Mercury*, 1 Feb. 1712 [notice from West announcing sale of ninety-two tickets and arrangements for division of the proceeds]. There were further ancillary schemes which derived from the lottery, including one which involved subscribing blank tickets from the first 1711 lottery, with an additional 12d per ticket, and then balloting for what year in which their principal would be repaid (*Post Boy*, 27 Feb. 1711). Another, designed to benefit widows and orphans, involved subscribing ten blanks and nominating three lives. For the first life, a subscriber received £6 pa. If this individual died, they received £12 pa, and £18 pa for the third. This represented a minimum return of around 9% pa. (*Tatler*, 10 Feb. 1711.)

[85] *Daily Journal*, 5 Sept. 1722; *London Journal*, 25 May 1723; *Daily Journal*, 9 Sept. 1724; *CalM*, 9 Aug. 1731.

[86] For one example, see NRO, MC 2782/A/1& 2, pocket diary of Augustine Earle, 1757–8, 1759–60. Earle was a commissioner of the excise, a member of the Society for Antiquaries, and owned the Heydon manor in Norfolk. John Heaton Delaval, the energetic improving owner of Hussey Delaval in the north-east of England, followed

through the post, and the standardized printed letters issued by lottery offices informing clients of the fate of their tickets in the draw are to be found in many a set of estate and family records, usually (all-too-predictably) notifying them that their tickets had been drawn blanks.[87]

Lottery office keepers continually sought ways to sustain and expand their businesses. Apart from aggressive self-promotion and publicity, one means was, like West, through offering sales of shares of tickets of ever-decreasing fractions. In 1719 Andrew and William Bell, who had premises in Cornhill at the heart of the City of London – the most common location for lottery offices throughout the eighteenth century – sold eighth shares of tickets for 8 sh.; tickets in the lotteries of that year cost £3 rather than the more usual £10. The Bells boasted that for an investment of 8 sh. you might win £2,500.[88] Later in the eighteenth century, lottery offices offered shares as small as 64ths, before, that is, parliament decreed (in 1787) that sixteenths were the smallest permitted share.[89]

Lottery office keepers developed other products designed to extend lottery participation. These included, notoriously, in the 1720s the hiring of tickets for a specified time, a practice which was known as 'riding a horse'. It quickly produced complaints that it was causing the ruin of large numbers of people lured into gambling sums that they could ill afford to lose. In 1724 one London newspaper urged:

> … its hoped Methods will be taken to prevent the Hiring of Horses and other pernicious Practices, which were carried on in Exchange Alley during the Drawing of the last Lottery, to such as Height, that many Persons have thereby been utterly ruined … The Horses, which, 'tis said, would have from 40 to 50 a Day upon the Hire, bore an excessive Price, particularly, the last Day of drawing they were at a Guinea an hour.[90]

Two years later, it was declared in the press that hiring of tickets had been 'as fatal to the inferiour Rank, as the S.[outh] S.[ea] Scheme was to those of higher Rank'.[91] This assessment was almost certainly exaggerated, although we have no way of telling who mainly took advantage of this

the same practice somewhat later in the eighteenth century (for which, see Northumberland Record Office, Delaval Papers, 2 DE 35/17, lotteries, 1771–1805).

87 The various uses of standardized printing by lottery offices to achieve gains in efficiency are emphasized by James Raven in *Publishing Business in Eighteenth Century England* (Woodbridge, 2014).

88 *Post Man and the Historical Account*, 11–13 Aug. 1719.

89 Bodl., John Johnson Collection: Lotteries vol. 6 (3), Notice of State Lottery for 1774 for W. Hodges & Co.

90 *CalM*, 12 Oct. 1724.

91 *CalM*, 21 Nov. 1726. See also ibid., 27 Sept. 1726, for comment on the intensity of demand for 'horses'.

practice; but it was certainly more than those of so-called inferior rank.[92] Hiring of tickets continued throughout the 1730s and into the early 1740s, before parliament prohibited it through legislation passed in 1743 and 1744, under a penalty of £500. Yet, as Dickson notes, such was the ingenuity of lottery office keepers that confronted with this prohibition, they merely turned to another practice – lottery insurance, a slippery subject to which we will return later.[93]

One other product that lottery offices offered was only indirectly related to the official lottery, although it piggybacked directly on the official draw. These were schemes involving so-called chances. 'Chances' cost less than a ticket or share thereof, and usually paid correspondingly lower sums if the associated number won a prize in the lottery draw.[94] While they appear to have initially emerged on a sizeable scale in the 1720s, they flourished markedly in the 1770s and 1780s, becoming ever-more elaborate in design and prominently promoted by lottery office keepers, until they were suppressed at the beginning of the 1790s by a combination of legislative and judicial action.[95] The reason for their suppression appears to have been that some of them were fraudulent; more importantly, they represented unwanted competition to the official lottery.

[92] See e.g. KARC, North Papers, EK/U471/A50, personal expenses of Lady Arabella Furnese, 1714–27, entry for 15 Sept. 1724, which reads: 'Pd my sister Saunderson my share for ye Hiring of ye chance of two Tickets in the lottery for one Day 0-11-0.'

[93] Dickson, *Financial Revolution*, p. 507. Dickson suggests that the reason behind this was not concern about encouragement of gambling by the lesser sort, but the potential impact on ticket prices; money used to hire tickets would otherwise have been used to buy them, thus helping to inflate prices.

[94] An alternative model was that they paid the same sums as the lottery proper, but not the lowest-denominated prizes.

[95] See *MChr*, 9 Jan. 1782, 'letter from MEANWELL' bemoaning the ingenuity by which lottery keepers invented schemes involving 'chances' and lured the credulous into gambling away sums they could not afford. Two such schemes, offered by, respectively, Messrs Sharman and Co. and Margay & Co., were advertised in the *Morning Post and Daily Advertiser*, 16 June 1780. Sharman and Co.'s scheme was offered chances at four prices – a guinea, half a guinea, 7s., and 4s. If the number was drawn a £10 or £20 prize, the purchaser of the chance was to be paid a sum somewhat less than their initial stake, while if it was drawn a capital prize it won a much larger sum. In the case of one of the schemes – where the chances cost 7s – it looks like its organizers owned the actual tickets corresponding to the numbers for sale, which is why the largest prizes were the same as in the official lottery. Margray & Co.'s scheme was a half guinea one based, first, on the Irish lottery. If the number drew a blank or £10 prize in this lottery it went forward to stand in the English lottery. Prizes consisted of numbers of presumably undrawn English lottery tickets. For the campaign to suppress this aspect of the lottery market, see Bob Harris, 'Selling the Lottery in Britain, c.1694–1826', in Ric Berman and William Gibson (eds.), *The Lantern of History: Essays in Honour of Jeremy Black* (Goring Heath, Oxon, 2020), pp. 86–110.

By the final decades of the eighteenth century, lottery offices accounted for the bulk of sales of tickets to the public. This position was underlined by the establishment of a system of licensing of lottery offices in 1779, also aimed at regulating their activities more closely and, as alluded to earlier, the move to a system from 1785 whereby lottery contractors bid for the right to sell tickets, and, under treasury oversight, determined the design of the lotteries. Forty-seven separate businesses took out lottery licenses in 1779.[96] By the last two decades of the eighteenth century, there were probably many more, if, that is, we include the many shadowy unlicensed ones.[97] There were also, by this date, licensed offices in several of the largest provincial towns and cities. Provincial lottery offices seem to have first emerged in the 1750s – for example, in Bristol and Edinburgh.[98] Thomas Bish, probably the leading lottery contractor of the later eighteenth and early nineteenth centuries, had licensed offices in London, Edinburgh, and Manchester; while by the 1790s there were licensed offices in Exeter, Bath, Bristol, Birmingham, Newcastle, Liverpool, and Norwich.[99] In the 1770s, provincial lottery agencies (as opposed to offices proper) were widespread. In several cases these were printers of provincial newspapers, who used their newsmen – the people who distributed the paper in its locality – to collect orders for tickets.[100] After 1782 licensed lottery businesses were allowed to have as many agents as they chose. In c. 1800, J. Branscomb & Co., to take one example, had forty-three country offices, from Aberdeen in north-east Scotland, Exeter in the south west, and Yarmouth on the Norfolk coast, although not a single one in Wales.[101] Witnesses appearing before the 1808 parliamentary committee on the laws relating

[96] *PA*, 4 Aug. 1779 [notice, Lottery Office, 27 July 1779].

[97] One contemporary claimed in 1787 that there were as many as 700 unlicensed lottery offices. (TNA, T1/652/68–75, memorial on lotteries, n.d., but 1787.) The *St James's Chronicle* claimed in its issue of 10 Jan. 1775 that there were 'no less than 300 lottery offices' distributed throughout the capital, while in December of the same year (7 Dec. 1775) it declared that there is 'scarce a street, court or Alley without three or four of these open Gambling Houses'.

[98] *WEP*, 28 Aug. 1758, advertisement for J. Hazard, lottery office keeper.

[99] *The Salisbury and Winchester Journal*, 9 Dec. 1799, advertisement for Bish entitled 'Profit Without Risk'. See also *EdinA*, 25 Nov. 1791, which listed those licensed to sell tickets in the state lotteries.

[100] *Northampton Mercury*, 3 Jan. 1774; *Reading Mercury and Oxford Gazette*, 17 Jan. 1774; *Leeds Intelligencer*, 9 May 1775. John Ware of Whitehaven, printer of the *Cumberland Pacquet*, appears to have been operating as a very occasional lottery agent at the turn of the nineteenth century. CRO, Carlisle, DA/276A & B, John Ware Account Books, 1799–1802, 1802–1805.

[101] The full range of places were: Aberdeen; Bath; Bristol; Birmingham; Bury; Bolton; Coventry; Chatham; Chester; Chichester; Dorchester; Derby; Dundee; Exeter; Edinburgh; Gloucester; Glasgow; Gosport; Hull; Lancaster; Liverpool; King's Lynn;

to the lotteries uniformly reported that the system of agencies had spread markedly from 1802 with more frequent lotteries. One estimate in the early nineteenth century put their overall number at as many as 3,000.[102] By this date there can have been remarkably few places in Britain, large or small, that did not boast lottery agents or within relatively close proximity.[103]

Two sets of lottery records dating from the early nineteenth century amply confirm this picture of relentless geographical expansion. They are, first, the lottery register books of Norwich stationer and local lottery agent John Craske, which cover the lotteries of 1813–1816 and 1821–1824; and, second, books covering the last few lotteries in the 1820s of Glasgow stationer Thomas Murray, who acted as an agent for the important London lottery business of John and James Sievewright.[104] Somewhat frustratingly Craske's records give only sporadic indications of the addresses of the purchasers of tickets. Most of his clients, nevertheless, appear to have hailed from Norwich, usually buying the smallest available shares of tickets, sixteenths. There are also scattered references, however, to places across Norfolk – Ashwelthorpe, Aylsham, Beccles, Bungay, Burnham Market, Hethersett, Dereham, Mendlesham, Wymondham, and so on. Stray letters interpolated in the leaves of the books reveal how easy it was for someone living outside of Norwich to

Marlborough; Newark; Newport, Isle of Wight; Norwich; Northampton; Newcastle; Nottingham; Plymouth; Portsea; Reading; Salisbury; Stamford; Shrewsbury; Sherborne; Weymouth; Wolverhampton; Winchester; Worcester; Warrington; Yarmouth; York. CRO, Barrow-on-Furness, Soulby Collection, handbill for J. Branscomb, n.d. but c. 1800.

102 TNA, IR55/13, Return to the Honourable House of Commons Pursuant to an Order for 'An Account of the Number of Lotteries Drawn under Act of Parliament since 1811 Inclusive, Together with the Amount of Revenue Derived Severally from the Same, Shewing also the Terms Upon Which the Said Lotteries were Disposed of to the Contractors' (1816).

103 Their spread can be traced at the local and regional level in the advertisement columns of the provincial press. See e.g. *The Bury and Norwich Post; or Suffolk, Norfolk, Cambridgeshire and Ely Advertiser*, 21, 24 Jan., 7 Feb. 1810, which contained notices for lottery agents in Bury St Edmunds (2), King's Lynn, Norwich (3), Colchester, Hadleigh, Woodbridge, Downham Market, Saffron Walden, Yarmouth, and Ballingdon. Most were involved in the book, printing, or newspaper trades, or some combination thereof, which makes perfect sense in terms of the structure and operation of provincial bookselling and printing, its close business and personal links to, respectively, the capital's print-publishers and news industry, and their reliance on the postal services. They were also used to acting as agents, for example, for medical remedies.

104 NRO, BR80/1 & 2, lottery register books of John Craske, 1813–25; NRS, Court of Session Productions, CS96/2105, John and James Sievewright, lottery contractors, London, Thomas Murray, stationer, Glasgow, lottery ticket sales book, 1824–6.

purchase tickets from Craske. Carriers – those relatively unheralded heroes of economic progress in this period – were one important means. They transported letters and money to his office, and then returned with the ticket(s) to its purchaser. Given the exponential growth of carrier services in this period, especially in the decades after 1760, their increased professionalization and organizational sophistication and efficiency, remarkably few places can have remained entirely inaccessible to the lottery business, although the density of connections varied regionally, broadly following quite closely the advancing frontiers of urbanization and early industrialization.[105]

Similarly, only a minority of entries in the Glasgow lottery books include addresses for purchasers of tickets. Murray had his own agents in, respectively, the booming industrial frontier town of Paisley, the important Clyde ports of Greenock and Port Glasgow, Ayr, the county town of Ayrshire, and the Ayrshire manufacturing centre and port of Irvine. Even based on the relatively sparse information provided, the geographical coverage of Murray's business was strikingly extensive. It reached throughout much of west-central Scotland (Airdrie, Stirling, Renfrew, Strathaven, Kirkintilloch, Neilston, Pollockshaws, Beith, Cumbernauld, Dumbarton, Balfron, Hamilton, Kilwinning, Partick, Cambuslang, Ayr, Port Dundas, Eaglesham, Dunblane, Sanquhar, Stewarton, Saltcoats, West Kilbride), and even into and across remote parts of Argyllshire (Dunoon, Campbeltown, Arran, Inverary, Fort William, Oban, Tobermory on Mull, and Arrochar).[106]

There is one other important type of intermediary in the lottery marketplace deserving of brief mention – commercial lottery societies. These appear to have flourished again particularly in the 1780s. Essentially what they involved was sharing the cumulative gains of any capital prizes and smaller prizes between subscribers according to the sum invested.[107] Such schemes in one sense go back to those run much earlier in the century by individuals such as goldsmith banker Matthew West. However, they can also be seen as a scaling-up of the many lottery clubs

[105] D. Gerhold, The Growth of the London Carrying Trade, 1681–1838', *Economic History Review*, 41 (1988), 392–410; G. L. Turnbull, 'Provincial Road Carrying in England in the Eighteenth Century', *Journal of Transport History*, 4 (1977), 17–39; Bob Harris and Charles McKean, *The Scottish Town in the Age of the Enlightenment* (Edinburgh, 2014), pp. 109–11.

[106] There were even individuals from Frankfurt-am-Main and Huddersfield.

[107] Jackson, *A Guide to Adventurers*, which promoted one such society, the Amicable Society of Lottery Adventurers, and warned about the many, fraudulent imitative schemes.

which flickered into existence in many places, and which were often, but far from exclusively, linked to taverns and public houses. One anonymous individual who toured the main wheat-growing counties in England in the early autumn of 1775, which were in the south and east, reported: 'I think the People are all made after Gambling, for I scarce saw one Public-house without a lottery club.'[108] In 1786, a newspaper report told of one small club, numbering five members, which met at the White Hart in Woodford, on the north eastern edge of London, who had scooped a £20,000 prize, setting off wild celebrations in every public house in the village.[109] Some lottery clubs had formal rules or articles of association[110]; but the vast majority did not, hence they have left only faint traces of their existence. Lottery and indeed other clubs undeniably contributed very significantly to extending the market for official lottery tickets among the middling and labouring classes, although evidence for this is, frustratingly, almost entirely confined to occasional newspaper reports and pieces of publicity produced by the lottery office keepers.[111]

The market, therefore, for lottery tickets expanded phenomenally in this period, both in terms of geographical scope and social depth, although we will have more to say about the latter in the following chapter. The lottery benefited from the early, broadening, and intensifying commercialization of British society, and especially from the transformation in communications by road and through the expanding, thickening network of the postal services. It is a story of market integration, entrepreneurial energy, and creativity, and businesses which were very quick to exploit new possibilities for promoting consumption of goods and products, including, most importantly perhaps, the changed world of print which had been ushered into newly vigorous life by the end of pre-publication censorship in 1695.

[108] *PA*, 28 Sept. 1775, letter signed with the initials 'S. G.'. The Craske lottery book contains relatively regular references to purchases by a number of Norwich lottery clubs, some of which clearly met in a tavern – e.g. 'R. Club: Imperial Arms', 'Swan Inn Club', 'Lamb Lottery Club' – and some which may well have done – e.g. 'Club at Mr Pattens', 'Angel Club', 'Club at Compasses' and so forth. What is not clear is how many were actually lottery clubs, or existing associations, members of which on occasion bought lottery tickets collectively.

[109] *Reading and Oxford Gazette*, 13 Mar. 1786. I owe this reference to Eamonn O'Keeffe.

[110] See e.g. SCA, NC/59, Rules and Orders Agreed Upon to be Kept and Strictly Observed by an Amicable Society for Raising a Sum of Money in Order to be Adventured in Every State Lottery for the Equal Benefit and Advantage of Every Member of the Said Society, 28 Mar. 1755.

[111] See further on this, ch. 4, pp. 201–2.

3.4 Publicizing the Lottery

From the beginning, the press, print, and the fortunes of lotteries were tightly bound up together, as emphasized by Ann Murphy, the leading modern historian of the early lotteries, and Natasha Glaisyer.[112] As referred to earlier, the terms of state lotteries were published first in the official newspaper, the *London Gazette*, from whence they were speedily reprinted in the pages of the capital's proliferating newssheets. Banker John Campbell could readily assume already in 1711 that his client, Lord Yester, would have read about the first lottery of that year in the newspaper the *Post Man*.[113] It was not long before schemes of lotteries were regularly appearing in a rapidly expanding and maturing provincial press, as well as in the more slowly developing Scottish one.[114] As with stock prices, and often based on the same source – commodity and stock price currents – metropolitan and provincial newspapers reported the fluctuating prices of tickets and blanks. They commented on demand for tickets, the state of the draw, the numbers of winning tickets, and the identity of the lucky winners of the big capital prizes. On 7 December 1747, the Edinburgh weekly newspaper the *Caledonian Mercury* reported not just the numbers of all the tickets which had won large prizes in the last two days, but the identities of several local lottery winners:

> We hear No. 38818, drawn On Saturday last a Prize of 1,000 l. is the Property of Mr Manship, a wholesale Linnen Draper in Princess Street; that the 5,000 l. drawn on the 23d, is the Property of Mr. North, Clerk of the Merchant Taylors Company; and that one of the 1,000 l. drawn this Lottery is the Property of Mess. Fairholm and Company, Merchants in Edinburgh.

The *Chester Chronicle* reported on 9 May 1775 that local man Faithful Thomas, deputy constable of Chester Castle, had won £300 in Cox's Museum Lottery, while a week later (on 15 May) the *Salisbury Journal* was reporting on a similar win by a local watchmaker. Alongside what was a veritable barrage of newspaper coverage an enormous volume of printed ephemera poured forth from the presses of metropolitan printers to promote and inform about the lottery and exploit contemporary interest therein: printed schemes; books listing the prizewinners or benefits from the lottery draw; so-called number books – numerical books in

112 Murphy, *Origins*, p. 95; Natasha Glaisyer, *The Culture of Commerce in England, 1660–1720* (Woodbridge, 2006), esp. pp. 155, 168–9, 179.
113 Coutts & Co. Archives, Letter Book 6, fo. 20r, Campbell to Lord Yester, 24 Feb. 1711.
114 The *Caledonian Mercury*, for example, published the full scheme of the lottery of 1721 (*CalM*, 27 June 1721), but Scottish papers, such as the *Scots Courant*, had contained various reports on the lotteries from at least 1711.

which to record the fate of tickets, handbills, and so on. By the later eighteenth century, as printer-publishers sought to feed the buoyant demand for pocket books of dizzying variety, so appeared lottery pocket books, presumably in which you could record the fate of your numbers.[115] Much earlier the capital's coffee houses moved promptly to provide accounts of the state of the draw for anxious ticket owners, each claiming greater expedition and accuracy than the rest. Lists of drawn numbers, prizes and blanks, were produced daily during the draw, even by the hour, and, for a fee, could be sent to ticket owners outside the capital.[116] In the early nineteenth century, similar lists were being sent free through the post under the franks of the post office clerks of the road.[117]

Lottery office keepers, meanwhile, increasingly advertised their services in the provincial as well as metropolitan press, also inserting 'puffs' – paid for paragraphs purporting to be news – aimed at stimulating interest in the lottery. By the end of the century schemes of lotteries routinely appeared in *all* of the metropolitan and provincial newspapers. They were also being distributed in the form of single-sheet publications by stage and mail coachmen.[118]

With the continued expansion and growth of the provincial press, but also the significantly increasing English provincial and Scottish circulation of London papers after 1764, in newsprint lottery businesses had at their ready disposal a very powerful engine of publicity, indeed.[119] In 1787 a separate newspaper office, staffed by sixteen people, was established at the general post office in London, such was the volume of newspapers with which it now had to cope. In the year ending 5 January 1791, 3,944,093 London papers were dispatched through this office. In the same period in 1808–1809 this figure had risen to 7,421,320, while in 1810–1811 it reached 8,598,987.[120] From his

115 Hertfordshire Archives and Local Studies, Sworders of Stocking Pelham and Almshoebury, E. 1845, *Ladies Lottery Pocket Book* (1777). Thanks are due to Hazel Tubman for pointing this out to me.

116 See relevant notices in, *inter alia*, *Spectator*, 1, 24 Oct.; *British Mercury*, 8, 15, 22 Oct.; *Post Boy*, 11, 23 Oct. 1711.

117 RMA, Post 24/2, Articles to the Circulated to the Clerks of the Road, 27 Mar. 1811

118 The rise of specialist advertising agencies in the capital made this placing of advertisements throughout the provincial as well as metropolitan press much simpler. For which, see Victoria E. M. Gardner, *The Business of News in England, 1760–1820* (Basingstoke, 2016), p. 64.

119 See Harris, 'Selling the Lottery'.

120 RMA, Post 24/1, number of newspapers passed through the General Post Office, London, 5 Jan. 1790–5 Jan. 1791; Post 24/2, an account of the number of newspapers sent by the vendors through the News Paper Office for the last three years, 1809–11.

'London Newspaper Office' in Dumfries in the early nineteenth century, bookseller George Johnstone boasted of his ability to supply London newspapers on the same terms as when ordered through London agents.[121] This growth of provincial circulation, and that of the press more generally, were despite sharp increases in the late eighteenth and early nineteenth centuries of prices of newspapers driven by successive increases in stamp duty. By 1800 there were around 100 provincial papers in existence, in addition to a metropolitan press comprising morning and evening dailies, tri-weeklies, and weeklies.[122] The expansion in numbers of Scottish newspapers may have been rather less impressive before the early nineteenth century. Nevertheless, by the final decade of the eighteenth century nearly 7,500 Edinburgh papers were being sent out weekly into the rest of the country through the post, the bulk of them northwards and westwards.[123] The rising numbers of coffee and subscription reading rooms across Britain – such as the Union New Room established in the small Cumbrian town of Ulverston in 1820 – made this abundance of newsprint readily available to the provincial middling sort – the growing ranks of professionals, merchants, manufacturers and tradesmen who, cumulatively and increasingly energetically and systematically, reshaped much of provincial urban culture and townscapes in their own image.[124] Even the coffee room attached to the George Inn in the small south-west Scottish port town of Stranraer in 1811 furnished customers with two London daily papers and two Scottish weeklies.[125] Meanwhile, clubbing together to subscribe to a newspaper was an increasingly common practice among members of the skilled labouring classes by at least the 1790s.[126]

[121] *The Dumfries and Galloway Courier*, 2 July 1811. See also Johnstone's notice in the same paper, 23 June 1812.

[122] For general guides to the development of the press in this period, see Hannah Barker, *Newspapers, Politics and English Society 1695–1855* (Harlow, 2000); Jeremy Black, *The English Press in the Eighteenth Century* (Beckenham, 1987); C. Y. Ferdinand, *Benjamin Collins and the Provincial Newspaper Trade in the Eighteenth Century* (Oxford, 1997). There is no modern comprehensive study of the Scottish press, but see relevant comment in Bob Harris, 'Scotland's Newspapers, the French Revolution and Domestic Radicalism, c.1789–1794', *Scottish Historical Review*, 84 (2005), 38–52; Alex Benchimol, Rhona Brown and David Shuttleworth (eds.), *Before Blackwood's: Scottish Journalism in the Age of Enlightenment* (London, 2015).

[123] RMA, Post 30/2, account of Edinburgh's newspapers sent to the country in a week, n.d. but later 1790s.

[124] Subscription reading rooms from at least the 1790s typically offered a range of metropolitan, provincial, and foreign, including sometimes colonial, newspapers.

[125] *The Dumfries and Galloway Courier*, 16 July 1811.

[126] See, *inter alia*, E. S. Chalk, 'Circulation of XVIII-century newspapers', *Notes and Queries*, 169 (1935), p. 336; M. J. Smith, 'English Radical Newspapers in the French

By the 1770s, if not significantly earlier, therefore, even the most casual of newspaper readers would have been struck by the sheer volume of lottery advertising and other lottery-related material in the periods leading up to and during the lottery draw. By the early nineteenth century, it was unmissable – such was its prominence – both in terms of volume and form, with most issues of provincial papers immediately before and during draw containing notices from at least two lottery contractors or business, many of them (unusually) spanning more than a single column in width and often involving use of large, bold type.[127] How much money was expended on this and other forms of publicity is unclear, but it must have been a good proportion of the normal expenses of lottery businesses.[128] The accounts of John Craske, the Norwich lottery agent of the 1810s and 1820s, include regular entries for posting bills, day boards (presumably advertising boards), circulars, entries which read 'Bill Town' and 'Bill Fair' (meaning handbills for circulation around Norwich and at fair time), as well as for 'advertisements', which were almost certainly notices in the Norwich and other regional newspapers. These local activities were essentially supplemental, however, to the massive campaigns of the big London lottery contractors by the early nineteenth century. In 1816, the treasury estimated that 'upwards' of ten million lottery bills 'of all sizes' had been printed in the previous year.[129] The printing expenses of the lottery contractors for the third lottery of 1809 amounted to over £13,600.[130] This, recall, is in addition to peppering the metropolitan and provincial newspapers with puffs and advertisements.

Lottery entrepreneurs were, in brief, masters of advertising, employing newspapers, placard men, sandwich men, wall posters, advertising vehicles (so-called errand carts), as well as handbills of ever-greater ingenuity, verbally and visually, in an effort to conjure into being and

Revolutionary Era, 1790–1803', unpublished PhD thesis, University of London, 1979; Bob Harris, *The Scottish People and the French Revolution* (London, 2008), p. 46. It was the fears of the propertied classes about the politicization of the lower orders in the 1790s that made such practices unusually visible, but they may well have occurred earlier.

127 For the early nineteenth century, see e.g. *Kelso Mail*, 10, 14, 17, 21, 24, 28 Apr.; 16, 19, 20, 26 June; 3, 7, 17, 31 July; 14, 21, 25 Aug.; 1, 8, 25 Sept.; 2, 6, 23 Oct.; 6, 20, 24 Nov.; 15, 29 Dec. 1817.

128 For discussion of this, see Harris, 'Selling the Lottery'.

129 TNA, IR55/10, draft return to the House of Commons, 1817.

130 TNA, T/64/324, Report of the Four Auditors Appointed to Inspect the Accounts Delivered by Richardson, Swift & Co. for Expences in the Third Lottery for 1809, Drawn 19th October 1810, in Which they were the Contractors (1811).

to sustain public interest in the lottery. A very common technique was to publicize winning tickets bought at particular lottery offices. This was done in newspaper puffs and advertisements, on lottery tickets themselves, and in handbills (from a small page in size to slips of paper) rushed off the presses (see Figure 3.1).

The invention and diversity of lottery handbills increased markedly in the early nineteenth century. Prior to that, the purpose of the lottery handbill was mainly informative, typically providing details of the key features of the current lottery scheme, the location and address of the lottery office, and also promoting their 'lucky' credentials through listing winning numbers bought there in recent years. An increasingly common feature (see Figure 3.2) was to list the names, occupations or backgrounds, and geographical origins of winners. The message conveyed was that winners came from across Britain and all parts of society. The lottery was (perhaps unsurprisingly) presented as notably socially inclusive, that the capital prizes might be won just as readily by a porter, say, or a servant as a merchant or member of the gentry. The possibility of winning did not depend on rank or wealth; the lottery engaged the hopes and dreams of everyman and everywoman.

As Rob Barnham has shown, a small handful of London printing firms specialized in producing lottery handbills.[131] Many of those handbills which have survived from this period were commissioned by Thomas Bish, the major lottery contractor. No one else was quite able to match him and his collaborators for their invention and wit in the opening decades of the nineteenth century, although several other major lottery contractors ran them close. Bish promoted utilization of acrostic verse, tales, wheels of fortune, hieroglyphics (see Figure 3.3), and such like, although it was for J. Sievewright that the caricaturist George Cruickshank produced a series of character sketches to advertise the lottery. After 1810 the printers of lottery handbills, exploiting the new potential offered by the iron press, pioneered the use of wood-engraved illustrations, new display types, the use of colours, and large, poster-sized formats (see Figure 3.4). As one contemporary observed: 'It is to the managers of the lotteries that we owe the merit of the Brobdingnagian style of printing.'[132] Handbills were commonly given

[131] Rob Barnham, 'Lottery Advertising 1800–1826', *Journal of the Printing Historical Society*, new ser., 13 (2009), 17–60.

[132] W. H. Pyne, *The Costume of Great Britain* (London, 1808), p. 23, quoted in Barnham, 'Lottery Advertising', 48. The use of new larger types was also rapidly adopted by provincial printers in the early nineteenth century, transformed local print advertising.

Figure 3.1 Rapidly printed handbills, such as this one produced for Thomas Bish, advertising 'big wins' in the current lottery draw at specific lottery offices were a common publicity device employed by their keepers. Bodleian Libraries, University of Oxford. John Johnson Collection, Lotteries Vol. 2 (10).

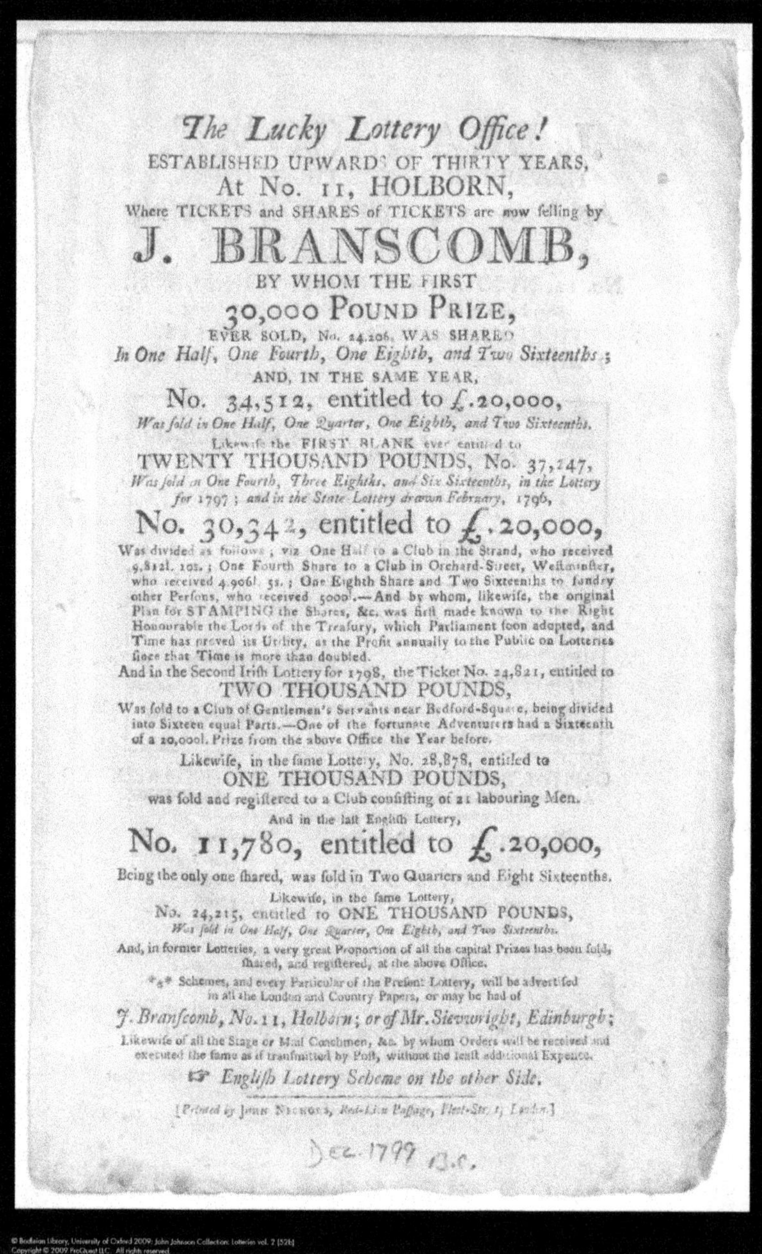

The Lucky Lottery Office!

ESTABLISHED UPWARDS OF THIRTY YEARS,

At No. 11, HOLBORN,

Where TICKETS and SHARES of TICKETS are now ſelling by

J. BRANSCOMB,

BY WHOM THE FIRST

30,000 POUND PRIZE,

EVER SOLD, No. 24,206, WAS SHARED

In One Half, One Fourth, One Eighth, and Two Sixteenths;

AND, IN THE SAME YEAR,

No. 34,512, entitled to £.20,000,

Was ſold in One Half, One Quarter, One Eighth, and Two Sixteenths.

Likewiſe the FIRST BLANK ever entitled to

TWENTY THOUSAND POUNDS, No. 37,147,

Was ſold in One Fourth, Three Eighths, and Six Sixteenths, in the Lottery for 1797; and in the State Lottery drawn February, 1796,

No. 30,342, entitled to £.20,000,

Was divided as follows; viz. One Half to a Club in the Strand, who received 9,812l. 10s.; One Fourth Share to a Club in Orchard-Street, Weſtminſter, who received 4,906l. 5s.; One Eighth Share and Two Sixteenths to ſundry other Perſons, who received 5000l.—And by whom, likewiſe, the original Plan for STAMPING the Shares, &c. was firſt made known to the Right Honourable the Lords of the Treaſury, which Parliament ſoon adopted, and Time has proved its Utility, as the Profit annually to the Public on Lotteries ſince that Time is more than doubled.

And in the Second Iriſh Lottery for 1798, the Ticket No. 24,821, entitled to

TWO THOUSAND POUNDS,

Was ſold to a Club of Gentlemen's Servants near Bedford-Square, being divided into Sixteen equal Parts.—One of the fortunate Adventurers had a Sixteenth of a 20,000l. Prize from the above Office the Year before.

Likewiſe, in the ſame Lottery, No. 28,878, entitled to

ONE THOUSAND POUNDS,

was ſold and regiſtered to a Club conſiſting of 21 labouring Men.

And in the laſt Engliſh Lottery,

No. 11,780, entitled to £.20,000,

Being the only one ſhared, was ſold in Two Quarters and Eight Sixteenths.

Likewiſe, in the ſame Lottery,

No. 24,215, entitled to ONE THOUSAND POUNDS,

Was ſold in One Half, One Quarter, One Eighth, and Two Sixteenths.

And, in former Lotteries, a very great Proportion of all the capital Prizes has been ſold, ſhared, and regiſtered, at the above Office.

*** Schemes, and every Particular of the Preſent Lottery, will be advertiſed in all the London and Country Papers, or may be had of

J. Branſcomb, No. 11, Holborn; or of Mr. Stevenright, Edinburgh;

Likewiſe of all the Stage or Mail Coachmen, &c. by whom Orders will be received and executed the ſame as if tranſmitted by Poſt, without the leaſt additional Expence.

☞ *Engliſh Lottery Scheme on the other Side.*

[*Printed by* John Nichols, *Red-Lion Paſſage, Fleet-Street, London.*]

Figure 3.2 By the end of the eighteenth century, lottery businesses used handbills to provide increasingly detailed information about the diverse social identities and often places of residence of winners at their offices. They emphasize how common was collective purchase of tickets, especially (but certainly not exclusively) among the lower orders. Bodleian Libraries, University of Oxford. John Johnson Collection, Lotteries Vol 2 (53b), Image 1.

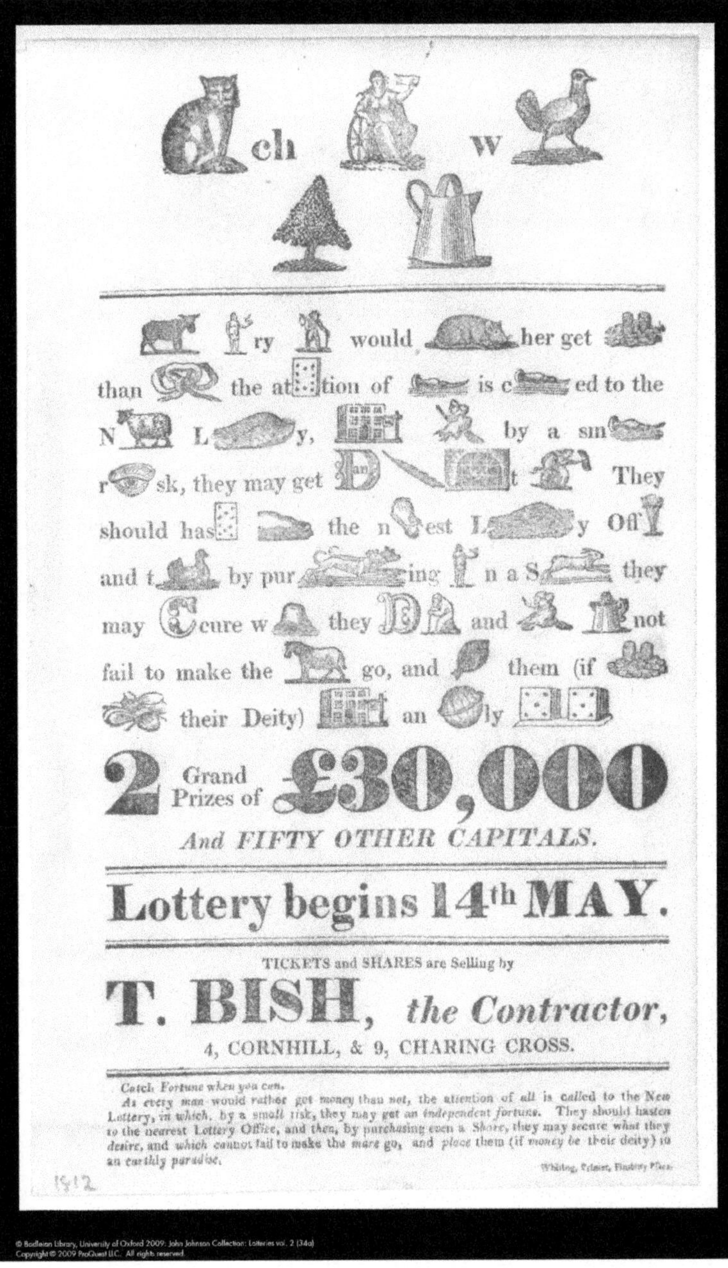

Figure 3.3 Use of hieroglyphics was just one of the new features of lottery handbills in the early nineteenth century as contractors such as Thomas Bish strove to maintain public interest in and demand for lotteries through extensive and intensive use of publicity. Bodleian Libraries, University of Oxford. John Johnson Collection, Lotteries Vol. 2 (34a).

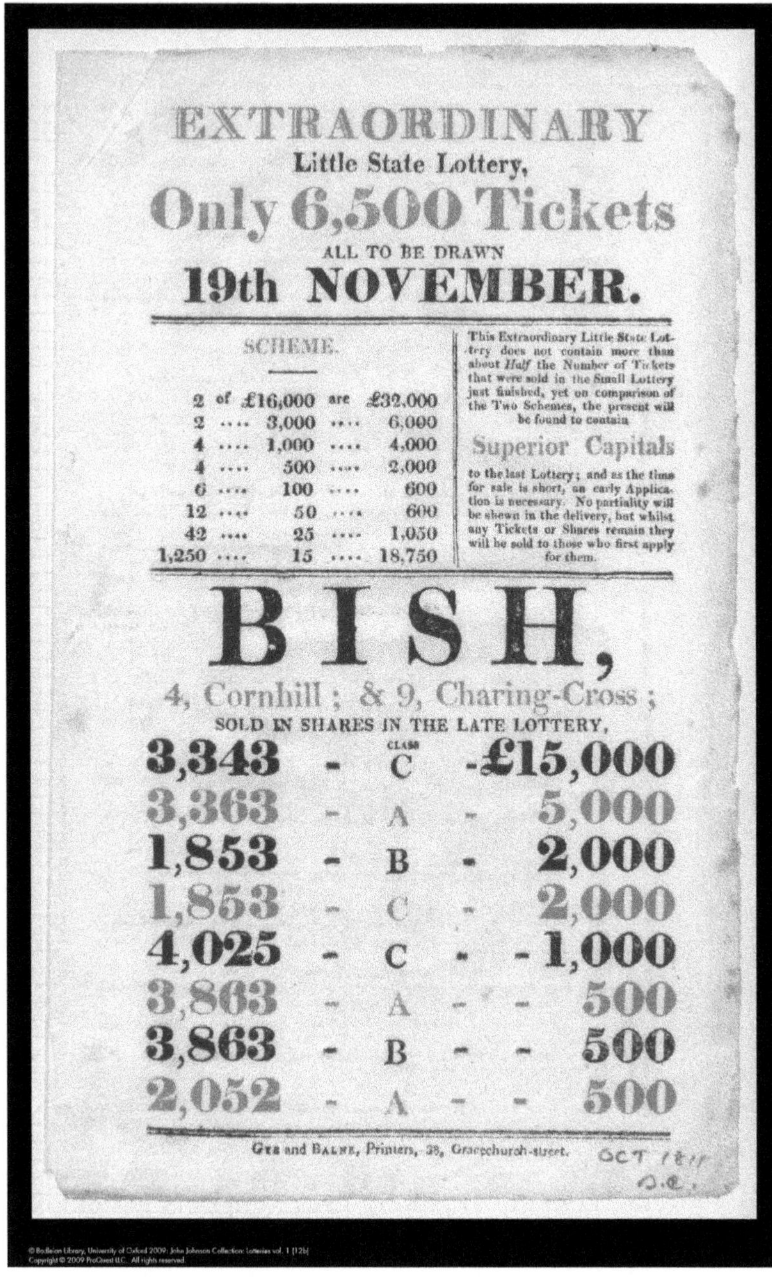

Figure 3.4 Lottery handbill printers of the early nineteenth century were very quick to exploit the potential offered by the iron press, new display types, the use of colours – this handbill was in black and red – and larger formats. Bodleian Libraries, University of Oxford. John Johnson Collection, Lotteries Vol. 1 (12b).

simple headings, picked out in prominent, bold type: **'Where to Get Rich'**, **'Luck's Progress'**, **'Do You Want Money?'**, **'How to grow Rich'**, **'Temple of Wealth'** are just some of those which were used. In 1820, such was the pervasiveness of this material that one sternly disapproving individual decided to compile an album of lottery handbills for his children and grandchildren as a record of the 'systematic series of tricks, puffs & deceptions' engaged in by the lottery office keepers to help promote their businesses and the lottery and what, he declared, was the shameful credulity of the public who seemingly allowed themselves to be thus imposed upon 'in these enlightened times' with, moreover, the connivance of the country's rulers.[133]

Much of this ephemeral print was, as already referred to, designed for the provinces. Lottery contractors supplied their provincial agents with posters and handbills which had been specially customized for their use (see Figures 3.5 and 3.6). But agents – such as John Soulby, printer in Ulverston, Westmorland, or Thompson & Son, Manchester booksellers, both of whom worked at different times for Bish – also produced their own handbills for circulation within their local town and region. It was the job of the provincial agent to ensure that their town and its environs were plastered with conspicuously displayed lottery handbills and advertising boards. The big London lottery contractors employed people to travel around the country systematically checking up that their agents were being sufficiently assiduous in this regard, and, where they were not, to remedy any deficiencies. In the early nineteenth century, lottery posters were a common, highly visible part of the townscapes of Britain.

With the frequency of lotteries increasing markedly after 1803, lottery contractors and offices were, in truth, battling against growing lottery exhaustion and, almost certainly, an increasingly saturated market. One response was tinkering with lottery design – by introducing novelty elements, seeming to increase the chances of winning the capital prizes, or increasing the ratio of prizes to blanks.[134] The principal one, however, was highly conspicuous publicity.

133 BL, 8225 bb. 78.

134 Changes to lottery design can be followed in TNA, IR55/19. Common devices included the addition of certain fixed prizes – i.e. the first number drawn above a £20 prize to gain an extra £3,000; small prizes for the first 500 blanks drawn on each day of drawing; inclusion of a supplementary lottery; reducing the range of numbers, having two tickets per number, so holders of both could win two large capital prizes; and so forth.

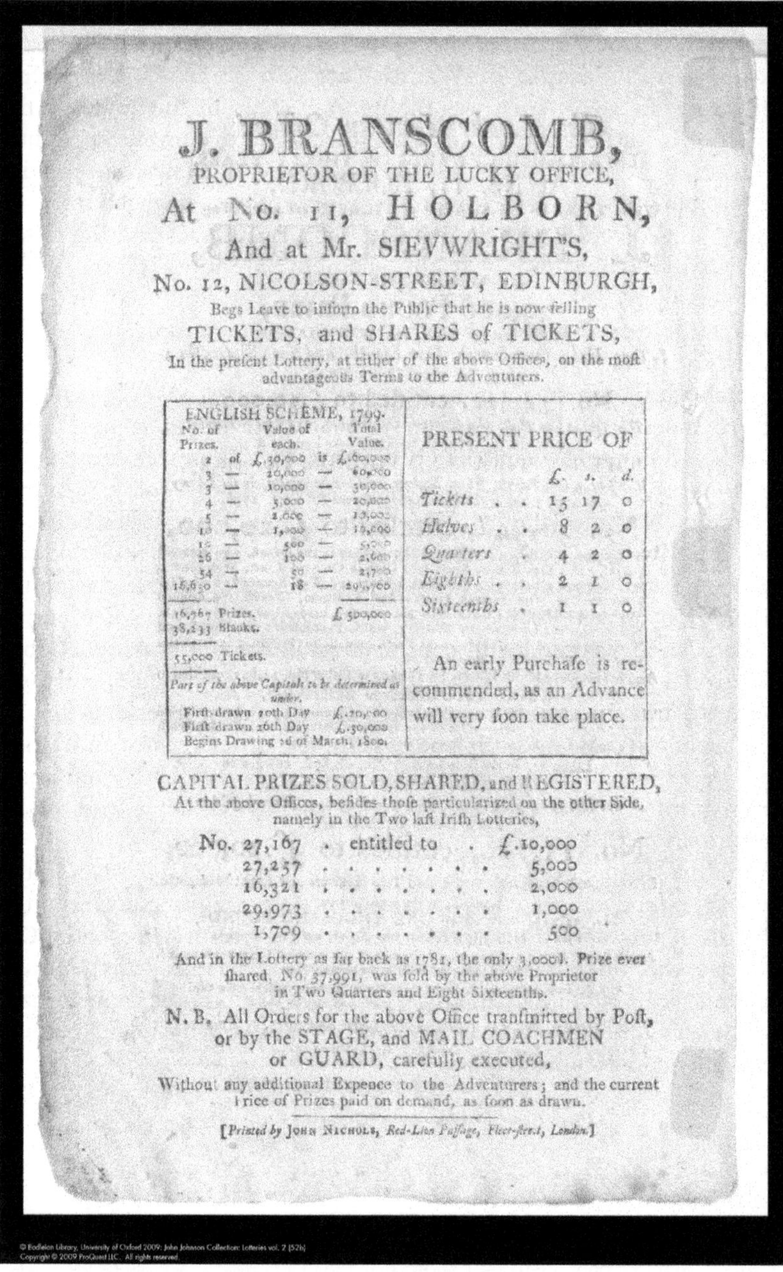

J. BRANSCOMB,
PROPRIETOR OF THE LUCKY OFFICE,
At No. 11, HOLBORN,
And at Mr. SIEVWRIGHT'S,
No. 12, NICOLSON-STREET, EDINBURGH,
Begs Leave to inform the Public that he is now felling
TICKETS, and SHARES of TICKETS,
In the prefent Lottery, at either of the above Offices, on the moft advantageous Terms to the Adventurers.

ENGLISH SCHEME, 1799.

No. of Prizes.		Value of each.		Total Value.
2	of	£.30,000	is	£.60,000
3	—	20,000	—	60,000
3	—	10,000	—	30,000
4	—	5,000	—	20,000
5	—	2,000	—	10,000
10	—	1,000	—	10,000
10	—	500	—	5,000
26	—	100	—	2,600
54	—	50	—	2,700
16,650	—	18	—	299,700
16,767 Prizes.				£ 500,000
38,233 Blanks.				
55,000 Tickets.				

Part of the above Capitals to be determined as under.
First drawn 20th Day £.20,000
First drawn 26th Day £.30,000
Begins Drawing 2d of March, 1800.

PRESENT PRICE OF

	£.	s.	d.
Tickets . .	15	17	0
Halves . .	8	2	0
Quarters .	4	2	0
Eighths . .	2	1	0
Sixteenths .	1	1	0

An early Purchafe is recommended, as an Advance will very foon take place.

CAPITAL PRIZES SOLD, SHARED, and REGISTERED,
At the above Offices, befides thofe particularized on the other Side, namely in the Two laft Irifh Lotteries,

No. 27,167	. entitled to .	£.10,000
27,257	. . . .	5,000
16,321	. . . .	2,000
29,973	. . . .	1,000
1,709	. . . .	500

And in the Lottery as far back as 1781, the only 3,000l. Prize ever fhared, No. 37,991, was fold by the above Proprietor in Two Quarters and Eight Sixteenths.

N. B. All Orders for the above Office tranfmitted by Poft, or by the STAGE, and MAIL COACHMEN or GUARD, carefully executed,
Without any additional Expence to the Adventurers; and the current Price of Prizes paid on demand, as foon as drawn.

[*Printed by* JOHN NICHOLS, *Red-Lion Paffage, Fleet-ftreet, London.*]

Figure 3.5 By the end of the eighteenth century, London lottery office keepers had an increasingly large network of provincial agents, although Sievwright's in Edinburgh was almost certainly a licensed office. The handbill also advertises clearly the importance of the postal services to the lottery and lottery businesses. Bodleian Libraries, University of Oxford. John Johnson Collection. Lotteries Vol. 2 (53b), Image 2.

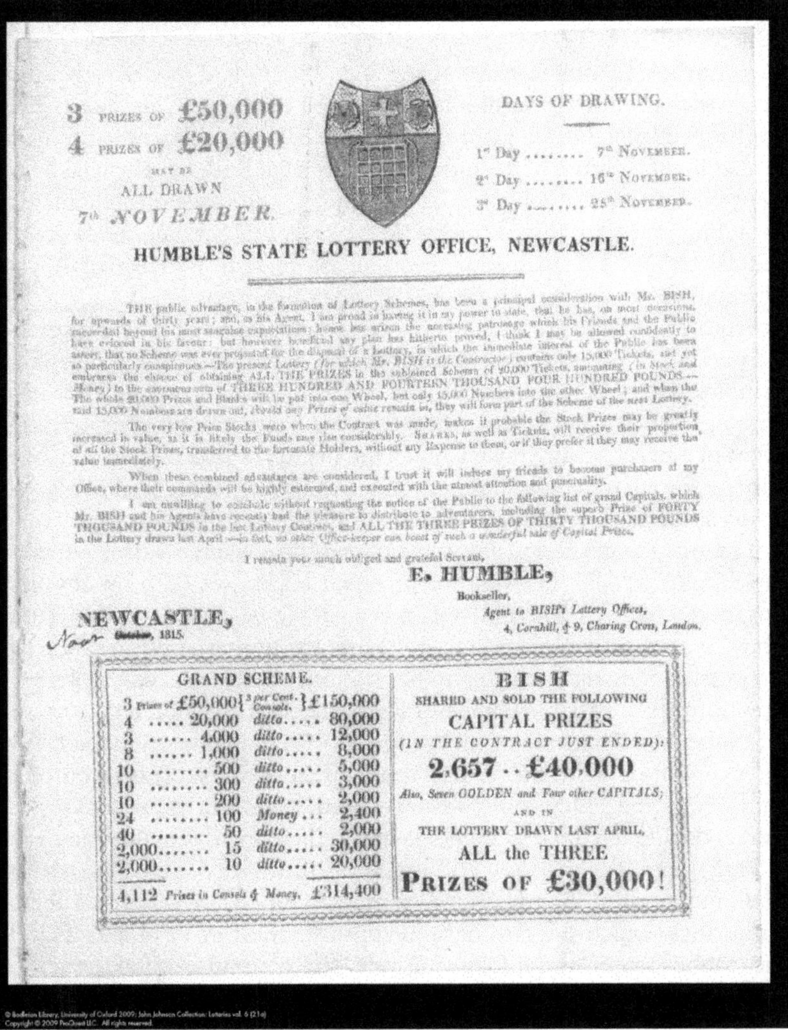

3 PRIZES OF £50,000
4 PRIZES OF £20,000
MAY BE
ALL DRAWN
7th NOVEMBER.

DAYS OF DRAWING.

1st Day .... 7th NOVEMBER.
2d Day .... 16th NOVEMBER.
3d Day .... 25th NOVEMBER.

HUMBLE'S STATE LOTTERY OFFICE, NEWCASTLE.

THE public advantage, in the formation of Lottery Schemes, has been a principal consideration with Mr. BISH, for upwards of thirty years; and, as his Agent, I am proud in having it in my power to state, that he has, on most occasions, succeeded beyond his most sanguine expectations; hence has arisen the increasing patronage which his Friends and the Public have evinced in his favour: but however beneficial any plan has hitherto proved, I think I may be allowed confidently to assert, that no Scheme was ever projected for the disposal of a Lottery, in which the immediate interest of the Public has been so particularly conspicuous.—The present Lottery (for which Mr. BISH is the Contractor) contains only 15,000 Tickets, and yet embraces the chance of obtaining ALL THE PRIZES in the subjoined Scheme of 20,000 Tickets, amounting (in Stock and Money) to the enormous sum of THREE HUNDRED AND FOURTEEN THOUSAND FOUR HUNDRED POUNDS.—The whole 20,000 Prizes and Blanks will be put into one Wheel, but only 15,000 Numbers into the other Wheel; and when the said 15,000 Numbers are drawn out, should any Prizes of value remain in, they will form part of the Scheme of the next Lottery.

The very low Price Stocks were when the Contract was made, makes it probable the Stock Prizes may be greatly increased in value, as it is likely the Funds may rise considerably. SHARES, as well as Tickets, will receive their proportion of all the Stock Prizes, transferred to the fortunate Holders, without any Expense to them, or if they prefer it they may receive the value immediately.

When these combined advantages are considered, I trust it will induce my friends to become purchasers at my Office, where their commands will be highly esteemed, and executed with the utmost attention and punctuality.

I am unwilling to conclude without requesting the notice of the Public to the following list of grand Capitals which Mr. BISH and his Agents have recently had the pleasure to distribute to adventurers, including the superb Prize of FORTY THOUSAND POUNDS in the last Lottery Contract, and ALL THE THREE PRIZES OF THIRTY THOUSAND POUNDS in the Lottery drawn last April:—in fact, no other Office-keeper can boast of such a wonderful sale of Capital Prizes.

I remain your much obliged and grateful Servant,

E. HUMBLE,
Bookseller,
Agent to BISH's Lottery Offices,
4, Cornhill, & 9, Charing Cross, London.

NEWCASTLE,
Nov 1815.

GRAND SCHEME.

Prizes		Value		Total
3	Prizes of	£50,000	3 per Cent. Consols.	£150,000
4	......	20,000	ditto	80,000
3	......	4,000	ditto	12,000
8	......	1,000	ditto	8,000
10	......	500	ditto	5,000
10	......	300	ditto	3,000
10	......	200	ditto	2,000
24	......	100	Money	2,400
40	......	50	ditto	2,000
2,000	......	15	ditto	30,000
2,000	......	10	ditto	20,000
4,112	Prizes in Consols & Money.			£314,400

BISH
SHARED AND SOLD THE FOLLOWING
CAPITAL PRIZES
(IN THE CONTRACT JUST ENDED):
2,657 .. £40,000
Also, Seven GOLDEN and Four other CAPITALS;
AND IN
THE LOTTERY DRAWN LAST APRIL,
ALL the THREE
PRIZES OF £30,000!

Figure 3.6 Lottery handbill printed for Thomas Bish and distributed through his many provincial agents, in this case the Newcastle bookseller, Edward Humble, 1815. Provincial agents were key figures in promoting the services of lottery businesses in their locality, including ensuring that lottery handbills and posters were prominently displayed in their local towns. Bodleian Libraries, University of Oxford. John Johnson Collection, Lotteries Vol. 6 (21a).

3.5 Lottery Insurance and the Role of Parliament and the Law

Two further, related features of the state lottery and its derivative products which require discussion have been left deliberately until last. These are, respectively, lottery insurance and the role of parliament and the law in shaping the nature of the lottery marketplace. Both have crucial light to shed on underlying concerns of this book – the place and character of gambling and the range of attitudes towards this activity. They are also central to the wider story of the role of the lottery in British society, especially from the middle of the eighteenth century.

From 1719 there grew up a very extensive business of lottery insurance. It operated in several main ways, although behind this was a vastly more complex reality.[135] Clearest cut, and relatively uncontroversial, was insurance against drawing a blank. In return for payment of a premium in the event of a ticket being drawn a blank the insurer would return to its owner either a sum of money or another, undrawn ticket. The crucial point is that it was assumed that the individual insuring the ticket was its possessor.[136]

The other main form, discussed already in Chapter 2, was altogether more controversial: insuring for prizes or blanks, or both, in any list of numbers whatever. In reality this was a simple bet on the outcome of the draw. It also, in contrast to lottery insurance proper, did not require the purchaser or insurer to be in possession of the relevant ticket. The premiums paid rose during the draw as the odds lessened on a particular outcome; and if a stated number drew a prize or blank, or, indeed, either on a certain day – whatever had been agreed – the successful purchaser won a cash prize. One could 'insure' for any sum, and premiums rose day by day during the draw as numbers and capital prizes remained undrawn.

Parliament, the treasury, and in the 1770s the city magistrates, sought to eliminate or at least restrict lottery insurance. The actions of the city authorities, which seem to have begun in earnest in 1774 and included the establishment in the following year of a committee of aldermen and common councilmen to enforce the law against lottery insurance, reflected an upsurge in concern about the lottery among sections of metropolitan opinion.[137] 'Every evening these gaming-schools', as one

135 There is a contemporary description of and guide to the pricing of the various sorts of insurance in *The Lottery Display'd, Or The Adventurer's Guide* (London, 1771), esp. pp. 33–7.

136 Insurance schemes could depart from this simple model. Thus, in 1719 one scheme offered to purchase 100 tickets for £200; their cost would have been £300. If any of the tickets were to draw prizes, the depositor of the tickets could buy them back for £300 for up to one month after the end of the draw. *Daily Courant*, 27 Aug. 1719.

137 The City of London petitioned parliament lamenting the destructive effects of the lottery in 1773 (*Annual Register* (1773), p. 84).

contemporary dubbed the capital's many lottery offices, 'are filled with footmen, journeymen, apprentices, and mechanics'.[138] All forms of lottery insurance were made illegal in the Lottery Regulation Act of 1782, one of the final measures of the tottering North administration.[139] This proved counterproductive, serving merely to depress the profitability of the lottery, and also leading to the burgeoning creation of illegal lottery offices, as well as to a welter of vexatious, fraudulent actions in the courts.[140] MPs, led by the Middlesex MP and reform-minded, William Mainwaring, had another go in 1786, although this failed, almost certainly owing to concerns about the extensive powers that it would have given to magistrates and officers of the law. Pitt the Younger, or rather George Rose as treasury undersecretary, guided an alternative, more acceptable measure through parliament in 1787, which legalized insurance of tickets by their owners where these were registered with licensed lottery offices.[141] In 1791 effective action was also taken against schemes that involved the sale of 'chances' where neither tickets nor shares were owned by their sellers. Newspapers advertising such schemes were deemed by the judges in the Court of King's Bench to be liable to prosecution, although they were subsequently given immunity from this by legislation passed in 1792.[142]

Illegal insurance, however, continued to flourish. During 1790–1791 there appears to have been considerable discussion within government circles about how best to suppress it, and an unsuccessful lottery bill in 1790, in which George Rose again had a large hand as treasury undersecretary, contained clauses aimed at suppressing advertising of illegal lottery offices, whether by means of newspapers or handbills.[143] In 1791 Thomas Wood, secretary to the Lottery Board, proposed a new

138 *MChr*, 11 Oct. 1775, letter signed 'NO GAMBLER'.

139 For fuller discussion of this measure, see ch. 5, below, pp. 00.

140 TNA, T1/652/68–75, memorial on lotteries, n.d., but 1787; *Considerations on Lotteries, and Proposals for their Better Regulation* (London, 1786).

141 This aspect of the Act was controversial and opposed by some, including the Earl of Stormont and Lord Loughborough in the Lords, as inevitably supporting gambling by licensing insurance. See *Morning Herald*, 10 Feb. 1787. See also *Gazetteer*, 6 Feb. 1787; *PA*, 6 Feb., and 9 Feb. 1787, where it was claimed that Pitt's persistence in pursuing what it claimed was an unpopular measure was motivated by his wish to make good bargains with the lottery contractors in future over the price of tickets.

142 TNA, IR72/34, Board of Stamps, Miscellaneous Books, Solicitor's Department, Lottery Cases: Law Opinions, 1787–1799, King v Smith, 1791, Case for the Opinion of the Court.

143 The original bill included clauses which would have imposed a £50 penalty on newspapers advertising illegal lottery shares and penalties on persons found hawking handbills or papers containing proposals or schemes relating to the lottery by summary process. Prosecutions were to be made in the name of the attorney general. The bill was opposed particularly by Lord Loughborough and the Lord Chancellor. One feature that

type of draw which, in his view, would have prevented such betting, but this was rejected by Pitt on the grounds that it would have raised doubts about the fairness of the draw and thus depressed sales of tickets. Wood put this solution forward again in 1796 and 1811, with the same result.[144] Following the establishment and reporting in 1792 of a Commons committee on the efficacy of the laws on the lottery, ministers had another go at suppressing it in 1793 when they changed the arrangements regarding who was permitted to record the results of the draw – with the aim of closing down the opportunities for such schemes to operate – and amended the law concerning prosecution of offences against the lottery laws.[145] In 1802, the Addington ministry reduced the duration of draws with the same goal in mind. Some argued that the lottery laws were, as one contemporary put it, 'far too mild', also noting that they were undermined by their dependence on informers.[146] In 1809 the Perceval ministry further reduced the duration of lottery draws to, where possible, a single day, which seems to have had an effect, although it may also have simply led to an increase in illegal private lotteries, the so-called Little Goes.[147] There were plenty of prosecutions of people for offering illegal insurance, as well as 'Little Goes', in the years between c. 1790 and the 1810s, which after 1793 were the joint responsibility of the Commissioners of the Stamp Duties and magistrates. The former met the costs of such prosecutions, including payments to informers.[148] Ironically, the suppression of 'chances' in

aroused opposition was its supposed attack on the press, by rendering vulnerable to prosecution. A second was the provision for arrest and prosecution of offenders without the issuing of an affidavit specifying the offences committed by individuals. Although it passed, in amended form, the Commons, it was defeated in the Lords. See esp. *Diary or Woodfall's Register*, 11 May 1790; *WEP*, 1 June 1790

144 TNA, T64/324, T. Wood to William Pitt, 1796; T. Wood to George Harrison Esq., 16 May 1811; same to same, 17 May 1811.

145 33 Geo III, c. 62. The alteration in the law concerning prosecution appears to have been driven by the abuse of existing powers by informers. In a bid to prevent this, any legal action for recovery of penalties had henceforth to be initiated in the name of the attorney general. Persons committed as rogues and vagabonds were to remain incarcerated for a period of not less than one month and not exceeding six months and until the final drawing of the lottery for which the offence had been committed. There was no right of appeal and no power of removal to a higher court.

146 BL, Add MS 59309, fo. 52, Mr <Wasteneys?> to Lord Grenville, 25 Feb. 1807.

147 42 Geo III, c. 119; 49 Geo III, c. 94. A summary description of Perceval's policy is provided in a footnote in *The Quarterly Review* (October 1815), p. 139. I am grateful to Edward Hicks for this reference. One person who considered that Perceval's new regulations had had a positive effect was William Wilberforce, for which see SCA, Papers of Samuel Roberts, RP/1/11, William Wilberforce to Samuel Roberts, 22 May 1815; RP/1/13, same to same, 25 Jan. 1816.

148 See University of Nottingham, Manuscripts and Special Collections, Portland Papers, Pw F 3930, Richard Ford to the duke of Portland, 14 Nov. 1794; PP, 1817 (104),

1791 was almost certainly in part responsible for the continued existence of illegal schemes, since these were cheaper than tickets in the official lottery, and prices of tickets also rose in the early nineteenth century. These schemes were partly filling a gap that had been inadvertently created in the market.[149]

Who commonly took advantage of the myriad lottery insurance schemes is impossible to say. They operated, as already mentioned, on a very large scale in the British capital. Whether they spread elsewhere is unclear, although before 1782 'chances' were regularly purchased in the provinces through the services of London lottery offices and their agents. In 1793 a parliamentary committee claimed, probably optimistically, that magisterial vigilance had eliminated insurance schemes outside of London.[150]

Even after 1782, contrary to what was sometimes claimed by contemporaries, lottery insurance flourished among social groups other than merely the 'poor', although that was a very loosely employed term in any case. In 1793 John Turton was prosecuted under a complaint made by a Rebecca Levi.[151] Levi had insured the number 215 with Turton, paying him 17s11d. Her winnings, when the number drew a prize in the state lottery, were 32½ guineas. The cause of the prosecution was that Turton had only paid out 20 guineas. Turton was a shopkeeper who probably turned to lottery insurance to bolster a failing business, but lacked sufficient capital to meet his obligations to winners. What is significant in this context is the amount of money that Levi paid to 'insure' her number. A witness before a parliamentary committee in 1792–1793 spoke of sums as great as between £300 and £400 being insured, while in 1808, before another parliamentary committee, it was claimed by one lottery office keeper that the middling class and a great many gentlemen and ladies continued to insure tickets, a claim also made

Lottery and Little-Go Acts, A Return and Account of the Number of Prosecutions and Convictions under the Lottery Act and Little Go Act during the Last Fourteen Months, 1817. See also PP, 1816 (510), Report from the Committee of the State of the Police of the Metropolis, with, the Minutes of Evidence Taken Before the Committee; and, An Appendix of Sundry Papers, 30–1, minutes of evidence of Nathaniel Conant.

149 This was implicitly recognized in a memorandum produced by the Lottery Office in November 1808, where the author suggested allowing shares smaller than 16ths, 24th, and 32nds, since this 'would prevent the lower classes from throwing away that sum in insurances, which would enable them to purchase a small share'. TNA, IR55/13, untitled memorandum, Lottery Office, 12 Nov. 1808.

150 House of Commons, Report From the Committee Appointed to Enquire How Far the Laws for Preventing ILLEGAL INSURANCES, and Other Evils, Which Have Been Found to Attend the Drawing of STATE LOTTERIES, are Effectual to the Object Proposed by Them, 12 Mar. 1793, 19.

151 LMA, Middlesex Justices, Sessions Papers, MJ/SP/1793/04/140, examinations of John Turton, vagrant, and Rebecca Levi, 1793.

by other witnesses.[152] In 1786 the press reported that a 'lady of high rank' from the West End had sent a messenger into the city with the purpose of insuring a single number for the astonishing sum of 4,000 guineas to win a prize; a lottery office had supposedly taken the bet, but only for 2,000 guineas.[153] There is no way of knowing whether this was merely press exaggeration, but what may be significant is that the lower figure appeared credible. At the bottom end, it was a matter of a premium of 4 or 5d on the first day of drawing to pay half a guinea, with sums rising each day thereafter. It was commonly stated that licensed lottery offices continued to operate illegal insurance schemes well after 1782, indeed, that many of them felt themselves compelled to do so in order to remain profitable.[154]

For all, however, that lottery insurance proved enticing to individuals from diverse backgrounds, illegal insurance appears to have been resorted to most regularly by the metropolitan labouring classes; and in the minds of a growing number of people a strengthening association existed between lottery insurance, poverty, or more specifically as it was coming to be designated in some quarters, 'indigence' and a bit later 'mendicity'. In 1786, one writer blamed such schemes for inducing 'a frenzy pervading all orders of people, mechanics, labourers, servants, servant-maids, and I am told even chimney sweeps'. These people, the same writer continued, 'have been urged on step by step, to risque [sic] every farthing they had reserved, or could by any means obtain, in this destructive kind of gaming'.[155] Metropolitan magistrates such as Patrick Colquhoun furnished details of cases involving ruinous speculation in lottery insurance by the poor, frequently by women, thereby shattering the home and family stability, and by gentlemen's servants. Colquhoun, who adopted a strictly paternalistic stance – he talked of 'sheltering the inferior classes from the mania of the Lottery' – wrote about the issue at length in his widely read *Treatise on the Police of the Metropolis*.[156] Servants were portrayed as especially susceptible to ill-judged speculations. The 1802 Act Against Little Goes talked explicitly of these being used to defraud 'servants, children, and unwary persons' of 'great sums'. At times, it feels as if these stories were selected precisely because they

[152] House of Commons, Report from the Committee … Illegal Insurances, 25; PP, 1808 (182 & 323), Reports from the Committee on the Laws Relating to Lotteries, 32, 47. It was also claimed that the high prices of legal tickets and shares drove people to insurance.

[153] *Salisbury Journal*, 27 Mar. 1786.

[154] PP, 1808 (182 & 323), Reports from the Committee on the Laws Relating to Lotteries, 22, 26, 42, 44.

[155] *Considerations on Lotteries*, p. 14.

[156] Colquhoun, *Treatise on the Police of the Metropolis* (7th ed., London, 1806), pp. 151–70.

confirmed prevailing constructions of poverty; and to this extent they were filtered, both consciously and unconsciously. Yet illegal lottery schemes with their 'morocco men and women' (so called because of the red morocco leather covered books that they carried, in which were recorded the numbers insured) were very much part of a highly commercialized world of popular gambling, which often involved fraud and defied attempts to suppress or control it, and which pervaded the capital's streets, inns, coffee rooms, and shops.[157]

Given their common association with deception and fraud, the success of illegal insurance might seem, at first glance, to be puzzling. It operated, nevertheless, with the tolerance, if not full connivance and support, of local communities – one reason why it was incredibly hard to eliminate. One factor in their popularity may have been that winnings were paid immediately – where they were paid at all, that is. Their credibility also relied to a significant extent on their relationship to the official lottery. This was even true to some extent of the Little Goes where this relationship was evidently much more remote. All this said, the official lottery, as hinted at earlier, often seems to have hovered on the margins of legality, and, as Paul Langford has emphasized, was quite commonly associated with frauds of various sorts – counterfeiting of tickets, selling fake promises to deliver tickets, providing false information on the lottery draw so as to buy prize-winning tickets as blanks, selling tickets which had already been drawn blanks, promoting and operating bogus insurance schemes and schemes of chances.[158] This, however, was fraud at a remove from the operation of the actual lottery draw; the reputation of this was never under real question, something that was crucial to the credibility of the lottery.[159]

A recurrent aim of lottery regulation was limiting the spread of lottery adventuring to those deemed best able to assess the risk involved – in other words, those with sufficient income and education – and protecting the poor against the supposedly destructive consequences of a lottery habit. A second goal was that of protecting state and public lotteries from competition – be this from foreign or private lotteries, or lottery-derived products such as 'chances'. The record in relation to the latter is again one of strictly limited achievement.

157 This is explored in further detail in Chapter 2, above, pp. 102–6.

158 Paul Langford, *A Polite and Commercial People: England 1727–1787* (Oxford, 1989), pp. 572–4. See also, for contemporary comment on this, Richard King, *The New CHEATS of LONDON Exposed: or, The FRAUDS and TRICKS of the TOWN Laid Open to BOTH SEXES* London, 1780, pp. 47–8.

159 There is a hint that contractors winning too many of the capital prizes in 1810 and 1811 led to scepticism about the fairness of the draw. For which, see TNA, T64/324, Mr Walsh to Spencer Perceval, 5 June 1811.

Take the example of private lotteries: these were prohibited from 1698 in a series of statutes. An Act passed in 1721 imposed particularly severe penalties on those operating or advertising private lottery schemes, whilst at the same time bringing their prosecution under the summary powers of magistrates; and the 1739 Gaming Act, which included lotteries within its terms, has been described by one historian as 'extremely strong'.[160] Yet there is no evidence of other than very occasional prosecutions under its terms, despite the fact that private lotteries disposing of stock and goods, including paintings, were very common.[161]

One reason why few prosecutions occurred is that private lotteries of this kind were generally small scale, so escaped notice, or more likely were deemed insufficiently threatening to other tradesmen or shopkeepers to prompt action. The close proximity of the worlds of formal or fixed and informal trade – selling from stalls or at fairs – was a source of recurrent tension in many places throughout this period, but this can disguise their continued interdependence. Why initiate action against another business when one might well want to engage in a similar practice in the future? Large private cash lotteries, which had been a feature of the 1690s, were seemingly eliminated by the early 1720s. Whether this was owing to legislative prohibition, and the threat of prosecution, or rather diminishing demand, is moot; or, as likely, insurance schemes and 'chances' came more than to fill the gap.

3.6 Conclusion

Official and public lotteries flourished despite, therefore, rather than because of any protection afforded by the lottery and gaming laws. The courts were a relatively ineffective means of suppressing sales of foreign lottery tickets and various lottery-derived products and activities – most

[160] Davison, 'Public Policy in an Age of Commercial Expansion', p. 83.

[161] Edinburgh goldsmith and jeweller, Alexander Aitchison sold some of his stock using a series of very well-publicized annual lotteries between 1780 and 1784. William Irvine Fortescue, 'Edinburgh Goldsmiths and Radical Politics, 1793–94: The Case of David Downie', *Book of the Old Edinburgh Club*, new ser., 9 (2012), 39–40. In 1744, one Francis Baker of London was prosecuted under the terms of the 1739 Gaming Act for holding a lottery for the disposal of £3,000 worth of large tea tables, tea kettles, lamps and stands, coffee pots and waiters, silver and gold watches, diamond earrings, rings, and place. LMA, City of London Magistrates, Sessions Papers, CLA/047/L1/13/1744/008, information, 10 Oct., summons, 4 Dec. 1744. When the bookseller Samuel Fancourt proposed to dispose of his circulating library through a lottery, he referred his scheme to the Lottery Office, which declared it illegal, so he felt compelled to turn to another plan. K. A. Manley, 'The Road to Camelot: Lotteries, the Circle of Learning, and the 'Circulary' Library of Samuel Fancourt', *The Library*, 7th ser., 8 (2007), 398–422.

obviously 'lottery insurance' – which either competed with the official lotteries or extended the social reach of the lottery marketplace well beyond what was desired by the government and authorities.

The lottery's success was built, in the first place, on its credibility with the public. This, significantly, endured despite its common association with frauds of various kinds and the occasional failed lottery, such as in 1697 or 1757. Nor did the fact that redemption schedules for the Queen Anne lotteries of 1711–1712 were not honoured, because of the failure of taxes imposed to raise the requisite funds, dampen enthusiasm for the lottery in the early part of our period, although this also owed a good deal to the success with which ministers managed a conversion operation for relevant lottery orders in 1717. Second, and more importantly, the lottery's success was a consequence of the efficiency of the lottery marketplace and its ever-growing accessibility. As we have seen, by the early nineteenth century, the lottery had succeeded in casting its net far and wide. Residents of small villages in Norfolk and industrial villages in west-central Scotland had by then come well within its giant reach. This, in turn, owed much to transformations in communications – an expanding road and postal network, multiplying coach and carrier services, the diversification and increasing power and reach of the newspaper press, and the ebulliently creative world of London trade printing and publishing. It also derived from the very rapid development from the 1690s in London of sophisticated primary and secondary markets in public and private stocks. The lottery was quickly enfolded within this world, and this ensured that before 1769 undrawn tickets, as well as blanks and prizes, were readily tradeable and thus a highly liquid investment. The rise of the lottery was, in sum, a triumph of market integration and private enterprise; the role of the state and para-state bodies such as the Bank of England was distinctly secondary.

Historians, such as Paul Langford, and also a good many others – John Brewer, Maxine Berg, John Styles, Beverly Lemire, to name only a few of the more prominent – have emphasized the depth, extent, and profound social, cultural, as well as economic effects of the commercialization of British society in this period.[162] The flourishing of the lottery was parasitic on this process. It successfully piggybacked, for example, on existing

[162] Langford, *Polite and Commercial People*; John Brewer, *The Pleasures of the Imagination: English Culture in the Eighteenth Century* (London, 1997); John Brewer and Roy Porter (eds.), *Consumption and the World of Goods* (London, 1993); Maxine Berg, *Luxury and Pleasure in Eighteenth-Century Britain* (Oxford, 2005); John Styles, *The Dress of the People: Everyday Fashion in Eighteenth-Century England* (New Haven and London, 2007); Beverly Lemire, *Fashion's Favourite: The Cotton Trade and the Consumer in Britain, 1660–1800* (Oxford, 1991).

commercial networks and businesses, such as, most notably, those of provincial booksellers and printers, from whose multiplying ranks were drawn the majority of lottery agents. Such individuals often combined different commercial roles as agents for a variety of products and businesses – patent medicines, perfumery, art supplies, newspapers and periodicals, as well as, of course, books, pamphlets, and prints. Provincial newspaper printers had their own regional networks of distribution, through the so-called newsmen who operated on local circuits, carrying newspapers and goods with them. These were readily exploited to expedite local lottery business. The lottery was also, however, itself further powerful evidence of the strength of these commercial impulses and the irrepressible ingenuity of the lottery entrepreneurs who competed for business and profit in what was an intensely competitive market.

While supply-side factors are, therefore, crucial in explaining the rise and success of the lottery in Britain in the long eighteenth century, the demand side is equally important. As the next chapter will show, the success of the lottery also derived from how quickly and extensively the lottery habit became entrenched amongst a broad cross section of, first, metropolitan society and then the upper and ever-expanding middling classes in the rest of the British Isles, as well as, whatever the intentions of the authorities, people well below this on the social scale.

4 Lottery Adventures and Adventurers

From its inception in the 1690s the market for official lottery tickets in eighteenth-century Britain had an important transnational dimension. Its domestic growth was still more remarkable. As we began to see in the last chapter, and as we will see further below, the domestic growth owed much initially to the emergence of a transparent and credible secondary market in securities, one that continued to expand despite, as Anne Carlos and Larry Neal emphasize, the shock waves produced by the collapse of the South Sea Bubble in 1720.[1] Lotteries, indeed, enticed people into participating in this new financial world. The continued expansion of lottery adventuring thereafter depended, as was argued in the previous chapter, on the ever-increasing speed and extent of the circulation of goods, people, and information in Britain between the later seventeenth and early nineteenth centuries, together with the continued growth, wealth, and profound influence of London, its 'overgrown' capital.[2]

If the rise of the lottery between 1694 and 1826 can be reconstructed in a good amount of detail, harder to identify – in more, that is, than merely impressionistic ways – are those who adventured in it, how regularly, and on what sorts of scale. Several pieces of fairly systematic data survive to which we can turn, although these mostly date from the early eighteenth century. Missing are large-scale, continuous records of who bought tickets, and in what quantities, or, indeed, any kind of equivalent of the household surveys on which modern studies of lottery participation are usually based. The difficulty also reflects the nature of participation in the lottery. This, as we saw in the previous chapter, depended on intermediaries of various kinds, which, amongst other

1 Ann M. Carlos and Larry Neal, 'The Micro-Foundations of the Early London Capital Market: Bank of England Shareholders During and After the South Sea Bubble, 1720–25', *Economic History Review*, lix (2006), 498–538.

2 The phrase was used by Andrew Armstrong, an Edinburgh woollen merchant, in his journal, recording a visit he made to London. Edinburgh Central Library, Y DA 1861.789, Journal of Andrew Armstrong, 1789–93, entry for July 1791.

things, meant that the person who bought the ticket might well not be the ultimate owner. This is much less problematic, however, than the pervasiveness of various collective forms of purchase. In addition to lottery clubs and commercial lottery schemes, this might simply entail acquaintances getting together on an ad hoc basis to purchase a ticket, as in the case in 1768 of Hull's Robert Carlisle Broadley, and seven other people, including two married couples, or slightly later the Hampshire gentleman, Tristram Huddleston Jervoise, who was a regular purchaser of tickets in conjunction with various family members and acquaintances.[3] It might involve the purchase of tickets, or shares therein, for children, such as undertaken by the Treasury Secretary, William Lowndes, in the 1710 lottery, or Francis Wright of Eyam, Derbyshire, who bought shares of tickets in the final third of the eighteenth century through her sister, Mary, a resident of Westminster.[4] The widespread, regular occurrence of these types of purchase should be borne in mind in what follows.

It is, therefore, necessary to be clear from the outset about the scope of the coverage of the present chapter. The principal focus is on purchases *in* Britain of tickets in official and public lotteries. Those by the Irish, British colonials, or foreigners are not explored here, albeit they almost certainly accounted for a significant proportion of the total. Similarly, adventuring by Britons in foreign and Irish lotteries is referred to only in passing. Purchases of foreign, especially Dutch, lottery tickets may have taken place on a considerable scale in the early eighteenth century. As John Blount complained in 1713: 'The great Numbers of the Tickets in the Dutch Lottery w[hi]ch have been brought into and sent for from England have contributed very much to keep down the Price of the Tickets in the English Lottery.'[5] Selling tickets in foreign lotteries was prohibited by parliament in 1722, although prosecutions under this legislation seem to have been very rare, and examples can fairly easily be found of individuals buying foreign lottery tickets, and indeed tickets in various Irish charitable lotteries, well after that date.[6] Tickets in the

3 University of Hull, Brynmor Jones Library, DP/146, journal and personal account book of Robert Carlisle Broadley of Hull, entries for 4 Oct., 29 Nov. 1768; HRO, Papers of the Jervoise Family of Herriard, 44M69/E11/130, account and notebook of Tristram Huddleston Jervoise, 1785–1794.

4 Hoare's Bank, HB/8/9/2, accounts with respect to purchase and sale of Lowndes family lottery tickets, 1710–21; DRO, D5430/32/2/2, Mary Sisum, London, to Mrs Francis Wright, 15 Nov. 1791; D5430/32/2/12–15, lottery accounts of Mrs Francis Wright, 1793–5.

5 BL, Add MS 70155, fo. 49, Blount to Edward Harley, 8 Dec. 1713.

6 See e.g. Lancashire Archives, DDKE/9/124/29, Thomas Banks to Ralph Banks, 30 Apr. 1724; 41, same to same, 14 July 1724 [refers to fate of tickets in the Dutch lottery]; NRS, Innes of Stow Papers, GD113/4/109/452, Mr Allan Whiteford, his

official Irish lottery, which was held between 1780 and 1800, were sold legally in Britain after 1782, and the battle between promoters of the British and Irish lotteries in the British market was fiercely joined.[7] Also omitted are purchases of 'chances' and the other forms of 'lottery insurance', which, as noted in the previous chapter, massively extended the market for lottery-derived or related products, especially (although not exclusively by any means) among the metropolitan lower orders. Because of this selectivity, and the plenitude of missing data, conclusions reached about the changing constituencies of lottery adventurers are necessarily partial and somewhat tentative.

Motivations of lottery adventurers, our second main focus, are still more elusive. Historians who examine speculative financial activities tend to view these primarily from the perspective of the investments themselves. Investors, past and present, rarely record their motivations. Economic historians assume that investing was based predominantly on the rational calculus of actual and probable financial benefit to the investor. It would be silly to dismiss this approach, and, as we will see, the terms of lotteries significantly influenced their fortunes and demand for tickets; contemporaries were well able to see a bad deal when it was put before them; equally, they could appreciate a very good deal, as was the case with the Queen Anne lotteries of 1711–1712. We might usefully recall, however, the great twentieth-century economist John Maynard Keynes' introduction of the notion of 'expectations' into discussions of investment. The investor, he suggested (in 1910),

> will be affected, as is obvious, not by the net income which he will actually receive from his investment in the long run, but by his expectations. These will often depend upon fashion, upon advertisement, or upon purely irrational waves of optimism or pessimism. Similarly, by risk we mean, not the real risk as measured by the actual average of the class of investment over the period of years to which the expectation refers, but the risk as it is estimated, wisely or foolishly, by the investor.[8]

We are contemplating, in brief, highly subjective appraisals of risk and reward, as well as the altogether more intangible, yet no less influential, realms of hope and beliefs about fortune or luck. The latter were crucial

account of two tickets in the Dutch lottery, 1729; Northumberland Record Office, ZBL 240, John Frederick Perregan to Sir Edward Blackett, Paris, 22 Dec. 1771, refers to the purchase of two tickets in the French royal lottery; NRS, Court of Session Papers, CS96/3307 printed notice, 'Scheme for the Better Supporting of the Charitable Infirmary in the Inns-Quay, Mercer's Hospital and the Hospital for Incurables on Lazer's Hill, Dublin, 1767'.

[7] Rowena Dudley, *The Irish Lottery, 1780–1801* (Dublin, 2005).

[8] Quoted in Robert Skidelsky, *Keynes: The Return of the Master* (London, 2009), p. 62.

features of lottery adventuring. Take the example of Samuel Johnson's biographer – the writer, journal keeper, and rather sporadically employed lawyer, James Boswell: in February 1791 Boswell bought a lottery ticket from a London lottery office keeper. Rather than looking at the number, he sealed it up in a paper. The following evening the lottery office keeper circulated a handbill publicizing that a ticket purchased at this office had won a prize of £5,000. Boswell, who had originally intended leaving his ticket uninspected until the draw was completed, became exercised by the intoxicating notion that his ticket must have been one of only a few hundred sold at this office on the previous day. Fired by this thought, he was unable to persist in his intention; consequently, he peeked at the last two numbers on his ticket, which, sadly for him, were not those of the winning ticket. 'I have', he wrote, '*remanded my ticket to its secresy*' (my emphasis).[9] The heavily ritualistic character of Boswell's lottery purchase highlights the frequent *non-rational* – which is not the same thing as irrational – dimensions to participation in the lottery.

Entertaining hopes of winning a capital prize in the lottery meant indulging in dreams – in Boswell's case, so he tells us, that of clearing his considerable debts. Dreams or fantasies are deeply personal, reflecting very closely an individual's peculiar circumstances – thus for Boswell his financial indebtedness. There is, nonetheless, an important sense in which they are socially constructed. Recent work by social psychologists has shown how social identity is shaped by values which are classifiable as extrinsic and intrinsic.[10] Intrinsic values are those which are not dependent on praise or reward from other people; typically, they concern relationships with family, community, and self-acceptance. By contrast, extrinsic values focus on status and self-advancement, and are closely bound up with how others see us. What is important for present purposes is that both sets of values have been shown to cluster in remarkably consistent patterns within and between countries. The balance between them and how they operate are strongly shaped, in other words, by the particularities of any given social environment. An issue this raises is whether important features of eighteenth-century British society served to enhance the salience of extrinsic values, and how far this might furnish another explanation for the lottery's success.

9 *Letters of James Boswell: 8 January 1778–19 May* 1795, ed. Chauncey Brewster Tinker, 2 vols. (Oxford, 1924), ii, pp. 420–2: James Boswell to Edmond Malone, 10 Feb. 1791.

10 Tom Crompton, September 2010, 'Common Cause: The Case for Working with Our Cultural Values', WWF, Oxfam, Friends of the Earth, CPRE, Climate Outreach Information Network, wwf.org.uk, cited in George Monbiot, *How Did We Get into This Mess?* (London, 2016), n. 1, p. 332.

The discussion of lottery adventuring which follows is divided into two main sections. The first seeks to identify who adventured in the lottery, how regularly, and on what sorts of scale. The second focuses on the question of motivations. The first section is organized along chronological lines. This reflects a key change in the form of the official lottery from 1769.[11] Prior to that date, most official and public lotteries were not winner-take-all affairs. Instead, blank tickets normally brought a return, in some cases, as we will see below, a good one. From 1714, this was usually paid in the form of annuities or government stock of a sum less than the face value of the ticket (typically between c. 60% and 80%) and paying interest of between 3% and 4%. Blanks and prizes could be sold following the draw. Several lotteries before 1769, however, paid prizes in cash, and in a small number of these – two in 1719 and the lottery of 1757 – blanks paid nothing. The latter were thus simple gambles on winning a prize. From 1769 all official lotteries were winner-take-all affairs, in which prizes were usually paid in cash or, less frequently, consols (consolidated government stock). The difference between the two basic forms – before and after 1769 – has an obvious bearing on the shifting nature of lottery adventuring.

4.1 Who Played the Lottery: The Picture before 1769

To date, historians investigating participation in the lottery in the long eighteenth century have focused overwhelmingly on the formative decade of the 1690s, one which saw successive waves of private lotteries and the staging of two official lotteries in, respectively, 1694 and 1697.[12] What they show is how rapidly lottery adventuring took hold amongst a broad cross section of metropolitan society, as well as those with close links to it. Anne Murphy estimates that tens of thousands of people – men and women – invested in the 'Million Adventure' of 1694. She also emphasizes how far during this decade lotteries and lottery adventuring spread to the provinces.[13]

[11] The different forms of the official lotteries in this period are described in detail in C. L'Etrange Ewen, *Lotteries and Sweepstakes: An Historical, Legal and Ethical Survey of Their Introduction, Suppression and Re-establishment in the British Isles* (London, 1932).

[12] Anne L. Murphy, *The Origins of English Financial Markets: Investment and Speculation before the South Sea Bubble* (Cambridge, 2009); Anne L. Murphy, 'Lotteries in the 1690s: Investment or Gamble?', *Financial History Review*, 12 (2005), 227–46; Lee K Davison, 'Public Policy in an Age of Economic Expansion: The Search for Commercial Accountability in England, 1690–1750', unpublished Ph.D. thesis, University of Harvard, (1990), esp. chs. 1 & 2.

[13] Murphy, *Origins*, pp. 155–8.

Significantly extending, however, the prominence and visibility of the lottery in British society were a new cluster of official lotteries held between 1710 and 1714, especially those in 1711–1712. This was a consequence, in the first place, simply of their scale. Between 1711 and 1714 the government used lotteries to borrow over £9 million. Never again would lotteries be as important as a source of government funds.[14] Second, it reflected the very favourable terms offered to investors in these lotteries by successive Lords Treasurer, Sidney, Lord Godolphin in 1710 and Robert Harley between 1711 and 1714. Such terms were necessitated by the sharp tightening of credit conditions during the later stages of the War of the Spanish Succession.[15] They also reflected the ambition of Harley and the new Tory ministry which assumed office in 1710 to reduce dependence for public borrowing on Whig-dominated chartered bodies – the Bank of England and the East India Company.[16]

The lotteries of 1711–1712 were of two sorts. There were, in both years, a £10 lottery and what was known as a classis lottery in which tickets had a face value of £100.[17] Godolphin's 1710 lottery, the first held since 1697, involved the issue of 100,000 £10 tickets, and promised holders of blanks 14 shillings per annum for thirty-two years (a return of 7 per cent *per annum*). In the lotteries of 1711–1712, blanks and prizes paid an annual interest rate of 6 per cent, with, in Peter Dickson's apt phrase, 'the further bait' of a promise to repay the principal sum within thirty-two years.[18] The ratio of prizes to blanks was also almost ten times greater than in 1710.[19] The classis lotteries, moreover, produced only winners; there were no blanks and *minimum* rates of return were 6.3%

[14] Lotteries accounted for about a third of long-term debt incurred by the government during the War of the Spanish Succession (1701–1714). While the percentage increase of the funded debt created by the lotteries remained of a similar order between 1719 and 1726, the sums involved were much smaller. Thereafter the proportion of public borrowing funded by the lotteries fell significantly. By 1755–1768, a period which included the Seven Years' War, the proportion had fallen to 9.4%. Lotteries by this period were increasingly adjuncts to public borrowing, while the workhorse of the funded debt was the 3% consol. François R. Velde, 'Lottery Loans in the Eighteenth Century' (2013), Table 1, p. 3, accessed electronically, 29 Jan. 2018 [www.ehes.org/velde.pdf].

[15] P. G. M. Dickson, *The Financial Revolution in England: A Study in the Development of Public Credit, 1688–1756* (London and New York, 1967), esp. pp. 62–75.

[16] This goal was also reflected in the establishment of the South Sea Company in 1711.

[17] The classis lotteries were modelled broadly on Dutch lotteries, although they were less complicated.

[18] Dickson, *Financial Revolution*, p. 74.

[19] In 1710, prize tickets constituted c. 2.6% of the total number, while in the £10 lotteries of 1711 and 1712 the equivalent proportion was 20%.

and 6.6% *per annum* in respectively 1711 and 1712.[20] The order of repayment in the classis lotteries simply followed the order in which the tickets were drawn, while in the £10 lotteries it was worked out by a separate draw of indicator tickets which referred to tranches of consecutively numbered lottery tickets. Where a ticket came in the schedule for repayment determined the immediate market value of blanks and prizes following the draw.[21]

Given the very attractive terms offered to investors, demand for tickets in the lotteries of 1711–1712 was unsurprisingly intense. In the case of the first lottery of 1711, the £10 one, the subscription for tickets filled up in a matter of just a few hours, leaving many people disappointed.[22] Subscriptions to the other lotteries of 1711–1712 also filled very rapidly, a development facilitated by the fact that from 1711 payment was in four parts, with discounts being offered for early payments.[23] Tickets on which just a single payment (or several) had been made – 'scrip' as it was termed – could be traded on the secondary market. It was through this secondary market that most people in 1711–1712, as in other years, obtained lottery tickets.

The Queen Anne lotteries had a very wide appeal. Based on data drawn from a sampling of City of London Orphans' Court inventories, Peter Earle emphasizes how investments in these lotteries were made by a much broader cross section of London's middling sort than in the case of the lottery of 1694. Around a third of Earle's sample of inventories relating to individuals who died between 1710 and 1720 included lottery tickets. One of these was that of the soap-maker, Caleb Booth, who died in 1713; as much as a third of Booth's assets, measured by appraised value, were invested in the lotteries of 1712 and 1713.[24]

20 Tickets in both lotteries were divided into five classes. The classes were uneven in size, and the number and size of prizes differed between the classes, as did the minimum return. Thus, in the first class, the smallest prize was £5 and £10 respectively in 1711 and 1712. This sum then rose in steps of £5 until in the fifth class it was £25 and £30, respectively. Overall returns on investments in these lotteries thus depended on the distribution of your tickets between the classes and whether any of these drew large prizes.

21 For which, see NA, DD/SP/6/9/21/3, an account of her Grace the Duchess of Newcastle's ten tickets in the classes, 27 Sept. 1711.

22 Coutts & Co. Archives, Letter Book 6, 13 Jan. 1710–1714 Oct. 1712, 29 r., John Campbell to <Simon?> Clarke, 17 Mar. 1711, which notes that the initial subscription had filled before three o'clock on the first day and that 'many are disappointed'.

23 Coutts & Co. Archives, Letter Book 6, 55 r., John Campbell to Col. James Campbell, 17 May 1711; 164 v., John Campbell to Sir James Wishart, 29 Apr. 1712.

24 Peter Earle, *The Making of the English Middle Class: Business, Society and Family Life in London, 1660–1730* (London, 1989), pp. 151–2.

James Macdonald estimates that the lottery loans of this period may have led to as much as a doubling of the overall number of public creditors.[25] Any such figure depends heavily on assumptions made about the distribution of numbers of tickets purchased by investors; nevertheless, Macdonald's suggested order of increase is entirely plausible.[26]

Members of the landed, mercantile, and professional elites invested heavily in the lotteries of 1711–1712. Among them was the wealthy London physician John Radcliffe. A large investor in government debt and stocks, Radcliffe committed substantial sums to both lotteries of 1711 and at least one of those of 1712. He paid over £19,500 for 200 tickets in the classis lottery of 1711, which placed him among the largest investors.[27] Another was Sir Richard Hill, who served for nine years as deputy paymaster of the forces in Flanders under William III and as envoy to Turin under Queen Anne. At his death in 1726, Hill possessed £30,698 in Bank stock; £5,006 in East India stock; £20,625 in South Sea stock; £19,000 in South Sea annuities; as well as having substantial sums invested in bonds and mortgages.[28] Through broker Moses Hart, Hill regularly bought and sold stocks in the 1710s and early 1720s. He started quite cautiously in his purchases of lottery tickets, procuring several tickets in the 1710 lottery and thirty-six tickets in the 1711 £10 lottery. In 1712, however, he invested in 1,000 £10 tickets and 66 tickets in the classis lottery, representing an investment of over £7,600, including brokerage.[29]

Hill was an active investor, speculating in financial markets overseas as well as in London, who sought to make money through frequent trading. The pattern, nevertheless, of wealthy individuals – including, in Peter Earle's phrase 'the elite members of the middle station' – committing significant sums to the Queen Anne lotteries as part of building a broader financial portfolio was a common one, and could be illustrated many times over.[30] To give one further example: Dudley North, son of the

[25] James Macdonald, 'The Importance of Not Defaulting: The Significance of the Election of 1710', in D'Maris Coffman, Adrian Leonard and Larry Neal (eds.), *Questioning Credible Commitment: Perspectives on the Rise of Financial Capitalism* (Cambridge, 2013), p. 135.

[26] Taking just the two £10 lotteries of 1711–1712, the total number of tickets issued was 330,000. To reach a figure of 20,000 for the number of investors, the average number of tickets bought would need to be 16.5. Given the data presented below on ticket purchases in these lotteries, this seems reasonable.

[27] Bodleian Library, Radcliffe Trust Papers, MS D. D. Radcliffe, c.12/1&2, financial papers.

[28] SRO, Attingham Collection, 112/1/2866, Richard Hill, 'Mon Etat at Lady day 1726'.

[29] SRO, 112/1/1934, Sir James Bateman to Richard Hill, 2 Apr. 1711; 112/1/1719, lists of numbers etc. of sixty-four bills in class lottery of 1712; 112/1720, lottery orders for 1712.

[30] Earle, *Making of the English Middle Class*, p. 151.

famous Turkey merchant of the later seventeenth century of the same name, derived much of his income from money lent out on mortgage and bond, which earned him interest of between 4% and 5%. But he was also a very substantial holder of government and especially South Sea stock – he held £31,108 of the latter in 1723. While the record of his lottery adventuring is slightly unclear, he bought 20 tickets in the 1710 ten-pound lottery, 2 classis tickets in 1711, and 100 tickets in the 1712 ten-pound lottery. He continued to purchase significant quantities of lottery tickets in later years, in 1719, 1724, and 1726.[31]

Two sets of data, however, enable us to be altogether more systematic in reconstructing lottery adventuring in 1711–1712. The first, and most comprehensive, is a record of holders of lottery orders from 1711 to 1712, who exchanged these in 1717 for 5 per cent stock managed by the Bank of England as part of a conversion operation. This is not a perfect source because lottery orders were traded following the draw; and the market for these appears to have been quite active around the time of the conversion.[32] Most people, however, seem to have held on to their lottery orders from 1711 and 1712. Almost all of those in possession of such orders opted for the conversion, presumably because, as the very successful and very wealthy city financier Sir James Bateman informed Lord Stair, this secured their principal, albeit at the cost of accepting lower interest payments.[33]

Table 4.1 represents the subset of subscribers who were credited with £2,000 or more of 5 per cent Bank stock in 1717. The numbers in this table are not straightforward. People quite often had multiple occupations, such as, for example, that of merchant and financier. Certain categories clearly overlapped – for example, women and gentility, or, indeed, as in the case of Johanna Cock, bankers/brokers and women. Cock was a substantial dealer in Bank of England and other stock. The most capacious and porous category is the largest – the 'genteel'. The designations of 'gentleman' or 'esq.' were by this period being

[31] KARC, North Manuscripts, EK/U471/A255–60, accounts of Dudley North, 1708–23; Hoare's Bank, HB/1/6. North purchased 333 tickets in 1719, while he bought 20 tickets in both the lotteries of 1724 and 1726. He sold most of the 333 tickets in 1719 before the draw, 185 of them to the partners of Hoare's Bank.

[32] As suggested by BL, Add MS 74,062, account book of Sir Robert Walpole, 1714–1718. The entries are not entirely clear in their meaning, but Walpole was selling class lottery orders in late 1716; he was also very actively trading in 1714 lottery orders. Another person who bought 1711 lottery orders in 1717 was Sir George Saville, who purchased orders costing £1,300. NA, Savile Papers, DD/SR/211/178, Sir George Savile's Book of Accounts, 1715–1721, 1717, fo. 14.

[33] Bateman is quoted by Dickson, *Financial Revolution*, p. 87.

Table 4.1. *Subscribers for £2,000 or more worth of 1717, 5 per cent lottery stock*

Occupation/designation	No./%
Gentility (i.e. baronet, knight, gent., esq.)	445 (47%)
Peer/peeress	16 (2%)
Professionals (incl. military/naval)	39 (4%)
Merchants	132 (14%)
Tradesmen/manufacturers/artisans	80 (9%)
Bankers/brokers	31 (3%)
Women	109 (12%)
Other	11 (1%)
Unknown/unclear	78 (8%)

Sources: Bank of England Archives, Ac 27/332–6, 5% Annuities 1717 Lottery Ledgers, 1717–1719; Ac 27/330–1, 5% Annuities 1717 Lottery, alphabet ledgers, A-H & I-Z.

claimed by a wide variety of individuals, not just those from a landed background.[34] Merchants and professionals are undercounted because of the vagaries of contemporary designations. Leading members of the mercantile classes, for example, who had achieved high civic status and social titles – typically that of knight or baronet – were usually listed under their honorific status.[35] Presumably much depended in this context on the assumptions and practice of the clerks who recorded this information.

Despite these limitations, this data furnish powerful further evidence for the strength of the appeal of the 1711–1712 lotteries to the capital's wealthy citizens and residents, as well as, indeed, to Dutch and other foreign investors. Among the largest subscribers, measured by the value of their stock, were prominent representatives of the capital's tightly interlocking financial, mercantile, and political elites, several of whom had close links with the merchant and financial classes in Amsterdam, frequently acting as their agents in financial and commercial transactions in London.[36] Two of the very largest subscribers were Justus Beck, the Bank of England director and financial dealer (£93,203), and Dennis

[34] P. J. Corfield, 'Class by Name and Number in Eighteenth Century Britain', *History*, 72 (1987), 38–61.

[35] These include, *inter alia*, Sir Lambert Blackwell; Sir Justus Beck, baronet; Sir Gilbert Heathcote, knight and alderman; Sir Isaac Shard, knight; Sir James Bateman, alderman and knight; Dennis Dutry, baronet.

[36] Dickson has emphasized the participation of foreign speculators in the lottery loans of 1710–1714, and the dominance among these of Dutch investors (Dickson, *Financial Revolution*, pp.308–9).

Dutry, the Huguenot wine importer who quickly turned to merchant banking (£40,199), both of whom were Dutch-born. Another Dutch-born financier who was very active in the lotteries in these years was Sir Matthew Decker, although his holding of lottery orders from 1711 to 1712 was relatively low in value by 1717.[37] Others included among this group of large investors comprise a veritable roll call of the city's financial titans: Sir Theodore Janssen (£35,530), Abraham Craiesteyn Sen. (£38,586), Sir Gilbert Heathcote (£22,376), Sir Peter Meyer (£14,646), Sir James Bateman (£2,659), and Sir Lambert Blackwell (£9,160), to name only a few. Several private bankers feature prominently: Henry Hoare (£40,977), George Middleton (£10,972), Sir Richard (£8,997), and Francis Child (£7,536); and, most obviously, Elias Turner and George Caswell of the Sword Blade Company, who were closely involved with Harley in devising his financial measures in 1711–1714.[38] Individuals such as Hoare, Turner, and Caswell acted as intermediaries, and on their own behalf. Distinguishing what proportions of the sums for which they were credited represented which activity is impossible, as is usually tracing the complex chains of relationships that lay behind large-scale financial speculations of this period, which typically involved partnerships of various kinds, as well as provision of credit.[39]

Two other well-represented groups were people of French Huguenot extraction and members of the Sephardi Jewish financial elite. The former included, in addition to Sir Theodore Janssen, several merchants and financiers – such as various members of the Desbouverie family – Sir Edward (£25,770), Sir Christopher (£13,391) – John de Remy de Montigny (£30,074), John Girardot De Tillieux (£14,870), and Richard Du Cane, who would become MP for Colchester in 1715 (£5,907) – as well as a good number of widows, spinsters, and gentlemen, many of whom were residents of Westminster. Among the Sephardi Jews were Joseph (£20,484) and Anthony Da Costa (£36,952), Joseph Henriques (£8,020), and Isaac Fernando Nunes (£12,951). From the outset, members of this international community were, perhaps unsurprisingly given their broader financial interests, conspicuously active in the rapidly developing market for lottery tickets.

[37] It was £4,461. For Decker's heavy involvement in the 1711–1712 lotteries, see Bob Harris, 'Lottery Adventuring in Britain, c.1710–1760', *English Historical Review*, 118 (2018), 305.

[38] George Caswell was credited with £41,404 in his own name, while Turner and Caswell together were credited with (£89,051), the second highest figure behind Justus Beck.

[39] For which, see esp. Larry Neal, '"*I Am Not Master of Events*"' *The Speculations of John Law and Lord Londonderry in the Mississippi and South Sea Bubbles* (New Haven and London, 2012).

As already noted, many individuals who invested in the lotteries in 1711–1712 were already active in the stock market. Among the leading subscribers were a substantial number of rentiers, for whom building a financial portfolio was an increasingly important aspect of securing for themselves a regular, reasonably secure income, a group which included a significant proportion of widows and spinsters. Few members of the peerage invested significant sums, a pattern in line with their investments in other public and government stocks.[40] Two who did, however – Lord Cowper and the Earl of Orkney, a Scottish representative peer – had sizeable holdings of other stocks.[41] Two peeresses who adventured deeply were Margaret Cavendish, Duchess of Newcastle, and the Duchess of Marlborough, although the latter's involvement was hidden because her tickets were held in the names of others.[42] Various landed men feature – the wealthy Cumberland landowner, Sir James Lowther (£11,541), for example, or William Chetwynd (£10,976), the youngest son of John Chetwynd, who began his public life in the diplomatic service before entering parliament as a Whig in 1715. Of the MPs who adventured in these lotteries, most were office holders, lawyers, or navy and military men, again a pattern reflected in investment in other public stocks.[43] In the case of the future Prime Minister, Henry Pelham (£10,520), the habit of lottery adventuring appears to have continued into later years, while his participation reveals that the fears of some individuals, such as Daniel Defoe, that the partisan hostility of some Whigs to these lotteries might undermine them proved to be well wide of the mark.[44] Another prominent Whig who was a lottery adventurer in this period was the writer Joseph Addison.[45] More striking still, however, are the numbers of tradesmen, shopkeepers, and manufacturers who

[40] Dickson, *Financial Revolution*, pp. 265–6, 280–1, 295–6. [41] idem, p. 281.

[42] NA, Portland of Welbeck (4th Deposit), DD/4P/50/13–14, list of Duchess of Newcastle's lottery tickets and receipt for same, 1711–1712; DD/$P/6/9/21, accounts and receipts re. investments in lotteries etc., 1712. For the Duchess of Marlborough's lottery purchases, see BL, Blenheim Papers, Add MS 61472, fo. 182, orders on the lottery 1711 for £1,000 payable as underwritten, and fos. 189–90, 'An Account of my Money Sept the 15th 1715'. In 1731, the newspapers were reporting that the duchess had purchased 1,000 tickets in that year's lottery (*CalM*, 22 Nov. 1731).

[43] Dickson, *Financial Revolution*, p. 267.

[44] *The Letters of Daniel Defoe*, ed. George Harris Healey (Oxford, 1955), pp. 316–7: Daniel Defoe to Robert Harley, 9 Mar. 1711. The criticism was, it appears, levelled against the schedule of prizes and supposed deficiencies in the sums likely to be raised by the taxes appropriated to defray the cost and payments. Defoe was proposing writing a tract to counteract what he described as 'Coffee house clamour', which might be circulated throughout England and into Scotland.

[45] *The Letters of Joseph* Addison, ed. Walter Graham (Oxford, 1941), p. 266: Joseph Addison to Joshua Dawson, 18 Dec. 1711, where Addison comments, 'I can not forbear telling you that last week I drew a prize of a thousand pound in the *Lottery*.'

committed large sums to these lotteries. Their presence reflected the capital's broadening economic base, the rising wealth of its diversifying and growing middle class, and, as importantly, their willingness to diversify their assets in pursuit of good returns.

What of the wider group of adventurers – in other words, including those who were credited with stock of a value of less than £2,000? A sample comprising 1,190 of all of those credited with stock in this issue reveals that nearly a third (31.4%) were from the titled nobility, or knights, gentlemen, and esquires.[46] Bankers and merchants made up 4.3% and professionals, including military men, 6.6%. Tradesmen and shopkeepers were fairly well represented at 10.2%, as were artisans and manufacturers (13.7%). Occupational categories can easily disguise diverse circumstances, and some individuals listed as tradesmen, manufacturers, shopkeepers, and artisans may well have boasted substantial wealth and incomes, albeit not at the levels commonly seen among the city's mercantile elite. It is no coincidence that mercers, drapers, haberdashers, brewers, and distillers are well represented, given that these occupations included individuals and businesses operating on a large scale by this period.[47] What most stands out, however, is the range of the occupations represented, listed in Table 4.2. This underlines the fact that the lottery's appeal already by this date reached well down into and across metropolitan society, something which would almost certainly be strongly reinforced had we got data concerning purchases of shares of tickets through the sorts of scheme being offered by the goldsmith banker, Matthew West, in 1711–1712, as well as several other consortia of goldsmith bankers.[48]

Another notable feature of this sample is the proportion of women – 24.1%. This is in line with the numbers of female investors in other government and public stocks.[49] Taking a slightly different sample, however – comprising all entries in the first of the ledgers for the 1717 lottery stock – women may well have constituted a little above a third of subscribers, which is rather higher than in respect of other public

[46] The sample comprises all entries in the first 150 pages of the first and third ledgers for the 5 per cent lottery stock.

[47] For which, see Earle, *Making of the English Middle Class*, ch. 4 'Business'.

[48] For these schemes, see ch. 3, p. 147.

[49] Amy M. Froide, *Silent Partners: Women as Public Investors during Britain's Financial Revolution, 1690–1750* (Oxford, 2017), Table 5.1, Female investors in Government Securities, 1692–1747, p. 123, which shows the proportion varying between at the low end 12% and the high 30.16% for the 5% lottery stock of 1717. See also Carlos and Neal, 'Micro-Foundations of the Early London Capital Market', esp. 525; Carlos and Neal, 'Women Investors in Early Capital Markets, 1720–1725', *Financial History Review*, 11 (2004), 197–224.

Table 4.2. *Occupational breakdown of sample of subscribers to 1717, 5 per cent lottery stock, tradesmen, shopkeepers, manufacturers, artisans, miscellaneous*

Tradesmen and shopkeepers

baker (4); bookseller (4); butcher (5); butter seller (1); cheesemonger (2); cider merchant (1); corn chandler (1); draper (3); druggist (4); glass seller (1); haberdasher (3); hosier (1); innholder (3); ironmonger (1); laceman (1); linen draper (5); looking glass seller (2); malster (1); meal factor (1); mealman (1); mercer (10); merchant tailor (5); milliner (4); oilman (1); perfumer (1); poulterer (1); salesman (3); salter (6); ship's chandler (1); stationer (1); tallow chandler (3); tinman (1); toyman (1); upholsterer (3); victualler (8); vintner (10); woollen draper (3)

Manufacturers and artisans*

armourer (1); blacksmith (1); brewer (5); carpenter (1); carver (1); coachmaker (1); clockmaker (2); combmaker (1); cooper (7); cordwainer (1); currier (1); cutler (4); distiller (12); dyer (3); engraver (2); farrier (1); founder (1); girdler (1); glassmaker (1); glazier (1); glover (1); hatband maker (1); jeweller (2); joiner (2); lacemaker (1); last maker (1); leather dresser (1) locksmith (1); mason (1); mathematical instrument maker (1); paint stainer (1); painter (1); periwig maker (7); pewterer (2); plasterer (1); razor maker (2); ropemaker (2); sailmaker (1); silversmith (1); skinner (1); smith (1); soap boiler (1); soapmaker (1); spectacle maker (1); staymaker (1); stocking maker (2); sword cutler (2); tailor (8); toymaker (1); watchmaker (9); wheelwright (2); weaver (28); woolcomber (1)

Misc.

bricklayer (1); butler (1); coachman (4); carman (1); cook (2); gardener (1); pastry cook (1); servant (8); writing master (1)

stocks and government securities; the amount of stock they owned was also significantly greater than in the three major stock companies (the Bank of England, East India Company, and South Sea Company).[50] At the same time, the average value of their subscriptions was lower than that of men, and they were less well represented (at 11%) among the top cohort of subscribers (those subscribing for stock of £2,000 or above in value). These findings seem to indicate that, amongst other things, women who did not normally participate in the stock market were drawn into modest lottery adventures in 1711–1712, a pattern reflected in other records.[51] The feminization of the stock market, which has recently been

[50] Dickson's estimate, based on a sample, is 34.7% (Dickson, *Financial Revolution*, p. 282). Froide's (see n. 49 above) is slightly lower at 30.16%.

[51] The records and accounts of Hoare's Bank include several women who appear to have bought only a single or a few tickets in the Queen Anne lotteries, and who feature as purchasers of tickets on only one occasion. See e.g. Hoare's Bank, Ledger 14, which records payments for tickets in the £10 lottery of 1711.

closely linked to investment in South Sea stock, entered an important earlier phase in its development with the Queen Anne lotteries.[52]

Moreover, the overall picture revealed by the registers of 1717 lottery stock is (reassuringly) consistent with that which emerges from our second set of data: two lists of prize-winners in the classis lotteries of 1711–1712.[53] Combined the latter contain a total of 2,249 entries, representing around 1,314 individuals. Tables 4.3–4.5 break down this data according to, respectively, occupational and status categories, place of residence, and the frequency with which individuals appear.

This set of data reveals even more sharply than the first the overwhelming importance in the early eighteenth century of London and its commercial and financial classes. This is even clearer if we include the 'proximity effect', as reflected in the numbers of people who were residents in neighbouring counties. Equally strongly underlined is the existence of large numbers of people from well outside the financial and mercantile elites, who were drawn into participating in the lottery in 1711–1712. Among the winners of major capital prizes in the 1711–1712 classis lotteries were several widows and spinsters, including one London widow who scooped the largest prize of £20,000, as well as a dyer, woollen draper, ironmonger, soapmaker, glover, and skinner.

One further significant pattern is only partially disclosed (in Table 4.5). Most people appear just once in the lists of prize-winners, although a substantial minority appear on two or more occasions. This almost certainly reflects how many people restricted their lottery adventuring in 1711–1712 to just one or several tickets. As already noted, many of these were very likely newcomers to the rapidly developing financial markets of the early eighteenth-century British capital.

The lotteries of 1711–1712 represented, as already emphasized, attractive investments, over and above the prospects they offered of winning large prizes. We cannot simply assume, therefore, that the patterns of adventuring exhibited in them were replicated in later official and public lotteries; the terms of these later lotteries were for a start significantly less favourable. Extant data with which to trace lottery adventuring after 1712 is frustratingly sparse. Records survive of subscriptions to several lottery issues, for example, that of 1745, analyzed recently by Amy Froide.[54] A problem with these, not fully acknowledged by Froide, is that the subscribers often sold their tickets on the secondary

[52] Ann Carlos, Erin Fletcher, Larry Neal, and Kirsten Wandschneider, 'Financing and Re-Financing the War of the Spanish Succession and then Re-financing the South Sea Company' in Coffman et al. (eds.), *Questioning Credible Commitment*, p. 163.

[53] TNA, E401/2599 & 2600.

[54] Froide, *Silent Partners*, pp. 125–30.

Table 4.3. *Occupations and status of prizewinners in the 1711 and 1712 classis lotteries*

hereditary peers (3.27%)
peer 22; baronet 21

gentility (41.55%)
knight 35; gentleman/Esq 511

women (8.67%)
wife 8; peeress 8; spinster 40; widow 54; other 4

commerce/finance (25.72%)
merchant 280; factor 8; broker 3; goldsmith banker 47

professions (4.49%)
legal
scrivener 4; serjeant at law 1; Lord Chief Justice 1
church
clergyman 2
medical
physician 13; surgeon 11; apothecary 13
military 13
other
accountant 1

tradesmen/shopkeepers (11.33%)
mercer 21; linen draper 17; distiller 12; grocer 11; haberdasher 9; druggist 8; brewer 7; vintner 5; woolen draper 5; cheese-monger 4; glass seller 4; ironmonger 4; silkman 4; stationer 4; upholsterer 3; confectioner 3; fishmonger 3; laceman 3; hosier 2; innholder 2; leather seller 2; tobacconist 2; baker 1; bookseller 1; butcher 1; chapman 1; coffeeman 1; corn chandler 1; fruiterer 1; haberdasher of hats 1; jeweller 1; milliner 1; oylman 1; undertaker 1; victualler 1; whalebone seller 1

artisans (5.1%)
peruke maker 6; salter 5; skinner 4; weaver 4; cooper 4; tailor 3; watchmaker 2; wire drawer 2; clockmaker 2; cloth worker 2; cordwainer 2; currier 2; dry salter 2; dyer 2; glover 2; pewterer 2; scarlet dyer 2; armourer 1; cloth drawer 1; coach wheel wright 1; coachmaker 1; felt maker 1; gold and silver wire drawer 1; gunmaker 1; leather dresser 1; mason 1; periwig maker 1; printer 1; silk throwster 1; silversmith 1; soapmaker 1; staymaker 1; sugar baker 1; sugar refiner 1; sword cutter 1; tanner 1

other
mariner/sailsman 5; packer 4; malster 1; cook 1; clerk 13; unclassified 16

institutions
Oriel College 1; Amicable Society for a Perpetual Insurance Office 1

Table 4.4. *Addresses of prizewinners in the 1711 and 1712 classis lotteries*[*]

(1) City	(2) Westminster	(3) Middlesex/ Southwark/ Surrey/ Essex/Herts	(4) Provincial England & Wales (excluding 3)	(5) Ireland	(6) Continental Europe
687	149	356	103	5	21

[*]Some of the entries for individuals – most commonly, peers or major office holders, such as the Attorney General, Sir Edward Northey – did not include addresses, and these are here excluded. Others gave an address such as Bank of England or Navy Office, and these have been included under the appropriate category.

Table 4.5. *Frequency with which names appear among prizewinners in the 1711 and 1712 classis lotteries*

1x	2x	3x	4x	5x	6x	7x	8x	9x	≥10x
942	183	77	29	27	7	7	10	1	19

market; indeed, this was, as we saw in the previous chapter, a ready way of turning a quick profit. More promising for present purposes are records and accounts kept by several private banks, among them Hoare's Bank. Information from these also allows us to begin to trace patterns and habits of lottery adventuring for a sizeable cohort of individuals over a significant length of time.

Clients of the private banks were, as noted in the last chapter, mostly wealthy and often from a landed background. We are, it goes almost without saying, concentrating on people who bought lottery tickets, not on those who did not, who may have comprised a majority of bank clients.[55] At this level, decisions about investing defy simple

[55] Because of the way in which the Hoare's Bank ledgers are organized, determining the proportion of their clients who bought lottery tickets is very difficult. Two series of ledgers exist for this period. One contains accounts of customers each with a sufficiently large volume of business to take up several double-page spreads in a single ledger. The other series contains records for customers who engaged in only a few transactions. The dates covered by the ledgers overlap because this was dictated by the amount of business transacted by an individual. Anne Laurence has found that only 17% of customers were active in the stock market in 1717, rising to 25% in 1719, and 30% in 1729. She includes lottery purchases and prizes in her calculations, but does not distinguish these from other stock. Ann Laurence, 'Women Investors, "That Nasty South Sea Affair" and the Rage to Speculate in Early Eighteenth-Century England', *Accounting, Business and Financial History*, xvi (2006), 249; Ann Laurence, 'The Emergence of a Private Clientele for Banks in the Early Eighteenth Century: Hoare's Bank and Some Women Customers',

explanations. Why someone was happy to put their money into the lottery and another not is almost impossible to say at this distance. One can speculate on the existence of alternative avenues of investment, or the disposition to take risks, or religious views and disapproval of gaming. Worth noting, however, in this context is that the clients of Hoare's Bank included a good many people who were deeply committed to the cause of the Church of England, high church philanthropic activities, and the reformation of manners. It was supporters of the latter who had been behind the legislation to prohibit all lotteries in 1698. Yet, several such people, including a number of clergymen, such as, most notably perhaps, the one-time non-juror, influential religious apologist, and promoter of charity schools, Robert Nelson, were regular lottery adventurers.[56] Even with their limitations there is much to be learnt about the lottery and lottery adventuring from these records.

The partners of Hoare's Bank were, as we saw in the last chapter, active in the lottery market on a fairly large scale, buying and selling tickets for a substantial minority of clients. Anne Laurence suggests that this activity spiked in 1711–1712 in terms both of volume and value.[57] This is almost certainly correct, and reflects the strong appeal of the lotteries in these years. Their involvement continued on a substantial scale after that date, at least until the middle of the eighteenth century, when consolidated lottery accounts appear to have ceased to be kept by the bank's clerks, or do not survive.[58] In the £10 lottery of 1712, the partners bought 2,272 tickets for at least 119 individuals. Levels of activity, measured by volume and numbers of individuals, if not value, remained broadly similar in the lotteries of the 1720s. As late as 1755 the bank's partners bought 527 tickets for 49 clients.[59]

Most of these individuals were buying small numbers of tickets. This pattern is clearer if we exclude the Queen Anne lotteries. Take the lottery

Economic History Review, lxi (2008), 570. It is clear, however, that the numbers involved in lottery adventuring were significantly higher in certain years.

56 Other clerical lottery adventurers among the Hoare's Bank clients included Charles Briscoe; Dr Joseph Barton; Samuel Arnold; Matthew Postlethwayt; and William Lupton. Thomas Milles, Bishop of Waterford and Francis Hutchinson, Bishop of Down and Connor, in Ireland, were also regular purchasers of lottery tickets.

57 Laurence, 'Women Investors', 249–50.

58 The bank continued to purchase lottery tickets for clients in the later eighteenth century, but on a diminishing scale.

59 Data derived from Hoare's Bank, HB/1/6, Ledger for Plate, including accounts and lists of names of customers for whom lottery tickets were bought and sold by the partners, 1697–c. 1730; HB/5//H/1–2, Money Lent Ledgers, including accounts of purchase of lottery tickets and lottery annuities from 1710 to c. 1725; HB/8/G/11, record of payments to the bank to complete the remaining sums due upon receipts for tickets in the lottery, 1755.

Table 4.6. *Lottery ticket purchases by clients of Hoare's Bank, 1723–1737*

Lottery	<5 tickets	5–10 tickets	11–20	>20
1723	33	26	2	8
1726	40	31	11	19
1731	64	18	5	2
1733 Charitable Corporation	52	30	5	12
1737 Westminster Bridge	48	25	5	3

Sources: HB/1/1/6, Ledger for Plate, c.1697–1730; HB1/1/2, Money Lent Ledgers, 1710–c.1725; HB/8/9/10, accounts re. Westminster Bridge lotteries, 1737–9.

of 1723, in which the bank's partners bought tickets for sixty-nine people: twelve bought a single ticket, while only eleven bought more than ten. The picture for other lotteries is similar (see Table 4.6).

Harder to assess is how regularly individuals purchased tickets. Focusing on lotteries held during the early Hanoverian period (1714–1760), a majority (63%) of the bank's clients who are recorded as having bought tickets appear just once in the accounts. This seems to indicate occasional involvement, although they could have been buying tickets elsewhere – for example, from lottery office keepers or from friends and acquaintances. Those whose involvement was more frequent included the widow, Jane Bonnell, whom we met briefly in the last chapter. As described by Laurence, Bonnell was lured into speculating in South Sea stock in 1719–1720, losing what was, for her, a significant sum of money.[60] Thereafter she restricted her financial investments to regular lottery purchases, although on a fairly modest scale; the highest number of tickets that she bought at one time was eight (in 1724).[61] There are plenty of similar cases. Amy Castleton, another widow, bought eight tickets in the 1731 lottery, twelve in 1736, and five in the Westminster Bridge Lottery of 1737. In 1731 she subsequently sold seven blanks and a £20 prize, thereby nearly recovering the cost of her initial investment.[62] Even among the fairly wealthy many were adventuring with relatively small (but still far from insignificant) sums, carefully adjusting their choices about how to spend their money according presumably to the likely material and, indeed, psychological benefits (of which more later).

[60] Laurence, 'Women Investors', 256, 259–60.

[61] Hoare's Bank, HB/1/6, which shows Bonnell purchasing eight tickets in 1723, five in 1724, one in 1726, three in 1731, two in 1736, and two in the Bridge lottery of 1737.

[62] Hoare's Bank, HB/1/6 and Ledger L/45, account of Mrs Amy Castleton, July 1731–June 1732.

The ledgers, meanwhile, of Drummond's Bank, clients who included prominent members of the Scottish landed and professional elites – the Dukes of Atholl and Queensberry, for example – reveal much the same general picture: most lottery ticket purchases were small scale. The bank's partners, for example, bought 601 tickets in the 1724 lottery for at least 56 of its clients. Of these, forty-one (73%) bought fewer than ten tickets, many of them between three and one.[63] The pattern was essentially the same in the 1755 lottery.[64] The dowager Duchess of Atholl bought a single ticket, as did the Tory MP for Gloucestershire, Norbone Berkeley. It may well be, moreover, that on the relatively few occasions where larger numbers of tickets were purchased some, even most, were for individuals other than the recorded buyer. The diplomat and MP, Andrew Mitchell, used the bank to make the first payment on fifty tickets in 1755, but the bank's clerks noted him as having made the last one on only twelve. He may have sold the part-paid tickets, or made payment on them by other means; or he may have been acting as an agent for others.[65] The Earl of Breadalbane made the first payment on ten tickets, five of which were for his wife. Another peer who did the same was the Earl of Hillsborough. Both were regular lottery adventurers.[66]

Several clients of Drummond's Bank may well have adventured more deeply in the lottery. The Earl of Stamford, for example, bought fifteen tickets in 1755 in his own right, while the 'Earl of Stamford & Company' bought another twenty-five; the account for the latter was also credited with nearly £700, the proceeds of a prize that had been won in a Brussels lottery. Lady Betty Germain, the courtier, political hostess, and widow of gambler and soldier, Sir John Germain, began by buying twenty tickets in the same lottery, purchasing a further twenty on each of three separate transactions. This pattern may well indicate her inability to resist further involvement, or, as likely, her simple wish for such. She also appears to have been trading in blanks and prizes. Like a good many other wealthy widows, she had accumulated a considerable financial portfolio, and her lottery adventuring is best viewed primarily as an extension of this activity.[67]

One further point about lottery adventuring in this early part of our period, and indeed later, needs underlining here. How we assess the

[63] RBS Archives, DR/427/4–6, Drummonds Bank, Customer Account Ledgers, 1724–6.

[64] RBS Archives, DR/427/34–5, Drummonds Bank, Customer Account Ledgers, 1755–6.

[65] Op. cit..

[66] See n. 53, above. NRS, GD 112/21/77, personal account books kept by John, Lord Glenorchy, later 3rd Earl of Breadalbane, 1733–1752. This shows Breadalbane purchasing six lottery tickets in 1734; four tickets in the Westminster Bridge Lottery of 1737; two lottery tickets in 1742, 1744, 1745, and 1750, respectively.

[67] RBS Archives, DR/427/34, Drummonds Bank, Customer Account Ledger, 1755.

character of any lottery adventure depends, as already implied, on the broader speculative activities, incomes, and wealth of the individuals concerned. Unfortunately, these all too crucial contexts can only be glimpsed very sporadically. In late 1731, Thomas, Lord Hervey spent £112 on ten lottery tickets, subsequently selling seven blanks and a £20 prize, yielding a total sum of £64, which amounts to a loss of just over 50% of his initial investment. In the early 1730s Hervey was buying and selling large quantities of East India and South Sea stocks, and the balance on his account with Hoare's Bank stood at a little more than £17,000.[68] In 1724, the Bristolian commercial magnate and religious dissenter, Sir Abraham Elton, bought 100 tickets, and his son may well have bought a similar quantity. Both men were conspicuously wealthy – the elder leaving £100,000 at his death. The Duke of Kingston, another very wealthy man, bought sixty-four tickets in 1724 and fifty in 1726.[69] Wealth alone, however, was not a strong predictor of a disposition to financial speculation, or, indeed, lottery adventuring.

Participation, therefore, in lotteries became well entrenched in Britain in the first half of the eighteenth century amongst a broad cross section of the landed and other elites, and almost certainly many among the middling sort, although the latter trend remains much less consistently visible. Here, as we began to see in the previous chapter, family, kinship, and other kinds of network – commercial, political, professional, or social – served both to extend and underpin this development. Participation could be emulative, a matter of copying the behaviour of others within one's networks or circles of acquaintance. In April 1711, for example, Charles Medlycott, H. M. Commissary in Lisbon between 1709 and 1714 informed Peter Delaporte, shortly to become a director of the South Sea Company, that Medlycott's wife wished to place £100 in the lottery. Evidently someone within their circle in the Portuguese capital had been lucky in an earlier lottery, presumably that of 1710.[70] Participation among kin and acquaintances was commonplace, as in the case of James Harris of Hampshire and his brothers.[71] While Londoners were prominent among the early lottery adventurers, lottery adventuring

[68] Hoare's Bank, Ledger L/18, account of the Right Hon. Lord Hervey, Sept. 1731–Mar. 1734.
[69] Hoare's Bank, HB/1/6.
[70] Northamptonshire Record Office, Northampton, Cockayne MSS, C. 2922, Charles Medlycott to Peter Delaporte, 14 Apr. 1711. I am very grateful to Dr Aaron Graham for drawing this letter to my attention.
[71] HRO, 9M73/G306/8, Thomas Harris, Lincoln's Inn to James Harris, Salisbury, 1 Dec. 1737; 9M73/G347/77, Thomas Harris, Lincoln's Inn, to Elisabeth Harris, 14 Jan. 1752.

spread well beyond the British capital, facilitated by personal connections of different types to the metropolis, and, increasingly by the mid eighteenth century, by means of lottery office keepers and the expanding reach of the postal services. It also spread well down the social scale. In 1751 a £2,000 prize was won by Wapping Friendly Society, while an £1,000 prize was won by a club of porters who met in a tavern in Cannon Street.[72] By the mid eighteenth century shopkeepers such as Thomas Turner from East Hoathly in Sussex and Abraham Dent from Kirkby Stephen in Westmorland can be found purchasing tickets (or shares thereof).[73] Turner's adventure in the 1757 lottery was a joint collaboration with his brother, while his wife engaged in a separate such gamble. Winner of the top prize of £20,000 in the 1726 lottery was the surgeon and later mayor of King's Lynn in Norfolk, John Goodwyn, who had his portrait painted by Arthur Pond in which he was depicted holding the winning ticket.[74] An engraved portrait was produced of John Alder, the 'fortunate Cooper of Abingdon', who was also depicted with the winning ticket, which brought him a prize of £20,000, prominently grasped in his right hand. On 10 December 1751, the *Aberdeen Press and Journal* informed its readers that an Aberdonian merchant had won two lottery prizes, one of £500 and another of £20.[75] A good many lottery adventures may have been ad hoc affairs, but for a growing number of people they had become a habit.

One further example illustrates very clearly several of these conclusions. This is that of George Drummond, six-time Lord Provost of Edinburgh, exemplary Whig loyalist figurehead, and sometime reluctant factotum of the Argyll interest in the Scottish capital. Drummond is today best remembered for having presided over the founding of the Edinburgh Royal Infirmary and Edinburgh medical school and the plans for the redevelopment and extension of Edinburgh, which began to unfold from the early 1750s but which were, it appears, under contemplation from as early as 1725.[76] From a merchant background, Drummond was until the early 1720s engaged in a trading co-partnership with his close political ally

[72] *London Daily Advertiser or Literary Gazette*, 16 Nov. 1751; *WEP*, 16 Nov. 1751.

[73] *The Diary of Thomas Turner, 1754–1765*, ed. D. Vaisey (Oxford, 19856), pp. 63–5, 113; CRO, Kendal, WDB 63/52, Abraham Dent, shopkeeper, Kirkby Stephen, non-business papers, state lottery ticket, 1760 and WDB 63/53, notification that ticket in the state lottery had drawn a blank, 19 Nov. 1760.

[74] *Daily Post*, 19 July 1726.

[75] In 1747, the press reported that the Edinburgh merchants, Messrs Fairholme and Company, had won a prize of £1,000 (*CalM*, 7 Dec. 1747).

[76] Alexander Murdoch, 'Drummond, George (1687–1766), accountant-general of excise in Scotland and local politician' (2004), accessed electronically, 10 Jan. 2017 (https://eproxy-prd.bodleian.ox.ac.uk: 4563/10.1093/ref.odnb/8065).

James Nimmo and John Campbell of Skipnish, brother of Daniel Campbell of Shawfield, the MP for Glasgow burghs. The failure of this trading venture seems to have left him entangled in heavy debts, and the shadow of these debts and financial pressures features heavily in the tortured spiritual diary he kept between 1736 and 1738, when he found himself out of political favour, having been dismissed from his post in the Customs commission in 1736.[77] This records his (probably temporary) alienation from the 'people in power', his pessimism about the spiritual and wider condition of his country, and also his intense, introspective spirituality, and belief in God's direct providence as a controlling influence on his life. Drummond was ever on the look out for signs of God's favour, interpreting repeated setbacks in his life, including his troubled relationship with his ailing, querulous mother, his dismissal from the customs administration, as further trials of faith, which engendered in him a mood precariously balanced between deep gloom and a brittle, but profound, optimism.[78] In respect of God's intentions for him, he was regularly consulting a woman whom he believed had direct access to God's mind.[79] At one point, he appears to have believed that God might have intended the Westminster Bridge Lottery as the vehicle for his worldly salvation and easing of his financial troubles. As he wrote in the entry in his journal for 12 July 1736: 'The Thames Bridge lottery has been, often thrown in my thoughts as a way in which the Lord may work a complete deliverance for me, and its daily, floating in my mind.'[80] The idea was later scotched by his spiritual confidante, who informed Drummond that the Lord had revealed to her that 'He is not to meddle in it [i.e. the lottery], It is not the way he is to be delivered.'[81] It is reasonably clear that it was only when his financial circumstances improved – in the 1750s – that Drummond began to engage in lottery adventures. Two advantageous marriages, the first in 1739 and more emphatically in 1755, when he wed an English

[77] University of Edinburgh, Special Collections, Dc. 1. 82 & 83, Diary of George Drummond, 1736–1738.

[78] See e.g. his entry for 15 Mar. 1738 (DC. 1. 83, f. 11): 'My situation still lyes heavy upon my thoughts. The furnace I have been, I may say, constantly in, now the Eighteenth year running, has been a constant threatning to unhinge all my affairs in life, and to expose me to want and disgrace. This has been uniformly my trail – I have been often, months, years years together, That I would not reasonably count upon one day free of discredite. I have been more established in believing that discredite would not happen since Prestonpans communion 1736 than in all the preceding course of the tryal. But its still the same tryal, and in every new shape it appears in, its always so contrived as to make it appear impossible to Reason That I can be delivered, so its now. But, hitherto, The Lord has helped, and The God to whom nothing is impossible, changes not.'

[79] An extensive record of her communings with God was interpolated by Drummond at various points in his journal.

[80] DC. 1. 82, f. 5. [81] DC 1. 82, f. 319.

widow and Quaker who brought with her a fortune of £20,000, were key elements in his improved financial circumstances. He began playing the lottery in the year following the second of these marriages, purchasing three tickets in that year, later (in February 1757) selling a £50 prize and two blanks to Drummond's Bank. He purchased twenty-five tickets in the so-called Guinea lottery, so denominated because the tickets cost a guinea. This was, as noted above, unusual for this period, a winner-take-all lottery paying cash prizes, and was not, importantly in the present context, a success with most potential investors. In subsequent years, he appears to have stuck to purchasing three or four tickets, although he bought only one in 1763.[82] His case reminds us not only that the relationship between religion and lottery participation could be a complex one, but once again underlines the fact that financial prudence and the lottery were definitely not incompatible bedfellows.

4.2 Playing the Lottery: The Picture after 1769

We can thus establish with some clarity the basic contours of lottery adventuring in the first half of the eighteenth century. Constructing a similar picture for the later eighteenth and early nineteenth centuries is an altogether bigger challenge. Relevant data are still more fragmentary. Parliament ordered the collection of information about different aspects of the lotteries in the early nineteenth century and conducted several enquiries, in 1793 and again in 1808, into the laws governing the operation of the lotteries, from which we can glean important bits of information. We also possess several sets of lottery records of provincial lottery agents from the 1810s and 1820s, referred to in the previous chapter.

One other helpful guide is a body of certificates sent to lottery managers testifying to the ownership of lost tickets which drew prizes. Owners of these tickets who wished to claim their prizes were required to swear an affidavit before a magistrate detailing the numbers of lost tickets and the circumstances surrounding their loss. Around 300 of these survive from between 1717 and 1825 in the treasury papers in the National Archives at Kew, all but a handful dating from after 1763.[83] As with the other data to which we have already referred, this is skewed heavily

[82] RBS Archives, DR/427/7-50, Drummonds Bank, Customer Account ledgers, 1727–1765.

[83] TNA, IR55/1 & 2.

towards the upper end of the cohort of lottery adventurers. It also has the by-now familiar limitations in respect of specifying the social status of the claimants.

Be that as it may, of the 300 or so of these individuals around a third possessed or at least *claimed* genteel status. Most of them were residents in or near to London. There were notably few titled claimants. One was the Earl of Hillsborough, who, as we saw earlier, was a regular lottery adventurer; he bought five tickets in 1772. Others were the 7th Viscount Montagu and the 1st Baron Eyre in the Irish peerage. London merchants and bankers were well represented (at a little over 16%). There were relatively few professionals, among whom were several clergymen and an Irish bishop. A good number of those claiming genteel status were those whom historians have become used to categorizing as the 'urban gentry', an expanding social stratum in Britain in this period. They included Allan Ramsay, the King's Painter under George III; the poet William Cowper; Bristol merchant and banker Isaac Elton; brothers John and Richard Leaper from Derby, the latter of whom became the town's mayor; and the Wapping biscuit maker William Curtis, who, following a successful political career in the City of London, including becoming Lord Mayor, earnt (or at least received) a knighthood, and who became a close companion of the Prince Regent, the future George IV. The figures for the genteel are, if anything, an underestimate because, as with our earlier sets of data, women are identified solely by address and marital status. There were smaller numbers of tradesmen and artisans, a handful of farmers, and a single yeoman. Samuel Greg, the Manchester Unitarian and early mill owner was a claimant, as was his fellow Mancunian, Thomas Agnew, a carver and gilder. So were two Glasgow bankers, for a ticket drawn in the 1822 lottery (which was actually drawn in March 1823); Richard William Batty, a surgeon in the 53rd regiment of foot, serving in the West Indies, whose tickets in the 1799 lottery were either lost at sea, taken by the enemy, or 'otherwise lost'; a Berwick tobacconist and a Brentford brickmaker, both of whom bought tickets in the 1778 lottery; a Leicestershire grazier who lost his ticket in the 1772 lottery in (appropriately) Smithfield market; a Bruges merchant, Dionysius Pillipers de Brouwer, who bought two tickets through two London merchants in 1767; and a Maidstone hatter who won a £50 prize in 1763.

The relative absence of members of the landed elites is potentially misleading. Lottery ticket purchases among this group appear to have remained relatively commonplace in the later eighteenth century, and probably for rather longer. Several members of the Blackett family from the north-east were regular lottery players in the later eighteenth century, as was the improving Northumberland landlord John Heaton

Delaval.[84] So too was William Philp Perrin, son of a Jamaica plantation owner, who had properties in London, Kent, and Derbyshire, and who lived at Tanhurst, near Dorking, Surrey.[85] The Earl of March, an obsessive gambler, was a sedulously habitual lottery adventurer.[86] Alexander Duff, second son of the 3rd Earl of Fife, seems to have been likewise, informing his aunt, Lady Grant in 1799: 'I am always dabbling a little in the lottery.'[87]

Lorraine Daston argues that the middle classes abandoned the lottery from the later eighteenth century, under the influence of 'evolving constellations of middle class attitudes towards time, risk, and familial responsibility'.[88] The growing impact of Evangelical religion, and the new codes of respectability with which it was associated, make this prima facie a very plausible scenario. Whether anything of the kind occurred, or how fast and how widely, however, is impossible to say. This is about more than the existence of 'unrespectable' middle class, an oft overlooked (but far from insignificant) group.[89] What eludes us, more saliently, are participation rates – in other words, what sort of percentage of, say, merchants 'dabbled' in the lottery. David Hancock's group of highly successful overseas merchants from the central decades of the eighteenth century, many of who came south to London from Scotland in pursuit of fortunes, appear to have avoided such speculations; their risk-taking, which was a crucial ingredient of their pursuit of wealth, took different forms.[90] On the other hand, merchants and others among the prospering middling ranks are easily found adventuring in the lottery in the later eighteenth and early nineteenth centuries, as we have already begun to see and will see further below. John Longsdon was sent by his father to London in 1811 to act as agent for the family shirting business; another

[84] Northumberland Archives, Blackett (Wylam) MSS, ZBK/C/2/1/3, Letter Book of Christopher Blackett, 1784-8; ZBL 266/1, diaries of John Erasmus Blackett, 1789– ; Delaval Family Papers, 2. DE 35/17, lottery tickets and letters and papers about lotteries, 1771–1805.

[85] DRO, D239/M/F/15894–15918, *The Naturalist's Diary* kept by William Philp Perrin, 1773–1780, 1783, 1793–1808.

[86] On March, see E. Beresford Chancellor, *The Lives of the Rakes: "Old Q" and Barrymore* (London, 1925).

[87] NRS, GD 248/1, Alexander Duff to Lady Grant, n.d., but 1799.

[88] Lorraine Daston, *Classical Probability in the Enlightenment* (Princeton, NJ, 1988), pp. 160–1.

[89] The categories of 'respectable' and 'unrespectable' are almost certainly too rigid, in any case, certainly before the central decades of the nineteenth century, albeit they work reasonably well with certain groups.

[90] David Hancock, '"Domestic Bubbling": Eighteenth Century London Merchants and Individual Investment in the Funds', *Economic History Review*, 2nd ser., 47 (1994), 679–702.

son, John, was sent to Liverpool. John embraced the 'commercial life', but he was entirely happy to keep his father informed of the price of lottery tickets.[91] The civil engineer, Thomas Townshend, who lived in King's Lynn, and who was John Rennie's assistant on the construction of Waterloo Bridge, purchased lottery tickets in the early 1820s.[92] The picture is not as straightforward as some historians appear to assume.

That shares or portions of tickets were commonly purchased – from the middle of the eighteenth century, if not earlier – pushed the lottery market much deeper down into and across society. In 1790 an Edinburgh woollen merchant recorded in his diary that a ticket in the lottery for that year, which had drawn a prize, had been sold by an office on the Scottish capital's South Bridge.[93] A quarter of the winning ticket had been bought by one of that city's serried ranks of writers (i.e. lawyers); 16ths by, respectively, a 'gentleman' in Alloa, a Leith baker, a club of nineteen tradesmen in Glasgow, a writer from Dumfries, and a maid servant from the Grassmarket. The latter, he noted, had in the previous year won a lottery prize of £500, which rather begs the question of why she apparently remained a servant maid. (Maybe she liked her job.) In 1786 the lottery office keepers, Richardson & Goodluck, advertised that prizes of £20,000 and £10,000 had been sold at their offices. These had been shared by, respectively, a club of thirty-two people from near Farnham, Surrey (a quarter); a club of twenty-seven people from a village near Tunbridge Wells (a quarter); a club of five people from Woodford, Essex (a quarter); a gentleman from Argyle Street in London (an eighth); a gentleman in Chelsea (an eighth); a society of ladies and gentlemen from Cornhill, London (a sixteenth); a club of twenty from Limehouse in the east of London (a half); a gentleman from Berkeley Square (a quarter); a society of ladies and gentlemen in

91 DRO, D3580/C/150, John Longsdon to his father, 7 Feb. 1811. His oldest brother, James, was counselled by his father on his thirteenth birthday: 'I pray God will prolong my life to train your [i.e. James and his brothers'] infant minds to the love of Religion, Truth, Industry & Honour.' (D3580/C/17, James Longsdon to Master James Longsdon, 17 Sept. 1799.)

92 NRO, Papers of Thomas Townshend, civil engineer of South Lynn, MC 905/1–54, 799x7. See also Lancashire Record Office, DDX 2743/MS797, Richard Blood, Lancaster, to Thomas Barrow, merchant, 24 Jan. 1801, advising him that he had purchased for him two half tickets in the English lottery; PKCA, Richardson of Pitfour Papers, MS 101, bundle 41, Robert Steele jnr., London, to Robert Richardson, Bideford, debiting John Richardson & Co. with the cost of a third of a ticket. The Richardsons were Perth linen merchants. See also bundle 13, same to same, 27 Mar. 1792, informing Robert that Robert Jobson, cashier to the Dundee Bank, had won an eighth of a prize of £20,000 in the lottery.

93 Edinburgh Central Library, Y DA 1861.789, journal of Andrew Armstrong, 1789–1793, 96r, entry for 1 Mar. 1790.

Exchange Alley (a sixteenth); and an eighth and sixteenth respectively to two gentlemen.[94] Sales of shares were briefly prohibited by statute in 1734, although with no apparent effect; from 1787 they were available in halves, eighths, and sixteenths.

We remain largely in the dark about how far or when purchases of tickets and shares thereof became a regular event in the lives of the labouring classes, or, indeed, where. Scattered references to groups among them clubbing together to buy tickets occur at various points, although such references are often fairly unspecific about the identities of those involved. In 1719 it was reported that a box club of journeymen weavers from Spittalfields, having accumulated 90l in stock, unanimously agreed to purchase 4 lottery tickets.[95] In 1747 sailors were apparently using their prize money to buy such a quantity of tickets that bets were being laid in London that at least two of the £10,000 prizes would be won by them.[96] In 1786, the father of one Mary Eaton's illegitimate child was identified as Henry Aylesby, a staymaker, who belonged to a lottery club which met at the Horse and Groom in Whetstone's Park, near Lincoln's Inn Fields in Holborn.[97] Critics of the lottery, who grew in number and vehemence from the end of the eighteenth century, commonly alleged that many among the metropolitan poor were being driven to penury and crime by lottery addiction. If this occurred, it is very likely that this was not so much because of participation in the official lottery, but derivatives thereof, such as lottery insurance and the private lotteries – the so-called Little Goes – which proliferated from the end of the eighteenth century.[98] This was a matter of cost, for the sums involved in playing the derivatives were typically substantially lower, as well as in London ready accessibility. Data from the early nineteenth century indicating the distribution of sales of tickets between wholes and shares reveals that sixteenths, the smallest share, steadily grew as a proportion of the whole.[99] This may tell us less than we

[94] NRS, GD 174/601/1, printed notice, lottery 1786.
[95] *Weekly Journal*, 17 Oct. 1719. [96] *CalM*, 26 Oct. 1747.
[97] LMA, St Clement Danes parish, pauper settlement, vagrancy and bastardy examinations, 31 Mar. 1783–3 Aug. 1786, examination of Mary Eaton, 22 July 1784.
[98] See ch. 3, pp. 168–9.
[99] PP, 1817(203), 'An Account of the Number of Tickets Sold and Shared in the Lotteries Drawn during the Last Two Years, Distinguishing Whole Tickets, Half Tickets, Quarters, Eighths, and Sixteenths'; 1819 (241), 'An Account of the Number of Tickets Issued and Shared in the Lotteries Drawn During the Last Two Years, Distinguishing Whole Tickets, Half Tickets, Quarters, Eighths, and Sixteenths'. If we take the third lottery of 1815, 14,000 tickets were issued, although how many were sold is unknown. 10,641 were sold as shares. Of these, 55% were sold as sixteenths; 13% as eighths; 20% as quarters; and 11% as halves. One Glasgow lottery agency sold 1,168 tickets in the first lottery for 1823, of which 31% were sold in sixteenths; 7% as eighths;

might suppose. We cannot assume that sixteenths were mainly sold to people below the top third of society.[100] The evidence may well, in fact, indicate otherwise – that instead the availability of such shares served to expand and extend the market for tickets among the broad middling ranks. This was the consistent message of witnesses before a parliamentary committee on the lottery laws in 1808. Thomas Swift, a lottery office keeper and stock broker of many years' standing, told the members of this committee that the proportions of smaller shares sold had increased in recent years *because of* the rising prices of tickets.[101] He suggested that the nature and identity of purchasers had not changed significantly. We cannot of course take testimony of this sort at face value; the MPs to whom he was talking were generally hostile to the lottery; they sought evidence that the lottery was damaging to society. The long term and very appreciable rise in nominal prices of tickets is incontestable, however. In 1808, a Cumbrian gentlewoman paid £24 for a ticket; the normal price paid in the 1750s was between £11 and £12.[102] Even a sixteenth – at, say, £1.10s in 1808 – represented a considerable financial commitment for someone whose annual income may have been between £50 and £200. Swift painted a picture of purchasing lottery tickets as entirely rational, controlled, and regular, in which people, who were emphatically not from the poorer classes, ventured relatively modest sums. He claimed that collective purchase of sixteenth shares was 'exceedingly rare, not above one Ticket or Share in 1000'.[103] Other witnesses before the committee claimed that the 'greater proportion' of lottery adventurers were members of the 'middling orders'.[104] Another witness, in response to the question whether the poor frequently purchased shares to tickets, answered that he knew 'very few instances of it'.[105] This was no doubt gilding the pill for the MPs, by deliberately downplaying the participation of the lower orders, but it may well not have been so far from the truth.

11% as quarters; and 50% as halves. (NRS, CS96/2106, Volume marked 'Tickets Shared).

100 For such a view, see Paul Langford, *A Polite and Commercial People: England 1727–1787* (Oxford, 1989), p. 572.

101 PP, 1808 (182 & 323), Reports From the Committee on the Laws Relating to Lotteries, 23. This claim was repeated by other witnesses, including Peter Richardson, a lottery office keeper and stock broker of forty years' standing (ibid., 21]

102 CRO, Carlisle, D. Sen. 5/5/1/9/48, J[ohn] Mobbs to Mrs Kitty Senhouse, 7 Mar. 1808;

103 PP, 1808 (182 & 323), Reports From the Committee on the Laws Relating to Lotteries, 23.

104 PP, 1808 (182 & 323), Reports From the Committee on the Laws Relating to Lotteries, 24.

105 PP, 1808 (182 & 323), Reports From the Committee on the Laws Relating to Lotteries, 43.

People of higher social rank had long purchased shares of tickets. This was a sensible way of spreading risk or, indeed, multiplying the (admittedly slim) chances of winning a capital prize. Table 4.7 lists the purchasers of several divided tickets sold for the state lottery in 1775, most of who were of solidly middling status.

Northumberland gentleman John Heaton Delaval, referred to above, bought plenty of single tickets over the years, but a good many shares as well. In 1788, for example, he purchased four quarters, six eighths, and six sixteenths; while in the following year, he bought one quarter, five

Table 4.7. *Divided tickets in the state lottery for 1775*

3891
30 Aug., ⅛th, Mr Scott, minister, Leith
22 Sept., 1/16th, James Innes, Royal Bank of Scotland
17 Oct., ¼, James Mclean, merchant, Stranraer
20 Oct., 1/16th, Alexander Anderson, chairman
24 Oct., 1/16th, John Gordon, writer (i.e. lawyer)
1 Nov., 1/16th, Thomas Williams, grocer, Edinburgh
2 Nov., ¼, Alexander Brown, timber merchant
8 Nov., 1/16th, Thomas Ruthven, writer, Edinburgh
3893
30 Aug., 1/16th, Mr Scott, minister, Leith
22 Sept., 1/16th, James Innes, Royal Bank of Scotland
25 Sept., 1/16th Mrs McAllum, North Loch Parks
6 Oct., 1/16th, Mrs Thomson, Writer's Court, Edinburgh
17 Oct., ¼, James Mclean, merchant, Stranraer
20 Oct., 1/16th, James Bouthron, merchant, head of Cowgate, Edinburgh
24 Oct., 1/16th John Gordon, writer, Edinburgh
1 Nov., 1/16th' Miss Jean Alves, da. of shipbuilder, Leith [?]
8 Nov., 1/16th, Thomas Ruthven, writer
11 Nov., 1/16th, Miss Margaret Davidson, Edinburgh
13 Nov., 1/16th, James Gerraly <...?> at the Abbey
3895
30 Aug., 1/16th, Mr Scott, minister, Leith
22 Sept., 1/16th, James Innes, Royal Bank of Scotland
9 Oct., 1/16th, Margaret Halket, Edinburgh
17 Oct., ¼, James Mclean, merchant, Stranraer
20 Oct., 1/16th, Archibald Henderson, mason, Edinburgh
24 Oct., 1/16th, Robert Brown, wright, Edinburgh
26 Oct., 1/16th, Capt. Loyd Hill
3 Nov., ¼, Charles Innes
7 Nov., 1/16th, William Smith, Canongate

Source: NRS, Innes of Stow Papers, GD 113/5/417

eighths, and thirteen sixteenths.[106] In the early nineteenth century sixteenths were, it is true, bought by artisans and others from among the labouring classes. They included, for example, a weaver from nearby to Hamilton; a Campsie slater; a Beith corkcutter; an Airdrie shoemaker; a tailor from Stewarton; and even a labourer from Renfrew.[107] However, they continued to appeal to people of middling status and above. In 1823, for example, a General Lamont of Rothesay and his wife separately bought sixteenth shares, as did a Lady Keith of Queen Street, Edinburgh. Others in the west of Scotland who did likewise in the early 1820s included George Jardine, the Professor of Logic and Rhetoric at the University of Glasgow, several writers (lawyers), military officers, manufacturers – including an Ayr chair manufacturer – various tradesmen, as well as a banker from Paisley.[108]

Lottery adventuring remained, therefore, common among the British propertied classes of the early nineteenth century, even if what proportion of them is unclear. It had also spread further down into society, to encompass some among the labouring classes. What, however, can we say about the motivations which underpinned these lottery adventures? Why were many people so readily susceptible to the lottery's appeal?

4.3 Motivations

As has already been emphasized, prior to 1769 by far the majority of official and public lotteries were not a simple gamble. This was part of the reason, Anne Laurence argues, that the lottery proved attractive to women looking for a relatively secure investment, that and the fact that lottery investments were highly liquid.[109] Even where a ticket drew a blank in the draw, it still yielded a steady income, and, if the investor were content to hold on to the resulting annuity or government stock, over time they would realize their capital with some interest. As the Hampshire gentleman, Thomas Jervoise, was informed in 1721: 'As to ye New Lottery, people seem desirous enough of entering into it because ye losses can be but little for all 10£ tickets for if they get no prize they

106 Northumberland Record Office, Delaval Family Papers, 2 DE 35/17, esp. fo. 17.
107 NRS, CS96/2105.
108 NRS, CS96/2105. The majority of entries in these records do not give occupations and are on occasion disarmingly imprecise – i.e. 'a tall pleasant gentleman'.
109 Anne Laurence, 'Women, Banks and the Securities Market in Early Eighteenth Century England', in Anne Laurence, Josephine Maltby and Janette Rutherford (eds.), *Women and their Money, 1700–1950: Essays on Women and Finance* (London and New York, 2009), pp. 46–58, esp. p. 48.

loose [sic] but 40 a ticket …'[110] Moreover, most lottery adventurers, as we have seen, committed relatively modest sums to it, and even then they frequently sold the blanks and (if luck was theirs) prizes immediately following the draw; or they sold their tickets before the draw took place in order to benefit from often steep rises in prices. Froide has noted that the spinster Gertrude Savile, sister of the MP and owner of the Rufford estate in Northamptonshire, Sir George Savile, did the latter with some success in the 1740s and 1750s.[111] In 1748, for example, she bought ten lottery tickets at a cost of £10.4.6 each. One was drawn blank, which she sold for £5.13, while the other nine she sold before they were drawn for the total sum of £105.1.6. For her this was fairly typical behaviour. In 1753 she made the first payment on sixty lottery tickets, selling twenty before the second payment became due. She then appears to have sold a further thirty-eight tickets on which the second payment had been made.[112] Savile's scrupulously kept, detailed personal accounts suggest someone who was more than usually careful about spending money; her lottery adventures were thoroughly consistent with this disposition.

The terms of any particular lottery had a strong bearing on its success, as, before 1769 at least, did the financial conditions in which they were held. This again emphasizes how far lottery adventuring prior to 1769 should be seen in the first place in terms of wider personal investment strategies. Some lotteries failed, as occurred in 1697, 1726, and 1757. The circumstances surrounding the almost complete failure of the 1697 Malt tax lottery – only 1,763 out of 140,000 tickets issued were sold – have been examined in considerable detail.[113] A combination of low yields – much lower than in the case of its immediate predecessor, the 1694 Million Adventure – uncertainties about redemption dates, a background of financial crisis and political gloom, and the higher returns readily available on other kinds of investment, produced what has been described recently as 'one of the largest failures – if not the largest – in financial history'.[114] That payments owing on the 1694 lottery had been suspended in the interim hardly helped. The promised schedules of payments and redemptions for several later lotteries, for example, those of 1711–1712, went unrealized, usually because the yields of the taxes on which these relied proved insufficient. Significantly, however, the underlying credibility of the lottery was not thereby undermined, presumably

[110] HRO, 44M69/F6/7/8, Matthew Lamb to Thomas Jervoise, 27 June 1721.
[111] Froide, *Silent Partners*, p. 137.
[112] NA, DD/SR A4/45, Gertrude Savile Accounts, 1736–1748.
[113] Georges Gallais-Hamonno and Christian Rietsch, 'Learning by Doing: The Failure of the 1697 Malt Lottery Loan', *Financial History Review*, 20 (2013), 259–77.
[114] Gallais-Hamonno and Rietsch, 'Learning by Doing', 267.

because of the success of several conversion operations managed by the government, such as that in 1717, and the basic resilience of the market in lottery tickets and orders.

The failure of the 1726 lottery, meanwhile, has been attributed to the fallout from the collapse of the South Sea Bubble.[115] This seems unconvincing since the lottery of 1724 was successful. More likely it was the consequence of its structure, and, as in 1697, the relatively limited benefits it promised to adventurers.[116] The 1757 lottery was, as emphasized earlier, a winner-take-all affair; and while the capital prizes were larger than normal, the ratio of blanks to prizes was also unusually high. As one newspaper put it, this was too much of a 'gamester's lottery' to attract many adventurers.[117] That lottery insurance developed quickly from 1719, a year again in which two lotteries were only prize lotteries – blanks returning nothing – and remained crucial to the profitability of the lottery thereafter indicates how many adventurers sought to limit potential losses. When in 1782, all lottery insurance was prohibited, five years later this prohibition had to be relaxed to allow owners of registered tickets to insure these, precisely because this practice was a crucial contributor to the lottery's profitability.[118]

An important explanation, therefore, for the success of the state lottery was that it was embedded within, and developed alongside, rapidly maturing, expanding financial markets located in and around Exchange Alley in London. These expedited the growth of the lottery marketplace, but also helped to underpin the long-term credibility of official lotteries. Lottery adventuring grew from practices and habits of financial investment which spread quickly among the elites and the prospering middling sort, first within metropolitan society and then beyond. However, what this fails to capture is the sheer extent and depth of the enthusiasm for the lottery, or, indeed, how this only intensified after 1768 when the lottery became a simple gamble. If, as was (and is) commonly stated, the British in this period were 'lottery mad', we have yet really to explain why.

The lottery generated intense interest and expectations. An (admittedly) basic measure of this is the rising premiums paid for tickets as the draw approached ever closer and the sharply rising sums paid for

115 Jesse Molesworth, *Chance and the Eighteenth Century Novel: Realism, Probability, Magic* (Cambridge, 2010), 20.
116 C. L. Ewen, *Lotteries and Sweepstakes in the British Isles* (London, 1932), p. 248.
117 *Gazetteer*, 10 Aug. 1762. For the Guinea lottery, see Lucy Sutherland, 'The City of London and the Devonshire-Pitt Administration, 1756–7', in *Politics and Finance in the Eighteenth Century: Lucy Sutherland*, ed. Aubrey Newman (London, 1984), pp. 86–7.
118 See ch. 3, p. 167.

undrawn tickets during the draw if the largest capital prizes remained undrawn.[119] Another is the sheer quantity of coverage it received in the metropolitan and provincial newspapers, from reporting on the terms of the lotteries, the state of the draw, winning ticket numbers, to the identities of the winners of the main capital prizes. While some of this reportage was paid for by lottery office keepers, this was not true of most. The strength of the appeal of lotteries as devices for gambling or speculating is abundantly apparent, as indicated by the proliferation of lottery-related schemes – chances and lottery insurance of various kinds, the 'Little Goes' of the later eighteenth and early nineteenth centuries – and the popularity of private lotteries as ways of selling goods and stock despite their being prohibited by law after 1698.[120] A report in a newspaper from 1777 detailing the many products relating to the lottery, and the many businesses taking advantage of its popularity – lottery handkerchiefs, lottery barbers, lottery shoeblacks, and so forth – may have been largely apocryphal, but the point it was making was about contemporary 'lottery mania', which was emphatically not invented.[121]

A major ingredient of the lottery's appeal were attitudes towards and beliefs in good fortune and luck. Lottery advertising was relentless in emphasizing 'lucky' lottery offices – 'Lucky Turner, or the Lad for the Prizes', 'E. Humbles Lucky Office', 'Fortune's Favourite Eyton', 'Pidding and Co.'s, The First Office in the World for Luck'.[122] Lottery office keepers were, as we saw in the last chapter, very quick to advertise the fact that winning numbers had been bought at their offices; notice of this was even printed on the lottery tickets which they distributed after 1785. One early nineteenth-century cartoon by Thomas Rowlandson, titled 'THE LOTTERY OFFICE KEEPER'S PRAYER', featured the eponymous lottery office keeper kneeling in prayer before the Goddess Fortuna beseeching good fortune for his schemes in winning prizes; the point being that it was a reputation for such which drew custom; without

119 See e.g. *CalM*, 28 Dec. 1747, which reported that ticket prices had risen to nearly £30 with only a few days left in the draw and 'several of the great prizes' remaining yet undrawn; NRS, GD124/16/129/3, William Flint to John Jamieson of Alloa, 7 Dec. 1780, reporting that he had bought on his own initiative a second lottery ticket at £19.10 because 'if I had waited for your answer [i.e. in a letter], which could not be sooner than ten days, and by that time Tickets might be selling at betwixt Thirty and Forty pounds, if the £20,000 prize remained in the wheel till that time'.

120 See ch. 3, esp. p. 172.

121 BL, LR 26 b.1 (5), newspaper cutting on 'the ingenious sett of Lottery merchants', 13 Oct. 1777. See also *PA*, 14 Oct. 1777, which reported: 'The Infection for Gambling is become so general and contagious, that on Saturday at Clare Market there was Lottery Meat, Lottery Butter, Lottery China, and even Lottery Potatoes. This is a fact.'

122 For examples, see Bodl., John Johnson Collection, Lotteries, Vols. 1–10.

it the prospect was rapid decline and failure. Lotteries were also very closely associated with fortune telling, a practice which continued to occupy a significant place in metropolitan and wider society throughout this period, despite being illegal under the terms of the 1744 Vagrant Act.[123] As Daston notes, Henry Fielding's play *The Lottery* (1732) portrayed ticket buyers requesting lucky numbers, and the play's heroine is persuaded by a fortune-teller that she is going to win the capital prize, in this case £10,000.[124] Seventy years later, the ubiquity of the fortune-tellers during 'lottery time' led London magistrate Patrick Colquhoun to exclaim:

> The extent to which this mischief goes in the Metropolis is almost beyond belief; … The folly and phrenzy which prevail in vulgar life, lead ignorant and deluded people into the snare of adding to the misfortunes which the Lottery occasions, by additional advances of money (obtained generally by pawning goods or apparel) paid to pretended astrologers for suggesting *lucky numbers*…[125]

William Henry Lyttelton, in attacking the lottery in the Commons in the early nineteenth century, spoke of it 'leading to gross superstition' and of lists of lucky numbers being passed from hand to hand.[126] Tales of 'lucky' numbers surface occasionally in the archives. John Craske, the Norwich lottery agent, received the following letter in 1825 from a Mrs Rackham of Aylsham in Norfolk:

> I conclude from an early application I may have an opportunity of selecting any number I may prefer in the ensuing lottery, but as I cannot be at Norwich at present and want two sixteenth shares I write the following numbers, from which you may probably be enabled to vend two 1773 3949 and 3771 if I can have none of those send the highest & the lowest number you have …[127]

[123] It was linked to fraud and criminality, but was dependent on a tenacious sub-stratum of popular belief. See e.g. Old Bailey Proceedings Online (www.oldbaileyonline.org. version 7.2, 27 Mar. 2015), Dec. 1743, trial of Margaret Skylight (t17431207–1); Feb. 1758, trial of Mary Robinson (t1750222–50); Jan. 1763, trial of Ann Read (t17630114–17); Jan. 1800 (trial of Elizabeth Lovel (t1800115–39); Jan. 1815, trial of Thomas Nott, alias Charles Smith (t18150111–106); Sept. 1811, trial of Charlotte Anthony Harriet (t1816098–120).

[124] Daston, *Classical Probability*, p. 156.

[125] Patrick Colquhoun, *A Treatise on the Police of the Metropolis* (7th ed., London, 1806), p. 129. Colquhoun emphasized that the 'delusion with regard to Fortune Tellers' was not confined to 'vulgar life', but also prevailed among 'ladies of rank, fashion and fortune'. Fortune teller, Richard Morris, made his living telling fortunes in Derbyshire and Shropshire in the eighteenth century. Most of the clients were, apparently, women, but businessmen also visited him to ask about the potential of commercial schemes. *The Life and Mysterious Transactions of Richard Morris* (London, 1799).

[126] *Public Ledger*, 5 May 1819.

[127] NRO, BR80/2.

For at least one lottery in 1817, the lottery contractors distributed handbills informing people of which numbers were available at which lottery offices, testimony to the importance to many people of securing their 'fancy' number.[128] The teacher of mathematics, Samuel Clark, took the trouble of writing a tract designed to expose the non-existent logic of a very widely publicized scheme in 1775 – John Molesworth's 'Calculations' – for selecting winning numbers.[129] Short-run fluctuations in gains and losses were explained by probability and probability alone. As Clark remonstrated: 'Chance alone, by its Nature, constitutes the Inequalities of Play, and there is no need to have Recourse to Luck to explain them.'[130] It was, however, not what most people evidently wished to hear.

Hopes for good fortune (or luck) were thus an essential currency of the lottery; and they were not readily exploded. As one Yorkshire gentleman shamefacedly admitted in 1739: 'I have been so frequently in Lotterys without Encouragement that I am almost ashamed of persisting, but I find, let them be upon so disadvantageous a foot, one cannot help desiring to be in fortune's way…'[131]

What we, therefore, need to begin to explain is why dreams of and belief in luck were influential. Several historians have portrayed this period as one which saw significant shifts in conceptions of fortune, and in attitudes towards risk.[132] This is sometimes presented in terms of secularization – a weakening belief in direct providence – and a growing conviction in the manageability of life and its uncertainties. Belief in supervening providence left no real room for the notion of luck. As one puritanically minded individual put it towards the beginning of our period:

> 'Tis therefore the veryest folly, and madness in the world for a man of reason to conclude of good and evill luk [sic]; upon beginning things &c. on such as they call good and evill lucky days, or from Good and Bad Signs (of which no reason can be given) Judic. Astrolog: Divinat: &c. – This is horid paganism and strikes

[128] Lancashire Record Office, DDX 818/32–33, handbill for J. Sivewright for lottery of 30 Apr. 1817; handbill for G. Carroll for lottery of 30 Apr. 1817.

[129] Daston, *Classical Probability*, p. 156. The Molesworth scheme was also promoted in Dublin in 1777, and then from 1783 by a Benjamin Wells (Dudley, *Irish Lottery*, p. 54). For a recent discussion of this scheme, see Natasha Glaisyer, 'Calculation and Conjuring: John Molesworth and the Lottery in Eighteenth Century Britain', *Journal for Eighteenth Century Studies*, 42 (2019), 135–55.

[130] Quoted in Daston, *Classical Probability*, p. 156.

[131] Hoare's Bank, HB/8/T/11, 1733/4-53, George Fox to Benjamin Hoare, 22 Sept. 1739.

[132] Daston, *Classical Probability*, pp. 151–3. See also Roy Porter, *Enlightenment, Britain and the Creation of the Modern World* (London, 2000), pp. 208–9.

point blank at the very Face of Divine Providence. See Leveticus 19–26. Deuteronomy 18.10

Belief in direct providence – that God intervened in the lives of individuals – was behind religious objections to lotteries which had commonly been voiced before 1700, but which were altogether rarer in the eighteenth century. How far, how deeply, and how widely such a shift in belief occurred is very difficult to say, even if, that is, we could agree on how to measure this.[133] Providentialism remained pervasive, and was far from simply residual.[134] The London earthquakes of 1750 provoked an outburst of breast-beating about the moral and religious condition of society, and calls for moral revival. When a soldier prophesied a third earthquake and the end of the world in 1750, fashionable London took to its coaches. As one contemporary described it:

Such was the Panick that above 1000 coaches & Six and four set out yesterday with whole familys to avoid Providence & 20000 or 30000 Inhabitants spent the whole Night in the feilds [sic] fearing the Crush & fall of the Houses & as many sat up all night not to be caught nappinging however the apprehension of a sudden visitation had that Effect that our Churches for several Days past and especially yesterday were scarce every known to be so crowded.[135]

Attachment to Enlightenment values and convictions can appear to be very weak at times, as only lightly superimposed on older attitudes and views. The London accountant, Stephen Monteage, was a regular lottery adventurer in the central decades of the eighteenth century, and someone for whom the lottery exerted a particularly strong appeal. He attended the lottery draw in person on several occasions, and in most years keenly followed the drawing of the capital prizes. Monteage was a man of profound religious convictions; he was a frequent attender at sermons delivered by the Calvinist Methodist George Whitefield in 1739–1740.

133 On this, see esp. J. C. D. Clark, 'Providence, Predestination, and Progress: Or, Did the Enlightenment Fail?', *Albion*, 35 (2003), 559–89. See also Timothy Alborn, *Regulated Lives: Life Insurance and British Society 1800–1914* (Toronto and London, 2009), where the author writes (on p. 3): 'Although insurance companies may have shared responsibility with policemen and health inspectors for a rise in what one mid-Victorian called a tendency to become "shockingly safe in all relations of life and death", they did so in ways that competed rather than converged with the efforts of others who specialized in minimizing risks to people's lives, health and property. *Because of this, the "great change" under way at the end of the nineteenth century failed to transform society as fully as contemporaries either hoped or feared it would. Gambling and enterprise survived the domestication of risk …'*

134 Clark, 'Providence, Predestination, and Progress'.

135 Bristol Record Office, Letters and Papers of Jarrit Smith MP, AC/JS/89-10a-k, bills of legal costs and receipts from D. A. Thomas to Jarrit Smith for legal work and expenses, letter accompanying Thomas's account for 1750, Thomas to Smith, 5 Apr. 1750.

Every time he bought a lottery ticket, or share thereof, he implored God's blessing. As he recorded in his journal on 5 November 1741, after having bought eighth shares in four tickets from one lottery office keeper: 'And pray God to give me his Blessing therein. For nothing comes by chance But according to his sole will & pleasure, Amen.' In the entry for 23 June 1763, having examined his eight tickets and found them all to be blanks, he wrote: 'Gods will be done & Lord Give me faith & Patience ...'[136] It was almost as if the draw itself was a test of his religious faith. The eighteenth-century press, meanwhile, hardly created a picture of a society governed by regular laws in which superstitious beliefs held limited sway; or rather it offered up sharply contradictory messages in relation to attitudes and beliefs, and the sway of reason.[137]

Yet, whatever the changes which did take place in notions of providence, or as a result of steps undertaken to minimize uncertainty and the impact of misfortune in peoples' lives – pre-eminently through the burgeoning device of insurance – the more pressing reality for the majority of people in this period, across many different spheres of life, was, as suggested in the Introduction to this book, that of frequent, sharp, and unforeseen fluctuations in circumstances – whether these be the consequence of illness, injury, the death of family members, poor harvests, credit squeezes, trade depressions, changes in fashion, and so on. Against such a background, staking money on the possibility of a win in the lottery may have seemed entirely reasonable, albeit the chances of gaining the big prizes were very slight. For all that people such as Henry Fielding viewed lotteries as essentially a tax on the weak minded and foolish, their view was driven precisely by their felt need to deny that chance or luck (if one chose to believe in such a thing) had any part in separating the lives of the propertied classes from those of the poor, or, indeed, could be and often was the difference between getting by and destitution.

Ross McKibbin has portrayed popular gambling in late nineteenth and early twentieth century Britain as a matter of mastery of particular kinds of knowledge, and enjoyment in that sense of mastery.[138] Other common forms of popular gambling – playing games of bowls and skittles for small stakes in the backyards of inns, for example – were basically recreational. The same cannot be said of betting on numbers, which flourished among, for example, the American urban poor in the nineteenth and twentieth centuries. What is represented in such a context is different;

[136] LMA, MS 20519, journals of Stephen Monteage.
[137] As emphasized in Jeremy Black, *The English Press in the Eighteenth Century* (1987).
[138] Ross McKibbin, 'Working Class Gambling in Britain 1880–1939', in Ross McKibbin, *The Ideologies of Class: Social Relations in Britain 1880–1950* (Oxford, 1991), pp. 101–38.

and we enter a different order of explanation, one that is about imagination and belief and, however challenging this is for the historian, psychology. Modern studies of gambling and lotteries talk about the hold they can exert within 'closed systems' – in other words, ones within which prospects of movement upwards socially are very limited – and of lotteries as a kind of safety valve that allows 'repressed wishes' to escape.[139] One can see this kind of process at work, or being encouraged, by contemporary lottery advertising, that the lottery worked, or so it was claimed, precisely to bring the impossible within the realms of the possible. And yet, the notion of a 'closed system' does not seem quite to fit British society in the long eighteenth century. Rather than horizontal social boundaries being starkly etched in society, social order in eighteenth-century Britain is and was commonly portrayed as an intricate series of narrow, very porous gradations. Nor does the idea of constricted prospects by itself offer much scope for considering the expanding, diversifying urban middling ranks and their motivations.

One contemporary who was eminently clear about the main reason for the success of the lottery was the Scottish moral philosopher, Adam Smith. 'That the chance of gain is naturally over-valued', he declared, 'we may learn from the universal success of lotteries ... The *vain hope* of gaining some of the great prizes is the sole cause of the demand' (my emphasis).[140] Modern research tends to support him, to the extent that it demonstrates the existence of a cognitive bias: people are likely to be risk-averse in the case of unlikely losses, but risk-seeking in the case of improbable gains. The latter, apparently, is even more the case where these gains can produce an elevation in social standing and where, even in cases of very low probability, the unlikely exists in the realm of the actual – in other words, where people can see cases of lottery success. This they could do in the regular reporting of lottery wins in newspapers and in the publicity relentlessly produced and circulated by lottery office keepers.[141] Just as today, lottery wins were the common talk of 'the town'.[142]

139 Edward C. Devereux Jr., *Gambling and Social Structure* (New York, 1980), p. 118.

140 A. Smith, *An Inquiry into the Nature and Causes of the Wealth of Nations*, vol. 1, ed. A. S. Skinner (Oxford, 1987), p. 125.

141 Charles T. Clotfelter and Philip J. Cook, *Selling Hope: State Lotteries in America* (Cambridge, MA, 1989).

142 See e.g. LMA, MS 20519, journals of Stephen Monteage, 8 June 1763 [where Monteage records having been in the St Martin Le Grand Coffee House where he heard that the number 31,184 had been drawn the £10,000 prize in the lottery]; *The Diary of John Hervey, First Earl of Bristol, 1688–1742* (Wells, 1894), pp. 95, 114, 219, letters from Lady to Lord Bristol, 15, 26 Oct. 1719, 13 Aug. 1722, which all refer to how in fashionable London circles 'nothing talkd of but lottery ticketts' – i.e. lottery wins.

Contemporary comments offer further support for Smith's view, but qualify it in one very important way. That is, they hint at something more arresting: a high degree of self-consciousness sometimes about hopes of winning, a sense of knowingly indulging in fantasies about good fortune. Horatio Sharpe, a former governor of Maryland living in London, sent a letter to his former secretary about a ticket for him that he would buy in the British state lottery: 'You may dream of thousands till it is ended, for I shall make a gambling purchase for you.'[143] In 1774, Peter Lascelles suggested to the Nottinghamshire clergyman, John Finch, that he might like to find someone else to buy his lottery tickets. 'I am not', Lascelles wrote, a 'Child of Fortune/or else I shou'd not have been the Vagabond I am at present … as Luck only is concerned, and judgement is quite out of the Question, suppose you was to employ a more fortunate agent than your friend Peter to make the purchase, some cunning Wight endowed with the gift of second sight …'[144] A year earlier, he instructed Finch:

> You must by no means be so rash as to think of building a house on the strength of a prize in the Lottery, for all our airy schemes are vanished like the baseless Fabrick of a Vision, that is to say, our ticket is a blank, and I design to inclose it in a letter to W, that he may keep as a momento to our Folly, or our credulity if you like better to soften the expression.[145]

The light tone suggests that this was not meant entirely seriously, nor the injunction to employ an agent with second sight. Lottery dreams may well have often been exactly of this kind for some people, entertained and distanced at the same time. What is highlighted by this is the importance of subjective pleasures of participation; these, crucially, were not determined solely by winning or losing.

Nevertheless, relentlessly emphasized in the increasingly elaborate lottery puffs and handbills of the later Georgian era was the extraordinary value of the major capital prizes (see Figures 3.1–3.6). For a fairly modest investment, or so it was claimed, riches were within the lottery adventurer's reach. The messages were often, and unsurprisingly, contradictory. Playing the lottery was not gambling, in that there was no loser, other than of course the unsuccessful adventurer. Someone had to win; and why should it not be you; fortune was after all blind. Winning did not entail sacrificing one's identity, or that was another of the common messages of these notices. Instead, it was to turn present hopes into

143 Quoted in Millikan, *Lotteries in Colonial America*, p. 60.

144 University of Nottingham, Manuscripts and Special Collections, NeD 657/7, Peter Lascelles to Rev. John Finch of Kirklington, near Newark, 22 Oct. 1774.

145 University of Nottingham, Manuscripts and Special Collections, NeD 657/2, Lascelles to Finch, 1773.

reality. One of Bish's handbills, headed 'Luck's Progress', depicted a series of scenes beginning with 'Consultation', in which a couple of indeterminate but clearly modest social status were seated around a table in a dilapidated room conferring on 'how to better our condition, and rise in the world'. The final scene, 'Exaltation', depicted them in a grand carriage with coach driver and postillion, the result of winning one of the £30,000 prizes.[146] Another handbill, this one comprised purely of text, and headed 'HOME QUESTIONS FOR Private Consideration', began with the following interrogatories:

If you are a person of fortune, do you experience that it is fully commensurate, not only to the support of your establishment, according to your rank, but with the enjoyments also of the whole routine of fashionable amusements?
If of either of the learned professions, do you find your emoluments from it present a fair prospect of your ultimately acquiring affluence?
If engaged in mercantile and commercial pursuits, do you feel that your CAPITAL is adequate to your wishes of extending your Speculations?
If a subordinate branch of trade be your pursuit, do you find that your industry is likely to produce you, after a series of years, a comfortable competency?
If dependent on either manual labour, servitude, &c. for support, do you perceive any prospect of ever bettering your condition?[147]

A big lottery win might mean the difference between persuading a 'flinty hearted father' to accept one's suit for a bride; it might equally mean, if you were a servant maid, returning home from the metropolis to offer succour to your aged parents, as the lucky ticket turned dependency into independence – 'that great sweetener in life'.

The fantasies on which the lottery flourished were powerful precisely because they sprang from ambitions that were widely entertained and nurtured in society – even if, or perhaps because, they were often frustrated. Stories of social mobility may have been more common in certain periods than others, or certainly more actively commented upon in the press and print, for example, during the frenzied climax of the South Sea Bubble or in the later eighteenth century, when the 'nabobs', those who returned with ostensibly and sometimes actual dazzling fortunes from India, attracted much negative commentary. But less dramatic stories of financial and business success, and pursuit of social status, were endlessly recycled in contemporary print culture, for example, in obituaries

[146] Bodl., John Johnson Collection, Lotteries, Vol. 1 (15). [147] BL, 8229 K 8 (76).

in newspapers and periodicals which described wealth and social recognition gained over a lifetime. They were also sufficiently frequently enacted in many a local community to be credible; money did after all perform repeated acts of social alchemy.[148] In world where much – an increasing amount, indeed – was staked on appearances and displays of the correct 'taste' and manners, money palpably did buy status. Pursuit of a fortune thus became even more of a social imperative. As a Nottingham gentleman reported to his niece in 1780: 'This morning Mr Wright the Banker married his Fifth Daughter to a Mr Edwards An Irish Gentleman. The Lady is only eighteen, *but it is an Advantageous match in point of fortune*' (my emphasis). In the same year, he wrote to another relation with the news that a Captain Wrightson was or had been married to a Miss Bland. Miss Bland was 'extremely young, not at all handsome but' – and here was the nub – '*has a fortune to outway everything*' (my emphasis).[149] A good many people in the later eighteenth century bemoaned the fact that money seemed to 'outway everything'; but what they were singularly unable to do was to deny its effects.[150]

What mattered ultimately, however, were not so much the actual prospects of upward social mobility; rather it was the *habit and instinct* to imagine this. The lottery contributed to this reflex because it very directly symbolized the social solvent that was money. There was no real reason to believe that one would win, whatever the lottery promoters incessantly claimed. But, as Addison noted, into the space that reason might otherwise have filled something other flowed – 'caprice' was the term he used.[151] The world of the lottery was quite literally a world of fictions, and, indeed, one literary scholar has argued that there existed a close connection between the rise of the novel and the lottery, although they admit not one susceptible to proof.[152] Lottery fantasies were not, they argue, about money *per se* as about imagining yourself within a plot, and novels provided a resource and encouragement to think in these

[148] Work on social mobility in eighteenth-century Britain has been curiously limited, and tended to focus overwhelmingly on the top of society, on which, see Introduction, no. 88, p. 24.

[149] NA, Foljambe of Osberton, DDFJ/11/1/5, correspondence of John Hewett, 1780–1784, fo. 16, John Hewett to Ann Warde, Nottingham, 31 Jan. 1780; fos. 85–6, John Hewett to Mary Arabella Foljambe, 31 Dec. 1780. See also *Caledonian Mercury*, 28 Dec. 1736, where it was reported: 'Last Week Capt. Macdonald, an Officer in a marching Regiment, a Gentleman of a very ancient and worthy Family in North Britain, was married to the only Daughter of Mr Bennet, a wealthy Wine Merchant in St. James's, Haymarket, who had the 10,000I. Prize in the last State Lottery.'

[150] On which, see esp. James Raven, *Judging New Wealth: Popular Publishing and Responses to Commerce, 1750–1800* (Oxford, 1992).

[151] *Spectator*, 9 Oct. 1711.

[152] Molesworth, *Chance and the Eighteenth Century Novel*, esp. pp. 32–3.

terms.[153] To be clear – or as clear as one can be in this context – when they talk here about the novel it seems that they have in mind less the 'novel' as an influential new literary genre, than a world view of which the novel was an exemplum.[154] Yet, as the handbill 'Luck's Progress', referred to above, makes clear, it was access to money that was the key to transforming fiction into reality.

Lotteries thus depended for their appeal on widespread recognition that chance or fortune, whether for good or ill, played a significant role in the lives of most individuals and families, and that it did not discriminate socially. Yet, persistent and widespread fascination with the lottery need not challenge the view that the middling ranks, or, indeed, many among the landed classes, were preoccupied with reputation and orderliness in their lives, along with propriety and virtue. The Lincolnshire surgeon and man midwife, Matthew Flinders, father of the famous navigator of the same name, for example, had, if the record of his diary is to be believed, prudence and moderation inscribed at the very core of his being. He entertained a profound sense of his dependency on God's providence. 'I am', he soberly recorded on New Year's Day 1778,

> Convinced a sufficiency is a very desirable thing, but far from being the whole necessary to human happiness, we ought with all humility and resignation to demean our selves to the divine will and to follow after that plan w.ch Reason & the scriptures point out as most excellent.[155]

If this were not itself sufficiently humbling a thought, he even managed to rationalize the deaths of several infant children as 'a blessing', since as he wrote, 'We have naught in a natural sense, but my industry in Business to depend on.'[156] His diary scrupulously records his income and expenditure for each year; money matters, having it, saving it, freeing himself of debt, collecting debts, preyed constantly on Flinders' mind. This did not prevent him, however, from buying shares in lottery tickets on several

153 Ibid., p. 8, where the author declares: 'The lottery, more than any other form of speculation, that is, offered ordinary people fictional capital – the fantasy, however unlikely, of participating in a narrative of significant events, with plot lines borrowed from novels.'

154 Molesworth, *Chance and the Eighteenth Century Novel*, p. 26. Not only is the term 'novel' very broadly defined by Molesworth, although it clearly carries connotations of a new inclusiveness and new kinds of narrative, he is also pretty unspecific about who he thinks played the lottery. Terms such as 'ordinary people', or 'people of modest or even low incomes', are hardly precise.

155 LA, FLINDERS/1, Account Book and Journal of Matthew Flinders senior, Jan. 1775–Dec. 1784, entry for 1 Jan. 1778.

156 Op. cit., entry for Oct. 1776.

occasions, just as on occasion he played games of cards for small stakes.[157]

Attitudes towards the lotteries were far from straightforward, although for some they were: as a form of gambling lotteries were to be eschewed. Quakers, for example, were strictly enjoined to desist from lottery adventuring; so too were Methodists. That said, some Quakers bought lottery tickets in this period.[158] Moral reformers at the beginning and end of our period opposed the lottery as a form of and encouragement to gambling, although opposition to the lottery does not appear to have been a particular priority for the Evangelicals or other moral reformers of the later Georgian era. The notion that on seeing the slave trade abolished (in 1807), the great Evangelical reformer, William Wilberforce, turned his attentions to the lottery is (disappointingly) untrue. If anything, he was rather unconcerned about the lottery, viewing Spencer Perceval's reforms in 1809 as having eliminated its worst aspects.[159] The efforts of moral reformers tended instead to focus on extending religious and moral instruction to the labouring poor or devising other means of supporting them in 'habits of sobriety, industry and virtue'.[160] One should treat the cause, which was character, not the symptom, which might be gambling.

Plenty of churchmen, meanwhile, adventured in the lottery without apparent fear of damage to their reputations; ministers of the Kirk drank from the same, morally murky waters. The fact that lotteries were on occasion allowed by parliament for public purposes can only have reinforced an idea in the eyes of many that the lottery was different to other forms of gambling. It might be rationalized for one as patriotic, as serving the national interest. It is not dissimilar to the ways in which the lottery today gains legitimacy through its association with 'good' causes. Lotteries flourished in colonial North America. The modern historian of these lotteries has detected very little opposition to them in a society in which, in New England at least, the Puritan inheritance continued to exert strong influence.[161]

[157] See e.g. *op. cit.*, entries for 31 Jan., 17 Mar., 27 Nov. 1775; May 1776; 23 Jan. 1777; July, Dec. 1783.

[158] E.g. Edward Wakefield, a London insurance broker and Quaker, who bought a ticket in 1801 (TNA, IR55/2).

[159] See esp. SCA, RP/1/11, William Wilberforce to Samuel Roberts, 22 May 1815; RP/1/3, same to same, 25 Jan. 1816; RP/12/14, same to same, 10 Feb. 1817; RP/1/16, same to same, 21 Mar. 1817; RP/1/22, same to same, 7 Sept.–8 Dec. 1818.

[160] The phrase comes from Patrick Colquhoun, *A New and Appropriate System of Education for the Labouring* People (London, 1806), p. 64.

[161] Millikan, *Lotteries in Colonial America.*

Yet, while lotteries might not necessarily imperil a commitment to virtue or that most vaunted of eighteenth-century personal qualities, moderation, lottery fantasies were not thereby suppressed. Take Edinburgh burgess, Andrew Armstrong, who had recorded in his journal the winners of a ticket sold at an Edinburgh lottery office in 1790. Why did he do this? He recorded other bits of information about lottery winners.[162] Was the real fantasy thus one of reinforcement of prevalent values and expectations and their subversion at the same time? Armstrong was in many ways a fairly typical representative of a section of the provincial urban middling sort – an avid attender of sermons, which he recorded in great detail in his journals, and intensely preoccupied with his own spiritual and moral condition. Visiting London, he attended sermons preached by the famous Evangelical preacher, William Romaine. In one entry, he noted the death of a fellow Edinburgh merchant, James Laing – 'a very industrious sober man'. This was the version of manhood that held Armstrong in its grip. His journal had an explicitly and monitory religious function:

> Let me indulge the pleasing idea, that when I am numbered with the Dead – this my Journal may be of use to some Soul – May the numerous egotisms and follies it contains be forgotten with the Author. Let the pious Advices, the earnest exhortations the awful warning here from his memory recorded fail not in their effect![163]

Or was Armstrong's fantasy a fundamentally capitalist one – to wit, that worldly success might depend on a spirit of adventure as well as good judgement and prudent accounting? Intriguingly, one of the suggestions about alterations to the lottery made in the early nineteenth century in order to reduce opportunities for dangerous gambling was that rather than have lotteries with small numbers of very large prizes, the prize money should be distributed into more and more modest prizes.[164] Such prizes might help the middling ranks with their businesses or allow them to marry. This was one version of the fantasy of the middling sort; it was, however, not the one that seems to have become associated with the lotteries of this period.

4.4 Conclusion

There are few simple conclusions to be drawn from this survey of lottery adventuring. Partly this is because so much about lottery adventuring in

[162] Edinburgh Central Library, YDA1861.789, Journal of Andrew Armstrong, f. 175, entry for Feb. 1791 where he records: 'During this month Provost Elder got a prize in the state lottery of £5000.' 'Provost Elder' was John Elder, the Lord Provost of Edinburgh.

[163] *Op. cit.*, f. 249.

[164] BL, Add MS 59309, fo. 52, Mr Wasteneys to Lord Grenville, 25 Feb. 1807.

Britain in the long eighteenth century remains stubbornly hidden from our gaze. That which comes into clearest view is (predictably) that of members of the propertied classes, and, even more so, the landed, commercial, and financial elites whose records have been carefully preserved in family archives or whose accounts were inscribed in the weighty ledgers of the private banks. How people viewed their lottery adventuring reflected closely their personal circumstances, which included their wealth and its security, as well as value judgements which were both highly subjective but also socially and culturally conditioned. Viewing participation in the lottery, as its contemporary critics did, as basically irrational does not take us very far at all; nor, as importantly, does the idea that Britons in this period showed a marked disposition to gamble.

More helpful is to think about the relationship between the lottery and the widening and deepening commercialization of British society in this period. At one level, at least before 1769 the success of the lottery reflected new habits of speculation and investment linked to the development from the 1690s of an expanding, credible, and reasonably transparent secondary market in private and public stocks. More broadly a growing range of people, especially among the middling sort, could be said in the long eighteenth century to have speculated on the idea of 'good fortune' – even if, as in the case of our London accountant, Stephen Monteage, they did not see it as such – together with the fantasies which this notion aroused. One very common fantasy in this period was that of the taming of uncertainty through protocols of self-regulation or devices such as insurance. Yet with contemporary capitalism presenting multiple, diverse faces, and with forms of property and wealth proliferating in ever less substantial forms, it was never quite that simple. Contradictions, in fact, abounded. For those growing numbers among the landed and broad middling classes who risked quite literally all in pursuit of wealth in the Caribbean or India in this period, the dream was to broker these gains into a social position or a life of comfortable independence once back home. The lottery in this instance was one with disease and death, but also – that is, if one had the luck to survive or to secure and maintain the patronage of the well placed and well connected – tantalizing opportunities for the rapid accumulation of wealth. The parallels were not lost on one contemporary, who wrote back, in rather solemn mood, to his Wiltshire home from Bengal in 1773:

> Money getting is the sole End we come here for, but we must labor much harder for it now than formerly, such immense Fortunes are not to be made, those Golden Days are past; we always hear of those that succeed, but never think at the same Time how many fail in the Pursuit; I may say with Propriety our coming here is like adventuring in the Lottery Wheel, but with the difference that we have

many more Blanks to a Prize, ten at least, if one out of ten succeeds, it is very well according to the course of things ...[165]

As the same correspondent also noted, a good many women, from a variety of backgrounds, also travelled to India to stake their fortunes on gaining a winning ticket in the lottery wheel of marriage in Calcutta and Madras.[166] Consciously pursuing good fortune was the inescapable condition of many.

At the same time, the new financial world of the eighteenth century embraced gambling. This was true in more ways than just nurturing the rise of the lottery, or, indeed, investors taking positions in volatile stock markets. The two, in fact, were frequently inseparable. It was possible to take out insurance, for example, on a third person's life, until, that is, it was prohibited by parliament in 1774 through the passage of the appropriately named Gambling Act.[167] Insurance brokers effectively took bets seemingly on anything – the outcomes of battles, the sex of the Frenchman (or woman), the Chevalier D'Eon, and so on. Commercial tontine schemes, which proliferated in the late eighteenth and early nineteenth centuries, were in one way merely a bet.[168] What the investor in these was gambling on was their or their nominee surviving longer than their fellow investors, as dividends and capital were shared between surviving stakeholders. Annuities, which were very widely sold to raise money in this period, were taken out on another person's life and premiums often took no account of age. In the 1745 lottery annuity, when an investor bought ten lottery tickets, they could nominate either their own life or that of another for the payment of the annual sum. Essentially the gamble here was against the government on your or your nominee's longevity. The Andover Lottery Tontine Society underlines the complex intermixing that was frequently the reality of financial devices in this period. Each member paid £10 for seven years, with the capital being invested in the public funds. The interest thereby earned was then used to buy lottery tickets, and the produce of this (if any) added to the capital. At the scheme's end, this capital was divided among

165 WSRO, Trowbridge, 4/3/318, John Kneller, 31 Jan. 1773.

166 WSRO, 4/3/318, same, Calcutta, 26 Dec. 1770.

167 Gregory Clark, *Betting on Lives: The Culture of Life Insurance in England, 1695–1775* (Manchester, 1999).

168 These schemes have yet to find their historian, but can be seen in part in terms of a wider proliferation of devices and bodies to encourage financial 'prudence' among the lower orders, including friendly societies and savings banks. There is some relevant comment in Moshe A. Milevsky, *King William's Tontine: Why the Retirement Annuity If the Future Should Resemble the Past* (Cambridge, 2015).

the survivors.[169] Devices to improve financial security did not necessarily eliminate gambling; rather they might well encourage it.

Examination of the lottery and lottery adventuring, finally, calls into question the idea that there were distinct cultures of gambling which may be mapped neatly on to different social groups. There was certainly a strong, indeed, strengthening, impulse to represent them as separate; but we should be wary of accepting this as reality. The reality was altogether messier. Social status, or, indeed, wealth and income were not by themselves the critical factors in determining if and how people adventured in the lottery. Even religion could be less influential than we might have anticipated. Part of the reason was that what the lottery represented depended so much on perspective. Was it gambling pure and simple, a patriotic investment, or a harmless flirtation with fortune? Contemporaries might and no doubt did answer these very differently. Preoccupation with securing money and 'independency' cut across social divides, even if what this meant in detail differed between, say, a younger son of a landed family, the widow of a merchant, or, indeed, a Maidstone hatter. The product of a commercializing society, the lottery also acted as a powerful mirror to it, albeit perhaps a rather distorting one. Nevertheless, what we see strongly reflected in it were profound, sometimes contradictory impulses which this society nurtured and on which it depended for its continued development. That some contemporaries chose not to see it in this way, to condemn the lottery as mere folly, tells us rather more about them than it does about the lottery's magnetic appeal in the long eighteenth century.

169 *The Salisbury Journal*, 16 Dec. 1799.

5 Gamblers and the Law

This chapter explores what at first sight seems to be a paradox. Britain in the eighteenth century boasted a veritable battery of laws circumscribing or proscribing different types and forms of gambling. Yet, much of this body of law remained a dead letter, and its effects were limited, if not entirely nugatory. As John Disney, author of an early-nineteenth century tract on the state of the law in relation to gaming, observed: 'Those laws, are, indeed, very seldom put into execution; very seldom, in comparison with the number of instances in which they are broken.'[1] Half a century earlier an anonymous writer bitterly declaimed against the inutility of the law:

> There is scarce a diversion that can corrupt our morals, nor a crime that seems like to affect the common safety, against which the Legislature hath not already provided by some or other punishment. Notwithstanding which, most of these diversions are as publicly taken and most of these crimes are frequently committed, as if they were not all under the magistrate's cognisance.[2]

Well might we conclude, together with moral reformers, that the challenge of regulating moral behaviour in an 'immense metropolis' in 'a wealthy and luxurious age' such as was London in the later eighteenth century, with its population nearing a million people, was immense.[3] As Margaret Jacob has recently stated: 'By the second half of the century, if not well before, the task of policing or spying on this [i.e. London] or any other great metropolis had become formidable.'[4] The creativity of urban life, about which Jacob eloquently writes, was not just, however, on the side of dissidence and subversion, but encompassed many initiatives

[1] John Disney, *The Laws of Gaming, Wagers, Horse-Racing, and Gaming Houses* (London, 1806), p. vii.

[2] Robert Bolton, *The Deity's Delay In Punishing the Guilty Considered, on the Principles of Reason* (London, 1751), p. iv.

[3] The phrases come from the *Report of the Committee of the Society for Carrying into Effects His Majesty's Proclamation Against Vice and Immorality, For the Year 1799* (London, 1799), pp. 5–6.

[4] Margaret C. Jacob, *The Secular Enlightenment* (Princeton, N.J., 2019), p. 15.

designed to achieve a better policed, more secure environment.[5] Groups of reformers and reforming magistrates periodically sought to drive out gamblers from their dens and the streets. Gaming was, nevertheless, just one of the targets of the vice police, and rarely, if ever, the most important. Campaigns against gaming houses were, as we will see below, sporadic, fairly short-lived, and ultimately achieved very little. The underlying story may be one of tenacious resistance to such efforts, and often of negotiation and collusion by the ostensible forces of order, or simply looking the other way. Nor was public opinion necessarily or in the main supportive of the rigorous application of the law in this sphere. For all that gambling might seem to threaten social order and the security of persons and property, it flourished at all levels of society, often in open defiance of the law. There was, as plenty of contemporaries noted, more than a hint of hypocrisy about efforts to suppress the gambling of the lower orders while that of their supposed superiors continued almost entirely uninhibited. Many people concluded (with reason) that reform needed to start from the top of society, with the so-called Great.[6]

5.1 The Law and Gaming

Viewed in the round, the law and, indeed, the courts conveyed a very clear and emphatic message about gaming; that, as Disney put it, it was 'a vice of importance, sufficient to excite their [legislators] attention, and to warrant strong penal laws to suppress it'.[7] Looked at more closely, however, the law was replete with contradictions, ambiguity, and uncertainties. Some derived from class bias, while others were a consequence of technical deficiencies, such as the multiplication of statutes and

[5] This has been a major theme in work on policing in the British capital in recent decades, for which, see *inter alia* J. M. Beattie, *Policing and Punishment in London 1660–1750: Urban Crime and the Limits of Terror* (Oxford, 2001); Tim Hitchcock and Robert Shoemaker, *London Lives: Poverty, Crime and the Making of a Modern City, 1690–1800* (Cambridge, 2015); Elaine A. Reynolds, *Before the Bobbies: The Night Watch and Police Reform in Metropolitan London, 1720–1830* (Basingstoke, 1998); Nicholas Rogers, 'Policing the Poor in Eighteenth-Century London: The Vagrancy Laws and Their Administration', *Histoire sociale/Social History*, 47 (1991), 127–47; Ruth Paley, '"An Imperfect, Inadequate and Wretched System"? Policing London Before Peel', *Criminal Justice History*, 10 (1989), 95–130.

[6] See e.g. *Daily Journal*, 30 July 1735*; Reflexions on Gaming, and Observations on the Laws Relating Thereto* (London, n.d., but prob. 1750), *passim*; *The Vices of the Cities of London and Westminster Trac'd from their Original* (London, 1751), esp. p. 7; *LEP*, 10 Jan. 1754; Thomas Erskine, *Reflections on Gaming, Annuities, and Usorious Contracts* (3rd ed., London, 1778), p. 10; Hannah More, *Thoughts on the Importance of the Manners of the Great to General Society* (London, 1788), pp. 117–8.

[7] Disney, *Laws of Gaming*, p. vii.

inadequacies in the drafting of legislation.[8] Most new legislation in this period regarding gaming was designed either to extend the scope of existing powers or reinforce the modes of their enforcement, to make them, in brief, less susceptible to frustration by an audacious, defiant, often well-organized gambling fraternity.

Under common law to play games of cards or with dice for reasons of recreation was perfectly legal.[9] On the other hand (hardly surprisingly), cheating at games for gain was not. Nor were debts accrued through gaming legally recoverable. Gaming houses were deemed nuisances under common law, while the courts also showed their disapproval of excessive gaming and its destructive consequences. It was, however, under statute rather than common law that most prosecutions relating to gaming occurred. The former, broadly, distinguished between, on the one hand, gamblers and specific types of gaming and, on the other, places of gaming, although the division was at times blurred.

To begin with gamblers, the key piece of legislation in this period was the Gaming Act of 1710 (9 Anne c.14).[10] For all its considerable importance, the circumstances behind its introduction and passage through parliament remain somewhat obscure.[11] It is entirely plausible that it

8 The problem of 'multiplicity', and the need for a wider rationalization and simplification of the law, were emphasized by Joshua Fitzsimmonds, *Free and Candid Disquisitions on the Nature and Execution of the Laws of England, Both in Civil and Criminal Affairs* (London, 1750), esp. p. 14. This call was taken up more broadly in the later eighteenth century.

9 *A New Abridgment of the Law. By Matthew Bacon, of the Middle Temple Esq* (5th ed., corrected, London, 1786), pp. 619–20; Frederick Edwards, *Brief Treatise on the Laws of Gaming, Horse Racing and Wagers* (London, 1839).

10 One commentator has claimed that this piece of legislation set the pattern for gaming control through to the 1960s, although this is a gross simplification. David Miers, 'Eighteenth Century Gaming: Implications for Modern Casino Control', in James Inciardi and Charles Faupel (eds.), *History and Crime: Implications for Criminal Justice Policy* (Beverly Hills, CA, 1980), p. 173. The Act applied to Scotland. Under an Act of the Scottish parliament dating from 1621 all money lost at cards, dice, and horse races and other games above 100 merks Scots was forfeit to the poor. The last decision of the Court of Session in relation to this Act was made in 1774.

11 See the comments in John Ashton, *The History of Gambling in England* (London, 1898), p. 51; David Miers, *Regulating Commercial Gambling: Past, Present, and Future* (Oxford, 2004), pp. 27–8; Roger Munting, 'A Social Opposition to Gambling in Britain: An Historical Overview', *International Journal of the History of Sport*, 10 (1993), 297. Some authorities suggest that the catalyst was a match between Sir William Strickland and Tregonwell Frampton, the keeper of the royal running horses at Newmarket, in which Frampton and others were tricked into sustaining heavy losses on betting on the race. It is unclear when the race was actually held, some putting the date as 1702 or 1703 and others 1708 or 1709. For the controversy surrounding the 'Merlin Match', see Roger Longrigg, *The History of Horse Racing* (London, 1972), pp. 52–5; Wray Vamplew, *The Turf: A Social and Economic History of Horse Racing* (London, 1976), pp. 199–201. One oddity, if this match were relevant, is that the Act did not explicitly mention horse racing, unlike its 1665 predecessor.

was the belated product of the movement for the reformation of manners, which gathered pace from the early 1690s, and which, as David Hayton has shown, gained considerable parliamentary support, especially (but not exclusively) from Tories.[12] A bill 'for the preventing of Gaming' had failed in 1698, when the moral reformers were at the height of their parliamentary influence, although an Act prohibiting lotteries was passed in the same year.[13] Having been lost in the Lords in the previous session owing to pressure of other business, the 1710 measure was re-introduced into the Commons by Sir John Hungerford, by this stage a Tory and supporter of Robert Harley.[14] Hungerford had promoted another abortive anti-gaming bill in 1709, this one to prevent the laying of wagers relating to the public.[15] It may well be, however, that the target and character of the 1710 Act were different, or rather became so. Supporters of the reformation of manners tended to focus their efforts on punishing the vice of the poor and instilling habits of virtue and industry in a new generation among the lower orders.[16] The principal objectives of this new measure were further to inhibit excessive gaming, its disruptive consequences, and the activities of those sharpers who preyed on the

[12] David Hayton, 'Moral Reform and Country Politics in the Late Seventeenth Century House of Commons', *Past and Present*, 78 (1990), 48–91.

[13] *Failed Legislation 1660–1800: Extracted from the Commons and Lords Journals*, ed. Julian Hoppit (Hambledon, 1997), pp. 220–1.

[14] By 31 March the bill still had not completed its second reading committee report. With 5 April being the last date for royal assent to be given to Acts during the session, there was insufficient time to complete the passage of the bill. The bill had received its first reading in the Commons on 13 December 1709, and had passed smoothly through the House, being taken to the Lords by Hungerford on 25 February 1710. The only specific reported amendment was an attempt to remove bowling and tennis from the list of affected games. *Journals of the House of Commons*, xvi, 241, 335; *Journals of the House of Lords*, xix, 120–1, 131, 134–5. William Pittis (*The History of the Present Parliament. And Convocation* (London, 1711), pp. 210–11) claimed that 'gamesters' had sought to oppose the bill, and were the source of the delays which eventually led to its defeat, but this seems doubtful given its legislative history.

[15] Parliamentary Archives, HL/PO/PU/1/1708/7&8An27, An Act to prevent the laying of Wagers relating to the Public.

[16] The literature on the societies for the reformation of manners is too substantial to list in detail here, but see *inter alia* Dudley W. R. Bahlman, *The Moral Revolution of 1688* (New Haven, Conn., 1957); A. G. Craig, 'The movement for the reformation of manners, 1688–1715', unpublished Ph.D. thesis, University of Edinburgh (1980); Faramerz Dabhoiwala, *The Origins of Sex: A History of the First Sexual Revolution* (London, 2012), ch. 2; Robert Shoemaker, *Prosecution and Punishment: Petty Crime and the Law in London and Rural Middlesex, c. 1660–1725* (Cambridge, 1991), ch. 9; Robert Shoemaker, 'Reforming the city: The reformation of manners campaign in London, 1690–1738', in Lee Davison et al. (eds.), *Stilling the Grumbling Hive: The Response to Social and Economic Problems in England, 1689–1750* (Stroud, 1992), pp. 99–120; Hitchcock and Shoemaker, *London Lives*, pp. 34–42.

fortunes of the suggestible gentry and their young heirs.[17] The Act, in short, was more about protecting landed estates and landed wealth from the snares of professional gamblers than eliminating gaming among the bulk of the population. That it passed at a moment of Tory political ascendancy was almost certainly not coincidental. Going through parliament during the same session were the Game Act and the Qualifications Act, both of which underwrote landed rule and privilege.[18]

The Gaming Act (1710) built on an earlier Act against excessive gaming dating from Charles II's reign (16 Car. 2, c. 14). This inflicted substantial penalties on those who gained money playing named games, or betting thereon, through cheating or deception. Moreover, sums above £100 gained by gaming or betting upon credit, as opposed to ready money, were not recoverable by law, while any person winning such sums would if brought to court forfeit three times the sum gained, with the informant gaining three times their costs. The 1710 Act reinforced the powers against and penalties attached to betting on credit and cheating at gaming. More significantly, it sought to deter gaming and betting for sums above £10 at any one time, by giving the loser the power to sue for recovery of the sum within three months, whilst also giving a third party the power to sue and recover three times the value of the sum lost. The most striking new powers under the Act, however, were those targeted against what it termed 'lewd and dissolute Persons' who 'live at great Expences, having no visible Estate, Profession or Calling to maintain themselves, but support those Expences by Gaming only'. In other words, it took aim squarely at those men who haunted taverns and resorts of the capital in search of prey among the gentry, especially callow young heirs. These individuals were adventurers who fashioned themselves as men of 'honour' and sported showy clothing. Under the Act two justices of the peace could, if they had 'just cause to suspect them', call such individuals before them, and if they could not account for themselves and

[17] The original bill appears to have included a clause which would have provided that any person keeping or maintaining a house or room for public gaming would be liable to a fine of £20 per day. It was pointed out that under this provision all public rooms and places of gaming, such as at Tunbridge Wells or Epsom would be liable to such a penalty, but also 'Bowling, Ninepins &c. The Consequence whereof will be that ruin of many Thousand Families, that never had Gaming for any Thing considerable.' HRO, The Jervoise Family of Herriard, 44M69/G2/188, 'Reasons for altering the Bill … for better preventing of excessive and immoderate gaming', n.d. (but prob. 1710).

[18] The Qualifications Act required county MPs to possess landed property worth at least £600, although its terms were readily and widely evaded (for which, see Paul Langford, *Public Life and the Propertied Englishman 1689–1789* (Oxford, 1991), p. 113). For the Game Act, see P. B. Munsche, *Gentlemen and Poachers: The English Game Laws 1671–1831* (Cambridge and New York, 1981).

their wealth, require them to find sureties for their good behaviour for twelve months. Should they be found to play or bet for any sum during that period they would be liable for a fine of 20 shillings and forfeiture of their recognizances. Equally notable was the severity of the penalty provided for those found guilty of assaulting or provoking a fight on account of any sum won by gaming or betting – a two-year prison term, but more significantly loss of all goods, chattels, and personal estate.

If excessive gaming, and defrauding of gullible heirs, was thus penalized or discouraged by the Gaming Act of 1710, certain games were later prohibited by name. Private (and, indeed, public) lotteries were made illegal in 1698, as referred to above. Further laws reiterating and strengthening the prohibition against *private* lotteries were enacted in 1711, 1718, and 1739.[19] In 1739, 1740, and 1745, specific games of chance were outlawed, with penalties being attached to those both offering and playing these games.[20] This was part of a wider campaign against gaming and gaming houses in the mid eighteenth century, to which we will return below. Such measures were quickly recognized to be ineffective: gamblers and gaming houses simply (and predictably) devised new games.[21] When in 1782 parliament passed a new gaming bill, drawing on the lessons of earlier failure it included a clause prohibiting games of chance in general terms. As its authors declared, quoting the influential jurist, Sir William Blackstone, 'particular descriptions will ever be lame and deficient unless all games of mere chance are at once prohibited'.[22] The real target of this bill was 'E.O.', a roulette type game which had been popularized after 1745 in reaction to the anti-gaming Act

[19] 10 Anne, c. 26 (Act for Suppressing Unlawful Lotteries and other Devices of the Same Kind); 8 Geo. I, c. 2 (Act for Suppressing Lotteries Denominated Sales, and other Private Lotteries); 12 Geo. II, c. 28 (Act for the More Effectual Preventing of Excessive and Deceitful Gaming).

[20] 12 Geo. II, c. 28; 13 Geo. II, c. 19 (Act to restrain and prevent the excessive increase of Horse Races, and for amending an Act made in the last session of parliament, intituled 'An Act for the more Effectual Preventing of Excessive and Deceitful Gaming'); 18 Geo. II, c. 34 (Act to explain, amend, and make more effectual the Laws in being, to prevent Excessive and Deceitful Gaming, and to restrain and prevent the excessive increase of Horse races). The 1739 Act named the games of hearts, pharaoh, basset, and hazard. The 1740 Act sought to prohibit dice or dice-like games, including 'passage' and excepting backgammon. The 1745 Act named 'roulet' or 'roly-poly'.

[21] *Reflexions on Gaming*, pp. 50–1. The MP for Bath, John Codrington, was warned by an pseudonymous correspondent, 'Timothy Telltruth' that any measure which named games would be easy to evade. The letter is undated, but probably refers to the 1739 Act, since Codrington did not sit after 1741. WSRO, 1178/606, 'Timothy Telltruth' to John Codrington Esq., Member of Parliament, n.d..

[22] LMA, MJ/SP/1782/04/024, Middlesex Justices, Sessions Papers, 23 Apr. 1782.

of that year, and which was *the* game of choice in metropolitan gaming houses of the early 1780s.[23]

Horse racing, regulated by a law passed in 1740 (13 Geo. II, c. 19), renewed and confirmed in 1745 (18 Geo. II, c. 34), represents a somewhat special case. The purpose of the 1740 Act was not to reduce gaming *per se*; rather, its goal was, as with a good deal of mid-century legislation and magisterial action, to restrict opportunities for popular leisure, which had expanded markedly in recent decades. It sought to do this by confining races and matches to those carrying a minimum prize or combined stakes of £50. Evidently there remained confusion about whether these Acts, in recognizing the legality of races carrying prizes of £50 or above, rendered betting on them legal. Nevertheless, betting on horse races was determined by the courts to fall firmly within the ambit of the Gaming Act of 1710.[24] Thus side bets of above £10 were not legal. Matches for sums above £50, however, were. Such anomalies only serve to highlight how legislators and the law were seeking to steer a decidedly torturous path, in that they were not trying to prohibit recreations, at least to the right kinds of people, or, indeed, gambling 'when practised innocently and as a recreation'.[25] The logic, such as it was, was articulated explicitly in a case heard in 1752 when a Middlesex grand jury indicted the keeper of a tennis court in Windmill Street for maintaining a disorderly house, 'because many Persons of Fashion used to come there, and play at tennis, and lay Betts'. Against the charge, it was pleaded that

> it was never reckoned Gambling for any Gentleman or Nobleman to have Cards played in their Houses, and that if such an opposite Opinion prevailed, all the Coffee Houses might, on the same Principle, be indicted for suffering Back Gammon or Chess to be played, which are no other than innocent amusements.

The verdict was found for the Defendant, 'as his Character was very good, and his Behaviour irreproachable'.[26] As was frequently pointed out, by permitting the official lotteries the authorities, moreover, applied a flagrantly double standard.[27] No wonder many contemporaries almost certainly shared the view of the Middlesex Court in 1752 that whatever

[23] See further below, pp. 248–50.

[24] Courts interpreted the law as narrowly as possible. See PP, Report From the Select Committee on Gaming (1844), *passim*.

[25] Dudley Ward and Viscount John Ward, *The Law of a Justice of Peace and Parish Officer* (2 vols., London, 1769), ii, p. 387.

[26] *Read's Weekly Journal*, 28 Oct. 1752.

[27] Money also of course came to the treasury through receipts from taxes on playing cards and dice.

the law said, its goal was not to prohibit the gaming of the elites or certainly the 'wealthy'.[28]

Meanwhile, wagers were deemed to be legal – meaning enforceable as contracts – where they did not tend towards a breach of the peace, were against the rules of good morals and sound policy, damage the character of a third person, or were contrary to law. A key judgement in this context was handed down in 1771 in the Court of King's Bench by Lord Mansfield as Lord Chief Justice in *Da Costa* v. *Jones*, a case involving a bet on the sex of the notorious Chevalier D'Éon. D'Éon, who lived as a woman, notoriously chose to keep their sex undisclosed. Mansfield and the other judges determined that to determine the outcome of the wager would be to damage the reputation of a third party – D'Éon – but also require the revelation of 'indecent evidence', to wit, details of D'Éon's body.[29] In another significant judgement the justices of the same court determined that a wager by two electors on the outcome of an election in the borough of Southwark in 1784 was not actionable because it might have a tendency to encourage bribery.[30] More bizarrely, a wager that Charles Stuart would be king in twelve months was deemed legal, although this finding was later queried by Lord Ellenborough.[31]

Judges tended to define the scope of legality in relation to betting as narrowly as possible, on occasion also making very clear their disapproval of gaming.[32] In 1799 judges in the Scottish Court of Session, the country's highest civil court, declared that determining the rights of parties involved in gaming was not something which properly fell within the remit of the court.[33] This was the position which would eventually be legislated for in England and Wales in the Duke of Richmond's Gaming Actions Discontinuance Act (1845).[34] At one level the posture of the

[28] See *Faro, and Rouge et Noir: The Mode of Playing, and Explanation of the Terms Used in Both Games* (London, 1793), esp. pp. 12–3.

[29] For the D'Éon case, see Gary Kates, *Monsieur D'Éon is a Woman: A Tale of Political Intrigue and Sexual Masquerade* (Baltimore, MD, 2001); Simon Burrows et al. (eds.), *The Chevalier D'Éon and his Worlds: Gender, Espionage and Politics in the Eighteenth Century* (London, 2010). For Da Costa v Jones, see Disney, *Laws of Gaming*, pp. 7–14.

[30] Allen v Hearn, 1 T R 56.

[31] PP, Report From the Select Committee on Gaming, 1844, Appendix, I, Substance of the Common and Statute Law Relating to Gaming, 223.

[32] See Lord Mansfield's comments in his address to the jury in the *Costa* v. *Jones* trial of 1777, where he declared 'his Abhorrence of the whole Transaction, and the more so their bringing it into a Court of Justice, when in it have been better settled elsewhere, wishing it had been in his Power, in concurrence with the Jury, to have made both parties lose ...' (*DA*, 3 July 1777; *Gazetteer*, 2 July 1777).

[33] PP, Report From the Select Committee on Gaming, 1844, Appendix, II, Extracts from Seventh Report of Commissioners on Criminal Law, 232–3.

[34] Vamplew, *Turf*, pp. 202–3.

judges and courts did not matter a jot because it was the 'law of honour', not that enforced by the courts, that ruled this world. The chasm between the law and the code of honour was one of the main reasons why the former was hopelessly ineffective in regulating the activities of most gamblers, certainly those who counted themselves as being among the 'quality'. As one Scottish legal authority despairingly concluded: 'While these mistaken notions remain, while game debts are falsely stiled debts of honour, the ruinous effects of gaming, let whatever laws be enacted, will never be sufficiently curbed.'[35] His was far from a lone voice.[36]

The class character of many anti-gaming measures was, then, as should by now be fairly apparent, as much, if not more, implicit than explicit. Part of the reason was that views among the elites on gaming were divided, a recurrent theme of this book. To some degree the actual content of the law was somewhat deceiving, as in the case of Acts prohibiting private lotteries. Such devices and games were viewed primarily to lure tradesmen and the lower orders, drawing them away from the industry and virtue that were viewed as their proper lot. In the case of games of chance the position was much more ambiguous; strictly speaking the law did not discriminate on social grounds. Thus, the 1745 anti-gaming Act, which proscribed 'roulet', also included a clause which stated that those winning or betting a sum of £10 at one go, or £20 within 24 hours, were liable to indictment within the next six months, and if found guilty were to be fined five times the sum won or lost. It was a different story needless to say in respect of their effects, for prosecutions of people of 'quality' for infractions under them were few and far between.[37]

It was a similar case in respect of our second main area of anti-gaming legislation – measures aimed against sites of gaming. Under a law dating back to the Henry VIII's reign (33 Hen. VIII, c. 9) keepers of gaming houses were liable to prosecution and a fine, as were those patronizing these establishments.[38] Under this statute the definition of gaming house was somewhat fuzzy, but the view that took hold was that a

[35] Robert Boyd, *The Office, Powers and Jurisdiction of His Majesty's Justices of the Peace and Commissioners of Supply* (2 vols., Edinburgh, 1787), ii, p. 563.

[36] Erskine, *Reflections on Gaming*, p. 10.

[37] Kent Justices suppressed 'E.O.' and 'G.S.' tables at Tunbridge Wells in 1751, while in the same year the Lords Regents wrote to the Mayor of Bath to suppress 'E.O' tables there (*GA*, 23 June, 12 Aug. 1751). However, gaming at Britain's multiplying resorts and spas appears to have been largely ignored by magistrates and reformers, although it did on occasion attract adverse comment.

[38] *A Help to Magistrates, and Ministers of Justice* (London, 1721), pp. 192–3.

gaming house was a place where for reasons of making money certain named and other unlawful games were played.[39] Where this left subscription gaming clubs, such as White's or Almack's, was moot, although (significantly) never tested in the courts. The powers available to magistrates against gaming houses were further broadened and strengthened by legislation passed in 1730, 1739, 1745, and in 1752 with passage of the Disorderly Houses Act.[40] As Disney declared: 'These statutes are so comprehensive, and the common law on the subject so plain, that it is scarcely necessary to state more than that Gaming-Houses are indictable, and to point out where the forms of these indictments may be found.'[41] Disney may have been correct in this conclusion, but there appears to have remained some confusion about the scope of these powers, hence in large part the effort in 1782 to secure new legislation to facilitate their suppression.[42] The problem again seems to have been the mode of prosecution and enforcement, and the ability to prevent efforts at frustrating this, for example, by preventing entry to premises, or suing out writs of *certiorari* to remove cases to higher courts, thereby delaying them, and allowing more time to pressurize witnesses. As we will see these were longstanding impediments to campaigns to suppress gaming houses.

What of popular gambling and gamblers? How far did the law seek to regulate their activities, apart from the measures so far discussed? Under 33 Hen. VIII, c. 9 members of the lower orders were in general prohibited from playing named games, while alehouses or taverns offering games for gambling were liable to prosecution as gaming houses.[43] As already mentioned, in the mid eighteenth century there was heightened concern about the leisure habits of the lower orders. Apart from a marked expansion of commercial leisure aimed at the lower orders, the crucial context was a series of crime waves which catalyzed widespread breast-beating about the effects of luxury and immorality, and in particular the supposed 'idleness' of the poor, viewed by a growing number of people, including the influential Westminster magistrates, Henry and Sir John Fielding, as the wellspring of growing crime. As John Beattie notes: 'It was not just a matter of rhetoric but of profoundest belief that immorality led men to crime to support their bad habits.'[44] Gaming

[39] For the different kinds of establishment that might fall under this definition, see Chapter 2, above, pp. 96–9. This definition of a gaming house continued to inform the law and actions of police into the nineteenth century.

[40] 2 Geo II, c. 28; 18 Geo. II, c. 34; 25 Geo. II, c. 36.

[41] Disney, *Laws of Gaming*, p. 114. [42] See below.

[43] The power of justices to compel players of unlawful games to enter recognizances that they would not in future do so was strengthened by 2 Geo. II, c. 28, s. 9.

[44] Beattie, *Policing and Punishment*, p. 120.

was also an exemplification of the threat and the dangers associated with the seemingly powerful lure of being 'fashionable', of what contemporaries termed 'extravagance', a fact confirmed by many a criminal biography published in the Ordinary of Newgate's account. From developing a taste for gaming the path to crime and perdition was a broad, straight one. As Charles Jones lamented: 'If the Ordinary of Newgate's Account be true, there is scarce an Execution that does not furnish us with Examples of Wretches, who place the principal Cause of their Calamities to Gaming and bad Company.'[45] Sir John Fielding was principal author of an Act passed in 1757(30 Geo. II, c. 24) which imposed new penalties on tavern keepers who allowed journeymen, apprentices, and labourers to game on their premises.[46] Sir John and his allies in the mid-century campaign against the vice of the lower orders, who included Saunders Welch, high constable of Holborn, brought into renewed focus the matter of alehouse licensing and the desirability of denying licenses to those who allowed gaming on their premises.[47] The urgency of using licensing of alehouses as a means of preventing gaming among the lower orders was a recurrent theme in eighteenth- and early-nineteenth century metropolitan policing, and would form a central element in a much broader renewed, national campaign for the reformation of manners in 1787.[48]

The 1757 Act was the most overtly class-discriminatory piece of anti-gaming legislation passed in the long eighteenth century, other, that is, than measures to regulate the lottery and the vagrant Acts (for which, see below). The lottery Acts, and their enforcement, are discussed elsewhere in this book. Suffice it to say here that the desirability of preventing the lottery adventures of the lower orders was fully recognized from early on

[45] Charles Jones, *Some Methods Proposed Towards Putting a Stop to the Flagrant Crimes of Murder, Robbery, and Perjury; and for the More Effectually Preventing the Pernicious Consequences of Gaming Among the Lower Class of People* (London, 1752), p. 24.

[46] Bob Harris, *Politics and the Nation: Britain in the Mid-Eighteenth Century* (Oxford, 2002), p. 300.

[47] See Sir John Fielding, *Extracts from Such of the Penal Laws As Particularly relate to the Peace and Good Order of the Metropolis* (new ed., London, 1768), p. 413. It was Welch who in 1748 informed the Middlesex Bench about the 'great Numbers of loose and disorderly persons' who on Sundays in the summer assembled in places in the environs of the capital to practice gaming of different kinds, and who were encouraging apprentices and others to neglect religious worship, and called for their assistance in preventing what he described as a 'growing evil'. (LMA, MJ/O/C/005, Middlesex Sessions, Orders of Court, May 1743-Feb. 1753.)

[48] See e.g. LMA, MJ/O/C/005, 16 July 1747, where the Earl of Chesterfield, one of the secretaries of state, wrote to Thomas Lane, chairman of the Middlesex Bench expressing the view the King 'is of Opinion that it would be of great use that no Licenses were granted for keeping of any Publick Houses of what Denomination Soever where Gaming of any Sort is carried on'. See also further below, pp.39.

by parliament and the courts. In the first half of the eighteenth century this was done through clauses in specific lottery Acts which sought to prohibit devices which extended the social constituency of lottery adventurers, such as hiring of tickets, schemes of 'chances' which depended on the outcome of the official lottery draw, and sales of very small fractions of tickets.[49] As a goal it became even clearer in the later eighteenth century when several Acts were passed by parliament which sought to prohibit various forms of lottery insurance and an Act which sought to eliminate the so-called small goes which was passed in 1802.[50] Lottery insurance and 'Little Goes' were viewed as no less than a 'contagion' in the metropolis, feeding the popular 'propensity for gaming' throughout the year. Both were among the main targets of the Society for the Suppression of Vice, founded in London in 1802. What is notable is how far hostility to gaming among the lower orders reflected wider attitudes, but was also led by the views and actions of professional magistrates seeking to reform policing, the Fieldings in the mid eighteenth century and their counterparts in the later eighteenth and early nineteenth centuries, among whom Patrick Colquhoun stood out in terms of the insistence with which he promoted his views. What united them was how they privileged the law and policing as the main instruments to enforce social and moral order on a populace in dire need of disciplinary regulation. As Sir John Fielding put it, while religion, education and good breeding might suffice to inculcate good habits among the 'superior sort', for the lower sort only the law would suffice.[51] Colquhoun put it more sharply, urging the necessity for 'a systematic superintending policy calculated to check and prevent the growth and progress of vicious habits'.[52]

Other legislation included anti-gaming measures. Most significantly, street gamblers – drivers of wheelbarrows who lured people into dice games, boys playing 'pitch and toss', those who ran gaming booths at fairs, or who assembled in the open air to game – were liable to summary conviction as 'rogues and vagabonds' under the terms of the 1744 Vagrant Act (17 Geo. 2 c. 6).[53] The Bankruptcy Act of 1705

[49] The sales of shares of tickets were prohibited in 1734, but this was soon given up. From 1787 the minimum share permitted was a sixteenth. Sales of chances were prohibited in 1718 (4 Geo. I, c. 9), and subscriptions for sales of chances or part chances in 1719 (5 Geo. I, c. 9). Hiring of tickets was forbidden in 1743 (16 Geo. II, c. 13).

[50] See Chapter 3, above, pp. 167–8.

[51] John Fielding, *An Account of the Origins and Effects of a Police* (London, 1758), p. viii.

[52] P. Colquhoun, *Treatise on Indigence* (London, 1806), p. 82.

[53] 5 Geo. IV, c. 83, sect. 4 (Vagrant Act) decreed 'that any person playing or betting in any street, road, highway, or other open and public place, at, or with any table, or instrument of gaming, at any game, or pretended game of chance, shall be deemed a rogue and

(3 Anne, c. 4) specifically excluded from any benefits of being awarded a commission of bankruptcy anyone who in one day had lost £5 or £100 in the year preceding their bankruptcy playing cards, dice, tables tennis, bowls, cockfighting, horse races or any other game or past time, or side bets on such activities. The authority of small debts courts, around fifty of which had been established by particularistic local legislation by 1800, and insolvent debtors Acts, under which imprisoned debtors were released under certain conditions pointedly did not cover debts incurred through wagers or gaming of any kind.[54] The small debts courts were viewed as crucial to sustaining the operations of credit within the burgeoning towns of a commercializing and industrializing society; they enforced a commercial morality in which there was no place for gaming.[55] There were also important efforts to decouple the business of insurance and gambling. The crucial piece of legislation was the so-called Gambling Act of 1774, which has been the subject of detailed study by Gregory Clark in his work on the development of the life insurance industry.[56] This prevented taking out life insurance policies on lives in which the beneficiary had no interest. It also sought to prohibit other, so-called wagering policies. There had been an earlier attempt to do this in a failed stockjobbing bill of 1773, one of several attempted measures in the central decades of the eighteenth century to give teeth to Sir John Barnard's famous 1734 Act which aimed to prevent time bargains in the financial markets, also seen by some as gaming.[57] The prohibition of wagering policies was in line with similar restrictions in respect of marine insurance, where legislation was passed in 1746 prohibiting no interest policies, which were again essentially a form of wager.[58] Such measures are a reminder of the shifting boundary line between commerce, finance, and gambling, even if some contemporaries urged the existence of a clear and supposedly self-evident distinction between them.[59] Finally gaol Acts, through which reform of prisons

vagabond, and any justice may commit him, on conviction, to the house of correction, there to be kept to hard labour for any time not exceeding three calendar months'.

54 Langford, *Public Life*, pp. 158–61; 51 Geo. III, c. 125, s. 39, Act for the Relief of Certain Insolvent Debtors in England (1811).

55 Margot C. Finn, *The Character of Credit: Personal Debt in English Culture, 1740–1914* (Cambridge, 2003), ch. 5.

56 G. Clark, *Betting on Lives: The Culture of Life Insurance in England, 1695–1775* (Manchester, 1999).

57 See esp. Philip Rawlings, 'Bubbles, Taxes and Interests: Another History of Insurance Law, 1720–1825', *Oxford Journal of Legal Studies*, 36 (2016), 799–827.

58 See Rawlings, 'Bubbles, Taxes and Interests'.

59 Richard Hey, *A Dissertation on the Pernicious Effects of Gaming* (Cambridge, 1783), esp. p. 80.

was pursued from the later eighteenth century, included clauses prohibiting jail keepers from allowing gaming among inmates.[60]

5.2 Non-enforcement of the Law against Gaming

The law and the courts showed, therefore, a fairly uniformly disapproving and reproving face to existing and prospective gamblers. And yet, as already stated, the singular truth is that the law was in this context mostly disregarded, sporadically implemented, and in the main ineffective. We need to understand why.

One important factor has already been mentioned: gambling was regulated – if such is the appropriate term – by the 'law of honour'. For any gentleman settling a bet was a matter of reputation; it cut to the heart of social status and the codes of behaviour which defined this. The rules which mattered were those set by convention and the participants, not the law; gentlemen expected to be judged by their peers, no one else – hence, for example, the expanding role of the Jockey Club as the body determining and enforcing the rules of horse racing, including the validity of certain bets.[61] Examples surface in court records of individuals bringing prosecutions for excessive gambling against people who had won more than £10 from them in gaming or betting on a game at one sitting. These appear to have been mostly people from the middling classes. In 1770, for example, in the Court of King's Bench, one Richard England, described as a 'yeoman', and late of the parish of St Luke, was prosecuted for unlawfully winning at one sitting around £25 with dice from a William Mundon. In the previous year the same court heard the case of a butcher from St Paul's Covent Garden who had gained £12.12 sh. in a game of cribbage.[62] One exception seems to have been the young Duke of Bedford, who was taken by three individuals (Richard Blackwell, Littleton Poyntz Meynell, and Henry Janssen) for £25,000 at the card game 'Bassett', although the grounds for the prosecution, in 1741, were for defrauding.[63] Cheating for gain was quite another thing, and it may well be that the vast majority of prosecutions for gaming brought by private individuals in this period were, indeed, against alleged cheats and fraudsters.[64]

[60] 24 Geo. III, c. 54 (Gaols Act, 1784). [61] See Chapter 1, above, pp. 54, 59.

[62] LMA, MJ/M/KR/001, Lists of Charges Returned to the King's Bench, 1769–1772, fos. 10, 16.

[63] LMA, MS/SB/P/0014, Middlesex Sessions, Process Register of Charges, Aug. 1734–Feb. 1742, 650.

[64] This conclusion is based on inspection of various sets of court records, esp. LMA, MSJ/C/C/01–03, Middlesex Sessions, Calendar of Summary Convictions, 1774–82,

This brings us neatly to the second main reason why anti-gaming legislation was honoured in the breach. It depended heavily on informers for enforcement. Informers were fiercely unpopular in the eighteenth century. As was feelingly noted at the end of the eighteenth century:

> The probability, or rather certainty of being charged with envious malicious, or fanatical motives: – The dread of incurring the imputation of singularity or officiousness; – the fear of becoming a butt for the poisoned arrows of slander, or the scarcely less-dreaded shafts of ridicule; – Even the reluctance naturally felt by an individual to bring himself into public notice, still more to render himself liable to the charge of volunteering an obnoxious service, and presumptuously seating himself as it were in the censorial chair: – All these causes, and many other might be assigned, must operate powerfully in preventing private men from presuming individually to undertake the enforcement of the laws against profaness and immorality.[65]

Informing was encouraged by financial incentives, for example, by London vestries and under specific statutes such as the Disorderly Houses Act[66]; London's stipendiary magistrates towards the end of the eighteenth century and in the early nineteenth century employed informers in efforts to prosecute so-called lottery vagrants, those who acted as agents for lottery insurances.[67] In the 1750s Sir John Fielding appears to have introduced a system of anonymous informing on gaming houses and other illegal popular entertainments using the penny post, an initiative for which he certainly claimed success.[68] Constables were periodically instructed to search for offenders against the gaming laws, but the overriding impression is that most of them acted reluctantly if at all. A common allegation was that they colluded with offenders. This was part of wider critique of the contemporary system of justice and its agents, including lawyers, for corruption or suborning by the criminal classes. As Beattie argues, reaching an appropriately balanced judgement on the performance and competence of constables and lesser officers of the law in this period is very difficult.[69] Some constables were notably

1783–93, 1794; MJ/SB/P/15, Middlesex Sessions, Process Register of Charges, Apr. 1742–Jan. 1751.

65 *Report of the Committee*, p. 7.

66 See e.g. Westminster City Archives, Clement Danes, vestry minutes, 5 Nov. 1767. The Disorderly Houses Act provided that householders who informed on gaming and other disorderly houses which led to a conviction would be paid their costs and a reward of £10 by overseers of the poor.

67 See Chapter 3, above, p. 168.

68 Fielding, *An Account of the Origin and Effects of a Police Set on Foot by his Grace the Duke of Newcastle in the Year 1753, upon a Plan Presented to his Grace by the Late Henry Fielding, Esq* (London, 1758), p. 30

69 Beattie, *Policing and Punishment*, esp. ch. 3 'Constables and Other Officers'.

active, pursuing and informing on large numbers of offenders, although such activism could easily provoke hostility and public opprobrium.[70] In 1750 the Court of Aldermen of the City of London noted that it was neglect of enforcement by lesser officers of the law that led to moral offences being committed 'with impunity'. Those found negligent in this respect were threatened with prosecution; their actions were also to be kept under closer scrutiny.[71] No doubt some constables were corrupt or negligent. They had, however, to make a choice between rigorous enforcement of orders from the bench or magistrates and the likely views of the communities of which they were a part. This might well mean looking the other way in the case of policing what might to some be viewed as vice and others harmless and legitimate recreation.

What all this meant was that concerted actions against gaming and gaming houses, as with other 'moral offences', required a great deal of will, and direction from above from determined reforming magistrates, quite often acting at the specific promptings of ministers of the state. The underlying motivation was usually concern about crime, since gaming was deemed to be a breeding ground of criminality and violent criminals. The result was that drives against gambling were rarely sustained for very long. This general pattern is revealed very clearly by examining in turn the three main anti-gaming campaigns of the eighteenth century, those of 1718–1722, the 1740s and 1750s, and the early 1780s. This also serves to disclose another major source of difficulty facing the forces of law and order – namely, the intensity and ingenuity of resistance mounted by gamblers and keepers of gaming houses.

5.3 Campaigns to Suppress London's Gaming Houses

The drive to suppress metropolitan gaming houses between 1718 and 1722 has recently been described in some detail by Tim Hitchcock and Robert Shoemaker.[72] As they suggest its origins remain somewhat hidden, although they note the relevance of a charge to the Westminster Grand Jury delivered by the chairman of the local

[70] See esp. Joanna Innes, *Inferior Politics: Social Problems and Social Policies in Eighteenth-Century Britain* (Oxford, 2009), ch. 7 'The Protestant Carpenter – William Payne of Bell Lane (c.1718–82): The Life and Times of a London Informing Constable'.

[71] LMA, COL/CA/01/01/158, Repertories of the Court of Aldermen, 1749–50, fos. 235–41, 3 Apr. 1750. This was part of a resolution to enforce the laws against vice and immorality, in response to the recently issued royal proclamation against vice. There was nothing new about calls to subject constables' actions (or rather inaction) to closer scrutiny. See e.g. LMA, MJ/O/C/003, Middlesex Sessions, Orders of Court, Jan. 1724-Jan. 1734, 14 Oct. 1728.

[72] Hitchcock and Shoemaker, *London Lives*, pp. 107–21.

magistrates, Bulstrode Whitelock, in 1718. In April of that year, Whitelock singled out the destructive consequences of gaming on the wealthy, but in October it was the effects on ordinary men that drew his attention. These comments were related to a contemporaneous crack-down on gaming and gaming houses. Hitchcock and Shoemaker note that sixty-seven indictments were prosecuted at the July Westminster Sessions for keeping unlawful games, although many of these were almost certainly not gaming houses *per se* but taverns and alehouses which provided or allowed unlawful games such as shuffle board and ninepins.[73] In December 1718 a committee of Middlesex justices was formed to report on the laws in force against persons keeping public gaming houses and bawdy houses, and to recommend the most effective and proper means to suppress them. This reported back to the bench in the following January, calling on justices to enforce the relevant powers under 33 Hen. VIII, c. 9, and also use the licensing of alehouses as another tool.[74] The next moves, which occurred in 1720, followed receipt of a letter sent to the Middlesex and Westminster justices from the Lords Justices, those responsible for government in the absence of the King, who was in his native Hanover at the time, calling on them to suppress gaming houses, night houses, and disorderly houses. The general background to this was heightened concern about violent attacks on and robbery of 'persons of quality' in Westminster, and attempts, led by magistrates, to reform the night watch. In response, the Westminster bench instituted frequent petty sessions in the autumn of 1720 to put the laws into operation.[75] At these sessions, justices issued warrants against gaming houses and common gamesters, and constables made their returns, typically on the following day. At one petty session, held on

[73] This followed an order in April 1718 to the High Constable of Westminster to 'make diligent search and true return of the names of all persons' who were guilty of profane swearing and cursing, and other 'immoral and disorderly practices'; drivers of wheelbarrows; singers of seditious ballads; printers of seditious and scandalous books and pamphlets; rogues, vagrants, and beggars; 'all such persons who keep and use common gaming houses, such as dice, tables, billiard tables, shovel boards, ninepin alleys and all other unlawful games whatsoever'; and those whose cellar doors obstructed public streets and thoroughfares. (LMA, MJ/SB/B/0075, Middlesex Justices, Session of the Peace and Oyer and Terminer Book, Jan.–Dec. 1718, Apr. 1718.) The Middlesex Bench had made an order for suppressing vice, immorality, and profaneness in January 1717, reference to which is made in LMA, MJ/SP/1720, Middlesex Sessions, Sessions Papers, 31 May 1720.

[74] LMA, MJ/O/C/001, Middlesex Sessions, Orders of Court, May 1716–Oct. 1721, 19 Jan. 1719.

[75] LMA, WJ/O/C/001, Westminster Sessions, Orders of Court, Apr. 1720–1728, fos. 4-4d, Oct. 1720. The campaign is described in *An Account of the Endeavours that have been used to Suppress Gaming-Houses, and of the Discouragements that have been Met with in a Letter to a Noble Lord* (London, 1722).

1 November, information was received against thirty gaming houses. What ensued was a battle to secure offenders, one in which the latter were mostly victorious through a combination of evasion, early information of any actions against them, and open defiance. A contemporary pamphleteer alleged that a further major impediment was the Westminster Court of Burgesses, which selected the high and petty constables, and beadles. The High Constable of Westminster was, it was said, compounding fines with keepers of gaming houses and other disorderly houses. Worse still grand juries were being summoned by the High Bailiff of Westminster, members of which showed favour to those being prosecuted, frequently finding the bills against them 'ignoramus' (rejecting them, in other words).[76]

Meanwhile, the keepers of gaming houses were threatening the justices and constables with counter legal actions, also raising a sum of money between them to defend prosecutions against them and their employees. They had taken more direct steps to deter and prevent raids, through the construction of hatches with iron spikes to street and inner doors, which were kept locked.[77] The gaming houses were guarded by men, described in one document as 'soldiers', who would refuse entry to justices and constables, and those of whom they were unsure.[78] At the same time, people were employed to give early notice of any intended raid.[79] Similar tactics were employed by keepers of gaming houses (as well as lottery insurance offices) throughout the eighteenth century and beyond. When constables, for example, from the police office in Marlborough Street, presided over by stipendiary magistrate, Nathanial Conant, raided a gaming house in Leicester Fields in 1796 they found the entrance secured by an iron swing gate, inside of which was another barred gate before which sat a porter. Behind this was a private door which had been painted to look like brickwork. When it was forced it was found to be lined on the inside with plate iron, described as 'very strong', and behind this was further 'thick deal door'. In the time it took to effect entry many of the people within escaped over the rooftops of neighbouring buildings,

[76] *Account of the Endeavours*, pp. 9–11.

[77] There appears to have been doubt about whether constables had the authority to break down doors when refused entry.

[78] The term was probably used because porters of gaming houses were apparently normally soldiers from the foot guards.

[79] These included so-called orderly men and runners, while link boys, chairmen, coachmen, and others would be rewarded financially if they brought intelligence of justices meetings or constables being abroad.

although one person fell through a skylight covered with snow and was 'extremely hurt'.[80]

The justices might have given up in 1720, or so it was claimed at the time, but for continued pressure on them to act from local householders.[81] The justices took to convening in private, in a largely unsuccessful bid to prevent keepers of gaming houses gaining early notice of planned raids. Confrontation between the justices and the gaming houses reached a climacteric in a raid on Vandernan's gaming house, located in Playhouse Passage, off Drury Lane, in late December 1721. Several individuals who had participated in the ensuing 'riott' absconded, but three men were indicted for assault on the constables in a case heard before the Old Bailey in February 1722.[82] What had happened was that a group of constables, armed with a warrant for searching gaming houses issued by ten Westminster justices, finding the door of Vandernan's open, had entered, but were driven back by men armed with swords. From a window, alehouse pots, brickbats, and a chamber pot had been rained down on the retreating constables. What was described as 'the Proclamation', presumably meaning the Riot Act, was then read, possibly on two separate occasions, which received the responses 'A T[ur]d of your Proclamation' and various other, similar cries. Soldiers were called for, one of whom climbed in at the window and opened the door. Two soldiers were left to guard it, but were subsequently ordered to retire by individuals pretending to be officers. While the constables were inside, having shut the outer door, a hostile mob collected. The melée apparently lasted from eleven at night until two o'clock in the morning. The three men were all found guilty.[83]

This was not the end of the matter, however, for two constables' assistants, Philip Cholmley and Edward Vaughan, were indicted for murder at the Old Bailey in 1722.[84] As Hitchcock and Shoemaker have shown, both were men with a long record of informing, and presumably they had been quite deliberately selected for this prosecution. The case against them was that they had aided a soldier who had fired his musket killing one Henry Bowes, a former tailor and Vandernan's boxkeeper. The constables' assistants were found not guilty, a key part of their defence being the presence in the court of several justices who testified

80 TNA, Treasury Solicitors Papers, TS11/931/3301, *Rex* v. *Thomas Moore*, 1799.

81 *Account of the Endeavours*, p. 13.

82 Old Bailey Proceedings, Accounts of Criminal Trials, 28 Feb. 1722 [*London Lives online*, t17220228–65].

83 Ibid.

84 Old Bailey Proceedings: Accounts of Criminal Trials, 12 Jan. 1722 (*London Lives online*, t17220112–43).

to the 'very good character' of the men. Equally striking, however, is the language deployed by the prosecuting witnesses, who described the party of constables and other law officers raiding the gaming house as no less than a 'mob' intent on violence.[85]

Hitchcock's and Shoemaker's conclusion is that the magistrates may have won the battle, but they lost the war.[86] It is a very reasonable assessment. They cite the fact that the Societies for the Reformation of Manners prosecuted 104 people for gambling in 1722, a figure which fell sharply in the next 2 years (42 and 23, respectively). In 1723 Sir John Gonson led a group of twenty-six Westminster and Middlesex justices who formed a society to suppress gaming houses.[87] A letter written by Gonson seven years later indicates that at the request of this society the state had provided funds to help defray the costs of combatting actions against constables arising from their actions against gaming houses and prosecuting gaming house keepers and gamblers. This, claimed Gonson, had enabled him and his colleagues 'to go on with great success in putting down so many of these pernicious Houses and encouraged the officers to do their duties …'. Gonson was calling for a similar order to be made to Treasury Secretary, Nicholas Paxton, because certain constables were currently facing prosecutions arising from the execution of warrants against the Phoenix Gaming House in the Haymarket.[88] The problems encountered by the justices evidently continued, including the impanelling of grand juries who protected gaming house keepers from prosecution.[89] Whether, for all Gonson's claims, gaming houses in and around Covent Garden diminished in number is doubtful. One writer favourable to the aims of the campaign in 1720–1722 emphasized that what its mostly sorry record showed was the need for magistrates to be armed with new powers to suppress gaming houses, a view which would resurface in the context of later magisterial drives against them.[90] Saunders Welch declared in 1758: 'The true reason of the long and successful reign of gamblers in this kingdom is, that there is not a punishment in law

[85] Much of the evidence concerned what had been said or shouted by the constables in the course of the raid.

[86] Hitchcock and Shoemaker, *London Lives*, p. 116.

[87] LMA, WJ/O/C/001, annotated list of justices, who entered into a society to suppress gaming houses in Middlesex and Westminster in 1723, at back of volume.

[88] TNA, State Papers Domestic, SP36/18/197, fos. 197–8, Sir John Gonson, Inner Temple to [?], 13 May 1730.

[89] LMA, MJ/O/C/003, Middlesex Sessions, Orders of Court, Jan. 1724–Jan. 1734, 14 Oct. 1725, order that the sheriff do not empanel any person keeping a victualing house, gaming house, or cook's shop, or selling strong spirituous liquors by retail on a grand jury.

[90] *Account of the Endeavours*, pp. 28–9.

adequate to the offence.'[91] For Welch, a major problem was that as misdemeanours, rather than felonies, gaming offences were bailable. This merely created time for the offenders to buy off the prosecutor or pressurize witnesses.

If concern about violent crime and robbery in particular framed and drove the actions of metropolitan justices against gaming houses in the early 1720s, this was similarly true in the 1740s and 1750s. As Beattie has noted the end of 1744 saw a sudden panic about violent attacks committed by a group known as the Black Boy Alley gang, so-called because of their base off Chick Lane in the populous city ward of Farringdon Without.[92] Early in October 1744 the lord mayor and aldermen of the city requested that the King intervene, and in response the secretaries of state instructed the Westminster magistrates to organize privy searches by their constables to discover the night cellars and in particular the gaming houses that were believed to shelter robbers and also encourage their offending. In a move which further demonstrates features apparent in 1718–1722, magistrates were ordered to hold frequent petty sessions and to arm their constables with warrants to enable them to arrest disorderly persons under the Vagrant Act of 1744, which had recently been passed to increase the penalties on anyone who fell within its definition of rogues and vagabonds, which, as we saw above, now explicitly included gamblers.[93]

One particular focus of concern were two gaming houses in Covent Garden run by two supposed peeresses, ladies Mordington and Cassilis. In January 1745, the chairman of the Westminster Sessions informed ministers of the difficulty posed by these ladies claiming the privilege of peers in resisting their efforts to suppress their establishments.[94] After hearing evidence from, among others, the reforming Westminster magistrate, Sir Thomas De Veil, the House of Lords passed a resolution removing the supposed privilege from the peeresses, ladies Mordington and Cassilis, which the former claimed protected her and her servants

[91] Welch, *Proposal*, p. 60. [92] Beattie, *Policing and Punishment*, pp. 406–9.

[93] Ibid., p. 407.

[94] TNA, State Papers Domestic, SP 36/65/159, affidavit of Daniel Carne, high constable of Westminster, relating to claims of Lady Cassillis that as a peeress she had a right to keep an illegal gaming house and to protect those frequenting it, being exempted from the jurisdiction of justice of the peace; SP 36/65/217, order of the Westminster quarter sessions for the chairman to present an account to the Duke of Newcastle of their actions in apprehending street robbers, and with regard to the gaming houses kept by ladies Mordington and Cassillis, 17 Apr. 1745. See also LMA, MJ/O/C/005, Middlesex Sessions, Orders of Court, May 1743–Feb. 1753, fos. 46v–47v, letter from the Middlesex Justices of the Peace to the Duke of Newcastle, 19 Oct. 1744.

from prosecution.[95] The 1745 anti-gaming Act included a clause specifically providing that 'No privilege of Parliament … be allowed to any person against whom any prosecution shall be had for keeping a common gaming house, or any place for playing at prohibited game'. We know much less about the scope of this renewed campaign against gaming houses than that of 1718–1722, and it would appear to have been more limited. Mordington's gaming house was suppressed, but with seemingly little impact on gaming in the capital.[96] It is hard to find evidence in court records of any significant spike in prosecutions for gaming in the mid-1740s.[97] In July 1745 the Court of Aldermen ordered the two marshalls of the city to use their efforts to suppress private and public gaming houses, and to bring their keepers and those found gaming in them before the magistrates.[98] The Middlesex Justices had informed the Duke of Newcastle in the previous October that they would need the assistance of parliament or ministers to make any real headway against the gaming houses, which may partly explain the passage of the anti-gaming Act of 1745.[99] Yet, just two years later, the Earl of Chesterfield was writing again to metropolitan justices about the threat to public order posed by gaming houses.[100] There was plenty of concern in the City of London during the central decades of the eighteenth century about the gaming of the lower orders as part of a broader effort to suppress, if possible, the burgeoning culture and business of metropolitan popular recreation. A major focus for magisterial action in this context were illegal fairs (Tottenham Court fair, Paddington fair, Bow or Green Goose fair, Welch fair, May fair, Mile End fair), which offered dramatic entertainments and gaming, the spas and resorts of St James Clerkenwell (Sadler's Wells, New Wells, Sir John Oldcastle's), the open area of Moorfields, and illegal horse races being staged in White Conduit Field in Islington.[101] While it emerged very clearly in the 1740s, this facet of

[95] *Journals of the House of Lords*, 26 (1741–6), 492.

[96] See the conclusion reached by Jones, *Some Methods*, p 21, where the author noted that remnant after suppression of houses simply dispersed across town.

[97] This conclusion is based on scrutiny of LMA, MJ/SP/B/0014 & 0015, Middlesex Sessions, Process Register of Charges, Aug. 1734–Feb. 1742, Apr. 1742–Jan. 1751.

[98] LMA, Col/CA/01/01/153, Repertory of the Court of Aldermen, 1744–1745, fo. 317, 23 July 1745.

[99] LMA, MJ/O/C/005, fos. 46v–47v.

[100] LMA, MJ/O/C/005, 16 July 1747.

[101] LMA, Col/CA/01/01/148–55, Repertories of the Court of Aldermen, 1740–50; LMA, MJ/O/C/005, *passim*. The order of the Middlesex Bench to suppress unlawful fairs was made a standing order in April 1748. Periodic action against the illegal fairs had been taken from at least 1718, for which, see Anne Wohlcke, *The 'Perpetual Fair': Gender, Disorder and Urban Amusement in Eighteenth-Century London* (Manchester, 2014), ch. 3 'Regulation and Resistance: Wayward apprenctices and other 'evil disposed persons' at London's fairs'.

policing of the British metropolis gained further momentum and expanded in scope in the subsequent decade, as we will see below.

Given the close connection which was believed to exist between gaming and crime, it is hardly surprising that the former once again became a significant source of magisterial and ministerial concern in the early 1750s, in the context of a much more serious panic about violent crime, which followed the end of the War of the Austrian Succession.[102] As the Westminster magistrate, Thomas Lediard, declared in 1754 it was to gaming houses and brothels that could be attributed 'half the vices that overspread the land, and terrify the peaceful subject'.[103] The intensity of the anxiety induced by the post-war crime wave culminated in the House of Commons establishing in 1751 the first committee ever appointed to examine in a general way the whole matter of crime and criminal administration, along with vagrancy and the workings of the poor laws. It also led Henry Fielding and others to write at length on the issue of crime and policing, as well as provoking major new initiatives in policing by Fielding and then his half-brother, Sir John, organized from their Bow Street magistrates' office, and underwritten by a substantial financial subvention from the state from 1753.[104] Other products of this same moment were the Disorderly Houses Act and Sir John Fielding's 1757 Act to impose penalties on tavern keepers allowing journeymen, apprentices, and labourers to game in taverns, referred to earlier.

For all that gaming, along with popular recreation, were identified as a major source of idleness and, therefore, crime, the successes and failures of policing action against gaming in the 1750s have yet to be systematically traced, if, indeed, this were possible given the intractable nature of many of the records. In 1750 the high constable of the Finsbury division in Middlesex called for the law to be put into execution against vagrants gaming and the prosecution of those found gaming in gaming houses,

[102] Beattie, *Policing and Punishment*, pp. 420–22; Hitchcock and Shoemaker, *London Lives*, pp. 194–232; Nicholas Rogers, *Mayhem: Post War Crime and Violence in Britain, 1748–53* (New Haven and London, 2012).

[103] *A Charge to the Grand Jury, at the Session of Peace held for the City and Liberty of Westminster, 16 Oct. 1754. By Thomas Lediard, Esq.* (London, 1754), pp. 25–6.

[104] Nicholas Rogers, 'Confronting the Crime Wave: The Debate over Social Reform and Regulation, 1749–1753', in Lee Davison et al (eds.), *Stilling the Grumbling Hive: The Response to Social and Economic Problems in England 1689–1750* (Stroud, 1992), pp. 82–7; Nicholas Rogers, *Mayhem*, ch. 7; Richard Connors, '"The Grand Inquest of the Nation": Parliamentary Committees and Social Policy in Mid-Eighteenth Century England', *Parliamentary History*, 14 (1995), 285–313; John Beattie, *The First English Detectives: The Bow Street Runners and the Policing of London, 1750–1840* (Oxford, 2012); John Beattie, 'Sir John Fielding and Public Justice: The Bow Street Magistrates' Court, 1754–1780', *Law and History Review*, 25 (2007), 93–100.

recommending that a list of offenders be compiled to ensure that prosecutions went forward.[105] The powers of the Disorderly Houses Act appear to have been relatively rarely invoked, presumably because they depended on householders coming forward with information against such places. The Fieldings's stark views about the impolicy of allowing popular recreations may not have been widely shared, or at the very least appeared blatantly socially discriminatory, which, indeed, they were.[106] Only once was action against gamblers at Ranelagh briefly contemplated, in April 1750 in the context of the London earthquakes which produced a short-lived spasm of moral anxiety among London's elites.[107] Calls were periodically made to regulate and police, if not suppress, the pleasure gardens which were patronized by the middling and lower sort. Yet whatever actions were taken they continued to flourish.[108] The campaign against popular and illegal fairs had somewhat better success, although it was a long haul and their cessation was certainly not permanent.[109] While the Middlesex bench in 1752 once again recommended to justices not to allow alehouse licenses to publicans who maintained skittle grounds and nine-pin yards, or allowed other games on their premises, how many keepers of gaming houses were prosecuted and gaming houses suppressed, or alehouses denied licenses because of allowing gaming, is currently hidden from view, although one suspects it was few, if any.[110] One John Seymour, who kept a house in Pope's Head Alley in Cornhill at the heart of the city, where billiards was played, was prosecuted in 1753. It appears that he had been singled out because of its visibility, that it was always open, and frequented by large numbers of people of varying social status. Yet even in this case, some of the witnesses appear to have been reluctant to come forward. One of them was an employee of Seymour's,

[105] LMA, MJ/O/C/005, fos. 197v–198v.

[106] For a statement of this priority, see John Fielding, *An Account of the Origin and Effects of a Police Set on Foot by His Grace the Duke of Newcastle in the Year 1753, upon a Plan Presented to his Grace by the Late Henry Fielding, Esq.* (London, 1758).

[107] LMA, MJ/O/C/005, fo. 195r. & v., 23 Apr. 1750, order appointing a committee to suppress gaming and other disorders at the Assemblies at Ranelagh, 26 Apr. 1750; *General Advertiser*, 24 Apr. 1750. Fielding also seems to have taken some action against 'sharpers' frequenting ridottos in the main pleasures gardens later in the 1750s (*Gazetteer and New Daily Advertiser*, 7 Apr. 1756).

[108] Warwick Wroth, *The London Pleasure Gardens of the Eighteenth Century* (reprint, London, 1979).

[109] The Middlesex Bench was forced to re-issue orders dating from 1755 against illegal fairs in May 1776. LMA, MJ/O/C/010A, Middlesex Sessions, Orders of Court, Feb. 1774–Dec. 1783, May 1776.

[110] LMA, MJ/O/C/005, fo. 253r., 9 Apr. 1752. In the previous year, the Middlesex Bench decided to enquire into whether any licenses had been granted to publicans who maintained skittle grounds (LMA, MJ/O/C/005, fo. 227v.).

so this is probably unsurprising. But another was a neighbour, called to prove that play took place 'at all hours'.[111] Getting witnesses to attest to gaming in gaming houses would long prove tricky, partly because most people wished to avoid trouble, but also because such places were not necessarily viewed as nuisances; rather they might be viewed as source of business and profit, for example, to landlords.[112] In 1755 the grand jury at a Middlesex general sessions called for action against keepers of cockpits, as well as horse racing staged at Tothill Fields and Belsize Park.[113] Sir John Fielding, meanwhile, who spearheaded efforts to suppress gaming and popular 'idleness' in the later 1750s, became very unpopular, although, as has been pointed out, he did win support from a group of moral reformers in London, many of whom appear to have been Methodists, who formed a new reformation of manners society in 1757.[114] The latter endured until 1762, by which date it claimed to have successfully prosecuted more than 10,000 people for various moral offences. Only a very small proportion of them, however, were for gaming.[115]

The battle against gaming houses and popular gambling was always, therefore, but a single element – or several – in much broader campaigns against criminality and vice, and this also needs to be borne in mind. Gaming was rarely at the very forefront of magisterial and policing priorities, and even when it was briefly it was never the sole one. Sir John Fielding, to take only one example, was at least as exercised about the problem of prostitutes and prostitution, and the criminality of juveniles lacking proper parental authority. Campaigners against vice pursued gamblers less intently than other categories of offence, such as prostitution, swearers and blasphemers, and Sabbath breakers. There was, in consequence, a continual threat of dilution of effort and loss of momentum in drives against gaming. This was to be evident in the last of the major campaigns against gaming houses to be considered here in any detail, that which began to take shape in 1781–1782.

111 LMA, CLA/043/LJ/13/1753/004, City of London Sessions, Sessions Papers, 20 July 1753.

112 See further below, p. 251. See also PP, Report of the Select Committee on Gaming, 1844.

113 LMA, MJ/SP/1755, Middlesex Sessions, Sessions Papers, Sept. 1755.

114 Hitchcock and Shoemaker, *London Lives*, p. 233.

115 John Wesley, *A Sermon Preached Before the Society for Reformation of Manners on Sunday, January 30, 1763. At the Chappel in West Street, Seven Dials* (London, 1763), p. 10. Of the 10,588 prosecutions, 40 were for unlawful gaming and profane swearing. This compares to 400 for Sabbath breaking and 550 for 'lewd women' and 'keepers of ill houses'.

In some ways, this is the most shadowy of the three. Yet, it exhibits a good deal in common with its earlier counterparts, in that at its heart was a group of committed reformist magistrates responding to public calls for action to suppress gaming houses. It also led to the most concerted attempt yet to furnish magistrates with effective powers to suppress gaming houses, in the form of the Gaming Bill of 1782, or as it is more correctly titled 'The Bill More Effectually to Prevent the Pernicious Practice of Gaming'.[116]

A major difference with the earlier drives is that this one does not appear to have coincided with a major panic about crime, which is not to say that concerns about the latter were very far from the surface of contemporaries' thinking. There may well have been a degree of anticipation here in relation to the end of the War of American Independence, and the effects of imminent post-war demobilization. Concern about gaming houses and their destructive effects certainly did not disappear in the 1760s and 1770s. In the spring of 1777, for example, a letter published in the *Morning Post*, observed that despite the severity with which the law treated playing at the dice game, hazard, this continued 'under the eye of [the] magistracy and to the utter disgrace of the public police'.[117] There was a rapid rise of gaming houses from 1777 to 1778 in which people played 'E.O.' ('Even and Odd'). We lack contemporary estimates of their numbers. The British Museum, however, has a collection of around seventy-six advertising cards of 'E.O.' and other gaming houses dating from c. 1782. Such cards were openly handed out on the streets as advertising.[118] It was the very visibility and flagrancy of these establishments that almost certainly in part provoked the drive to suppress them.

There was, however, considerably more to it. In the first place, there had been a sharp intensification in the 1770s of concerns about gambling among the middling and lower orders, one major focus of which was lottery insuring.[119] In early April 1776 it was reported in the press that a tradesman had lost 200 guineas at a 'noted gambling house' located near to St James's.[120] Two years later another paper reported that three merchant's clerks in the city had been dismissed for gambling with money belonging to their employers, while in 1780 'E.O.' tables were observed to be appearing in public houses frequented by people who

[116] This is discussed in more detail in Bob Harris, 'The 1782 Gaming Bill and Lottery Regulation Acts (1782 & 1787): Gambling and the Law in Later Georgian Britain', *Parliamentary History*, 40 (2021), 462–80.

[117] *Morning Post*, 3 Apr. 1777. See also *Public Ledger*, 28 Dec. 1774.

[118] *MChr*, 26 Mar. 1782.

[119] See Chapter 3, above, pp. 166–7.

[120] *MChr* 3 Apr. 1776.

were described as 'industrious day labourers'.[121] Second, and perhaps more importantly, gaming became the most visible symptom of the corruption and failures of the elites who had led Britain to failure in the war against the North American colonies. As Donna Andrew comments: 'In some curious way, the EO Table, and its extirpation, had become a symbol of what needed to be rehabilitated in the English Polity.'[122] Failure in war bred a mood of intense national introspection, and growing voices clamoured once more for moral reform. There was a much more intense, critical focus in the 1770s and 1780s on the dissolute habits of the fashionable. Vicessimus Knox, for one, believed that the Gordon Riots of 1780, which saw many of the key symbols of authority and financial power in London in flames, were attributable to 'the contempt thrown on the higher orders by various methods'.[123] A straw in the wind in this context was the passage in 1777 of the 'Act to restrain the raising of money by the sale of Life Annuities'. Sale of life annuities was a ready, and previously largely unregulated, way of raising money, which appears to have increased markedly in the third quarter of the eighteenth century. One of the clauses of the Act prohibited sale of life annuities on the lives of their grantors where they were aged under twenty-one, presumably to protect the fortunes of heirs of landed families against reckless expenditure, such as on gambling. One contemporary, who purported to be an MP, concluded of gaming bluntly: 'To this dreadful vice, must the loss of America be ascribed!'[124]

When metropolitan magistrates began to take concerted action against gaming houses in the early 1780s is unclear, although it was probably in 1781.[125] By the spring of 1782, groups of magistrates in the city and Middlesex were increasingly raiding such places, although Westminster magistrates were being criticized for their supposed inaction.[126] The magistrates, however, were running into difficulties. In March 1782, in

[121] *GEP*, 8 Jan. 1778; *MChr*, 17 Apr. 1780.

[122] Donna T. Andrew, '"How Frail are Lovers Vows and Dicers Oaths": Gaming, Governing and Moral Panic in Britain, 1781–1782', in David Lemmings and Claire Walker (eds.), *Moral Panics, the Media and the Law in Early Modern England* (Basingstoke, 2009), pp. 176–94.

[123] Quoted in Langford, *Public Life and the Propertied Englishman*, p. 469.

[124] *Hints for a Reform, Particularly in the Gambling Clubs. By a Member of Parliament* (London, 1784), p. 10.

[125] See LMA, MJ/SP/1781/May/018, Middlesex Sessions, Sessions Papers, warrant for arrest of Joseph Cooke, late of St James, Westminster, for unlawfully keeping a gaming table called an E.O. table, 29 May 1781.

[126] For a defence of the Westminster magistrates, see *Morning Herald*, 6 Mar. 1782, which reported that 'A great deal of ill founded invective has been lavished on the magistrates of the Westminster police, for not suppressing the various E.O. tables what are played within their jurisdiction.' The main magistrates involved appear to have been, in the

a case that had been removed from the Middlesex general sessions, the Court of King's Bench had acquitted two defendants charged with keeping a gaming house on the grounds of inadequate proof. Evidently, witnesses were not forthcoming to testify that gaming took place at various times.[127] Keepers of gaming houses subject to raids were also launching prosecutions against magistrates and constables in the courts.[128] It was against this background that at the April Middlesex general sessions it was agreed to form a committee to consider the state of the law relating to gaming in an effort to 'check the growing evil of gaming Houses in which E.O. and several other unlawful games are practised'.[129] The committee met on at least seven occasions in April and May 1782.[130] It sought the cooperation of the Court of Aldermen, which was duly forthcoming at the end of April.[131] It was members of the committee who drew up the draft bill which, with a few amendments, would become the Gaming Bill of 1782.[132]

Several of the details of this bill as passed by parliament merit our close attention. For, they underline again the scale of the challenges presented by efforts to drive the gaming houses out of existence. The key change would have been to move from prosecution of gaming house keepers by indictment before a jury to summary jurisdiction exercised by two

City, Alderman Hart, and Brass Crosby, and in Middlesex, Sampson Wright, William Hyde, and William Addington.

127 *London Courant*, 3 Apr. 1782.

128 See e.g. *London Chronicle*, 23–5 Apr. 1782, report on action in the Court of King's Bench for the recovery of EO tables and money seized by magistrates.

129 Information was presented at the April sessions against a Savile Robinson for six counts of keeping common gaming houses (LMA, MJ/SR/3146, Middlesex Sessions, Sessions Rolls, 8 Apr. 1782), which Robinson disputed on grounds of insufficient evidence.

130 LMA, MJ/O/C/010A, 11 Apr. 1782. The sessions appear to have appointed those magistrates present on 11 Apr. to the committee, but determined that it would be quorate with the presence of any three. The committee first met on 15 Apr. The magistrates who we know to have served were: Thomas Bishop (the chairman); William Addington; John Lewis; John Barnfather; Jeremiah Bentham, James Croft; George Mercer; James Paine; and Sampson Wright. The details can be followed in several extant minutes of their meetings (LMA, MJ/SP/1782/04/023–024, Middlesex Justices, Sessions Papers) and a later record of costs incurred in its service (MJ/SP/1785/05/034, Middlesex Justices, Sessions Papers, Charles Eyles's Account of the Expenses for Work for the Committee formed to Prevent Gaming and Gaming Houses, 1785).

131 For the debate among the aldermen on this request, see *Gazetteer and New Daily Advertiser*, 25 Apr. 1782.

132 On 22 May, having consulted with the Middlesex MPs, George Byng and John Wilkes, and William Mainwaring, the chairman of the Middlesex Bench and later county MP and formidable reforming magistrate, the Middlesex Bench submitted a petition to the House of Commons, presented by Wilkes, which called for new measures to be taken against gaming. It was Byng who on 5 June moved for leave to bring in the bill to parliament.

justices. Persons present in the gaming house were liable to a fine, while people publicizing the gaming houses, by writing or printing, were to be deemed a 'rogue and vagabond' under the Vagrant Act of 1744. This latter clause was aimed at the open advertising of the gaming houses, referred to above. Further clauses concerned the powers of search and seizure under warrants issued to constable by justices, including specifying that they had the power to break open the doors to gaming houses to effect entry; the summoning of witnesses, including rendering them liable to prosecution for perjury for their refusing or neglecting to appear when called; encouragement for offenders to turn King's evidence against their fellow gamblers; deterring people from obstructing efforts to suppress gaming houses; giving justices the authority to burn and destroy gaming implements and seize any monies discovered in raids, reward constable and other officers of the peace, as well as informers, for their assistance; removal of the power of issuing a writ of *certiorari* to remove a case to a higher court; and tightly restricting the circumstances and conditions under which a prosecution could be brought against any individual for actions taken in enforcing the Act and providing that if such prosecutions failed or were thrown out by the courts then the defendant would be awarded triple costs. The bill, in short, was a systematic attempt to tip the scales decisively in favour of the forces of law and order, and against keepers of gaming house and the gamblers.

Why the bill miscarried at the very last stage – it was never for some reason signed into law – or was not reintroduced in a later session is something of a puzzle. The campaign against gaming houses continued during 1782 and beyond, scoring some successes, although these were, apparently, hard won.[133] One possibility is that the bill was deemed to confer too much power on the forces of law and order. This was certainly the reason why a bill designed to help suppress illegal lottery insurance

133 Donna Andrew has counted a dozen reports in the press between April and December 1782 of magisterial action against the gaming houses (Andrew, 'How Frail', p. 183). One of the most high-profile cases was against Dr James Graham's Temple of Health, which was raided as a gaming house in July, and several individuals were taken up as keepers of EO tables and prosecuted. Four individuals were eventually found guilty, being sentenced to a year in prison and fines of £500 each. Another successful prosecution was against three individuals for keeping an EO table at 333 Oxford Street. However, a report in the vestry minutes of St James's Parish, Westminster, makes clear that the witnesses in this case had come under sustained pressure and inducements to withdraw their evidence and not appear in court. There was also a plan to seize one of the witnesses and prevent him from appearing. Westminster City Archives, Vestry Minutes, St James's Parish, 29 Mar. 1783. Such problems may be why on some occasions magistrates appear to have been willing to release offenders on promise of good behaviour and having destroyed their gaming equipment.

was rejected by parliament in 1786.[134] The bill as originally proposed by the Middlesex justices would have given constables the power to raid gaming houses merely on suspicion rather than first getting a warrant from a magistrate. This element would appear to have been removed by amendment in the Lords.[135] The battle against gaming houses was quickly subsumed by wider campaigns respectively to combat crime at the end of the war and for the reformation of manners. In the later 1780s the targets of anti-gaming action shifted to, once more, the licensing of alehouses in 1787, and the thorny matter of lottery insurance, which was the focus of new legislation in 1786–1787.[136] The horizons of supporters of the new reformation of manners campaign were notably broad, and their tactics were focused on ensuring proper leadership from above, liaising with magistrates, informing lesser officers of the law about their duties, exemplary prosecutions, certain legislative changes, as well as supporting various other initiatives designed to uphold moral order.[137] Gaming was only one of the concerns of such individuals, and almost certainly not among the most important.

However, this was not the full story, as the 1790s would reveal. For it was in that decade that the Lord Chief Justice, Lord Kenyon, would use his position to encourage further action to suppress gaming. Before becoming Lord Chief Justice, Kenyon was a member of the Proclamation Society, formed in 1788 to implement the royal proclamation against vice issued in the same year. As was mentioned above, judges earlier in the eighteenth century, such as Lord Mansfield, had on occasion made clear their intense disapproval of gaming. But where Kenyon was different was in how far he was prepared to allow moral principle to govern his actions and decisions in court.[138] One area in which this was apparent was in cases relating to adultery, another was gambling. There were limits to how far he could go, so in 1790 he and other judges were compelled to reiterate the legality of wagers subject to

[134] See Harris, 'The 1782 Gaming Bill'.

[135] *London Chronicle*, 27 June 1782, report of Commons debate of 26 June; *Morning Herald*, 1 July 1782, letter to the Lord Chancellor.

[136] See Chapter 3, above, p. 167. See also Harris, 'The 1782 Gaming Bill'.

[137] See esp. Joanna Innes, 'Politics and Morals: The Reformation of Manners Movement in Later Eighteenth Century England', in Eckhart Hellmuth (ed.), *The Transformation of Political Culture: England and Germany in the Late Eighteenth Century* (Oxford, 1990), pp. 57–118; M. J. D. Roberts, 'The Society for the Suppression of Vice and Its Early Critics, 1802–1812', *Historical Journal*, 26 (1983), 156–76.

[138] Douglas Hay, 'Kenyon, Lloyd, first Baron Kenyon (1732–1802), ODNB [http://doi.org/10.1093/ref:odnb/15431]

the usual conditions.[139] In 1795 he presided at the Guildhall over a case heard before a special jury brought under the Gaming Act of 1710 regarding the recovery of gambling debts. In delivering his verdict for the defendant, Kenyon sought to encourage prosecutions of gaming houses.[140] This evidently led a John Shepherd, of Bloomsbury, who described himself a 'gentleman', to initiate one such prosecution in the following year. This resulted in the conviction of Thomas Miller, keeper of a gaming house located off Leicester Square, who was sentenced to a fine of £500 and imprisonment for twelve months. Shepherd, Kenyon declared in court, deserved the thanks of the public for his actions, also awarding him his costs.[141] Cases involving gaming which came before Kenyon produced verdicts which were invariably hostile to gamblers, and which sought to give further force to the law against gaming. Most famously, in May 1796 Kenyon warned that not even 'the first ladies in the land' would be immune from prosecution in his court and that they would be made to 'exhibit themselves in the pillory'. In the event, it was before Nathaniel Conant at his police office in Marlborough Street in March 1797 that the society ladies Mrs Hobart, Lady Elizabeth Luttrell, and Mrs Sturt would be convicted for hosting and playing the unlawful game of faro at Mrs Hobart's house in St James's Square, each of them being fined £50, while the banker, Henry Martindale, was fined £200.[142] From his Bow Street police office Patrick Colquhoun was orchestrating prosecutions in the same period against people running or playing games of hazard. Under the terms of the 1745 anti-gaming Act, this was proscribed, and offenders were liable to conviction on information proved by just one witness before a justice. Several appeals, however, were granted against convictions by the Middlesex bench.[143] These most likely were on grounds of insufficient evidence. But in one case, that of Henry Cooper of Market Lane, in St James's parish, the story was rather different, and highlights another problem with the reliance on informers

[139] Disney, *Laws of Gaming*, pp. 19–20, quoting Kenyon in the case of Good v Elliot, 3 T. R. 693.

[140] *GEP*, 10 Mar. 1795. Goodwin and Co v De Heine and others, 1795.

[141] TNA, Home Office Papers: Judges' Reports on Criminals, HO47/22/30, fos. 161–70: Report by Lord Kenyon on three petitions on behalf of Thomas Miller, convicted at the Court of King's Bench in Jan. 1796, for keeping a gaming house, 11 Jan. 1798.

[142] Clare Walcott, 'Mrs Hobart's Routs: Town House Hospitality in 1790s London', *Huntingdon Library Quarterly*, 77 (2014), 453–77; Gillian Russell, '"Faro's Daughters": Female Gamesters, Politics, and the Discourse of Finance in 1790s Britain', *Eighteenth-Century Studies*, 33 (2000), 481–504.

[143] LMA, Middlesex Sessions, Sessions Papers, MJ/SP/1796/06/041, appeal of Joseph Atkinson, 1796; MJ/SP/ 1797/12/004, petition of James Chowder, 1797; MJ/SP/1798/01/88, petition of James Chowder, 11. Jan. 1798; MJ/SP/1798/01/92, petition of James Duffin, Jan. 1798.

to initiate prosecutions – namely, that their motives might easily be venal or vexatious. Cooper had been convicted on information of running a game of hazard in September 1798, and had been fined £200, with goods belonging to him to that value being seized. Cooper's story was that he had been entrapped by the witnesses into permitting the game to be played on his premises, and that he had never set up a hazard table for gain. The magistrate before whom he was convicted – it is unclear whether this was Colquhoun – had also failed to set out the names of the informants on whose evidence the conviction was based. The Middlesex bench believed Cooper and his conviction was duly quashed.[144]

In denouncing gambling Kenyon echoed a growing body of opinion that was hostile to fashionable gaming and increasingly critical of the immoral behaviour of the upper ranks, opinion further sharpened by the twin menaces of the French Revolution and the growth of domestic popular radicalism. In 1792, George III issued a new proclamation against vice, and William Ashurst's charge to the Middlesex grand jury in response attacked once again the gaming house as a potent social ill, although his was mainly an attempt at deterrence through persuasion. Whether the lead given by Kenyon and several of the London magistrates in the campaign to suppress gaming had a lasting or very significant effect on the fortunes of gamblers and gaming houses in the capital seems very unlikely. One writer later noted that prior to the French Revolution there had been around half a dozen gaming houses in London, although this may well have been an underestimate, but that there were nearly fifty in 1820.[145] Colquhoun's verdict in his *A Treatise on the Police of the Metropolis* was expressed in terms merely of a 'hope' that what he termed 'this iniquitous system of plunder' had been 'somewhat restrained' through the efforts of Kenyon and the 'meritorious vigilance and attention of the Magistrates', including, of course, himself.[146] In the same work, Colquhoun emphasized the rise since the 1770s of what he characterized as a 'System' of gambling, a network of gaming houses and lottery insurance offices that criss-crossed the capital and which now constituted a 'vast Machine of destruction'. Such a powerful 'Confederacy', with its 'immense pecuniary resources' was able to defy efforts to suppress it. Colquhoun was leading a call for much greater

144 LMA, Middlesex Sessions, Sessions Papers, MJ/SP/1798/10/180, 182a-f, 191, appeal of Henry Cooper, victualler, the Cock, Market Lane, St James's Parish against his conviction for setting up a fraudulent game of hazard, Sept.-Oct. 1798.

145 *The Gaming Calendar, To Which is Added Annals of Gaming* (London, 1820).

146 *A Treatise on the Police of the Metropolis* (7th ed., London, 1806), pp. 135–6.

magisterial activism to suppress gaming, and his comments were calculatingly alarmist; but they also reflected accurately the relative impotence of the police in the face of the gamblers.

5.4 Conclusion

Reformers and magistrates scored only the odd victory, therefore, against gaming and gamblers. Most anti-gaming laws were ignored. Many of their clauses were seemingly very rarely invoked, such as the powers to demand sureties from 'sharpers' for their future behaviour under 9 Anne, c. 14., or to fine alehouse keepers allowing journeymen, apprentices, and labourers to game on their premises under 30 Geo. II, c.24.[147] Thomas Erskine, for one, was of the opinion that the best thing to do with all these laws was to repeal them, and seek other means to suppress gambling.[148] Further work is needed on patterns of prosecutions and policing action in relation to gambling in taverns, on the street, and in other open-air sites. The problem is that much of this was in the form of summary justice, for which the records are fragmentary and often provide little information about the details of the offence for which a person was incarcerated or fined. Nevertheless, it seems highly likely that such activity, as in the case of attempts to suppress metropolitan gaming houses, depended heavily on direction from above, whether this came from reformist magistrates or the state. The same pattern was very evident in relation to enforcement of the lottery laws. Without such direction there was very little incentive to undertake action, as well as some potent disincentives, not least the likelihood of attracting the hostility of the gambling fraternity. Few tavern keepers were presented to grand juries or appear to have been subject to prosecution for allowing gaming on their premises. There was repeated encouragement to metropolitan magistrates to deny licenses to alehouse keepers who permitted gaming in their establishments. In 1782, for example, Thomas Townshend, the home secretary, sent a letter, dated 22 October, to William Mainwaring as chairman of the Middlesex bench, which, amongst others thing, called for greater vigilance in the renewal of licenses to publicans who were known to allow gaming. Five years later the committee of Middlesex justices appointed by the Middlesex general sessions to make recommendations relating to licensing of public houses included the resolution that no publican who allowed gaming on their

[147] For an example of the former power being used by John Fielding and Saunders Welch in 1756 against 'nine notorious sharpers', see *Gazetteer and London Daily Advertiser*, 7 Apr. 1756.

[148] Erskine, *Reflections*, p. 11.

premises be granted a license.[149] In 1802 Westminster magistrates issued new orders in relation to alehouse licensing.[150] Doubtless such calls produced a flurry of activity in response. In November 1782 in the Finsbury division in Middlesex thirty people were seized, of whom many had been discovered gaming in alehouses. The names of the publicans where this had been happening were passed to magistrates, and the publicans were duly ordered before them to be reprimanded and compelled to give sureties for their future good behaviour. In September 1783, the St Clement Danes vestry in Westminster recommended unanimously that the Holborn magistrates refuse licenses to the Spotted Dog in the Strand and the Coach & Horses which sat opposite from it.[151] But all this was small beer, and the impression created by the extant record is that very few licenses were refused or not renewed.[152] This was despite the fact that there was mushrooming of such establishments in many parts of the capital.[153] One astute response to the recommendations made in 1787 in relation to licensing and gaming, from the officers and inhabitants of Mile End, was that the problem lay with the quality of the magistracy itself, and in particular the number of trading justices. But they also argued that to talk about the character of publicans as if this was a significant factor was wide of the mark. For it was not poor character that drove them to offer gaming, but commercial competition; publicans were competing for customers.[154] If they could recognize this reality, so could others, which was no doubt another reason why prosecutions were relatively rare. Those among the poor who persistently openly gamed

[149] LMA, Middlesex Justices, Sessions Papers, MJ/SP/1787/07/102, draft minutes concerning licensing, with reference to skittle grounds, gaming, and ‘unlawful pastimes’, July 1787.

[150] Patrick Colquhoun, *Treatise on the Function and Duties of a Constable* (London, 1803), Appendix, No. 1, pp. 79–83.

[151] *London Chronicle*, 7 Nov. 1782; Westminster City Archives, St Clement Danes Vestry Minutes, 4 Sept. 1783.

[152] See e.g. PP, 1822 (261) XXI.523, Account of the Number of Magistrates Licences for Victuallers in the Metropolis, 1817–1822. Under the Alehouse Licensing Act of 1753 (26 Geo. II, c. 31), publicans who allowed unlawful games in their houses, or disorders therein, were liable to forfeit their recognizance entered into as a precondition of gaining a license, and be disqualified from keeping an alehouse for three years. The pattern in provincial towns was almost certainly similar.

[153] PP, 1817 (233) VII. 1, Select Committee of the House of Commons on the State of Police of the Metropolis, and Execution of the Laws for Licensing of Victuallers, 9.

[154] LMA, Middlesex Justices, Sessions Papers, MJ/SP/1787/07/110B, response by officers and inhabitants of Mile End to a letter from the clerk of peace, 12 July 1787. In 1718 an alehouse keeper from Thomas Ditton in Surrey complained that his indictment for keeping nine pins in his house was ‘an angry [i.e. vexatious] prosecution by reason all ale house keepers have nine pins in our hundred’. SHC, Surrey Quarter Sessions Records, Sessions Bundles, QS2/6/1718/Mid/69.

around London, such as the runaway apprentice, Thomas Slade, who left his master, a baker in Westminster, and was taken up 'playing and betting at unlawful games', were always vulnerable to arrest and detention. Suppression of this kind of activity appears to have been intermittent, however, and its impact short term.[155]

Britain's record in relation to policing gambling was remarkably similar in many ways to that of absolutist France.[156] If anything, the French authorities showed even more concern than their British counterparts about gaming, with royal decrees prohibiting particular games of chance being issued at the rate of around one every eight years throughout the eighteenth century. As with the mid eighteenth century British anti-gaming statutes, in theory these applied to everyone; in practice the position was much more ambiguous, and it was open gaming establishments that were the real target. As in Britain, French anti-gaming law sought to draw some very fine distinctions, which only added additional layers of challenge in enforcing it. Thus, to give one example, as a game of skill, billiards was legal, as were modest stakes placed on games. Laying bets on the outcome of games, however, was not. Keepers of halls could strictly observe the law, but this almost certainly meant losing business to less scrupulous rivals. The parallel with the case of publicans with their skittle yards and so forth in Britain is unmissable. The double standards were equally, if not more, apparent across the Channel. As referred to in an earlier chapter, the French official lottery was much more of a gambler's lottery than the British one, and, unlike its British counterpart, it was the state, not private interests, that managed the sale of tickets. Nor were the French authorities any more effective than their British counterparts in suppressing illegal gambling.

In Britain, this picture of inefficacy and evasion would continue into the nineteenth century. This was despite important, but by no means complete, shifts in attitudes towards the balance to be sought between protecting the liberty of individuals and enforcing order among the lower orders, with the period 1780–1820 often in this context being viewed as an important period of change. The expansion of policing powers can, in fact, be traced back rather further, as several historians have

155 See e.g. LMA, MSJ/O/C/C/1, Middlesex Sessions, Calendar of Summary Convictions, 1774–86.

156 John Dunkley, *Gambling: A Social and Moral Problem in France, 1685–1792* (Oxford, 1985), ch. 2 'Gambling and the Law'; John Dunkley, 'Illegal Gambling in Eighteenth Century France: Incidence, Detection and Penalties', *British Journal of Eighteenth-Century Studies*, 8 (1985), 129–37.

emphasized.[157] A key moment, nevertheless, was the passage of new vagrant Acts in 1822 and 1824, which amongst other things extended the powers of arrest to an even broader range of unwanted behaviours, including street betting.[158] Magistrates were also given reinforced powers to deny or remove licenses from alehouses in which gaming took place under the Victualling Act of 1834.

Part of the reason for the underlying continuities, apart from the energetic resistance of the gambling fraternity, was the continuing contradictory nature and social selectivity of the law, that and the fact that, while there was a growing body of people who sought tighter regulation of leisure, especially that of the lower orders, many members of the propertied classes continued to enjoy gambling of various kinds. The history of unrespectability has as much claim on the attention of the historian as that of respectability, although the latter has received altogether more notice. Being respectable was all very well, but, as in the case of horse racing and its attendant entertainments, including gambling, 'unrespectability' might bring welcome custom to towns throughout Britain. The nature of the law, or how it was understood by those tasked with enforcing it, continued to pose significant problems, particularly regarding the collection of evidence.[159] As in the eighteenth century, the law could be a site of resistance to policing actions, as well as conferring new powers on its agents. Yet the main problem was the sheer dynamism of the world of gambling, driven by buoyant and widespread entrepreneurialism, frequently sponsored by members of the propertied classes, and firmly embedded within the cultures of large sections of the labouring classes. Those who argued that the only real answer was attitudinal change were, in this sense, quite right, but this, as Colquhoun for one recognized, was in truth as much a fantasy as the proposition that the bulk of the population would not continue to make their own choices about how to spend their leisure time.

[157] Rogers, 'Policing the Poor'; Paul Lawrence, 'The Vagrancy Act (1824) and the Persistence of Pre-emptive Policing in England since 1750', *British Journal of Criminology*, 57 (2017), 513–31.

[158] Rogers, 'Policing the Poor'; M. J. D. Roberts, 'Public and Private in Early Nineteenth-Century London: The Vagrant Act of 1822 and its Enforcement', *Social History*, 13 (1988), 273–94.

[159] PP, Report from the Select Committee on Gaming, 1844.

Conclusion

A big challenge in writing any history of gambling is identifying exactly what it is that we are trying to understand. The frequently made claim that eighteenth-century England was in the grip of a 'gambling fever' or 'gambling mania', whatever its superficial plausibility, begs more questions than it answers. The notion, in any case, as was argued in the Introduction to this book, is so vague and timeless that its analytical utility is close to nil. Rather than attempting to assess whether it holds up at all, the approach employed in this book has been instead to ask why opportunities to gamble increased in Britain in the long eighteenth century; how widely, both geographically and socially; how this might have changed who commonly participated in gambling; and what were the implications of these shifts for its character and meanings. It has also sought to explore different ways in which gambling, in all its various forms, was related to broad patterns of social, cultural, and economic experience.

Gambling in a Commercial Society

An underlying theme has been the role of commercialization as a key driver of the expansion and extension of gambling opportunities. This is very clearly disclosed in the case of the lottery. In the 100 years or so following its introduction in 1694, the reach of the official lottery grew to encompass much of Britain, and, indeed, further afield – to Ireland, continental Europe, across the Atlantic, and to India among servants of the East India Company – as well as to nearly all sections of British society. By the early nineteenth century remote parts of rural society, including the Scottish Highlands, as well as most of urban Britain, had fallen under its spell. Lottery derivatives – 'chances', lottery insurance and 'Little Goes' (unofficial, illegal lotteries) – pushed lottery adventuring much further down into and across the metropolitan population, which by 1801 had climbed to around 900,000. It is not too much of a stretch to see the legal and illegal lottery businesses of later Georgian Britain as foreshadowing the large-scale commercial gambling enterprises of the later nineteenth- and early twentieth centuries. Their existence and operations underline how conditions developed in Britain after 1700 to support fairly sophisticated, highly organized gambling businesses which achieved something akin to a mass market in London and its immediate environs, spreading out from there to the rest of Britain. In France the state operated the royal lottery; in Britain – apart from the lottery draw, which was the responsibility of the Lottery Office, nominally overseen by the government-appointed lottery commissioners – the role fell to private commercial interests and businesses. The lottery offers a powerful case study in entrepreneurial ingenuity, increasingly efficient methods of transacting business, and exuberant salesmanship, but also the possibilities for making new markets created by a series of far-reaching, interlinked contemporary transformations to communications – to transport (the creation of new roads, multiplying carrier and coach services), postal services (cross posts, more extensive and regular posts, including six-day posts, penny posts, and from the 1780s the more rapid conveyance of newspapers and letters through the advent of mail coach services), and the unceasingly pro-generative worlds of print and newspaper publication.

Similar sorts of influence are readily discernable in the rise and development of several major, increasingly national sports after c. 1730 – notably, horse racing and cricket, but also, albeit to a lesser degree and following a somewhat different chronological trajectory, boxing (or pugilism, as it was more commonly known) and its near relation, pedestrianism. Here, however, the role of commercialization was combined with that of patronage from the landed and, to a lesser extent, urban elites. Each and all of these sports were very closely linked to heavy, often highly public betting or wagers normally engaged in by members of the fashionable elites and titled nobility, as well as widespread side betting amongst a much broader cross section of society. At the same time, they stimulated greater sophistication and variety in betting practices, although this can only be occasionally glimpsed in the historical record – for example, ante-post betting associated with the introduction of races for yearlings, such as the Derby and the Oaks, or betting on different aspects of cricketing contests staged at the Artillery Ground in London, such as which player would score the highest number of notches (i.e. runs). There also emerged a growing class of people whom we might label professional gamblers, individuals such as in the early nineteenth century William Scrope Davies, member of the metropolitan 'Dandy' set and associate of Lord Byron's.[1] For such people the main point of gambling, pretty much the only point, was money. The popularity of sports and sporting celebrities burgeoned from the 1790s, aided powerfully by the rise of a sporting press. Primed, however, by an expanding newspaper press and the canny publicity strategies of organizers of sporting contests, keen and widespread interest in these things was apparent earlier. In 1741 Ralph Verney (later 2nd Earl Verney) informed his father, Lord Fermanagh: 'There was near six thousand people at the great cricket match yesterday.' 'These matches', he lamented, echoing a view of popular leisure expressed ever more sharply by the mid eighteenth century, 'will be as pernicious to Poor People as Horse Races, for the contagion spreads.'[2] Eight years later, Josiah Tucker, the dean of Gloucester and writer on political economy, lamented the time spent in England 'by all sorts of manufacturers' – by whom he meant artisans and workers in manufacturing – at horse races, cockfights, and cricket matches, as well as bull baiting and electioneering.[3]

Taking a still broader perspective, a further major contributory factor to increasing opportunities to gamble, for people of all social ranks, was urbanization – defined both quantitatively (as the growing proportion of the population in towns) and qualitatively (in terms of the development of more mature, complex, and pluralistic societies and economies). Towns were crucibles of increasing social fluidity – multiple, overlapping social identities, and intensified competition for social status. They helped to foster new patterns and habits of consumption and leisure, while at the same time perpetuating, multiplying, and subtly transforming older ones as rural habits took root in urban settings. Larger, increasingly diverse, youthful and mobile urban populations resisted social control, whether from the elites, secular authorities, or the churches, mostly defying or simply ignoring the battery of laws which sought to constrain or suppress gambling, especially that of the lower orders. These patterns were – unsurprisingly given its gigantism, concentrations as well as diffusion of wealth, the diversity of its population, and its commercial leisure culture of unexampled vitality and breadth – most clearly evident in the capital. As it expanded relentlessly, both in terms of its

[1] For Scrope Davies and his gambling, see Phyllis Daine Deutsch, 'Fortune and Chance: Aristocratic gaming and England society 1760–1837', unpublished Ph.D. thesis, University of New York (1991), pp. 134–53.

[2] M. Verney (ed.), *The Verney Letters of the Eighteenth Century from the MSS at Claydon House*, 2 vols. (London, 1930), ii, p. 189: Ralph Verney to his father, 27 Aug. 1741.

[3] Josiah Tucker, *An Essay on the Advantages and Disadvantages which Respectively Attend France and Great Britain with regard to Trade* (London, 1749), p. 39.

geographical extent and population, London in the eighteenth century became only more disaggregated as a city, a dynamic, shifting jumble of different communities (loosely and variously defined) with their own distinctive temporal rhythms, habits, and patterns of interaction and mobility. Gambling was well rooted in many of these, flourishing in city coffee houses, Westminster taverns and gaming houses, and the many open spaces spread across the capital and its environs, while streets, courts, and alleys across the capital were home to legal and illegal lottery offices. Even the capital's prison yards were notable sites of gambling of diverse kinds.[4] If eighteenth-century London was, in the words of one historian, a 'gambler's paradise', this was not simply because it was home to fashionable elite gaming clubs.[5]

Urban growth and revival in this period were not uniform processes, either in respect of chronology or the resulting social and cultural configurations; and deep-rooted religious and cultural traditions left their heavy imprint. With the partial exception of Edinburgh, Scottish towns appear to have seen less and less intensive gambling than many places south of the border – a product of a combination of significantly lower incomes among the bulk of the population, a less mature economic base before c. 1760, and the influence of Presbyterian Calvinism in the west and central lowlands. The fragmentary record in this context is almost certainly a partial guide; silence is not the same thing as absence. Much gambling in Scotland and throughout Britain in this period occurred in the crepuscular light of the tavern, or elicited little contemporary comment. Specialization of towns, in respect of function and their economic base, was an important feature of urban development throughout Britain in this period.[6] High stakes and elite gambling were strongly associated with certain spa towns – pre-eminently Bath, which grew very rapidly on the back of its role in attracting the elites and those who aspired to fashionable living. Yet, most towns, large and small, irrespective of their leading characteristics, had their sites of fashionable recreation as well as popular license and unrespectability, the latter more or less well hidden in the shadows.

[4] Joanna Innes, 'The King's Bench prison in the later eighteenth century: law, authority, and order in a London debtors' prison', in Joanna Innes (ed.), *Inferior Politics: Social Problems and Social Policies in Eighteenth-Century Britain* (Oxford, 2009), pp. 251, 257–8

[5] Jane Carson, *Colonial Virginians at Play* (Williamsburg, PA, 1989), p. 19.

[6] P. J. Corfield, 'Business Leaders and Town Gentry in Eighteenth-Century Britain: Specialist Occupations and Shared Urbanism', *Urban History*, 39 (2012), 10–50.

As urban communities prospered and grew, inns, taverns, alehouses, and other drinking establishments increased in number, dramatically in some places in the early eighteenth century.[7] Many of these provided spaces and facilities for games of different kinds – bowling, billiard tables, and so forth – which patrons played for financial stakes or on which they made bets. Definite hierarchies of tone, ambition, and service existed among the proliferating drinking establishments; and at the apex were inns or taverns boasting large numbers of rooms, which often included a ballroom or large meeting space.[8] Yet, gambling attracted genteel, middling, and 'low' alike throughout the Georgian era. We saw in Chapter 2 that in the cricketing heartlands of England – Kent, Surrey, Sussex, and Hampshire, and also London – various taverns were linked to cricket grounds. In 1787 Hampshire magistrates ordered the suppression of seven Winchester drinking establishments for being 'gaming houses'. An anonymous letter written by a townswoman to the town's mayor in September 1787 complained bitterly about several of these:

> A Gaming House the Angel was and how my Children and Self was brought to the greatest distress and in want of bread by my Husbands being allways at that House and the Duke of York at Skittle Missipey [i.e. missisippi] or marvels and more porr Honest wifes and Children as my Neighbours are in the same distresst Condition by our Husbands consorting to the Angel and Duke of York who have three sorts of Games to intice our Poor unguarded Husbands to spend their time and money the Wheatsheaf and Coach and Horses are also the same gameing House marvels and Shuffel Board tables ...'[9]

In 1804, the mayor of the dockyard town of Plymouth received several anonymous letters denouncing the prevalence of billiard tables in the town. Many tradesmen might, or so the author of one of these letters declared, have 'realised a ... competence had it not been for frequenting these tables'. In response, the council issued a printed proclamation against allowing gambling with billiard tables, cards, dice, draughts, and shuffle boards in private and public houses, under the threat of fines

[7] There were, however, widespread efforts in England to tighten alehouse licensing in the 1780s. For which, see Peter Clark, *The English Alehouse: A Social History 1200–1830* (London, 1983), pp. 254–60; S. Webb and B. Webb, *The History of Liquor Licensing in England* (London, 1903), pp. 58–9.

[8] Clark, *The English Alehouse*; Bob Harris, 'Buildings, Associations, and Culture in the Scottish Provincial Town, c.1700–1830', in Mark Wallace and Jane Rendall (eds.), *Association and Enlightenment: Scottish Clubs and Societies, 1700–1830* (Lewisburg, PA, 2021), pp. 49–66.

[9] HRO, W/D3/324/3, anonymous letter to the mayor, Sept. 1787; 7, abstract of houses ordered by the magistrates to be suppressed, 25 Sept. 1787.

and other penalties.[10] In the mid eighteenth century, cabinet maker Thomas Allen kept a gaming table at one of his local inns in Bridlington on the Yorkshire coast.[11]

Tavern gaming was not new, boasting a long and colourful history.[12] Taverns had, to take just one example, commonly staged cockfights from at least the sixteenth century. This link remained a very strong one two centuries later. If anything, the connection strengthened in the early eighteenth century as cockfights were staged to coincide with proliferating race meetings, and the gentry became a regular presence in county and other towns. While often dependent on gentry patronage as breeders and owners of birds, cockfighting was another highly commercialized business, flourishing in towns regularly visited by gentry – for example, York or Beverley – but also in the increasingly populous and rapidly growing manufacturing towns, places such as Leeds and Halifax. Publicans played a crucial role in the staging of the majority of matches or 'mains' as they were termed, organizing publicity, and providing facilities – cockpens for the weighing and inspection of birds, and cockpits where the fighting actually took place with raked seating for paying spectators.[13] Competition between inns and taverns reinforced pressures on publicans to make provision for or allow gambling on their premises, one of the main reasons why, as mentioned in Chapter 5, sporadic attempts to clamp down on those where gaming took place had strictly limited impact.

The Changing Character of Gambling

Whether such developments, singly or in combination, changed the character as opposed to amount of gambling is harder to say. For some it may have – the 'problem gambler', to borrow an anachronistic term, was a product of metropolitan life and its intensive chronicling in the eighteenth century. Another who became much more visible was the 'sharper', who preyed on the unwary and gullible in inns and taverns, bowling greens, tennis courts, and billiard tables, or, at a lower level, in games played on streets and in parks

10 Plymouth and West Devon Record Office, Plymouth Borough Records, 1/680/33–35.

11 East Riding of Yorkshire Archives and Records Service, East Riding Quarter Sessions Records, QSF/171/B/6, 171/C/18–23, 171/D/7, files relating to a case against Thomas Allen of Bridlington, cabinet maker, for keeping a 'Roulet engine or Gaming Table called or known by the name of Odd and Even', 1750.

12 For one example, involving a vicar who lost his money gaming at cards and dice in Nottingham taverns in the sixteenth century, see Cameron Louis, 'The Wayward Vicar of Woollaton', *Transactions of the Thoroton Society*, 93–4 (1989–90), 29–33.

13 Iris M. Middleton, 'Cockfighting in Yorkshire during the Early Eighteenth Century', *Northern History*, 11 (2003), 129–46.

and other open spaces, although the term is probably better thought of as connoting an activity as opposed to identity or quasi-occupation.[14] They formed part of a distinctive metropolitan 'economy of make-shifts', which enfolded a highly mobile, rootless section of London's urban poor. Sharpers also hunted their prey in places far beyond the capital, including at fairs and race meetings, as well as in taverns.

One aspect that did see significant change was the participation of women. Insofar as historians have shown interest in this to date it has mainly been in respect of 'Gambling Ladies of Quality', such as Georgiana, Duchess of Devonshire.[15] There may have been more of this going on than we generally recognize. In 1765, the *London Evening Post* reported that the wife of a 'very eminent merchant' had lost notes and jewels to the value of £3,000 at a recent 'rout'.[16] Eleven years later, another London newspaper observed:

> Commerce is now the polite round game, and played to a higher pitch of gambling among the women than ever loo was. A new married countess lately lost twelve hundred pounds at one sitting; and a young lady of quality begins so much before her time, that she lost 500 the same night.[17]

Card playing at court and in court circles in the first half of the eighteenth century, in which women were very active participants, was, with the exception of the brief period between Christmas and Epiphany, probably mostly for relatively small sums.[18] Women in such circles did not just play cards, but dice games, such as hazard, and at ninepins and bowling.[19] Lady Anne Cust, who was a resident in Somerset, she and her husband having shut up their London house in Arlington Street as an economizing measure, continued in her new abode to play cards, subscribe to horse races, as well as on one occasion engaging in a wager with her sister-in-law for £1.1.6.[20] As emphasized in Chapter 1, elite women, who typically had income or funds which they controlled – whether it be

[14] See e.g. *A Brief Description of the Cities of London and Westminster* (London, 1776), pp. xxvi–xxvii.

[15] For the Duchess of Devonshire and her gambling, see esp. Deutsch, 'Fortune and Chance', ch. 2 'Dame Fortune's Decline: The Life and Times of Georgiana, Fifth Duchess of Devonshire'. The phrase 'Gambling Ladies of Quality' comes from the *GEP*, 22 May 1790.

[16] *LEP*, 16 Apr. 1775.

[17] *Morning Post*, 20 Mar. 1776.

[18] See Verney (ed.), *The Verney Letters*, i, pp. 16–17: Margaret Adams to Lord Fermanagh, 9 Oct. 1714, where the letter writer reports, 'I beg you'll tell Lady Fermanagh that if she pleases to come to town she may play at Court for a small sum.'

[19] See e.g. LA, Brownlow Papers, BNLW 4/6/18, account book of Eleanor, Viscountess Tyrconnel, 1715–19, which includes entries for ninepins, four doz. pearl counters, two pair of dice and a box, and losses, of several pounds, at cards and hazard.

[20] LA, BNLW 4/6/20/1, account book of Lady Anne Cust, 1715–19.

by virtue of payment of an annuity settled on them or some other source or, in the case of married women, a sum regularly given to them by their husbands – commonly frequented the gaming tables of Bath and other spas and resorts. Less clear is whether this was normally in mixed company, although gaming and card playing were activities which frequently drew men and women together socially. In the 1690s, when the men at court decamped to Newmarket for the races, the women remained in London. Lady Hervey, who took a very keen interest in her husband, John, Lord Hervey, 1st Earl of Bristol's matches and gambling – indeed, the impression gained from their regular correspondence is that their gambling was a shared enterprise – informed him on 9 April 1698: 'I have defered [sic] writing all day in hopes of a letter, and am now come to Lady Orkneys, where my Lady Jersey is, & they will not let me leave omber [ombre – a card game] any longer than just to keep to my old custom of writing every post ....' Usually through her husband Lady Hervey wagered quite significant sums of her own money on the Newmarket races in which his horses competed, before that is, like her husband, she brought this to an abrupt stop.[21]

However, in respect of social and geographical extent, and the number involved, much more important in enticing women to 'hazard their fortunes' were the official lottery and its various derivatives. The Queen Anne lotteries, as was shown in Chapter 4, encouraged greater involvement of women of diverse social backgrounds in the emergent financial markets of the early eighteenth century. Many of them were widows and spinsters, as were regular lottery adventurers in the mid eighteenth century, such as the spinster Gertrude Savile discussed in Chapter 4. It can be questioned whether these lottery women were really gambling, at least before 1769, since before that date tickets which drew blanks produced a return, albeit of lower value than what was paid for the ticket, and could be and regularly were sold to help defray any losses. They might rather be seen as shrewd, even prudent investors. Yet, the lottery's appeal was never simply a product of financial calculus, a weighing up of the chances of winning a prize against potential short-term losses; this would be to vastly underestimate the lure of the main capital prizes, the tantalizing thought that good fortune might be yours, and the 'lottery dreams' which were thereby stimulated. As Lady Mary Wortley Montagu informed one of her female correspondents: 'I have just now receiv'd ye Numbers of the Great Lottery which is drawing. I find my selfe (as yet)

[21] *The Diary of John Hervey, First Earl of Bristol, 1680–1742* (Wells, 1894), esp. pp. 127, 253–4, 277. See also ch. 1, pp. 42–3.

among the unlucky but *Thank God the great prize is not come out & there is room for hopes still*' (my emphasis).[22] There continued to be very large numbers of female lottery adventurers after 1769 when the lottery became a winner-take-all affair. Among the propertied classes, married women commonly had tickets purchased on their behalf by their husbands, or tickets or shares thereof were purchased in their joint names. However, the fact that tickets were often bought in the women's own names seems significant in this context. In 1791, for example, Hampshire gentleman, Thomas Hall, bought a half share of a ticket, while his wife purchased four sixteenths in her own name.[23] In 1774 a Mrs Gentle, the wife of a Newcastle brewer, was winner of an eighth of the main £20,000 prize in that year's lottery.[24] Occasionally we discern these women's independent involvement quite clearly. Thomas Turner, the Sussex shopkeeper, engaged in a lottery adventure in 1757 in the so-called Guinea Lottery, which, unusually before 1769, was a simple gamble on winning a cash prize. While his purchase of a share of a ticket was in collaboration with another person, this was not his wife, but instead his brother. His wife had her own separate adventure in combination with Mrs Hannah Atkins, a local widow.[25] Turner and his first wife famously did not get on, but plenty of examples exist of female kin and other networks being used to purchase lottery tickets, as we saw in Chapters 3 and 4. Women from the lower orders, including female domestic servants, were eager purchasers of lottery insurance and adventurers in the Little Goes which flourished in the capital from the late eighteenth century, after 1802 in flagrant defiance of the law. Lady Ongley's housekeeper was in 1777 fortunate to be acquitted of forgery of a receipt for payment of a bill from a tallow chandler, having used the money to engage in lottery insurance gambles.[26] (She was only acquitted on the grounds of previous good character and the relatively small sum involved.) Married women who wrecked the tranquility and economic well-being of the households of their industrious husbands were stock figures in criticism of the negative impact of the lottery – echoing anti-Methodist writings of the mid eighteenth century, albeit excessive piety was definitely not the issue in this case – while the fascination for the lottery among women of all social ranks was a source of frequent

[22] University of Nottingham, Manuscripts and Special Collections, Newcastle (Clumber) Collection, Ne C 15276, microform copy of a letter from Lady Wortley Montagu to Mrs Anne Justice, n.d. but post-1700.

[23] HRO, 44M69/F14/1/34, J. Pinnock to Thomas Hall Esq., 13 Nov. 1791.

[24] *Public Ledger*, 28 Dec. 1774.

[25] *The Diary of Thomas Turner 1754–1765*, ed. David Vaisey (Oxford, 1985), pp. 115, 116.

[26] *Morning Post*, 21 Feb. 1777.

comment. Female servants were among the winners of the largest capital prizes, such as the 'cook maid' who scooped a £10,000 prize in one of two cash lotteries staged in 1719.[27]

Shrill voices can be found throughout the eighteenth century denouncing the 'rage for gaming' and the havoc wreaked thereby on individual lives and society. Such voices were often those of people in London scrutinizing the unique society arrayed before them, with its capacity to bedazzle and perturb by turn, or they were those of the consciously conservative. Their responses were conditioned by a series of interconnected anxieties – about crime, social and political stability, the condition and quality of political leadership, and the wider moral health of the population. It is no accident that some of the most detailed contemporary comment on gaming comes from the pens of magistrates and other officials tasked with responsibility for policing London's turbulent, disputatious, uncomplying population. Much gaming was highly and, to its critics, troublingly visible. This, in turn, owed much to the burgeoning print media – newspapers, periodicals, novels, and a torrent of printed ephemera. An aspect of the lotteries in the early nineteenth century which attracted sharp criticism was the brazen publicity tactics of the lottery contractors and lottery offices, which were both visual and aural, and which had become an intrusive, clamorous presence, particularly (although not exclusively) in the metropolis. A reporter for the *Times*, John Tyas's first-hand description of Manchester on the eve of the notorious Peterloo massacre (16 August 1819) noted the many lottery handbills conspicuously posted on the city's buildings.[28]

Yet, 'gaming' was a more elusive, less easily definable target than its critics were willing to acknowledge. Its boundaries were not at all self-evident. What was 'gaming' and what was something other, simple recreation, for example, or reasonable pursuit of profit in financial or other markets, to a very significant degree lay – and still does – in the eyes of the beholder. As one of the witnesses before the 1844 parliamentary select committee on gaming observed:

> A wager may be a harmless thing in itself. It is the abuse of it which constitutes the evil. That which may be a matter of amusement with some, may, if it is carried to a great extent, become a matter of great imprudence, and may be a moral wrong to his family.

'Imprudence or the vice', they shrewdly continued, 'depends on a man's circumstances.'[29] What ultimately separated innocent recreation from

[27] *Diary of John Hervey*, p. 570.
[28] Robert Poole, *Peterloo: The English Uprising* (Oxford, 2019), p. 260.
[29] PP, 1844 (297), Report from the Select Committee on Gaming, Minutes of Evidence, pp. 2–3.

destructive gaming was the element of motivation or, as it was also on occasion expressed, 'character'. And therein lay the problem for many people. James Beattie, the Scottish 'common sense' philosopher, grimly warned: 'Persons who take pleasure in play seldom fail to become immoderately attached to it.'[30] The worlds of gaming and of Exchange Alley overlapped in various ways. At different moments 'gaming' on stocks attracted sharply adverse comment. In the 1760s and early 1770s (before the passage of Lord North's Regulating Act (1773)), this more often than not was focused on the only too evident manipulation of and speculation in East India stock, although such trading could be as much politically as narrowly financially motivated.[31] The Ayr Bank crisis of 1772 had its origins in complicated time bargains on £1.5 million worth of East India stock entered into by Alexander Fordyce of the Ayr Bank. In the immediate aftermath of the bank's collapse, which triggered a wider financial panic, detonating shock waves through the economy, the *Middlesex Journal* called for the 'total suppression of all the gambling in "Change-alley"'.[32] Fordyce was denounced as a Scot – anti-Scottish prejudice never lurked very far from the surface of much metropolitan opinion – but more pertinently a 'gamester', a 'prodigal upstart' whose personal ambition and pursuit of quick profit had led to disaster. One response was another attempt at rendering effective a prohibition on stockjobbing – meaning in this context options trading – initially imposed by parliament in 1734 under the terms of Barnard's Act, so called after its main author, the long-standing City of London MP Sir John Barnard.[33] Legislators periodically tried at least to create greater distance between finance and gambling in the case, for example, of the burgeoning insurance industry through important Acts passed in 1746 and 1774 pertaining to, respectively, marine and life insurance. The direction of travel in this respect, such as it existed, was hardly one way, and, as we saw in the case of the lottery market in Chapter 3, speculative trading of various kinds contributed significantly to supporting the profitability and success of lotteries, which is why ministers steered clear of intervention. In the early nineteenth century, this even included trades in so-called produces, essentially bets on the differences between the prices of lottery tickets as

[30] James Beattie, *Elements of Moral Science*, 2 vols. (Edinburgh, 1790), i, p. 352.

[31] Huw V. Bowen, 'Lord Clive and Speculation in East India Company Stock, 1766', *Historical Journal*, 30 (1987), 905–20; L. S. Sutherland and J. A. Woods, 'The East India Speculations of William Burke', *Proceedings of the Leeds Philosophical and Literary Society*, 11 (1964), 188–92; Lucy Sutherland and J. Binney, 'Henry Fox as Paymaster General of Forces', *Economic History Review*, 70 (1955), 229–57.

[32] *Middlesex Journal*, 13 June 1772.

[33] P. Kosmetatos, *The 1772–73 British Credit Crisis* (Basingstoke, 2018).

fixed by lottery contracts and their final price on the eve of the draw.[34] Options trading continued despite legislative prohibition, and it is not at all clear that the so-called Gambling Act (1774), which prohibited gambling life insurance policies – in other words, those taken out on the life of a third party in whom you had no interest – eliminated policy gambling by city brokers, an activity which merits deeper investigation.[35] The late eighteenth century saw a proliferation of large-scale commercial tontine schemes in which investors were basically betting on their own or their nominees' longevity. Pitt the Younger launched an official tontine loan in 1789. This was unsuccessful, but at least one contemporary was insistent that the basic idea behind it had been sound; the weakness in 1789 was the scheme, in which only the interest rather than capital *and* interest was transferred to survivors. The principle of relying on the propensity of people to 'hazard their fortunes' to entice lending to the state by the public was entirely sound, and might readily encourage it from across the social spectrum, or so they argued.[36]

In seeking to distinguish commerce and gaming much depended on how one defined an acceptable risk, and, indeed, how far you were prepared to acknowledge that economic progress relied on people being prepared to speculate in pursuit of profit and gain. One newspaper lamented in 1790:

> The same principle that operate in the West end of the town in producing gambling by cards, dice &c operates in the City by speculators in trade – All is resolved into gambling, and men in trade are no longer satisfied with slow, sure, and equal profits. They must be *men of fortune* by what they call *hits*.[37]

Great efforts were spent seeking to inculcate habits of industry and propriety among the commercial classes in this period. Yet, what was dangerous speculation and what commercially prudent behaviour were (and are) very difficult to pin down, other than that this depends on perspective and inherently tricky judgements about risks and the ability to mitigate these in various ways. Contemporary anxieties in this context may have only been added to by the fact that a great many people were, contrary to the claims of Jerrold Seigel, not ready to view economic

[34] TNA, T64/324, Mr Wood, 'On Produces of Lotteries', 31 May 1811.

[35] In the meantime, see G. Clark, *Betting on Lives: The Culture of Life Insurance in England, 1695–1775* (Manchester, 1988).

[36] University of Nottingham, Manuscripts and Special Collections, Portland Papers, Pl C 36/9/3, Observations upon a Plan of Finance by Thomas Cleghoun, Old Hall Green, Puckeridge, Herts, 3 Feb. 1798.

[37] *Gazetteer*, 4 Sept. 1790.

activity in terms of its own logic.[38] As Keith Thomas notes, while liberal economic thought may have made inroads into people's thinking and outlooks in the eighteenth century, this was 'repeatedly challenged' by different traditions.[39] Insistence on the strict moral probity, scrupulous religious beliefs, and philanthropic generosity of the mercantile classes was one indicator of the very considerable influence of the latter. Another was the persistent and persistently intense preoccupation with the concept of luxury and its supposedly deleterious effects. Even David Hume, who did much to provide a set of ideas which embraced materialism or 'plenitude' as it was termed – a task taken up by his friend and fellow Scot Adam Smith in *The Wealth of Nations* (1776) – acknowledged that luxuries could be divided into those which were harmless, which created greater amenity as well as wealth in society, and others which were vicious or destructive.[40] Forestalling in food markets – holding back supply from local markets or buying up local supplies to send to distant markets where prices were higher – was condemned in periods of short supply and climbing prices as an illegitimate form of speculation. This, it is true, was from the later eighteenth century increasingly challenged by defenders of 'free markets' as the best means to avoid shortages, but most people appear to have remained at best ambivalent on this point.[41] The proximity of gaming and some commercial markets, moreover, seemed all too apparent, even if little understood by those viewing them from the outside. One was the hop market, which seems to have been unusually prone to manipulative practices involving forward selling and monopolizing of supply, but also where many hop producers in the third quarter of the eighteenth century appear customarily to have bet on the annual produce of hop duties.[42]

[38] Jerrold Seigel, *Modernity and Bourgeois Life: Society, Politics and Culture in England, France, and Germany since 1750* (Cambridge, 2012), p. 46.

[39] Keith Thomas, *The Ends of Life: Roads to Fulfilment in Early Modern England* (pbk ed., Oxford, 2010), p. 145.

[40] James A. Harris, *Hume: An Intellectual Biography* (Cambridge, 2015), pp. 271–2.

[41] The literature on food markets and food protests is extensive, but a theme which emerges in some more recent scholarship is the degree to which the middling sort supported intervention to alleviate hardship of local populations, and also showed hostility to merchants and farmers who put profit above this imperative. See e.g. Adrian Randall and Andrew Charlesworth (eds.), *Moral Economy and Popular Protest: Crowds, Conflict and Authority* (Basingstoke, 2000); John Bohstedt, *The Politics of Provisions: Food Riots, Moral Economy and Market Transition in England, c.1550–1850* (Farnham, 2010).

[42] The banker, Alexander Fordyce, was involved in speculations in the hop market when his activities blew up in his face. The Mr Waddington who was found guilty of forestalling under common law by Lord Kenyon in the King's Bench in 1800 was a hop merchant. On which see Douglas Hay, 'The State and the Market in 1800: Lord Kenyon and Mr Waddington', *Past & Present*, 162 (1999), 101–62. On 8 Sept. 1778 the

The lottery signally exposed many of the contradictions, evasions, and flagrant double standards in contemporary views. Participation by the propertied in the lottery might be foolish, but was not destructive and ruinous like the adventuring of the lower orders. This relied on a negative, highly patronizing view of the capacity for reasoned judgement among the 'poor'. Lotteries brought in much-needed revenue, directly and indirectly, priming the system of public borrowing which underwrote the expansion of British power overseas and defence of trade and other strategic interests. Lottery adventuring could thus be viewed as a patriotic act; but to others it was a dangerously destructive form of gaming – to individuals, families, as well as the economy and society more broadly.

Gambling for high stakes, as outlined in Chapter 1, occurred throughout the whole period. It was already well entrenched in fashionable society by the later seventeenth century, although it may have reached a climacteric in the final third of the eighteenth century. Gambling of this kind has been identified by some historians as an important aspect of an 'aristocratic ethos', even as being crucial to its perpetuation.[43] This is linked to its being governed by the 'laws of honour', rather than the 'laws of the land'. Honour was the proper code of the gentleman. Yet, while 'deep play' was often characterized by social exclusivity – as in the subscription gaming clubs which operated blackballing systems of membership – this was often more apparent than real.[44] In truth, as with so much in Britain in this period, it was money ultimately that gained admission to this world. Gambling, in fact, threatened as much as shored up the exclusivity of an aristocratic elite, promoting what many viewed as an uncomfortable propinquity between the elites, people of very different social rank, and flagrant adventurers, as well as professional gamblers. Social rank remained a potent currency throughout this period, and there was a great deal of snobbery. Indeed, one historian has gone so far as to suggest that 'codes of deference and condescension ... sustained

Morning Post reported on the 'spirit of gaming' among the hop planters of Kent, Worcestershire, and Essex, declaring that 'no less than £50,000 was depending on wagers that the duty on the article this year will not amount to £100,000'. The figure was almost certainly exaggerated, but not the propensity of hop planters to lay bets on the amount raised by a particular year's hop duty or, indeed, much else. For which, see Hampshire Record Office, 12M98, Froyle hop duty betting books, 1798–1858. See also the series of letters published in the *Public Advertiser* under the pseudonym 'Civis' in 1773–4 on the speculative practices of hop merchants (*PA*, 16 Sept., 2 Oct., 20 Oct. 1773; 19 Jan., 5 Feb., 4 Mar. 1774).

43 See esp. J. C. D. Clark, *English Society 1688–1832: Ideology, Social Structure, and Political Practice during the Ancien Regime* (Cambridge, 1985), pp. 107–8.

44 Valérie Capdeville, *L'Âge d'Or des Clubs Londoniens 1730–1784* (Paris, 2008).

oligarchy in its most ruthless form'.[45] There was, it is true, often a very fine balance in Britain in this period between openness and the power of rank. This does not detract, however, from the deeper reality of a society in which social status, certainly below the level of the titled nobility, could be bought. Gambling might not immediately imperil the social status of nobleman or woman, but it could threaten to subsume the former within a wider, less comfortable identity, that of 'man of the world', where what really mattered was money and appearance, not rank *per se*.

Attitudes towards gaming *within* the landed elites were also more ambivalent, downright contradictory, and polarized than is often supposed. Recall here Lord Hervey, referred to above in connection with his wife: Hervey recorded a detailed critique of gambling in his diary, despite the fact that he adventured deeply in the lottery and was a prominent member of the Newmarket set of Queen Anne's reign. Gaming among the landed elites was commonly identified as a vice to which the young were especially prone. How far 'deep play' was engaged in at the English universities in the eighteenth century is unclear given our current knowledge of social life among the contemporary student body at Oxford and Cambridge.[46] The answer may well be not much, if we are to credit a letter written by the dean of Christ Church, Oxford, Cyril Jackson, to the Duke of Portland in 1786 regarding his son, the Marquis of Titchfield.[47] Titchfield had been the 'chief promoter' of a faro table which had been the constant occupation of a group of students during the previous two terms. It was, significantly, not only the scions of aristocratic families involved.[48] Jackson was confident that the source of Titchfield's behaviour was not Oxford but London and the 'habits & connections' he had developed there. Second, the occurrence needed to be put in its proper context. 'The love of company & I fear the love of cards have been too powerful for us to struggle against as we c.d have wished,' wrote Jackson.

45 Leslie Mitchell, *The Whig World 1760–1837* (London and New York, 2005), p. 17.

46 For the argument that the conduct of many students in Oxford in the eighteenth century was inspired by the metropolitan London fop, see Heather Ellis, 'Foppish Masculity, Generational Identity and the University Authorities in Eighteenth-Century Oxbridge', *Cultural and Social History*, 11 (2014), 367–84.

47 That said, Charles James Fox quickly lost something more than 80 guineas at gaming when he went up to Oxford, as he acknowledged to his father. BL, Add MS 51422, fos. 224–5, Charles James Fox to Lord Holland, n.d.. I owe this reference to Geraldine Porter.

48 University of Nottingham, Manuscripts and Special Collections, Portland Collection, Pl C 5012, Cyril Jackson, Christ Church, to the Duke of Portland, 16 July 1786, where Jackson informs the duke that he would have followed the normal regulations of the university 'Had the party consisted only of men in the same rank of life with Lord T. ... But there were others to whom it w.d have been ruin.'

Nevertheless, he continued: 'Y.r Grace will however understand me, as not meaning to say, that there has been any thing w.ch c.d be calld play before these two last terms – & even then it has not been high play – so much I believe I can say with certainty.'[49] Whether Jackson's assurance was securely founded is impossible to say at this distance, although it would hardly be the first or last of these to be based on partial knowledge.

That London and the snares of fashionable society were, nevertheless, the main problem was probably correct. James Harris, later Lord Malmesbury, reflecting back on his days at Merton College, Oxford, in the mid-1760s, remarked: 'The set of men I lived with were very pleasant but very idle fellows. Our life was an imitation of high life in London.'[50] Steering young men from the elites, perhaps especially younger sons, whose incomes and prospects quite often did not match their social expectations, clear of the hazards presented by the 'ways of London' and other similar environments was always challenging as they emerged into manhood.[51] The Gambling Act of 1710 was testimony to the fears of a Tory-dominated parliament about one such hazard – sharpers who frequented the taverns and gaming houses of the British capital on the prowl for likely victims among callow, young heirs of landed families. The grand tour presented another set of potential entrapments, although sex and sexually transmitted diseases were probably the more common. Conceptions of honour were at the same time subject to diverse interpretation. They attached not just to the individual but family. Prudence, as noted above, was relative, and could only be properly measured in light of the obligations of rank and wealth. The 3rd Duke of Atholl, whose expenditure on his estate and properties, forced on his successor a programme of financial retrenchment was not personally extravagant. Prudence was no less a social imperative for many among the landed elites than for the middling sort, and this meant eschewing feckless behaviour such as gambling away one's fortune and risking the reputation of family and its financial stability. Gambling as a consequence could easily divide landed families along generational lines, or, indeed, within the same generation, as in the case, explored in Chapter 1, of the Murrays of Atholl, one of eighteenth-century Scotland's leading magnate families.

None of this is to say that gambling was uncommon among the landed classes in this period. It was, however, not generally of a kind or on a

[49] Op. cit.. [50] Quoted in Ellis, 'Foppish Masculinity', 373.

[51] The phrase 'ways of London' was used by John Davidson in a letter regarding the young Duke of Hamilton to his mother, the duchess, written from Edinburgh, 7 Nov. 1776, NLS, Stuart Stevenson papers, MS 8262, fos. 259–60.

scale seen in the exclusive gambling clubs of the capital. Sir Brownlow Cust had an annual income in the early 1790s of around £9,000, a London residence, and was a member of White's. Yet, his typical losses at cards were of the order of a few pounds.[52] Even where it involved rather greater expenditure, such as in the case of horse racing – 'a ridiculous aping of great People', as one newly elected fellow of Magdalen College somewhat pompously termed it in 1778[53] – it could be as much an aspect of a wider commitment to rural sports as an aspect of elite, especially elite male, leisure and identity, as an occasion for betting. For some the two were indistinguishable in any case. The enduring popularity of cockfighting and the degree of personal (and financial) investment in hunting of various kinds among the landed classes are abundantly manifest and impossible to overlook. Such intense enthusiasms raise serious questions about viewing the 'bon ton' and the titled nobility and landed elites as one and the same.[54]

Motivations for gambling were diverse, as only too clearly apparent in respect of lottery adventures and adventuring, as we saw in Chapter 4. Whether it be lottery adventuring or other kinds of gambling, however, the values and meanings which people attached to these activities can only be properly understood in relation to the wider society of which they were a part. There are potential dangers of overgeneralization in this context, about, to take one example, the supposed characteristics of specific social groups. Equally, it is easy to be too rigidly deterministic in drawing connections between gambling and wider socio-cultural current and impulses. This book has focused in the main on those who gambled regularly, not those who did not. Nor has it said very much about occasional gamblers – such as the Dumfries merchant, William Grierson, who in the early nineteenth century staked the very modest sum of 2d on infrequent games of curling in which he participated.[55] Partly this is because the sources necessarily lead us elsewhere as we try and establish what gambling may have meant for those who were drawn to it. One of the other underlying themes of this book has been the influence of personal connections and particular social networks on, as well as locale and milieu to, gambling. Gambling milieu tended to

52 LA, BNLW 4/6/29/5, personal, household, estate expenditure accounts of Sir Brownlow Cust.

53 Lancashire Record Office, Dixon 16/4/1, J. Parkinson to Mrs Parkinson, Magd:[alen] Coll:[ege], Oxon, 8 May 1778.

54 As seems to be the case in Hannah Grieg's otherwise very illuminating book, *The Beau Monde: Fashionable Society in Georgian London* (Oxford, 2013).

55 John Davies (ed.), *An Apostle to Burns; the Diaries of William Grierson* (Edinburgh, 1981), entry for 24 Jan. 1795

reproduce their own sub-cultures, whether fully consciously in the form of rules, conventions, even specifically designed clothing, or as the product of entrenched, customary forms of behaviour. Gambling was seemingly common among the bachelor residents of the Inns of Temple and the officers of the British Army and East India Company army as well as civil service. One contemporary complained of the British community in Madras in 1779:

> Gaming is arrived to that height that it requires the most vigorous measures to break the spirit of it … I dined with the Governor [Sir Thomas Rumbold], a few days ago, when he proposed a rubber, which of course was readily assented to. The party consisted of the Governor, Mr Plumer, Lieutenants Low and Malcolm which was scarce begun when dinner came upon table, and kept 60 people waiting for its being finished.[56]

In the case of military men, this was almost certainly because of a sharpened emphasis on honour, but it was also a function of patterns of sociability particular to army life, and, perhaps, the number of younger sons of aristocratic and wealthy gentry families who found their way into its ranks. In 1793, in the opening stages of British participation in the French Revolutionary Wars, Lord Wallingford, later 8th Earl of Banbury, described life in a garrison town in the Austrian Netherlands for his mother. There was, he noted, 'gaming and drinking in abundance', such that many officers would, he opined, be unfit for service by the following spring. Wallingford was not himself a party to such behaviour; as an older officer – he was thirty – he was happy to retire to his room and a warm fire.[57] There were, it bears emphasizing, always choices to be made even within particular milieu, albeit they could be strongly constrained ones.

Another reasonable generalization is that much gambling reflected a society which was very sharply divided along gender lines, in which men and most women often occupied different spaces, and much male leisure was homosocial. Gambling among and between men was very often a public display of hyper-masculinity, or an explicit act of self-fashioning. This might entail demonstrating confidence in one's own judgement or knowingness, in relation to, say, the cockpit, or physical capacity and skill. Effecting an identity as a 'sportsman', which in this period might easily overlap with that of the 'man of pleasure', was one open to men of very different backgrounds, not just the gentry or, indeed, 'Turfites' such

[56] Devon Heritage Centre, Z6/335, Thomas Palk, Fort St George, to Robert Palk Esq, 15 Oct. 1779.

[57] HRO, Knollis family, earls of Banbury, 1M44/110/65, Lord Wallingford to his mother, 29 Nov. 1793.

as Robert Fletcher of Ballinshoe, who in the early nineteenth century sought out sporting contests on which he could gamble vast sums. It is fairly easy to lose sight of this because of the emphasis in much recent historical writing on this period on the rise and influence of 'polite' or 'virtuous' models of manhood. The French Revolutionary Wars and Napoleonic Wars undoubtedly saw a re-emphasis on male physical prowess and sports as training grounds for British military power, but these were never far from the surface of British culture and society in earlier decades. Cricketing contests frequently arose from challenges publicly issued by teams, from the elite level downwards. Gambling was often related to not losing face; and disputes were, tellingly, quite commonly settled by wagers. It is difficult to assess in this context whether wagers were acting as an alternative to violence, a further example of the civilizing influences at work in society which many historians see as a strong feature of this period.[58] Wagers could, however, as easily generate violence.[59] Whatever the case, the very close relationship between, on the one hand, gambling and, on the other, honour and reputation underlines its performative character. Settling a gambling debt was about enacting a consciously exaggerated code of honour. Among artisans and tradesmen betting typically derived from intensely competitive occupational or local cultures – 'the emulative spirit of Excellency' – which focused on the tavern or fairs, parish feasts and festivals, and the sports and games associated with these, and which may have been the particular (but by no means the exclusive) province of the young.[60] This was not a new impulse, although it was very powerfully perpetuated within expanding industrial regions among groups such as the handloom weavers. More novel was how particularly in London such behaviour might be fuelled by publicity and strategies of self-advertisement, such as encountered in Chapter 2 in the case of Westminster tavern keeper, Sam House. The rise of pedestrianism as a semi-professional, commercialized sport from the 1790s discloses the very close proximity and interdependency of these new and older worlds, and how much of the latter was subsumed within the former.

[58] See esp. Robert Shoemaker, 'Reforming male manners: public insult and the decline of violence in London, 1660–1740', in T. Hitchcock and M. Cohen (eds.), *English Masculinities, 1660–1800* (London, 1999), pp. 133–50.

[59] See e.g. University of Nottingham, Special Collections and Manuscripts, Mol 252, statement of events give by Sir Francis Molyneux that led to the duel between Lord Byron [5th Baron Byron, 1722–98] and William Chaworth, and the latter's subsequent death, c. 26 Jan. 1765; Mol 99, list of people attending a meeting of the 'Nottinghamshire Club' at the Star and Garter Tavern, Pall Mall, at which Lord Byron and William Chaworth fought a duel, 26 Jan. 1765.

[60] The phrase quoted comes from *Museum Rusticum et Commerciale*, Vol. 5 (1765), p. 231.

What of the various gaming houses which clustered around London's Covent Garden and St James's Street? What did they represent to those who frequented them, beyond the sorts of observation already made? No doubt they preyed on the desperate and the unwary, staying open for long hours and through the night into the next day. Those running them sought to entice merchants' and bankers' clerks, those who were entrusted with money, through provision of luxurious Sunday suppers.[61] It is tempting to suggest that what they really offered was a counter-culture of bravura, one which denied that industry and prudential accounting were the only routes to wealth, or that hopeless odds could not be vanquished. What they peddled was an illusion of independent manhood in the guise of the 'man of pleasure'. Perhaps more profoundly, somewhat like the lottery as discussed in Chapter 4, their appeal reflected, albeit less directly than the lottery, a widespread, often intense preoccupation with money and the social alchemy it could perform, or the deliberate subversion of the disciplines of an expanding capitalist economy, and the industry and probity which it seemed to demand, but rewarded all too capriciously. Honest graft, and scrupulous self-accounting did not always, or in many cases, bring the rewards promised by their keen proponents. The lesser or inferior gaming houses, to adopt Patrick Colquhoun's terminology, had something in common with the subscription gambling clubs of Westminster, such as Brooks's, in that they were theatres in which men sought to 'make a figure', or could readily convince themselves that this is what they were doing. For a brief moment perhaps, this is precisely what they did offer.

In pursuing the potential meanings and significances of gambling in the long eighteenth century, we come up, therefore, against a notably disparate set of realities. Several common themes emerge, but they are much more deeply etched in some places and milieu than in others, and entirely absent in others. This is perhaps unsurprising given the diversity of gambling in this period, together with the very diverse nature of contemporary society.

However, to return to the argument outlined in the Introduction to this book, with much gambling we can discern the effects of the magnetic force of notions of fashion and fashionability, the pursuit of independence and social status (often the same thing), but also the materialism of much contemporary society, the solvent power of money, and the very visibly enacted drama of social mobility, both upwards and downwards. The social meteors, those who accumulated vast fortunes and brokered

[61] Patrick Colquhoun, *A Treatise on the Police of the Metropolis* (7th ed., London, 1806), p. 441.

these into positions of social eminence, compelled attention beyond their number, while counter image was the disasters, felt at both an individual and collective level, inflicted by debt and the instabilities of the credit system. Beyond this also very relevant, although harder to recover, are attitudes towards risk and fortune, and the roles they played in shaping social and economic outcomes. That sets of values which were, on the face of things at least, thoroughly inimical to gambling were also strongly present, especially among particular social groups – those of industry, moderation, virtue, and propriety – need not undermine the argument, but may, in fact, only further strengthen it. Gambling could be a form of resistance to such imperatives, or, rather, an attempt to bridge the very considerable gap between independence and happiness, the anticipated rewards of such conduct, and the reality, which was their frequent, even increasing frustration. While we can easily exaggerate a shift from intrinsic to extrinsic social values in Britain in this period, with an urbanizing Britain, the possibilities for effecting self-consciously fashionable identities – 'the man of pleasure', 'man of the world', the 'nominal captain' and so forth – became open to a much wider cross section of society than hitherto. When the constables of St George's Hanover Square in London raided a public house located off Grosvenor Square in 1776 in search of disorderly persons, what they found was a 'sixpenny weekly club' comprised of thirty butchers, bakers, barbers' apprentices, and gentlemen's servants, the perpetual president of which was a woman described as being dressed 'quite in the *Ton*'.[62] Being a person of fashion was quintessentially a matter of outward appearances and outwardly directed conduct. That anxieties were equally common about appearances being deceptive, a mask hiding true circumstances and character, only further testifies to the depth of the impact of such developments.

A Polite and Commercial People?

If a good deal, therefore, of the story of gambling in the long eighteenth century in Britain is tightly bound up with parallel histories of commercialization and urbanization and their profound economic, social, and cultural effects, viewing society through the optic of gambling confirms but also seriously qualifies Britain's portrayal in this period as, in Langford's descriptor (borrowing from William Blackstone), a 'polite and commercial people'. Langford, to be sure, was referring to England and the period from 1727 to 1787, although subsequent usages

[62] *New Morning Post*, 22 Nov. 1776.

have been applied more broadly, to cover a longer period and places beyond England. This is about more than highlighting, important though this is, other realities, mentalities, and currents of opinion that sit very awkwardly at best with such a characterization; or, indeed, focus on gambling highlighting the many and frequent tensions and contradictions in patterns of contemporary behaviour and values. It is precisely these contradictions which can lead to very different conclusions being reached by historians about, say, the influence of Enlightened values and outlooks in this period. People's realities are usually messier than the categories which historians, in pursuit of general narratives, seek to impose on them; put it another way they did not see contradiction where we might see it. To take one relevant example, commercial tontine schemes may have been at bottom a type of gambling, but they could also readily be presented as a prudent means of saving for the future. Or consider the Londoner Stephen Monteage, who we met in Chapter 2: Monteage could rationalize the vagaries of the lottery wheel in terms of a very clearly articulated belief in God's specific providences. To many more people, however, in respect of the lottery it was the idea of luck (or good fortune) which proved irresistibly appealing, rather than looking to God. This might be seen in terms of broadly secularizing trends, but equally it was about the persistence of older, superstitious beliefs. Belief in 'lucky' numbers and consultation of fortune hunters, these were common companions of the lottery in this period. Politeness, meanwhile, as Langford was very well aware, was always about aspiration and, indeed, collective and individual self-promotion. But at the same time, among many of the middling sort it served as a form of evasion. For it both admitted and denied the sheer power of money at this and other levels of society, as well the volatility of personal fortunes; it was the mask which covered (if only partially) the oft-perilous struggle which consumed the lives of most people among the middling ranks for economic security, and a measure of prosperity and social status.

Against this general background, gambling occupied a deeply ambiguous position in British society. It attracted many, but at the same time repulsed others. Some gambling was harmless and an entirely legitimate form of recreation; other forms were altogether more pernicious and destructive in their effects. The real difficulty was drawing a firm line between them, or between habits which might be harmless at one level, but could easily become harmful. Historians of gender especially have shown how competing notions of gender identity could coexist in very close proximity. The worlds of eighteenth-century gambling exhibit this only too clearly, viewed both generally, as well as in the cases of specific individuals. Or, they show how very different models of masculinity coexisted at all levels of society. An intrinsic feature of politeness were the tensions which lay at its very heart, both in terms of what it was and how it might be reconciled with other, often more deep-rooted social and cultural values, which might be religious in derivation or entirely secular, such as those fostered by rural and athletic sports or within particular male homosocial milieu. This was (and is) about much more than politeness and resistance to its claims. If it had been this only, it would not explain the sheer vitality and persistence of gambling in this period.

Looking Forward

Finally, a theme to which this book has not been able to give the attention it properly merits, although a good deal about it has been said in passing, is how (and how much) the landscape and cultural economies of gambling changed in the early decades of the nineteenth century. Some historians point to the story in this period as being one of decline and increasing inhibition, as the middle classes strove to dissociate themselves from the perceived failings of their social inferiors and a dissolute aristocracy above them. At the same time, while gaming clubs continued to flourish in and around St James's, Westminster, indeed, only growing in number in the early decades of the nineteenth century, the fashionable London associated with these places mutated, becoming markedly less socially exclusive. As it did so, the aristocracy retreated, or a younger generation, which came to maturity during the French Revolutionary Wars and Napoleonic Wars, developed new, more sober, responsible habits and outlooks.[63] About the precise chronology of change, there is much less clarity. Was this well underway by 1830 or did the main phase of change occur in the middle decades of the nineteenth century? The decision by parliament to abolish the lottery in 1823 might seem to represent another significant element to this picture, albeit the motives for its action were at least as much financial as moral; the lottery was no longer profitable or important as an element of public finance.[64] Historians of gambling and popular leisure, meanwhile, tend to focus on developments in the second half of the nineteenth century, or certainly from the 1840s, when large-scale, commercialized urban popular gambling seems to re-emerge in London and the major provincial

[63] See Deutsch, 'Fortune and Chance'.

[64] James Raven, 'The Abolition of the English State Lotteries', *Historical Journal*, 34 (1991), 371–89.

industrial cities and towns.[65] The implication is that gambling became less of a feature of the lives of the labouring classes and poor in the earlier decades, that their opportunities to gamble diminished, an assessment for which studies of shifting patterns of work and general living standards and wages would indirectly at least seem to offer a degree of support.[66]

This book has suggested at various points that this picture can be overdrawn and relies in any case on some questionable assumptions, both in respect of the periods before and after c. 1830. This is about more than the all-too-real difficulties of defining gambling, the capacity of people to behave in contradictory ways, and the very real gaps in the evidence. It is also because the periodizations around which modern British history has traditionally been written today look increasingly insecure. A truer picture, if and when it is comprehensively reconstructed – and insofar as this is possible – will almost certainly be one of persistence, continuities and adaptation, as well as growth in certain regions of Britain and decline in others. In the period c. 1689–1830 London and its environs necessarily looms very large; in the nineteenth century, the large manufacturing towns and cities of Britain feature far more heavily. Gamblers and gaming houses continued to defy the law with impunity, and for much the same reasons as before c. 1800. Pedestrianism and horse racing flourished at least up to 1830, driven by powerful commercial forces and opportunism, and continued to provide many opportunities for betting including at gaming booths found on most racecourses at least up until 1820 and replaced thereafter by illegal betting booths. Profit in this context, and economic imperatives, tended to outweigh the aggressive moral disapproval of a section of local and national opinion. It was often a similar story with respect to fairs, which brought much wanted custom to towns, as well as disruption and unruliness. The members of the 1844 select committee on gaming concluded that betting had become much less common than in the previous century. What they had in mind was the declining habit among not just the landed classes to bet on almost anything – marriages, the longevity of a person's life, and political and military events – a facet of changing gambling practices which has yet to be charted or explained. Nevertheless, as the committee's report went on to state:

65 See e.g. Roger Munting, *An Economic and Social History of Gambling in Britain and the USA* (Manchester, 1996); Mark Clapson, *A Bit of a Flutter: Popular Gambling and English Society c.1823–1961* (Manchester, 1992).

66 The literature on the standard of living question in early industrial Britain is vast, but see the essays by S. Horrell and G. Clark and N. Cummins in Roderick Floud, Jane Humphries and Paul Johnson (eds.), *The Cambridge Economic History of Modern Britain, Volume 1: 1700–1870* (Cambridge, 2014).

> At present Wagers are chiefly confined to sporting events, *but the practice of Wagering is still deeply rooted in the habits of the nation, and the practical imposition of pecuniary Penalties for Wagers would be so repugnant to the general feelings of the people*, that such Penalties would scarcely ever be enforced … (My emphasis.)[67]

The imperatives of virtue and propriety, especially among the middle classes, but also sections of the labouring classes, were strongly reinforced in the opening decades of the nineteenth century, partly under the impact of the accelerated spread of Evangelical forms of religion, but also strengthening secular currents of improvement. The attitudes of many towards 'gaming' – as opposed to playing games for small stakes among those who could afford it and who had time for such recreations, which usually meant the polite – had, however, been critical throughout the eighteenth century. Gambling flourished despite such attitudes. Part of the reason is simply that, as we have seen, views differed, quite sharply, and were often contradictory; and there is good reason to believe that this continued to be the case in the subsequent century. The authorities and parliament could be notably cautious about infringing on personal freedoms, which is why calls for punitive policing powers were often resisted, again as they would be well beyond 1830. If the first half of the nineteenth century is often associated with the cult of respectability and religious revival, it also saw a strengthening conviction that the 'economy of private people' was their own affair. To adapt somewhat a conclusion of a modern historian of nineteenth-century horse racing, between the power and public expression of ideologies of middle class respectability and their effects on not just the labouring but also the middle and upper classes there existed very significant gaps.[68] It was in these gaps, aided by the continuing, even strengthening capacity of urban life to sustain cultural pluralism and competing status and gender hierarchies, that gambling would continue to flourish and adapt, while the meanings and values attached to it would also continue to evolve.

67 PP, 1844 (297), Report from the Select Committee on Gaming, v.

68 Mike Huggins, *Flat Racing and British Society 1790–1914: A Social and Economic History* (London, 2000), pp. 138–9. See also ch. 3 of the same work, 'The Middle Class Supporters of Racing'.

Select Bibliography

Manuscript Sources

Archives of the Honourable Artillery Company

Court Minutes

HAC Lottery Accounts 1775–7, HAC/As/G1/1 [Accounts of White, Benge & Co. of 16 Lombard Street].

Bank of England Archives

5 per cent Annuities 1717 Lottery, alphabet ledgers, A–H & I–Z, Ac 27/330–1.

5 per cent Annuities 1717 Lottery Ledgers, 1717–19, Ac 27/332–6.

Letter from H. Prideaux to Humphry Morice Esq., Norwich, 29 Dec. 1718, 16A2/2/20(2).

Bedfordshire Archives and Records Service

Wrest Park (Lucas) Papers, L29 & L30.

Blair Castle

Atholl Papers.

Bodleian Library

John Johnson Collection: Lotteries, vols. 1–10.

Radcliffe Trust Papers, financial papers, MS D. D. Radcliffe, c. 12/1&2.

Bristol Record Office

Letters and Papers of Jarrit Smith MP, AC/JS.

Presentments 1676–700, JQS/C/1.

British Library

Althorp Papers, Add MS 76154, 76596.
Blenheim Papers, Add MS 61472.
Memorandum book of Sir W. Calverley 1663–722, Add MS 27418.
Account book of Nicholas Carewe, afterwards 1st Baronet Beddington, Surrey, 1705–8, Add MS 30335.
Collections of handbills relating to lotteries
1768–826, LR 26 b 1.
1804–25, 1889 a 19.
1804–26, 8226 a 27.
1805–9, 8227 e 19.
1806–13, 8229 k 8.
1807–25, 1880 b 41.
1810–26, 8229 f 11.
Dropmore Papers
Papers of Lord Grenville relating to the Lottery, 1788–807, Add MS 59309.
Holland House Papers
Correspondence of 1st Lord Holland with his son, Charles James Fox, 1761–7, Add MS 51422.
Landsdowne Papers, Add MS 829
Private accounts of the duchess of Newcastle, 1757–76, Add MSS 33628.
Portland Papers
Taxes and Lottery, 1710–814, Add MS 70155.
Transcript of 'The Peninsular Memoirs of Lieutenant George James Sullivan', RP 8211
Verney Papers [microfilm copies]
Robert Walpole, MP
Account book of Robert Walpole, 1693–8, Add MSS 74245.
Walpole Papers
Account book of Sir Robert Walpole, 1714–8, Add MS 74062.

Coutts & Co. Archives

Letter Book 6, 13 Jan. 1710–14 Oct. 1714.

Cumbria Record Office, Barrow-on-Furness

Soulby Collection.

Cumbria Record Office, Carlisle

Lonsdale (Lowther) Papers, D/Lons.
Senhouse Papers, D. Sen.
John Ware Account Books, 1799–802, 1802–5, DA/276A & B.

Derbyshire Record Office

Fitzherbert Family of Tissington
The Naturalist's Diary kept by William Philp Perrin, 1773–80, 1783, 1793–808, D239/M/F/15894–918.
Longsdon of Little Longstone, Family and Estate Papers, Correspondence, D3580/C/–
Wright of Eyam Hall
Lottery accounts of Mrs Francis Wright, 1793–5, D5430/32/2/12–15.
Mary Sisum, London, to Mrs Francis Wright, 15 Nov. 1791, D5430/32/2/2.

East Sussex Record Office, Brighton

The Shiffner Archives
General and Personal Cash Accounts of Sir John Bridger, 1751–811, SHR/1372–85.

Edinburgh Central Library, George IV Bridge, Edinburgh

Journal of Andrew Armstrong, 1789–93, Y DA 1861.789.

Edinburgh City Archives

Acts of Council.
McLeod Collection.

Glamis Castle, Angus

Strathmore Papers.

Hampshire Record Office

Correspondence and Personal Papers of the Hall Family of Preston Candover.
Letters to Thomas Hall junior from James Pinnock of Lasham and Gower St., London, 1781–99, 44M69/F14/1/34.
Froyle hop duty betting books, 1798–858, 12M98.
Papers of the Harris Family, Earls of Malmesbury.
Letters to James Harris (and some to Elizabeth Harris) from his brother Thomas, 9M73/–.
Papers of the Jervoise Family of Herriard.
Account and notebook of Tristram Huddleston Jervoise, 1785–94, 44M69/E11/130.
Matthew Lamb to Thomas Jervoise, 27 June 1721, 44M69/F6/7/8.
'Reasons for altering the Bill … for better preventing of excessive and immoderate gaming', n.d. (but prob. 1710), 44M69/G2/188.

Papers of the Knollis family, earls of Banbury.
Lord Wallingford to his mother, 29 Nov. 1793, 1M44/110/65.
Winchester City Archives, Judicial Records, Quarter Sessions
Bundle of Papers related to licensing, 1787, W/D3/324.

Hoare's Bank, Fleet Street

Accounts regarding the Bridge lotteries, 1737–9, HB/8/G/10.
Accounts with respect to purchase and sale of Lowndes family lottery tickets, 1710–21, HB/8/9/2.
Bank Ledgers.
Ledger for Plate, 1697–c. 1730, HB/1/6.
Letters to partners, HB/8/T/11/–.
Money Lent Ledgers, 1710–c. 25, HB/5/H/1–2.
Record of payments to the bank to complete the remaining sums due upon receipts for tickets in the lottery, 1755, HB/8/G11.

Kent Archives and Records Centre

Filmer Manuscripts.
Letters from Bevisham Filmer to Sir Edward Filmer (3rd Bart.), 1733–7, U120/C25 & C26.
North Papers
Accounts of Dudley North, 1708–23, EK/U471/A255–60.
Personal expenses of Lady Arabella Furnese, 1714–27, EK/U471/A50.

Lancashire Record Office, Preston

Dixon 16/4/1, J. Parkinson to Mrs Parkinson, Magd:[alen] Coll:[ege], Oxon, 8 May 1778.
Hulton and Hulton
Various advertisements relating to the lottery, 1796–817, DDHU/53/82/10.
Kenyon Family of Peel Hall
Letters addressed to Ralph and Thomas Banks, DDKE/9/124.
Lancaster Library Collection
Richard Blood, Lancaster, to Thomas Barrow, merchant, 24 Jan. 1801, DDX 2743/MS797.
Minute book of the subscribers of Fullwood Moor Race Course, 1790–829, DDX 103/4.
Miscellaneous Records
Advertisements for Thomson & Son, booksellers, Manchester, lottery agents, c. 1807, DDX 818/32–3.

Lincolnshire Archives, Lincoln

Account Book and Journal of Matthew Flinders senior, Jan. 1775–Dec. 1784, FLINDERS/1.
Brownlow Papers, BNLW

Monson Papers

An account of the receipts and payments on the money collected for the Ladies Plate at Lincoln, 1733, 10/9/6.

London Metropolitan Archives

City of London Sessions, Sessions Papers, CLA/047.

Journals of Stephen Monteage, MS 20519.

Lists of Charges Returned to the King's Bench, 1769–72, MJ/M/KR/001.

Middlesex Sessions, Calendar of Summary Convictions, 1774–82, 1783–93, 1794, MSJ/C/C/01–03.

Middlesex Sessions, Orders of Court, MJ/O/C.

Middlesex Sessions, Process Register of Charges, Aug. 1734–Feb. 1742, Apr. 1742–Jan. 1751, MS/SB/P/0014–0015.

Middlesex Sessions, Session of the Peace and Oyer and Terminer Books, MJ/SB/B.

Middlesex Justices, Sessions Papers, MJ/SP.

Middlesex Justices, Sessions Rolls, MJ/SR.

Minutes of the Board of the Honourable Brotherhood, A/BLB/1 & 2.

Minutes of a Candlewick ward club from 1739, MS 2841, vol. 1.

Minutes of City of London dining club, MS 3406.

Minutes of the Centenary Club, MS 544, vol. 2.

Moneys paid in upon the civil list lottery ano. 1713 being the first payment, Col/CHD/LA/02/219.

Repertories of the Court of Aldermen, COL/CA/01/01/–.

Westminster Sessions, Orders of Court, WJ/O/C.

The National Archives

Accounts of Thomas Pitt, Jr, Lord Londonderry with George Craddock, 1714–16, Chancery Masters Exhibits, C108/416/14.

Bagnall v Overman, Court of Chancery Records, C6/372/12.

Board of Stamps, Miscellaneous Books, Solicitor's Department, Lottery Cases: Law Opinions, 1787–99, IR72/34.

Bonds and affidavits relating to lost prize-winning lottery tickets, 1717–87, IR55/1 & 2.

Chatham Papers, PRO30/8.

Catalogue of Sale of Contents of Sir George Colebrooke's house in Arlington Street, Christie and Ansells, 1778, Chancery Masters Exhibits, C104/146, Cullen v Queensberry.

Home Office Papers, Judges' Reports on Criminals, HO47/22/30.

Lottery Office Papers, IR55/13.

Memoranda and Draft Reports on Lotteries, 1802–25, IR55/10.

Memorial on lotteries, n.d., but prob. 1787, T1/652/68–75.

Minutes, Accounts and Vouchers of the Lady's Club, afterwards Arlington House Club, 1770–5, Chancery Masters Exhibits, C104/146, Cullen v Queensberry.

Papers on Schemes for Lotteries, 1809–19, IR55/19.
Papers Relating to Lottery Tickets, T64/324.
Register of Beneficiaries in a Lottery, 1712, E 401/2599 & 2600.
State Papers Domestic, SP36.
Treasury Solicitor's Papers, TS11.

National Library of Scotland

Account Book, 1771–96, of Alexander Anderson, merchant & burgess of Edinburgh, MS 8891.
Correspondence of Andrew Stuart, MS 8251.
Memorandum of wager in pocket book of David Bruce of Kinnaird, 14 Feb. 1753, Acc 6257.
Papers of the Honourable Company of Edinburgh Golfers, 36–42, Bet Books, 1776–826, Acc 11208.
Stuart Stevenson Papers, MS 8262.
Typescript Copy of a Manuscript Register of Leith Races, 1753–70, Acc 11594.

National Records of Scotland

Accounts and business letters addressed to James Ewart, 1762–4, RH15/66/7.
Commissary Court Papers, St Andrews Commissary Court, Register of Testaments, CC3/3/110.
James Ewart, Royal Bank, Edinburgh, lottery ticket notebook, 1763, CS96/3307.
John and James Sievewright, lottery contractors, London, Thomas Murray, stationer, Glasgow, lottery ticket sales book, 1824–6 & Volume marked 'Tickets Shared', CS96/2105 & 2106.
Letters from Hugh Warrender, London and Aston, to George Warrender, 1747–53, GD214/639.
Maclaine of Lochbuie Papers, GD174
Papers of the Campbell Family, earls of Breadalbane
  Personal account books kept by John, Lord Glenorchy, later 3rd earl of Breadalbane, 1733–41, 1742–52, GD 112/21/77 & 78.
Papers of the Erskine Family, earls of Mar and Kellie, GD124.
Papers of the Graham Family, dukes of Montrose, GD220.
Papers of the Hall Family of Dunglass, East Lothian.
  Diary of Sir James Hall of Dunglass, 1805, GD 206/2/315/15.
Papers of the Innes Family of Stow, Peebleshire, GD 113.
Papers of the Ogilvy Family, earls of Seafield (Seafield Papers), GD248.
'Scheme for the Better Supporting of the Charitable Infirmary in the Inns-Quay, Mercer's Hospital and the Hospital for Incurables on Lazer's Hill, Dublin, 1767', CS96/3307.
The John MacGregor Collection
  Act against Playing at Cards and Dice, etc. in Edinburgh coffee-houses, taverns, etc., 12 Apr. 1704, GD50/198.

National Register of Archives of Scotland

Hamilton Papers, NRAS 2177, Bundles 767, 2808, 2867, 3520–1, 3527, 4032.
Papers of the Macpherson Family of Blairgowrie, Perthshire, NRAS 2614.

Norfolk Record Office

Bradfer-Lawrence Collection, Account Current of Philip Case with Everard Browne & Co., 1767–9, BL/CS6/7/15.
Lottery register books of John Craske, 1813–25, BR80/1 & 2.
Papers of Thomas Townshend, civil engineer of South Lynn, MC 905/ 1–54, 799x7.
Pocket diary of Augustine Earle, 1757–8, 1759–60, MC 2782/A/1& 2.
Townshend Papers, BL/T/3/1/21.

Northumberland Record Office

Blackett (Wylam) Papers, ZBL
Delaval Family Papers
Lottery tickets & letters and papers about lotteries, 1771–805, 2 DE 35/17 .
Memorandum books of Ralph William Grey, 1731–50, 753, box 1, G
Swinburne (Capheaton) Papers
Sir John Swinburne, account and diary from 11 June 1730 to [?] Nov. 1744, ZSW 454.

North Yorkshire Record Office

Zetland Papers.

Nottinghamshire Archives

Foljambe of Osberton, correspondence of John Hewett, 1780–4, DDFJ/ 11/1/5.
Portland of Welbeck (4th Deposit), DD.
Savile Papers, DD/SR.
Photocopies of diaries of Joseph Woolley, framework knitter in Moore's Almanacs for 1801, 1803–4, 1809, 1813, and 1815, DD/311/1–6.

Perth and Kinross Council Archives

Kinnaird Papers, MS 100, Bundle 1064.
Richardson of Pitfour Papers, MS 101, bundle 41.

Plymouth and West Devon Record Office

Plymouth Borough Records.

Royal Bank of Scotland Archives

Account of James Campbell of St Germains with John Campbell for the purchase of lottery tickets, 12 May 1744, RB/1480/11/8.
Draft letter from John Campbell to John Campbell of Achalader, 20 July 1764, RB/1480/23/1.
Drummond's Bank, Customer Account Ledgers, DR/427/7–50, 1727–65.
Heywood Brothers Customer Account Ledger, 1791–4, HB/36/1.
Profit and Loss Ledger of Child & Co., 1769, CH/203/2/1.

Royal Mail Archives

Account of Edinburgh's newspapers sent to the country in a week, n.d. but later 1790s, Post 30/2.
An account of the number of letters and newspapers sent from London in 3 months, 1823, Post 30/4766.
An account of the number of newspapers sent by the vendors through the News Paper Office for the last three years, 1809–11, Post 24/2.
Articles to the Circulated to the Clerks of the Road, 27 Mar. 1811, Post 24/2.
Net produce of postage of letters in Scotland, Post 9/168.
Number of newspapers passed through the General Post .Office, London, 5 Jan. 1790–5 Jan. 1791, Post 24/1.
Printed notices.

Scottish Borders Archives and Local History Centre, Hawick

Hawick Old Kirk Sessions, minutes and accounts, 1711–25, CH2/1122/2.

Sheffield City Archives

Papers of Samuel Roberts, RP/1/11 & 13.
Rules and Orders Agreed Upon to be Kept and Strictly Observed by an Amicable Society for Raising a Sum of Money in Order to be Adventured in Every State Lottery for the Equal Benefit and Advantage of Every Member of the Said Society, 28 Mar. 1755, NC/59.
Wentworth-Woodhouse Papers, WWM.

Shropshire Record Office

Attingham Collection, 112/1.

Surrey History Centre

Surrey Quarter Sessions Records, Sessions Bundles, QS2/6.

University of Edinburgh, Special Collections

Diary of George Drummond, 1736–8, Dc. 1. 82 & 83.

University of Hull, Brynmor Jones Library

Journal and Personal Account Book of Robert Carlisle Broadley of Hull, 1768–73, DP/146.

University of Nottingham, Manuscripts and Special Collections

Papers of the Molyneux Family of Terversal, Nottinghamshire, Mol
Statement of events give by Sir Francis Molyneux that led to the duel between Lord Byron [5th Baron Byron, 1722–98] and William Chaworth, and the latter's subsequent death, c. 26 Jan. 1765, Mol 252.
List of people attending a meeting of the 'Nottinghamshire Club' at the Star and Garter Tavern, Pall Mall, at which Lord Byron and William Chaworth fought a duel, 26 Jan. 1765, Mol 99.
Newcastle (Clumber) Collection, Ne C.
Portland Collection, Pw and Pl.
The Mellish Collection, Me.

Westminster Archives

Coroner's Inquests, 1760–71.
Letter book of John Ewer, banker, 1731–3, Acc. 762.
St Clement Danes parish, pauper settlement, vagrancy and bastardy examinations, 31 Mar. 1783–3 Aug. 1786.
St. Clement Danes parish, vestry minutes.
St James's parish, vestry minutes.

Wiltshire and Swindon Record Office

Bennett Family of Pythouse, Tisbury.
Two letters written by John Kneller from Calcutta, 1770, 1773, 413/318.
Marquis of Ailesbury Papers, 1300/–.
The Codrington Family of Wraxall and Long Ashton, Somerset.
'Timothy Telltruth' to John Codrington Esq., Member of Parliament, n.d., 1178/606.

Published Primary Sources

An Account of the Endeavours That have been used to Suppress Gaming Houses, and the Discouragements that have been met with in a Letter to a Noble Lord (London, 1722).

The Letters of Joseph Addison, ed. Graham, Walter (Oxford, 1941).

An Address to the Sovereign, on the Ministers' Conduct in Rejecting the Petition of the Lieutenant of the Royal Navy (London, 1788).

Anderson, James, *General View of the Agriculture and Rural Economy of the County of Aberdeen, with Observations on the Means of its Improvement* (Edinburgh, 1794).

Arbuthnot, John, *An Inquiry into the Connections between the Present Price of Provisions, and the Size of Farms* (London, 1773).

Arnot, Hugo, *The History of Edinburgh, From the Earliest Accounts to the Present Time* (Edinburgh, 1788).

[Bacon, Matthew] *A New Abridgment of the Law. By Matthew Bacon, of the Middle Temple Esq* (5th ed., corrected, London, 1786).

Barlow, Joel, *Advice to the Privileged Orders in the Several States of Europe* (London, 1793).

Beattie, James, *Elements of Moral Science*, 2 vols. (Edinburgh, 1790).

Billingsley, John, *General View of the Agriculture of the County of Somerset, with Observations on the Means of Improvement* (London, 1798).

[Bolton, Robert] *The Deity's Delay In Punishing the Guilty Considered, on the Principles of Reason* (London, 1751).

Boswell: The Applause of the Jury 1782–1785, eds. Lustig, Irma S. and Pottle, Frederick A. (New Haven and London, 1982).

Letters of James Boswell: 29 July 1758 – 29 Nov. 1777, ed. Tinker, C. B., 2 vols. (Oxford, 1924).

Boswell's London Journal 1762–1763, ed. Pottle, Frederick A. (New Haven and London, 1950).

Boyd, Robert, *The Office, Powers and Jurisdiction of His Majesty's Justices of the Peace and Commissioners of Supply* (2 vols., Edinburgh, 1787).

Brodribb, G., *The English Game. A Cricket Anthology* (London, 1948).

Buchan, William, *Domestic Medicine: Or A Treatise on the Prevention and Cure of Diseases by Regimen and Simple Medicines* (London, 1769).

Calendar of Treasury Books 1660–1718, ed. W. A. Shaw, 32 vols. (London, 1898–1903).

Caulfield, James, *Portraits, Memoirs, and Characters of Remarkable Persons, From the Revolution of 1688 to the End of the Reign of George II, 4 vols* (London, 1820).

Champion, Richard, *Comparative Reflections on the Past and Present Political, Commercial and Civil State of Great Britain* (London, 1787).

Letters from Lady Jane Coke to her Friend Mrs Eyre at Derby 1747–1758, ed. with notes by Rathorne, Mrs Ambrose (London, 1899).

Colebrooke, H. T., *Remarks on the Present State of the Husbandry and Commerce of Bengal* (Calcutta, 1795).

The Letters of John Collier of Hastings 1731–1746, ed. Saville, Richard, Sussex Record Society, 96 (Lewes, 2016).

Colquhoun, Patrick, *Treatise on the Function and Duties of a Constable* (London, 1803).

A Treatise on the Police of the Metropolis (7th ed., London, 1806).

A New and Appropriate System of Education for the Labouring People (London, 1806).

Treatise on Indigence (London, 1806).

Considerations on Lotteries, and Proposals for their Better Regulation (London, 1786).

Diary of Mary, Countess Cowper, Lady of the Bedchamber to the Princess of Wales, 1714–1720, ed. Cowper, Hon. C. C. (London, 1865).

The Letters of Daniel Defoe, ed. Healey, George Harris (Oxford, 1955).

A Brief Description of the Cities of London and Westminster (London, 1776).

Disney, John, *The Laws of Gaming, Wagers, Horse-Racing, and Gaming Houses* (London, 1806).

Drake, F., *Eboracum: Or, the History and Antiquities of the City of York* (York, 1736).

Edwards, Frederick, *Brief Treatise on the Laws of Gaming, Horse Racing and Wagers* (London, 1839).

The Ill Effects of the Game of Rowlet, Otherwise Rowley-Powley (London, 1744).

An Enquiry into the Present Alarming State of the Nation. Shewing the Necessity of a Reform in Government, and a Speedy Resolution of Taxes; an Adequate Representation of the People; and Restoration of Triennial Parliaments (London, 1793).

Erskine, Thomas, *Reflections on Gaming, Annuities, and Usorious Contracts* (3rd ed., London, 1778).

Faro, and Rouge et Noir: The Mode of Playing, and Explanation of the Terms Used in Both Games (London, 1793).

Fellows, John, *Seasonable Words of Advice to All Such as Are Concerned in the Lottery; In Which Are Pointed Out the Evils that Have Attended on Gaming, Especially in Buying Chances, Policies, and Insuring* (London, 1780).

Fielding, John, *An Account of the Origin and Effects of a Police Set on Foot by his Grace the Duke of Newcastle in the Year 1753, upon a Plan Presented to his Grace by the Late Henry Fielding, Esq* (London, 1758).

Fielding, Sir John, *Extracts From Such of the Penal Laws. As Particularly Relate to the Peace and Good Order of this Metropolis* (London, 1768).

Fitzsimmonds, Joshua, *Free and Candid Disquisitions on the Nature and Execution of the Laws of England, Both in Civil and Criminal Affairs* (London, 1750).

Fordyce, J., *Sermons to Young Women*, 2 vols. (London, 1775).

Remembrances of Elizabeth Freke, 1671–1714, ed. Anselment, Raymond A., *Camden Fifth Ser.*, 18 (Cambridge, 2001).

Gale, Samuel, *An Essay on the Nature and Principles of Public Credit* (London, 1784).

The Gamester. A Benefit Ticket. For All That Are Concern'd in the LOTTERIES (London, 1719).

The Gaming Calendar, To Which is Added Annals of Gaming (London, 1820).

The Letters of John Gay, ed. Burgess, C. F. (Oxford, 1966).

An Apostle of Burns: The Diaries of William Grierson, ed. Davies, J. (Edinburgh, 1981).

Grosley, P. J., *A Tour to London: Or, New Observations on England, and its Inhabitants* (2 vols., London, 1772).

A Help to Magistrates, and Ministers of Justice (London, 1721).
Henderson, Ebenezer, *The Annals of Dunfermline and Vicinity from the earlier authentic period to the present time AD 1069–1878* (Glasgow, 1879).
The Diary of John Hervey, First Earl of Bristol, 1688–1742 (Wells, 1894).
Hey, Richard, *A Dissertation on the Pernicious Effects of Gaming* (Cambridge, 1783).
The Rake's Diary: The Journal of George Hilton, transcribed by Hillman, Ann (Curwen Archives Texts, Berwick upon Tweed, 1994).
Hints for a Reform, Particularly in the Gambling Clubs. By a Member of Parliament (London, 1784).
Historical Manuscripts Commission, *Fifteenth Report, Appendix, Part VI: The Manuscripts of the Earl of Carlisle, Preserved at Castle Howard* (London, 1897).
Historical Manuscripts Commission, *Fourteenth Report, Appendix, Part IV, The Manuscripts of Lord Kenyon* (London, 1894).
Howard, Thomas, Earl of Effingham, *An Essay on the Nature of a Loan. Being an Introduction to the Knowledge of Public Accounts* (London, 1782).
Jackson, R., *A Guide to Adventurers in the Lottery, or Plan of the Amicable Society of Lottery Adventurers* (n.d., but prob., London, 1785).
Jesse, J. H., *George Selwyn and his Contemporaries* (4 vols., London, 1882).
Jones, Charles, *Some Methods Proposed Towards Putting a Stop to the Flagrant Crimes of Murder, Robbery, and Perjury; and for the more effectually preventing the pernicious consequences of Gaming among the Lower Class of People* (London, 1752).
Journals of the House of Commons.
Journals of the House of Lords.
King, Richard, *The New CHEATS of LONDON Exposed: Or, The FRAUDS and TRICKS of the TOWN Laid Open to BOTH SEXES* (London, 1780).
The Lady's Preceptor, Or, a Letter to a Young Lady of Distinction upon Politeness Taken from the French of the Abbé D'Ancourt, and Adapted to the Religion, Customs and Manners of the English Nation (London, 1743).
The Lady's Year's Gift: Or, Advice to a Daughter in The Works of George Savile, Marquis of Halifax, ed. Brown, M. N., 3 vols. (Oxford, 1989).
[Lediard, Thomas]*A Charge Delivered to the Grand Jury, at the Sessions of the City and Liberties of Westminster, 16 Oct. 1754. By Thomas Lediard Esq* (London, 1754).
A Letter From the Grave, Communicated in a Vision By Mr Holman's Late Servant: Addressed to Servants of All Denominations (London, 1792).
A Letter to the Honourable House of Commons in Relation to the Present Situation of Affairs (1750).
Lewis, Erasmus, *A Letter to the Club at White's* (London, 1750).
The Life and Mysterious Transactions of Richard Morris (London, 1799).
The Life and Political Opinions of the Late Sam House: Interspersed with Curious Anecdotes and Amorous Intrigues of this Singular and Distinguished Character (London, 1785).
The Lottery Display'd, Or The Adventurer's Guide (London, 1771).
Love, Henry Davison, *Vestiges of Old Madras: Traced from the East India Company's Records Preserved at Fort St George and the India Office, and From Other Sources*, 4 vols. (London, 1913).

McCann, Timothy J. (ed.), *Sussex Cricket in the Eighteenth Century*, Sussex Record Society, 88 (Lewes, 2004).

Macky, John, *A Journey through England. In Familiar Letters. From a Gentleman Here to his Friend Abroad*, 2 vols. (2nd ed., London, 1732).

More, Hannah, *Thoughts on the Importance of the Manners of the Great to General Society* (London, 1788).

Museum Rusticum et Commerciale, Vol. 5 (1765).

The Diary of Sylas Neville 1767–1788, ed. Cozens-Hardy, Basil (London, New York and Toronto, 1950).

Observations on Mr Fielding's Enquiry into the Late Increase of Robbers &c (London, 1751).

Letters from Bath 1766–1767 by the Rev. John Penrose. With an Introduction and Notes by Mitchell, Brigitte & Penrose, Hubert (Sutton, 1983).

Pick, W., *An Authentic Historical Racing Calendar of all the Plates, Sweepstakes, Matches, &c, Run at York, From the First Commencement of Races There in the Year 1709, to the Year 1785 Inclusive* (York, 1785).

Pittis, William, *The History of the Present Parliament. And Convocation* (London, 1711).

The Correspondence of Richard Price: March 1778-February 1786, eds. Thomas, D. O. and Peace, W. Bernard, 2 vols. (Durham, N. C. and Cardiff, 1983–94).

The Correspondence of Alexander Pope, 1729–1735, ed. Sherburn, George, 5 vols. (Oxford, 1956).

Letters of John Ramsay of Ochtertyre 1799–1812, ed. B. L. H. Horn (Scottish Historical Society, 1966).

Gentle Reflections on the Short but Serious Reasons for a National Militia (London, 1757).

Reflexions on Gaming, and Observations on the Laws Relating Thereto (London, n.d., but prob. 1750).

Report of the Committee of the Society for Carrying into Effects His Majesty's Proclamation Against Vice and Immorality, For the Year 1799 (London, 1799).

A Frenchman in England 1784: Being the Mélanges sur L'Angleterre of François de la Rochfoucauld, ed. Marchand, Jean (Cambridge, 1933).

The Diary of Dudley Ryder, 1715–1716, ed. Matthews, W. (London, 1939).

The Memoirs of Susan Sibbald, ed. Hett, F. P. (London, 1926).

Sinclair, Sir John, *The History of the Public Revenue of the British Empire* (2nd ed., London, 1789).

Smith, Adam, *An Inquiry into the Nature and Causes of the Wealth of Nations*, ed. Skinner, A. S, vol. 1. (Oxford, 1987).

Strang, John, *Glasgow and its Clubs; Or Glimpses of the Condition, Manners, Characters, & Quiddities of the City, During the Past & Present Century* (London and Glasgow, 1856).

Joseph Strutt, *The Sports and Pastimes of the People of England (1801)*, ed. Cox, J. Charles (London, 1898).

The Diary of William Thomas of Michelston-Super-Ely, near St. Fagans Glamorgan, 1762–1795, abridged and edited by Denning, R. T. W. (Cardiff, 1995).

Serious Thoughts in Regard to Publick Disorders, with Several Proposals for Remedying the Same (London, prob. 1751).

[Trusler, Rev. J.] *Principles of Politeness and of Knowing the World. By the Late Lord Chesterfield Methodised and Digested* (London, 1775).

Trusler, Rev. J., *Principles of Politeness and Knowing the World, Containing Every Instruction Necessary to Complete the Gentleman and Man of Fashion* (16th ed., London, 1800).

Tucker, Josiah, *An Essay on the Advantages and Disadvantages which Respectively Attend France and Great Britain with regard to Trade* (London, 1749).

The Diary of Thomas Turner 1754–1765, ed. Vaisey, David (Oxford, 1985).

The Verney Letters of the Eighteenth Century from the MSS. at Claydon House, ed. M. Verney, 2 vols. (London, 1930).

The Vices of the Cities of London and Westminster Trac'd from their Original (London, 1751).

Ward, Dudley and Ward, Viscount John, *The Law of a Justice of Peace and Parish Officer* (2 vols., London, 1769).

Ward, Edward, *The London Spy* (London, 1698).

Weatherby, James, *Racing Calendar: Containing an Account of the Plates, Matches, and Sweepstakes, Run for in Great Britain and Ireland, in the Year 1779* (London, 1779).

Wesley, John, *A Sermon Preached Before the Society for Reformation of Manners on Sunday, January 30, 1763. At the Chappel on West Street, Seven Dials* (London, 1763).

Wilkinson, Tate, *The Wandering Patentee, or, The History of Yorkshire Theatres, from 1770 to the Present Time* (York, 1795).

A Parson in the Vale of White Horse: George Woodwards's Letters from East Hendred, 1753–1761, ed. Gibson, Donald (Sutton, 1983).

Seasonable Words of Advice to All Such as are Concerned In the Lottery (1780).

[Zouch, Rev. Henry] *Hints Respecting The Public Police: By H. Zouch, Clerk, A Justice of the Peace* (London, 1786).

Newspapers and Periodicals

Aberdeen Journal

Annual Register

Belfast Newsletter

The Beauties of All Magazines Selected (3 Vols., 1762–4)

British Apollo

British Mercury

British Spy, or New Universal London Weekly Journal

The Bury and Norwich Post; or Suffolk, Norfolk, Cambridgeshire and Ely Advertiser

The Cambridge Magazine

Chester Chronicle

The Commercial and Agricultural Magazine (6 vols., 1799–802)

Daily Advertiser

Daily Courant

Daily Journal

Daily Post

Diary, or Woodfall's Register
The Dumfries and Galloway Courier
Dundee, Perth and Cupar Advertiser
Edinburgh Advertiser
Edinburgh Magazine
[Eliza Haywood] *The Female Spectator*, Vol. I (1755)
Gazetteer or New Daily Advertiser
General Advertiser
General Evening Post
Hampshire Telegraph
Kelso Mail
Leeds Intelligencer
Leeds Mercury
The Literary and Fashionable Magazine (1806)
Lloyds Evening Post
London Chronicle
London Daily Advertiser or Literary Gazette
London Evening Post
London Gazette
London Journal
London Magazine
London Morning Penny Post
London Packet
Middlesex Chronicle
Middlesex Journal
Monthly Magazine (1821)
Morning Chronicle
Morning Herald
New Morning Post
Newcastle Journal
News Supplement
Northampton Mercury
Old Whig
Post Boy
Public Advertiser
Public Ledger
The Quarterly Review
Reading Mercury and Oxford Gazette
Read's Weekly Journal
The Salisbury and Winchester Journal
Scots Courant
The Spectator
St James's Chronicle
Sussex Weekly Advertiser
The Tatler

The Telegraph
The Times
The Universal Visiter [sic], *and Monthly Memorialist. For May 1756.* [...] Number V (1756)
Weekly Journal or British Gazetteer
Whitehall Evening Post
The World

Parliamentary Papers

House of Commons Sessional Papers, Harper Collection of Private Bills, 1695–814, vol. 6, A Proposal humbly offered to the honourable House of Commons, &c to be established by virtue of an Act of Parliament for an Annual Lottery till the whole National Debt are discharged and annihilated, 1751.
House of Commons Sessional Papers, vol. 19, Report from the Committee Appointed to Examine the Book, Containing an Account of the Contributors to the Lottery, 1753, And the Proceedings of the House Thereupon, 14 Mar. 1754.
House of Commons Sessional Papers, vol. 88, Report From the Committee Appointed to Enquire How Far the Laws for Preventing ILLEGAL INSURANCES, and Other Evils, Which Have Been Found to Attend the Drawing of STATE LOTTERIES, are Effectual to the Object Proposed by Them, 12 Mar. 1793.
1808 (182 & 323), Reports from the Committee on the Laws Relating to Lotteries.
1816 (510), Report from the Committee of the State of the Police of the Metropolis, with, the Minutes of Evidence Taken Before the Committee; and, An Appendix of Sundry Papers.
1817 (104), Lottery and Little-Go Acts, A Return and Account of the Number of Prosecutions and Convictions under the Lottery Act and Little Go Act during the Last Fourteen Months, 1817.
1817(203), An Account of the Number of Tickets Sold and Shared in the Lotteries Drawn During the Last Two Years, Distinguishing Whole Tickets, Half Tickets, Quarters, Eighths, and Sixteenths.
1817 (233) VII. 1, Select Committee of the House of Commons on the State of Police of the Metropolis, and Execution of the Laws for Licensing of Victuallers.
1819 (241), An Account of the Number of Tickets Issued and Shared in the Lotteries Drawn During the Last Two Years, Distinguishing Whole Tickets, Half Tickets, Quarters, Eighths, and Sixteenths.
1822 (261) XXI.523, Account of the Number of Magistrates Licences for Victuallers in the Metropolis, 1817–22.
1844 (297), Report From the Select Committee on Gaming.

Secondary Material

This includes only items relating directly to gambling or which were drawn on heavily in the writing of this book. For other items, see the footnotes.

Anderson, Earl R., 'Footnotes More Pedestrian than Sublime: A Historical Background for the Foot-Races in Evelina and Humphry Clinker', *Eighteenth-Century Studies*, 14 (1980), 56–68.

Andrew, Donna T., '"How Frail are Lovers Vows and Dicers Oaths": Gaming, Governing and Moral Panic in Britain, 1781–1782', in Lemmings, David and Walker, Claire (eds.), *Moral Panics, the Media and the Law in Early Modern England* (New York, 2009), pp. 176–94.

Andrew, Donna and McGowen, Randall, *The Perreaus and Mrs Rudd: Forgery and Betrayal in Eighteenth-Century London* (Ca., 2001).

Aristocratic Vice: The Attacks on Duelling, Suicide, Adultery and Gambling in Eighteenth Century England (New Haven and London, 2013).

Ashton, John, *The History of Gambling in England* (London, 1898).

Bahlman, Dudley W. R., *The Moral Revolution of 1688* (New Haven, Conn., 1957).

Bale, John, 'Cricket in Pre-Victorian England and Wales', *Area*, 13 (1981), 119–22.

Banner, Stuart, *Speculation: A History of the Fine Line Between Gambling and Investing* (New York, 2017).

Barclay, Katie, 'Illicit Intimacies: The Imagined 'Homes' of Gilbert Innes of Stow and his Mistresses (1751–1832)', *Gender & History* 27 (2015), 576–90.

Barnham, Rob, 'Lottery Advertising 1800–1826', *Journal of the Printing Historical Society*, new ser., 13 (2009), 17–60.

Barker, Hannah, 'A Devout and Commercial People: Religion and Trade in Manchester during the Long Eighteenth Century', in Elaine Chalus and Perry Gauci (eds.), *Revisiting the Polite and Commercial People: Essays in Georgian Politics, Society and Culture in Honour of Professor Paul Langford* (Oxford, 2019), pp. 136–52.

Beattie, J. M., *Policing and Punishment in London 1660–1750: Urban Crime and the Limits of Terror* (Oxford, 2001).

Berg, Maxine, *Luxury & Pleasure in Eighteenth-Century Britain* (Oxford, 2005).

Berry, Helen, 'Rethinking Politeness in Eighteenth-Century England: Moll King's Coffee House and the Significance of "Flash Talk"', *Transactions of the Royal Historical Society*, 11 (2001), 65–81.

Black, Iain S., 'Private Banking in London's West End, 1750–1830', *London Journal*, 28 (2003), 29–59.

Blyth, Henry, *Old Q: The Rake of Piccadilly* (London, 1967).

Borsay, Peter, *The English Urban Renaissance* (Oxford, 1989).

'London 1660–1800: A distinctive culture?', in Clark, Peter and Gillespie, Raymond (eds.), *Two Capitals: London and Dublin 1500–1840* (Oxford and London, 2001), pp. 167–84.

Boulton, W. B. , *The History of White's* (2 vols., London, 1892).

Bowen, Huw V., 'Lord Clive and Speculation in East India Company Stock, 1766', *Historical Journal*, 30 (1987), 905–20.

'"The Pests of Human Society": Stockbrokers, Jobbers and Speculators in Mid-Eighteenth Century Britain', *History*, 78 (1993), 38–53.

Brailsford, Dennis, *Bareknuckles: A Social History of Prizefighting* (Cambridge, 1988).

British Sport: A Social History (rev. ed., Cambridge, 1997).

Brenner, Reuven with Brenner, Gabrielle, *Gambling and Speculation: A Theory, a History, and a Future of Some Human Decisions* (Cambridge, 1990).

Breward, Christopher, 'Masculine Pleasures: Metropolitan Identities and Commercial Sites of Dandyism, 1790–1840', *London Journal*, 28 (2003), 60–72.

Brewer, John, '"The Most Polite Age and the Most Vicious": Attitudes towards Culture as a Commodity 1660–1800', in Bermingham, Ann and Brewer, John (eds.), *The Consumption of Culture 1600–1800: Image, Object, Text* (London and New York, 1995), pp. 341–61.

Bruce, Alistair, 'Betting Motivation and Behaviour', in Vaughan-Williams, Leighton and Siegel, Donald S. (eds.), *The Oxford Handbook of the Economics of Gambling* (Oxford, 2013), pp. 1–24.

Bruno, Bernard (ed.), *Lotteries in Europe: Five Centuries of History* (Brussels, 1994).

Cannon, John, *Aristocratic Century: The Peerage of Eighteenth Century England* (Cambridge, 1984).

Capdeville, Valérie, *L'Âge d'Or des Clubs Londoniens 1730–1784* (Paris, 2008).

Carlos, Ann M. and Neal, Larry, 'Women Investors in Early Capital Markets, 1720–1725', *Financial History Review*, 11 (2004), 197–224.

'The Micro-Foundations of the Early London Capital Market: Bank of England Shareholders during and after the South Sea Bubble, 1720–25', *Economic History Review*, lix (2006), 498–538.

Carlos, Ann, Fletcher, Erin, Neal, Larry and Wandschneider, Kirsten, 'Financing and Re-financing the War of the Spanish Succession and then Re-financing the South Sea Company' in Coffman, D'Maris, Leonard, Adrian and Neal, Larry (eds.), *Questioning Credible Commitment: Perspectives on the Rise of Financial Capitalism* (Cambridge, 2013), pp. 147–68.

Carr, Rosalind, *Gender and Enlightenment Culture in Eighteenth Century Scotland* (Edinburgh, 2014).

Carson, Jane, *Colonial Virginians at Play* (Williamsburg, PA, 1989).

Carter, Philip, *Men and the Emergence of Polite Society: Britain 1660–1800* (Harlow, 2001).

Chamley, Christophe, 'Interest Reductions in the Politico-Financial Nexus of Eighteenth-Century England', *The Journal of Economic History*, 71 (2011), 555–89.

Chancellor, E. Beresford, *The Lives of the Rakes: 'Old Q' and Barrymore* (London, 1925).

Clapson, Mark, *A Bit of a Flutter: Popular Gambling and English Society c.1823–1961* (Manchester, 1992).

Clark, Geoffrey, *Betting on Lives: The Culture of Life Insurance in England, 1695–1775* (Manchester, 1988).

Clark, Gregory, 'Debts, Deficits, and Crowding Out: England 1727–1840', *European Review of Economic History*, 5 (2001), 403–36.

Clark, J. C. D., *English Society, 1688–1832: Ideology, Social Structure, and Political Practice during the Ancien Regime* (Cambridge, 1985).

'Providence, Predestination, and Progress: Or, Did the Enlightenment Fail?', *Albion*, 35 (2003), 559–89.

Clark, Peter, *The English Alehouse: A Social History 1200–1830* (London, 1983).

British Clubs and Societies 1580–1800: The Origins of an Associational World (Oxford, 2000).

Clotfelder, Charles T. and Cook, Philip J., *Selling Hope: State Lotteries in America* (Camb., Mass., 1989).

Cowan, Brian, *The Social Life of Coffee: The Emergence of the British Coffeehouse* (London and New York, 2005).

Curtis, T. C. and Speck, W. A., 'The Societies for the Reformation of Manners: A Case Study in the Theory and Practice of Moral Reform', *Literature and History*, 3 (1976), 45–64.

Daston, Lorraine, *Classical Probability in the Enlightenment* (Princeton, NJ, 1988).

Deutch, Phyllis, 'Moral Trespass in Georgian London: Gaming, Gender, and Electoral Politics in the Age of George III', *Historical Journal*, 39 (1996), 637–56.

Devereux Jr., Edward C., *Gambling and Social Structure* (New York, 1980).

de Vries, J., *The Industrious Revolution: Consumer Behaviour and the Household Economy, 1650 to the Present* (Cambridge, 2008).

Dewald, Jonathan, *The European Nobility 1400–1800* (Cambridge, 1996).

Dickie, Simon, *Cruelty & Laughter: Forgotten Comic Literature and the Unsentimental Eighteenth Century* (Chicago, 2011).

Dickson, P. G. M., *The Financial Revolution in England: A Study in the Development of Public Credit, 1688–1756* (London, 1967).

Downing, Karen, 'Boxing, Manners, and Masculinity in Eighteenth Century England', *Men and Masculinities*, 12 (2010), 328–52.

Dudley, Rowena, *The Irish Lottery 1780–1801* (Dublin, 2005).

Dunkley, John, *Gambling: A Social and Moral Problem in France, 1685–1792* (Oxford, 1985).

'Illegal Gambling in Eighteenth Century France: Incidence, Detection and Penalties', *British Journal of Eighteenth-Century Studies*, 8 (1985), 129–37.

Earle, Peter, *The Making of the English Middle Class: Business, Society and Family Life in London, 1660–1730* (London, 1989).

Edwards, Peter, 'The decline of an aristocratic stud: The study of Edward Lord Harley, 2nd Earl of Oxford and Mortimer, at Welbeck (Nottinghamshire), 1717–29', *Economic History Review*, 69 (2016), 870–92.

Eles, Henry S. and Spencer, Earl, *Brooks's 1764–1964* (London, 1964).

Ellis, Heather, 'Foppish Masculity, Generational Identity and the University Authorities in Eighteenth-Century Oxbridge', *Cultural and Social History*, 11 (2014), 367–84.

Ellis, Joyce, '"On the Town"; Women in Augustan England', *History Today*, 45 (1995), 20–7.

Ellis, K. L., *The Post Office in the Eighteenth Century: A Study in Administrative History* (London, 1958).

Ellis, Markman, *The Coffee-House: A Cultural History* (London, 2004).

Evans, James E., '"A Scene of the Uttmost Vanity": The Spectacle of Gambling in Late Stuart Culture', *Studies in Eighteenth Century Culture*, 31 (2002), 1–20.

Ewen, C. L., *Lotteries and Sweepstakes: An Historical, Legal and Ethical Survey of Their Introduction, Suppression and Re-establishment in the British Isles* (London, 1932).

Fabian, Ann, *Card Sharps and Bucket Shops: Gambling in Nineteenth-Century America* (Ithaca, NY, 1999).

Fairfax-Blakeborough, J., *Northern Turf History, Vol. IV, History of Horse Racing in Scotland* (Whitby, 1973).

Finn, Margot C., *The Character of Credit: Personal Debt in English Culture, 1740–1914* (Cambridge, 2003).

Fletcher, Anthony, *Gender, Sex & Subordination in England 1500–1800* (New Haven and London, 1995).

Floud, Roderick, Humphries, Jane and Johnson, Paul (eds.), *The Cambridge Economic History of Modern Britain, Volume 1: 1700–1870* (Cambridge, 2014).

Ford, John, *Prizefighting: The Age of Regency Boximania* (Devon, 1971).

French, Henry and Rothery, Mark, *Mans's Estate: Landed Gentry Mentalities, 1660–1914* (Oxford, 2012).

Froide, Amy M., *Silent Partners: Women as Public Investors during Britain's Financial Revolution, 1690–1750* (Oxford, 2017).

Fulford, R., *Boodle's 1762–1962: A Short History* (London, 1962).

Gallais-Hamonno, Georges and Rietsch, Christian, 'Learning by doing: The failure of the 1697 Malt Lottery Loan', *Financial History Review*, 20 (2013), 259–77.

Gatrell, Vic, *City of Laughter: Sex and Satire in Eighteenth-Century London* (London, 2006).

The First Bohemians: Life and Art in London's Golden Age (London, 2013).

Glaisyer, Natasha, *The Culture of Commerce in England, 1660–1720* (Woodbridge, 2006).

'Calculation and Conjuring: John Molesworth and the Lottery in Eighteenth Century Britain', *Journal for Eighteenth Century Studies*, 42 (2019), 135–55.

Goulstone, John, *Hambledon: The Men and Myths* (Cambridge, 2001).

Greig, Hannah, '"All Together and All Distinct": Public Sociability and Social Exclusivity in London's Pleasure Gardens, ca. 1740–1830', *Journal of British Studies*, 51 (2012), 50–75.

The Beau Monde: Fashionable Society in Georgian London (Oxford, 2013).

Griffin, Emma, 'Popular Culture in Industrializing England', *Historical Journal*, 45 (2002), 609–35.

Hancock, David, '"Domestic Bubbling": Eighteenth Century London Merchants and Individual Investment in the Funds', *Economic History Review*, 2nd ser., 47 (1994), 679–702.

Harris, Bob, *Politics and the Nation: Britain in the Mid Eighteenth Century* (Oxford, 1992).

Harris, Bob and McKean, Charles, *The Scottish Town in the Age of the Enlightenment, 1740–1820* (Edinburgh, 2014).

'Lottery Adventuring in Britain, c.1710–1760', *English Historical Review*, 133 (2018), 284–322.

'Selling the Lottery in Britain, c.1694–1826', in Berman, Ric and Gibson, William (eds.), *The Lantern of History: Essays in Honour of Jeremy Black* (Goring Heath, Oxon, 2020), pp. 86–110.

'Buildings, Associations, and Culture in the Scottish Provincial Town, c.1700–1830', in Wallace, Mark and Rendall, Jane (eds.), *Association and Enlightenment: Scottish Clubs and Societies, 1700–1830* (Lewisburg, PA, 2021), pp. 49–66.

'The 1782 Gaming Bill and Lottery Regulation Acts (1782 & 1787): Gambling and the Law in Later Georgian Britain', *Parliamentary History*, 40 (2021), 462–480.

Harvey, Adrian, *The Beginnings of a Commercial Sporting Culture in Britain, 1793–1850* (Aldershot, 2004).

Harvey, Karen, 'The History of Masculinity, c. 1650–1800', *Journal of British Studies*, 44 (2005), 296–312.

The Little Republic: Masculinity & Domestic Authority in Eighteenth-Century Britain (Oxford, 2012).

Hay, Douglas and Rogers, Nicholas, *Eighteenth-Century English Society: Shuttles and Swords* (Oxford, 1997).

Hayton, David, 'Moral Reform and Country Politics in the Late Seventeenth Century House of Commons', *Past & Present*, 78 (1990), 48–91.

Hembry, Phyllis, *The English Spa, 1560–1815: A Social History* (Harlow, 1990).

Hitchcock, Tim and Cohen, Michèle (eds.), *English Masculinities 1600–1800* (London, 1999).

Hitchcock, Tim, *Down and Out in Eighteenth Century London* (Hambledon, 2004).

Hitchcock, Tim and Shoemaker, Robert, *London Lives: Poverty, Crime and the Making of a Modern City, 1690–1800* (Cambridge, 2015).

Holt, Richard, *Sport and the British* (Oxford, 1989).

Hoppit, Julian, 'Attitudes to Credit in Britain, 1680–1790', *Historical Journal*, 33 (1990), 305–22

Hoppit, Julian (ed.), *Failed Legislation 1660–1800: Extracted from the Commons and Lords Journals* (Hambledon, 1997).

'The Myths of the South Sea Bubble', *Transactions of the Royal Historical Society*, 12 (2002), 141–65.

Humphries, Jane, 'Household economy', in Floud, R. and Johnson, P. (eds.), *The Cambridge Economic History of Modern Britain, Vol. 1: Industrialisation, 1700–1860* (Cambridge, 2004), pp. 238–67.

Huggins, Mike, *Flat Racing and British Society 1790–1914: A Social and Economic History* (London, 2000).

'Popular Culture and Sporting Life in the Rural Margins of Late Eighteenth-Century England: The World of Robert Anderson, "The Cumberland Bard"', *Eighteenth Century Studies*, 45 (2012), 189–205.

'Racing Culture, Betting and Sporting Protomodernity: The 1750 Newmarket Carriage Match', *Journal of Sport History*, 42 (2015), 327–39.

Horse Racing and British Society in the Long Eighteenth Century (Martlesham, 2018).

Hunt, Margaret R., *The Middling Sort: Commerce, Gender, and the Family in England, 1680–1780* (Berkeley, CA., 1996).

Innes, Joanna, *Inferior Politics: Social Problems and Social Policies in Eighteenth-Century Britain* (Oxford, 2009).

Itzkowitz, David C., 'Fair Enterprise or Extravagant Speculation: Investment, Speculation and Gambling in Victorian England', *Victorian Studies*, 35 (2002), 121–47.

Jobey, George, 'Cockfighting in Northumberland and Durham during the Eighteenth and Nineteenth Centuries', *Archaelogia Aeliana*, 20 (1992), 1–25.

Joslin, D. M., 'London Private Bankers 1720–95', *Economic History Review*, 7 (1954–5), 167–86.

Kavanagh, Thomas M., *Dice, Cards, Wheels: A Different History of French Culture* (Philadelphia, Penn., 2005).

Klein, Lawrence E., 'Politeness and the Interpretation of the British Eighteenth Century', *Historical Journal*, 45 (2002), 889–98.

'The Polite Town: The Shifting Possibilities of Urbaness, 1660–1715', in Hitchcock, Tim and Shore, Heather (eds.), *The Streets of London: From the Great Fire to the Great Stink* (2003), pp. 27–39, 217–9.

Kosmetatos, P., *The 1772–73 British Credit Crisis* (Basingstoke, 2018).

Kruckeberg, Robert, 'The Royal Lottery and the Old Regime: Financial Innovation and Modern Political Culture', *French Historical Studies*, 37 (2014), 25–51.

Langford, Paul, *A Polite and Commercial People: England 1727–1787* (Oxford, 1989).

Public Life and the Propertied Englishman 1689–1798 (Oxford, 1991).

'The Uses of Eighteenth Century Politeness', *Transactions of the Royal Historical Society*, 6th ser., 12 (2002), 311–31.

Laurence, Anne, 'Women Investors, 'That Nasty South Sea Affair' and the Rage to Speculate in Early Eighteenth-Century England', *Accounting, Business & Financial History*, 16 (2006), 245–64.

'The Emergence of a Private Clientele for Banks in the Early Eighteenth Century: Hoare's Bank and Some Women Customers', *Economic History Review*, lxi (2008), 565–86.

'Women, Banks and the Securities Market in Early Eighteenth Century England', in Laurence, Anne, Maltby, Josephine and Rutherford, Janette (eds.), *Women and their Money, 1700–1950: Essays on Women and Finance* (London and New York, 2009), pp. 46–58.

Legay, Marie-Laure, *Les Loteries Royales dans L'Europe des Lumières (1680–1815)* (Lille, 2014).

Lockitt, C. H., *The Relations of French and English Society (1763–1793)* (London, 1920).

Longrigg, Roger, *The History of Horse Racing* (London, 1972).

Macdonald, James, 'The Importance of Not Defaulting: The Significance of the Election of 1710', in Coffman, D'Maris, Leonard, Adrian and Neal, Larry (eds.), *Questioning Credible Commitment: Perspectives on the Rise of Financial Capitalism* (Cambridge, 2013), pp. 125–46.

Manley, K. A., 'The Road to Camelot: Lotteries, the Circle of Learning, and the 'Circulay' Library of Samuel Fancourt', *The Library*, 7th ser., 8 (2007), 398–422.

McCloskey, D. N., *Bourgeois Dignity: Why Economics Can't Explain the Modern World* (Chicago, 2010).

McKibbin, Ross, 'Working-Class Gambling in Britain, 1880–1939', in McKibbin, Ross, *The Ideologies of Class: Social Relations in Britain 1880–1950* (Oxford, 1991), pp. 101–38.

Middleton, Iris, 'Cock Fighting in Yorkshire in the Early Eighteenth Century', *Northern History*, 40 (2003), 129–41.

Middleton, Iris and Vamplew, Wray, 'Horse Racing and the Yorkshire Leisure Calendar in the Early Eighteenth Century', *Northern History*, 49 (2003), 259–76.

Miers, David, 'Eighteenth Century Gaming: Implications for Modern Casino Control', in *History and Crime: Implications for Criminal Justice Policy*, eds. Inciardi, James and Faupel, Charles (Beverly Hills, CA, 1980), pp. 169–92.

Regulating Commercial Gambling: Past, Present, and Future (Oxford, 2004).

Milevsky, Moshe A., *King William's Tontine: Why the Retirement Annuity If the Future Should Resemble the Past* (Cambridge, 2015).

Millikan, Neal E., *Lotteries in Colonial America* (New York and Abingdon, 2011).

Mitchell, Leslie, *Charles James Fox* (Oxford, 1992).

The Whig World 1760–1837 (London and New York, 2005).

Molesworth, Jesse, *Chance and the Eighteenth Century Novel: Realism, Probability, Magic* (Cambridge, 2010).

Mortlock, D.P., *Aristocratic Splendour: Money & the World of Thomas Coke, Earl of Leicester* (Stroud, 2007).

Mullin, Janet E., *A Six Penny at Whist: Gaming and the English Middle Classes 1680–1830* (Woodbridge, 2015).

Munting, Roger, 'Social Opposition to Gambling in Britain: An Historical Overview', *International Journal of the History of Sport*, 10 (1993), 295–312.

An Economic and Social History of Gambling in Britain and the USA (Manchester, 1996).

Murphy, Anne L., 'Lotteries in the 1690s: Investment or Gamble?', *Financial History Review*, 12 (2005), 227–46.

The Origins of English Financial Markets: Investment and Speculation before the South Sea Bubble (Cambridge, 2009).

'Demanding "Credible Commitment": Public Reactions to the Failures of the Early Financial Revolution', *Economic History Review*, 66 (2013), 178–97.

Nacol, Emily C., *An Age of Risk: Politics and Economy in Early Modern Britain* (Princeton and Oxford, 2016).

Neal, Larry, *The Rise of Financial Capitalism: International Capital Markets in the Age of Reason* (Cambridge, 1990).

'The Evolution of Self- and State Regulation of the London Stock Exchange, 1688–1878', in Debin, M. and van Zanden, J. (eds.), *Law and Long-Term Economic Change: A Eurasian Perspective* (Stanford, CA, 2011), pp. 300–22.

"I am Not Master of Events" The Speculations of John Law and Lord Londonderry in the Mississippi and South Sea Bubbles (New Haven and London, 2012).

Newman, Aubrey (ed.), *Politics and Finance in the Eighteenth Century: Lucy Sutherland* (London, 1984).

Paul, Tawny, *The Poverty of Disaster: Debt and Insecurity in Eighteenth-Century Britain* (Cambridge, 2019).

Phillips, Nicola, *The Profligate Son: Or, a True Story of Family Conflict, Fashionable Vice and Financial Ruin in Regency England* (Oxford, 2013).

Porter, J. H. , 'Cockfighting in the Eighteenth and Nineteenth Centuries: From Popularity to Suppression', *Transactions of the Devonshire Association for the Advancement of Science, Literature and Art*, 118 (1986), 63–71.

Porter, Roy, *English Society in the Eighteenth Century* (London, 1982).

Enlightenment, Britain and the Creation of the Modern World (London, 2000).

Radford, Peter, *The Celebrated Captain Barclay: Sport, Money and Fame in Regency Britain* (London, 2001).

'Lifting the Spirits of the Nation: British Boxers and the Emergence of the National Sporting Hero at the time of the Napoleonic Wars', *Identities: Global Studies in Culture and Power*, 12 (2005), 249–70.

Randall, Adrian and Charlesworth, Andrew (eds.), *Moral Economy and Popular Protest: Crowds, Conflict and Authority* (Basingstoke, 2000).

Raven, James, 'The Abolition of the English State Lotteries', *Historical Journal*, 34 (1991), 371–89.

Judging New Wealth: Popular Publishing and Responses to Commerce in England 1750–1800 (Oxford, 1997).

Publishing Business in Eighteenth Century England (Woodbridge, 2014).

'Debating the lottery in Britain c. 1750–1830', in Zollinger, Manfred (ed.), *Random Riches: Gambling Past and Present* (Ashgate, 2015), pp. 87–104.

Rawlings, Philip, 'Bubbles, Taxes and Interests: Another History of Insurance Law, 1720–1825', *Oxford Journal of Legal Studies*, 36 (2016), 799–827.

Rendall, Jane, 'The Clubs of St James's: Places of Public Patriarchy, Exclusivity, Domesticity and Secrecy', *The Journal of Architecture*, 4 (1999), 167–89.

Reynolds, Elaine A., *Before the Bobbies: The Night Watch and Police Reform in Metropolitan London, 1720–1830* (Basingstoke, 1998).

Richard, Jessica, *The Romance of Gambling in the Eighteenth Century British Novel* (Basingstoke, 2011).

Richards, R. D., 'The Lottery in the History of English Government Finance', *Economic History*, 3 (1933–7), 57–76

Roberts, M. J. D., 'The Society for the Suppression of Vice and Its Early Critics, 1802–1812', *Historical Journal*, 26 (1983), 156–76.

'Public and Private in Early Nineteenth-Century London: The Vagrant Act of 1822 and its Enforcement', *Social History*, 13 (1988), 273–94.

Rodger, N. A. M., 'Honour and Duty at Sea', *Historical Research*, 75 (2002), 425–47.

Rogers, Nicholas, *Mayhem: Post-war Crime and Violence in Britain 1748–1753* (New Haven and London, 2012).

Russell, Gillian, '"Faro's Daughters": Female Gamesters, Politics, and the Discourse of Finance in 1790s Britain', *Eighteenth Century Studies*, 33 (2000), 481–504.

Schwarz, Leonard D., *London in the Age of Industrialisation: Entrepreneurs, Labour Force and Living Conditions 1700–1850* (Cambridge, 1992).

'The Standard of Living in the Long Run: London, 1700–1860', *Economic History Review*, 38 (1985), 24–41.

Seigel, Jerrold, *Modernity and Bourgeois Life: Society, Politics, and Culture in England, France, and Germany since 1750* (Cambridge, 2012).

Shepard, Alexandra, *The Meanings of Manhood in Early Modern England, 1560–1640* (Oxford, 2003).

Shoemaker, Robert B, *Prosecution and Punishment: Petty Crime and the Law in London and Rural Middlesex, c. 1660–1725* (Cambridge, 1991).

'Reforming the City: The Reformation of Manners Campaign in London, 1690–1738', in Lee Davison et al. (eds.), *Stilling the Grumbling Hive: The Response to Social and Economic Problems in England, 1689–1750* (Stroud and New York, 1992), pp. 99–120.

'Reforming male manners: Public insult and the decline of violence in London, 1660–1740', in Hitchcock, T. and Cohen, M. (eds.), *English Masculinities, 1660–1800* (London, 1999), pp. 133–50.

'Male Honour and the Decline of Public Violence in Eighteenth-Century London', *Social History*, 26 (2001), 190–208.

'The Taming of the Duel: Masculinity, Honour and Ritual Violence in London, 1660–1800', *Historical Journal*, 45 (2002), 525–45.

Stafford, William, 'Gentlemanly Masculinities as Represented by the Later Georgian *Gentleman's Magazine*', *History*, 93 (2008), 47–68.

Steedman, Carolyn, *An Everyday Life of the English Working Class: Work, Self and Sociability in the Early Nineteenth Century* (Cambridge, 2013).

Stone, Lawrence, *The Crisis of the Aristocracy, 1558–1641* (Oxford, 1965).

Stone, Lawrence & Fawtier Stone, Jeanne C., *An Open Elite? England 1540–1880* (Oxford, 1986).

Sutherland, Lucy and Binney, J., 'Henry Fox as Paymaster General of Forces', *English Historical Review*, 70 (1955), 229–57.

Sutherland, L. S. and Woods, J. A., 'The East India Speculations of William Burke', *Proceedings of the Leeds Philosophical and Literary Society*, 11 (1964), 188–92.

Swain, Peter, 'Pedestrianism, the Public House and Gambling in Nineteenth Century South-east Lancashire', *Sport in History*, 32 (2012), 383–404.

Temin, Peter and Voth, Hans-Joachim, 'Hoare's Bank in the Eighteenth Century', in Mokyr, Joel and Cruz, Laura (eds.), *The Birth of Modern Europe, 1400–1800: Essays in Honour of Jan De Vries* (Leiden, 2010), pp. 81–108.

Thomas, Keith, *The Ends of Life: Roads to Fulfilment in Early Modern England* (pbk ed., Oxford, 2010).

In Pursuit of Civility: Manners and Civilization in Early Modern England (New Haven and London, 2018).

Thompson, E. P., 'The Peculiarities of the English', *Socialist Register* (1965), 311–62.

Tosney, Nicholas, 'The Playing Card Trade in Early Modern England', *Historical Research*, 84 (2011), 637–56.

Underdown, David, *Start of Play: Cricket and Culture in Eighteenth-Century England* (London, 2000).
Ungar, Ruti, 'The Construction of the Body Politic and the Politics of the Body: Boxing as Battle Ground for Conservatives and Radicals in Late Georgian England, *Sport in History*, 31 (2012), 363–80.
Walcott, Clare, 'Mrs Hobart's Routs: Town House Hospitality in 1790s London', *Huntingdon Library Quarterly*, 77 (2014), 453–77.
Vamplew, Wray, *The Turf: A Social and Economic History of Horse Racing* (London, 1976).
Vickery, Amanda, *The Gentleman's Daughter: Women's Lives in Georgian England* (New Haven and London, 1998).
Webb, S. and Webb, B., *The History of Liquor Licensing in England* (London, 1903).
Welch, Evelyn, 'Lotteries in Early Modern Italy', *Past & Present*, 199 (2008), 71–111.
Whale, John, 'Daniel Mendoza's Contests of Identity: Masculinity, Ethnicity and Nation in Georgian Prize-Fighting', *Romanticism, 14* (2008), 259–71.
Whyman, Susan E., 'Paper Visits: The Post-Restoration Letter as Seen through the Verney Family Archive', in Earle, Rebecca (ed.), *Letters and Letter Writers 1600–1945* (Aldershot, 1999), pp. 15–36.
Sociability and Power in Late Stuart England: The Cultural Worlds of the Verneys 1660–1720 (Oxford, 1999).
The Useful Knowledge of William Hutton: Culture and Industry in Eighteenth-Century Birmingham (Oxford, 2018).
Wohlcke, Anne, *The 'Perpetual Fair': Gender, Disorder and Urban Amusement in Eighteenth-Century London* (Manchester, 2014).
Wroth, Warwick W., *The London Pleasure Gardens of the Eighteenth Century* (London, 1896).

Unpublished Theses

Davison, Lee K., 'Public Policy in an Age of Economic Expansion: The Search for Commercial Accountability in England 1690–1750', unpublished Ph.D. thesis, University of Harvard (1990).
Deutsch, Phyllis, 'Fortune and Chance: Aristocratic gaming and English society, 1760–1837', unpublished Ph.D. thesis, New York University (1991).
King, R. F., 'Aspects of Sociability in the North East of England 1600–1750', unpublished Ph.D. thesis, University of Durham (2001).
Middleton, Iris, 'The Developing Pattern of Horse Racing in Yorkshire 1700–1749: An Analysis of the People and the Places', unpublished Ph.D. thesis, De Montfort University (2000).
Tosney, Nicholas, 'Gaming in England, c.1540–1760', unpublished Ph.D. thesis, University of York (2008).

Online Sources

Clifford, Helen, 'Accommodating the East: Sir Lawrence Dundas as Northern Nabob? The Dundas Property Empire and Nabob Taste', (http://blogs.ucl.ac.uk/dist/1/files/2013/02/Aske-Hall-final-pdf-19.08.14.pdf).

History of Parliament Online (www.historyofparliamentonline.org) *London Lives, 1690–1800.*

Old Bailey Proceedings Online (www.oldbaileyonline.org. version 7.2, 27 Mar. 2015) *Oxford Dictionary of National Biography.*

Velde, François R., 'Lottery Loans in the Eighteenth Century' (2013), (www.ehes.org/velde.pdf).

Zollinger, Manfred, 'Entrepreneurs of Chance. The Spreading of *lotto* in Eighteenth Century Europe' (www.helsinki.fi/iehc2006/papers1/Zollinger.pdf).

Index